Advanced Motif Programming
Techniques

Advanced Motif Programming Techniques

Alistair George and Mark Riches

Prentice Hall

New York   London   Toronto   Sydney   Tokyo   Singapore

First published 1994 by
Prentice Hall International (UK) Limited
Campus 400, Maylands Avenue
Hemel Hempstead
Hertfordshire, HP2 7EZ
A division of
Simon & Schuster International Group

Printed and bound in Great Britain by
Redwood Books, Trowbridge, Wiltshire

Library of Congress Cataloging-in-Publication Data

George, Alistair.
    Advanced motif programming techniques / Alistair George and Mark
  Riches.
        p.   cm.
    Includes bibliographical references (p.   ) and index.
    ISBN 0–13–219965–3 (pbk.)
    1. X Window System (Computer system)   2. Motif (Computer file)
  I. Riches, Mark.   II. Title.
  QA76.76.W56G46   1994
  005.4′3—dc20   93–42977
                                                            CIP

British Library Cataloguing in Publication Data

A catalogue record for this book is available from
the British Library

ISBN 0–13–219965–3

---

2 3 4 5   98 97 96 95

Contents

Foreword

I recently had the good fortune to attend a small meeting in which a well-known computer industry entrepreneur and visionary was leading a discussion. He spoke at length about the need for innovation and urged everyone not to limit themselves to current-day standards. "Revolutions do happen", he concluded. Indeed, they do, although sometimes revolutions are only clear in hindsight and are often taken for granted once the results become part of the mainstream.

This book is a part of the continuing story of one such revolution in the UNIX computer industry that began in the latter part of the 1980s. A typical UNIX environment was primarily text-based at that time. Most hardware vendors had some type of proprietary window system, but the windows were used mainly to allow multiple character-based terminal emulators to be used at once. There was very little of what would be recognised today as a "GUI". There was virtually no widely available UNIX-based software. All that has changed since the introduction of the X Window System. The X Window System has affected every aspect of today's UNIX environment, both hardware and software.

One of the most promising of these changes is one that affects the way software is developed. One of the holy grails of the software industry has been "reuse", the idea that software could be based on standard off-the-shelf reusable components, in the same way that hardware developers can draw on a large supply of ready-made chips. In 1986, Brad Cox coined the phrase Software-IC in his book, *Object-Oriented Programming: An Evolutionary Approach*. According to Cox, a

Software-IC was the software equivalent of a hardware integrated circuit. Cox envisioned programmers using Software-ICs to build software from cheap, reliable, interchangeable components, just as hardware engineers do. Today, we are closer to Cox's vision than one might expect. It has been made possible, in part, by the acceptance of the X Window System.

Although X provided an industry-wide standard window system, those who tried to write significant applications using X's low-level API quickly found X to be difficult to use. Soon, everyone began to develop toolkits designed to make the task easier. Ultimately, the Motif toolkit described in this book was adopted by nearly all of the UNIX community. Industry-wide acceptance of Motif is significant because it shows that the vision articulated by Brad Cox over seven years ago is rapidly becoming a reality. X provides the basic substrate on which a component industry can be launched, and the Motif toolkit provides both common components and the "software bus" into which additional components can be plugged.

A quick glance through any contemporary UNIX magazine reveals many companies who sell custom widgets that can be plugged into applications based on the Motif toolkit. In keeping with Cox's vision, one company even produces a "widget data book" modelled on the IC data books used by hardware developers.

Finally, with Motif, developers can write software for a single software architecture, largely from standard off-the-shelf components, and produce a program that can be distributed on all UNIX platforms. The result is good for developers who can develop software more easily, for users who can choose from a wider variety of software at better prices, and for hardware vendors who can leverage the large amounts of available software to provide potential buyers with solutions they need.

Along with the widespread use of X and Motif comes the need for education and training materials for old and new programmers alike. Like the industry itself, the needs of the programming community have evolved over the years since X was first introduced. When I first began participating in seminars on X and Motif, many programmers came just to hear what this new technology was about, and had never tried to write any X-based software.

Today, while there are always new programmers who need to start with the basics, there are many people who have accumulated significant experience using X and Motif. At this point, it is common for those who attend seminars to have written at least some, and in many cases, a great deal of software based on X and Motif. Many come to exchange ideas, to learn new or more advanced techniques, or to learn how others have taken advantage of X and Motif. Many developers have now had an opportunity to try to write significant applications and are looking for ways to share their experience with others.

This book is an outgrowth of that trend. Alistair George and Mark Riches have spent several years building one of the most challenging types of applications one can develop for Motif, an application "builder". User interface builders take the "Software-IC" concept even further than Cox imagined by allowing programmers to construct interactively an application from a palette of ready-made components. Such tools are challenging to write because the programs not only have their own, highly interactive and graphical user interface, but they must also allow the user to manipulate and create a user interface for another application. Developing such a tool for Motif requires a thorough understanding of the toolkit as it is typically used by applications and also requires knowledge of many not-so-typical corner cases and internal implementation details. In this book, the authors draw on the knowledge they have developed from that experience and share their unique insights and ideas with the reader.

As this book goes to press, X and Motif are so widely used within the UNIX community that it is hard to remember what development was like before they appeared. It may be hard to appreciate the impact that these platforms have had on everyone's development because yesterday's revolutions quickly become today's mainstream technology. Revolution gives way to evolution. But as developers continue to build on and evolve this technology, everyone benefits. An important consequence of the growth of X and Motif is the ever-increasing number of programmers who are willing and able to share their real-world experiences to benefit others. By documenting what they have learned, the authors of this book are contributing to the ongoing evolution of X and Motif. I am sure many readers will benefit from their experience.

Doug Young
Principal Scientist, Silicon Graphics, Inc.

Preface

There is no shortage of books which provide an introduction to the Motif toolkit and explain, at least in outline, how to use it to develop graphical user interface (GUI) applications. However, no introductory text can hope to cover all the functionality of the toolkit, let alone describe its quirks and subtleties. Furthermore, Motif does not exist in isolation; it builds on the X toolkit (Xt and Xlib), and is in turn built on by application programmers. Strange things can happen at the interfaces and interesting things are possible.

This book is aimed squarely at programmers who have already done some application development in Motif, and are looking to broaden and deepen their skills and understanding. If you do not know what a widget is, this book is not for you yet. If, on the other hand, you need to know how to stop a scrolled list widget from resizing itself, how to get a form layout which really does what you want, or how to handle input and output in a drawing area, this book can help you.

This is not just a cookbook, although it can be used as such. It aims to explain why as well as how, to describe not just what is available (which is what the toolkit reference documentation does) but also what it is intended for and when it should be used. You can read this book cover to cover and gain an understanding of major features of Motif and the surrounding technologies, or you can dip in to find a solution to a problem or an explanation of a feature.

There seems to be a convention among authors of technical books that the technology which they describe should be regarded as perfect in every way. We do not follow this convention; difficulties inherent in the Motif toolkit are described, as well as work-arounds where known. We also describe some of the major design flaws (now, alas, fixed in stone) and ways of mitigating their effect. We do not by this intend to denigrate the Motif toolkit. In our view, it is now the safest bet for a base technology on which to build GUI applications, but programmers need ways of working with its warts, not denials of their existence.

Motif is not complete in itself. Many applications will also need to use features of the underlying X toolkit. Although there are many books which describe the X toolkit, they generally do so from the bottom up. Here, we work from the Motif toolkit down, showing how X and Motif mechanisms can be used in conjunction, rather than in isolation. The coverage of the X toolkit is in no sense comprehensive, but it is sufficient to meet some of the most common requirements and, as important, to allow you to approach X toolkit books and documentation with some confidence.

The book is structured into two parts: Part 1 covers the various widgets that comprise the Motif toolkit. Each of the widgets is discussed in turn and their uses, bugs and foibles are described. For many of the simpler widgets, this discussion is restricted to a few hints and tips, whereas some need an entire chapter to themselves. We also discuss Xt widgets that are part of the intrinsics (i.e. not the Athena widget set) and show how they fit together with the Motif widgets.

Part 2 concentrates on some of the additional mechanisms of the toolkits and on Xlib itself. A large proportion of this part is concerned with the low-level mechanisms for detecting and responding to events; these are more comprehensive than the predefined callbacks provided by Motif, if a little trickier to use. There are also chapters on the window manager, font lists and compound strings, input and traversal and an extensive examination of the selection and drag and drop facilities. The concluding chapter takes a brief look at internationalisation and some of the problems that it raises.

To a programmer who uses the Motif toolkit, a widget is just a black box. Part 2 opens the box a little by describing some of the ways in which Motif uses these underlying mechanisms. This is important; the same mechanisms are there for anyone to use, but where Motif assumes that they are used only in a certain conventional way, unrestricted use can cause chaos.

Examples

Some of the examples given in this book are complete programs. The majority, however, are fragments extracted from larger programs which illustrate the point in question without getting bogged down in pages of code. Whatever their origin, all the examples have been against the Motif 1.2 toolkit using the X11R5 server and client libraries on SunOS 4.1.

We have used the OSF Motif and MIT X distributions. Many hardware vendors modify these toolkits before they distribute them. This may have the effect of fixing some bugs; in our experience it is equally likely that you will find new, platform-specific ones. We welcome reports of bugs found in our examples (they are bound to be there), but please give us as much information as you can about the operating environment (hardware, OS and toolkit versions and so on) as you can.

London
December 1993

Alistair George
Mark Riches

Acknowledgements

We would like to thank family, friends, colleagues, employers and publishers who have allowed us to write this book with relatively little distraction.

X-Designer is a trademark of Imperial Software Technology.
X Window System is a trademark of The Massachusetts Institute of Technology.
UNIX is a trademark of AT&T Bell laboratories.
SunOS is a trademark of Sun Microsystems.

CHAPTER 1

Introduction

OSF/Motif is now the *de facto* standard user interface technology for applications that use the X window system to provide networked graphics. It is widely supported, if less widely loved.

The Motif widget set is the most widely used part of Motif. It provides a comparatively large and complex set of reusable user interface components, together with convenience functions to create and manipulate them. It contains widgets suitable for most common uses, and provides them with enough different resources so they can be adapted to work in a large variety of ways.

The size and complexity of the widget set means that while it is easy to get started with Motif, it is much harder to exploit it fully. Further, some of the more powerful features are provided not by Motif, but by the underlying X window system. This in turn has two layers, Xt and Xlib, so complete mastery requires knowledge of three separate technology layers, each of which has its own documentation set.

With all these different layers there is frequently more than one way to achieve a desired effect. Indeed, much of this book is taken up with examining various available techniques and identifying the most appropriate.

This book is designed to help you develop your skills as a Motif application developer in two ways: first, to gain understanding of the Motif widget set itself, and second, to understand how Motif, Xt and Xlib work together, and when they are working against each other.

1

1.1   OSF/Motif in context

OSF/Motif is a commercial product of the Open Software Foundation. Source code is available, but not freely available. OSF/Motif is usually described as having four components:

- The Motif widget set.
- A window manager, mwm.
- UIL, the Motif User Interface Language.
- The Motif style guide.

This book covers the Motif widget set, with some discussion of window managers in general and mwm in particular. We do not cover UIL explicitly, although much of the detail in the chapters on widgets is applicable, however the widgets are created. Equally we make little mention of the Motif style guide, except in passing. In the remainder of this book, 'Motif' usually refers to the widget set alone.

Motif is built on the X window system. The X window system is defined by the X Consortium, which is essentially a standards-making body. However, it supports the standards with a sample implementation from the Massachusetts Institute of Technology - MIT X - for which source is available. No fee is charged by MIT for the source, so it is usually available at low cost or for nothing.

Many platform vendors have licensed the OSF/Motif technology, and distribute all or part of it in binary form. Most of these vendors also distribute a binary Xt and Xlib implementation based on the MIT X, although some have their own implementations.

In this book, we assume that you have access to Motif, Xt and Xlib libraries and the Motif window manager, together with appropriate programmer's reference documentation.[1] We do not assume that you have source code for either Motif or X.

1.2   How to use this book

This book is not intended to be used in isolation, or by novices. To use this book, you will need at least Programmer's Reference Manuals for Xlib, Xt and Motif (detailed in the bibliography, or available as manual pages on your system). We assume that you know how to find the appropriate reference section for a function or widget class, even if not all of the information in the section is comprehensible. We also assume that you have written programs using the Motif widget set and intend to write more.

---

1. We also make some use of utilities such as xev. These are provided as part of the core MIT X distribution and usually installed in /usr/bin/X11. They are not essential.

You may find it useful to acquire copies of the standard texts on Xt and Xlib:

- Asente and Swick (1990).
- Scheifler and Gettys (1992).

These books provide comprehensive explanations of the Xlib and Xt topics that we can only touch on. They also achieve a commendable level of accuracy.

This book need not be read from beginning to end. It is arranged by topic and can be used as a reference or for problem solving, as well as a self-teaching aid. To help you find your way around, the next section briefly describes the contents of each chapter.

There are numerous code fragments in this book; these are not necessarily complete programs, but can easily be incorporated in your own code. There is no substitute for practical experience, and you are strongly recommended to find excuses to try the techniques described in the text.

1.3   Structure of the book

On the whole, each chapter of this book can stand alone. However, certain basic information is reviewed in Chapter 2. You should probably skim that chapter before attempting to read any other. The remainder of the book is in two parts.

Part 1 examines each of the Motif widgets in turn. As such, it has something of the character of a reference book, but it provides information that supplements the standard Motif references. Each chapter looks at a subset of the widgets, examining their interesting resources, along with their behaviour and use. If a particular resource is not listed for a widget then you can assume that the Motif documentation describes it adequately.

Chapter 6 looks specifically at the XmForm widget and contains many examples and techniques for achieving various layout styles. Chapter 7 deals with the XmScrolledWindow and XmMainWindow. This chapter contains an extensive worked example of application-defined scrolling.

Part 2 looks at the various supporting mechanisms provided by the toolkits. Each chapter in this part gives reasonably complete coverage of one topic area:

- Chapter 10 *Resources* discusses the mechanisms that Xt provides for setting resources on widgets.
- Chapter 11 *Translations and accelerators* introduces the facilities provided by Xt to dispatch incoming events to application code.
- Chapter 12 *Event handling* examines the whole area of detecting, responding to and sending events.
- Chapter 13 *Focus and traversal* looks at the mechanisms provided to control which widget gets keyboard input, especially Motif tab groups and the Motif keyboard traversal mechanism.

• Chapter 14 *Window managers* investigates the relationship between an application and the window manager. It shows you how to control (or at least influence) the way the window manager treats your application's windows and how to respond to messages from the window manager.

• Chapter 15 *Compound strings and font lists* covers Motif's support for strings with multiple fonts and directions.

• Chapter 16 *Drawing* is a whistle-stop tour of some of the drawing facilities provided by Xlib.

• Chapter 17 *Grabs* looks at ways of influencing the event-dispatching process by the use of grabs.

• Chapter 18 *Selections* lays the groundwork for the next chapter by looking at the mechanisms provided by X for inter-client communication via the selection facilities.

• Chapter 19 *Drag and drop* describes the simple but flexible mechanism which is provided by Motif.

• Chapter 20 *Internationalisation* looks briefly at the internationalisation support provided by X and shows how it can be built into an ordinary Motif application.

1.4   Conventions

• Source code is set in a sans-serif font. This includes function names in the body of the text (e.g. XmCreateForm()) and fragments of code as examples:

```
int main (argc,argv)
    int     argc;
    char   **argv;
{
    if (argc > 1) {
        printf ("Hello world\n");
        exit (1);
    }
}
```

• This code also illustrates the code layout conventions we eventually agreed on.

• The same format is also used for output messages:

```
Hello world
```

• Italics are used for *emphasis*.

• Widget class names are reproduced in full (e.g. XmPushButton). Additionally, ScrolledText, ScrolledList, PulldownMenu, PopupMenu, MenuBar, OptionMenu and MenuPane are used as if they were real classes.

- Resource names and enumeration values do not have an XmN or Xm prefix (i.e. they are as used in resource files).

- Occasionally we use a warning sign in the margin to indicate that there is something to watch out for - a stumbling block that will trip you up if you are unwary. The more exclamation marks, the greater the danger.

example

- This icon is used to indicate that the code example can be found in the example sources. The source code is structured by chapter and example name. In this case you should look for a directory named chapter1/example which will contain the source code and additional files required to build the example. Details on obtaining the example sources can be found at the end of the book.

1.5   A word on GUI builders

It would be unnatural if the developers of a Motif development tool did not mention GUI builders in a book on Motif. We developed X-Designer after years of frustration and pain coding graphical user interfaces by hand. When Motif appeared it soon became clear that this was a toolkit that, because of its complexity, was going to be difficult to write code for, but, because of its functionality and promised (now achieved) robustness, was going to be an appropriate vehicle and target for a proper code-generating graphical tool. The XmForm widget is an excellent example of this - it is hard to write code for it by hand, but it is useful enough that people still try. The X-Designer form layout editor lets developers design form layouts interactively, then generates the code to implement them. It modifies the XmForm 'on the fly' to show changes in the layout to the developer; this stresses the widget in ways uncommon in most applications, but causes us remarkably few problems.

The information in this book will help you get the best out of whatever tools are available to you and let you tackle problems that are outside the scope of even the most comprehensive tools, but it will not supplant them. If you can possibly raise the money, go out and buy a GUI builder of some sort; it will save you a lot of time and energy when doing basic interface design, and allow you to concentrate on areas that require real skill and expertise. Which tool you buy will depend on your requirements and preferences. We have already mentioned the name of a particularly good one, and will endeavour not to do so again.

CHAPTER 2

Basics

This chapter gives a brief review of the basic features of the X window system, the X toolkit intrinsics and the Motif widget set. An understanding of the topics covered in this chapter is needed in some of the later chapters. However, you do not need to understand everything here before moving on, and most of the topics should be familiar to you anyway. We recommend that you skim this chapter now, and come back later if you need to.

This chapter introduces many terms, identified by an *italic font*. These terms are useful entry points into the indices of related books such as Asente and Swick (1990) and Scheifler and Gettys (1992).

2.1 X basics

Applications access the features of X via Xlib, which provides a C binding for a procedural interface to the X protocol and related utility functions. We will often use Xlib as an adjective to describe a feature that is provided by the X protocol.

2.1.1 X servers and windows

A Motif application does not directly access input and output devices. Instead, it communicates (possibly over a network) with an X server.

An X server manages a device known as a *display*, which has a keyboard, a pointing device (mouse) and a number of *screens*, usually one. Multiple screens add little to the discussion, and the rest of this section assumes a single screen.

Clients (applications) can connect to a server, and then communicate with it by sending requests. In particular, a client can request that the server create and destroy *windows* on a screen. Every window has another window as its parent, except for the *root window* of a screen, which is created automatically by the server and covers the entire screen. A window created as a child of the root window is known as a *top-level* window.

Each window has a unique identifier, the *window ID*, assigned by the server when the window is created. There is no access control on windows. If you have the ID of a window, you can send requests to the server to manipulate it, and they will be honoured.

Windows are not visible on the screen when they are first created; a client must *map* them first. This need not be the client that created them.

Every window is clipped by its parent, and drawing operations within a window are clipped to the window. This means that the area of the screen that an application can use is limited to the area covered by its top-level windows.

Windows that have the same parent can overlap; the one that appears on top is determined by the *stacking order*.

2.1.2 Properties and atoms

A window has a fixed set of attributes, such as its size and position. It is also possible to hang arbitrary typed, named chunks of data on a window. These chunks of data are called *properties*. Properties are held by the server; if you have the ID of a window, you can change and query the values of its associated properties by sending requests to the server.

Property names (and many other things) are identified by character strings. To keep network traffic down, the requests you send to the server and its responses contain, not the string itself, but an equivalent integer called an *atom*. The server maintains the mapping between strings and atoms. If you have a string, you can ask the server to give you the equivalent atom, generating a new atom if necessary. Similarly, you can convert an atom back to the corresponding string. There are some predefined atoms, representing some commonly used strings such as "WINDOW" and "CURSOR". The fact that these atoms are predefined is just a performance optimisation. They do not have any special status.

2.1.3 Events

A client sends requests to the server. The server may send *events* to clients. Events are (usually) related to windows and a client asks the server to tell it about certain types of event on a window by *selecting* for the event type on the window. If no client selects for the event, the server does not report it at all. For most types of event, many clients can select for it on the same window and the server reports it to all of them.

To select for a type of event, the client specifies an *event mask*. A single event mask may select for more than one type of event and a single type of event may be selected for by many different event masks.

Some types of event are generated as a result of user actions; if the user moves the mouse, this will be reported as a MotionNotify event. Others may happen as a result of requests made by clients; if a client asks the server to map one of its windows, it will receive a MapNotify event to say that the server has done so. If one client unmaps or moves one of its windows, another client may get an Expose event, indicating that a formerly obscured window is now visible. A client can also generate a fake event on a window. It sends it to the server, which passes it on to the appropriate clients. A special type of event, the ClientMessage, is only generated in this way, and is used to allow two clients to communicate without having to know anything about each other except a common window ID.

2.2   X toolkit

This toolkit is variously described throughout the book as Xt or the intrinsics toolkit (or some combination of both).

2.2.1   Widgets and resources

The main purpose of Xt is to provide a set of facilities which can be used to create a proper user interface toolkit. Xt is an object-oriented programming system, where the objects are loosely known as *widgets*.[1] Every widget is an instance of a widget *class* and Xt provides a set of basic widget classes and a set of functions to manipulate them. However, the Xt widget set is not sufficiently comprehensive to be a real help in building applications.

The class of a widget defines its attributes, which are known as *resources*. Resources can be set in program code, by command line arguments or by values specified in *resource files*. If no value is specified, a default value specified by the widget author is used.

The inheritance mechanism in Xt is such that a new widget class inherits the resource list of its parent class, although the default values may be different, and the structure of the documentation for the Motif widgets reflects this inheritance.

Applications can exploit the Xt resource mechanisms by defining resource lists that are not bound to any particular widget; these are known as *application resources*.

---

1. Any O-O expert will gladly take an hour out to tell you why Xt is not truly object-oriented, although any two experts are unlikely to give the same reasons.

2.2.2 Widgets and windows

Like windows, widget instances are arranged in a hierarchy. The root of a *widget hierarchy* is usually a specially created instance of the ApplicationShell widget. The widget hierarchy and window hierarchy are similar, except that shell widgets create their windows as children of the root window, rather than as children of their parent widget's window. The term widget hierarchy is sometimes used to mean a tree of widgets rooted on a shell; that is, a tree of widgets corresponding to a top-level window and its descendants.

Widgets that have children are instances of the Xt widget class Composite, or a class derived from it. Composite widgets are responsible for *managing* the geometry of their children; the children can suggest their preferred size and position, but the parent has ultimate authority. Child widgets are ignored by their parent until they are explicitly managed by the application.

A widget's window is created when the widget is *realised*. Realising a widget also realises all its managed children, so it is normally only necessary to realise an application's ApplicationShell widget. Other shells and their descendants are normally realised automatically when they are popped up.

A widget's window is mapped by Xt if and only if the widget is managed and has its *mapped-when-managed* flag set True. This is the default, so managed widgets normally have mapped windows.

2.2.3 Callbacks and event handling

In Xt, events are normally detected using the *callback* mechanism. Callback functions are associated with specific occurrences on particular widgets, and are invoked when appropriate. Callback functions are normally invoked by *action routines* in widgets, which are themselves called by Xt when it detects certain event sequences. The mapping between event sequences and actions is maintained in a *translation table*.

An application can provide its own action routines and modify a widget's translation table so as to change the way it responds to events. An application can also install *event handlers*, which are functions that are invoked directly in response to certain events, rather than through the translation manager.

2.3 Motif

By Motif we mean the Motif toolkit, which contains a set of widgets, related convenience functions and functions for manipulating other sorts of entity used to support the widget set.

2.3.1   Compound strings and font lists

In many, but not all, places Motif uses *compound strings* to represent text. These are used with Motif *font lists* to represent strings which may be drawn using a number of different fonts, and possibly in both left-to-right and right-to-left directions.

Compound strings are used for all displayed text other than that in XmText and XmTextField widgets. For the most part they are part of the Motif programmer's burden, although they do have their uses.

2.3.2   Keyboard traversal

The *keyboard focus* determines which widget receives keyboard input. It can be moved between widgets using the mouse and, with the right *focus policy*, can also be moved between widgets in response to key presses.

Widgets can be grouped together into *tab groups*. Keyboard traversal within a tab group uses the cursor keys, and the Tab key is used to move between tab groups.

2.3.3   Drag and drop

Motif supports a *drag and drop* mechanism which allows the user to move data between widgets. A few of the Motif widgets use this to provide simple drag and drop by default, but applications can exploit it to provide more sophisticated facilities.

Motif drag and drop makes use of the X *selections*. These are little more than a set of conventions, but Xt provides functions which allow an application to use them correctly without needing any great understanding of the underlying basis.

2.3.4   Motif window manager

The Motif window manager, mwm, is responsible for controlling top-level windows. It allows the user to move, resize and iconise them.

Although Motif has its own window manager, the interface between applications and their window manager is independent of Motif, and (in theory) Motif applications will work with other window managers as non-Motif applications will work with mwm.

Part 1

Widgets

CHAPTER 3

Primitive widgets and gadgets

This chapter describes the various Motif primitive widgets - those derived from XmPrimitive - and concludes with a short section on their gadget counterparts. The widgets are ordered below by superclass, so that related widgets are together. Figure 3.1 shows the hierarchy of primitive widget classes.

The distinguishing feature of the primitive widgets is that they cannot have child widgets created for them.

3.1 XmPrimitive

XmPrimitive is the base class from which the other primitive widgets are derived. An XmPrimitive widget would never be instantiated; the class exists only to provide a common base class for those Motif widgets which cannot have children.

3.1.1 Interesting behaviour

XmPrimitive has translations and actions to support keyboard traversal and to handle highlighting when the enclosing shell gets the keyboard focus.

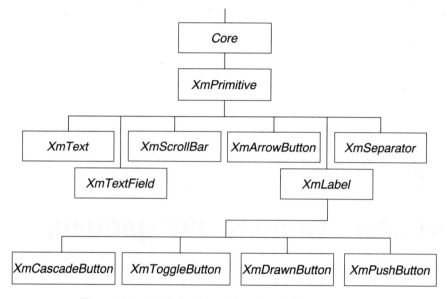

Figure 3.1   *XmPrimitive widget class hierarchy*

3.2   XmLabel

The XmLabel widget has two major roles. The first is as an output-only area which can display a compound string or a pixmap. The second is as a basis for the button widget classes that are derived from it. To support this second role the XmLabel widget class contains quite a number of features that are not really relevant to the XmLabel class itself, but which are used by its subclasses.

3.2.1   Interesting resources

accelerator

The accelerator resource is only used by instances of the button subclasses when they are inside a MenuPane. It defines a KeyPress event that will be automatically translated to an Activate action for this button if it is received anywhere inside the parent shell.

The accelerator syntax is an ill-documented subset of the translation syntax for a single KeyPress event, such as "Ctrl<Key>O". The event type must be 'KeyPress' (or a synonym: 'Key' or 'KeyDown') and only a few modifiers are allowed ('Ctrl', 'Shift', 'Lock', 'Meta', 'Alt' and 'Mod1' to 'Mod5').

Note that the XmLabel *accelerator* resource is very different from the Core *accelerators* resource.[1] The accelerators resource is covered in Section 11.4.

---

1. Remember that an XmPushButton in a menu can only have a single accelerator.

acceleratorText
>AcceleratorText defines the actual text that is displayed in the button to give the user a clue as to what the accelerator is. The toolkit does not require that the two resources bear any resemblance. For an accelerator of Ctrl<Key>O the acceler-atorText could be 'Control+O'. Note that this resource is a Motif compound string.

fontList
>Defines the font that will be used to display the text of the XmLabel. Refer to Chapter 15 for a full discussion of font lists and compound strings.

labelType
>Determines whether the text defined by labelString or the pixmap defined by labelPixmap is displayed.

labelInsensitivePixmap and labelPixmap
>If the labelType resource is set to PIXMAP; the actual pixmap displayed will depend on the sensitivity of the widget. A pixmap can be a full-colour icon, but Motif only provides routines to manipulate pixmaps that are one bit deep (i.e. they can show only two colours). If you want to use more than two colours in your pixmap you will need to do some Xlib programming, or use one of the many available pixmap manipulation libraries. We have used the XPM library supplied in the contrib section of the MIT X11 release to some effect.

labelString
>Defines the text that is displayed in the label. The text is a Motif compound string. See Chapter 15 for a full discussion of font lists and compound strings.
>The XmLabel widget makes a copy of the labelString resource. If you have created the compound string only for use by the XmLabel widget, you will need to free it after creating the widget or setting the resource with XtSetValues().

marginHeight and marginWidth
>These are the margins that the user and developer should modify to make the label larger and smaller. Manager parent widgets tend to modify the settings of marginLeft, marginRight, marginTop and marginBottom.

mnemonic and mnemonicCharset
>Mnemonics are another way for the user to activate a button in a MenuPane or MenuBar. They are displayed by underlining the first character in the labelString that matches the mnemonic in the character set specified by mnemonicCharset. Figure 3.2 shows an XmCascadeButton displaying a label with two charsets. The mnemonic is set to 'l' and the mnemonicCharset is set to the charset of the second string segment. See Chapter 15 for further discussion of font lists and compound strings.
>If the button is an XmCascadeButton in a MenuBar, the user can post the associated PulldownMenu with the mnemonic. If the MenuBar has the keyboard

Figure 3.2   *XmCascadeButton with a mnemonic and mnemonicCharset set*

focus, the user simply types the mnemonic. If the MenuBar does not have the focus, then <Alt>mnemonic can be used to post the MenuPane. Once the MenuPane is posted, the user can type the mnemonic for a particular button within the MenuPane and cause it to be activated.

 Mnemonics are KeySyms. The file keysym.h lists the valid KeySym values. In code specify them as:

```
XtSetArg (al[ac], XmNmnemonic, XK_l);
XtSetArg (al[ac], XmNmnemonic, XK_plus);
```

In a resource file specify them as:

```
mnemonic: l
mnemonic: plus.
```

3.2.2   Interesting behaviour

The XmLabel widget has a default translation for Button2 which starts a drag operation transferring the labelString and labelPixmap resources as targets COMPOUND_TEXT and PIXMAP, respectively. See Chapter 19 for a full discussion of drag and drop.

XmLabel widgets do not display a 3D border, although they do leave room for a border to be displayed.

Although ostensibly an output-only widget, the XmLabel widget has quite a number of Translations and Actions. A number of these are specifically designed to assist in the handling of menus.

3.2.3   Examples of use

XmLabels (see Figure 3.3) are used widely to provide captions for other widgets.

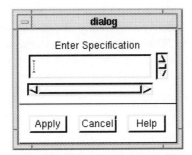

Figure 3.3   *XmLabel widget as caption to scrolled text*

3.2.4   Watch out for

 Setting the alignment resource has no effect if the widget is a child of an XmRowColumn. The XmRowColumn widget has its own alignment resource which is forced onto XmLabel children.

    Setting the labelPixmap resource has no effect unless the labelType is PIXMAP.

3.3   XmPushButton

The XmPushButton widget is widely used in Motif applications as a control which the user can click on to initiate an action within the application.

3.3.1   Interesting resources

activateCallback
Although obvious, this is the callback that does the real work.

defaultButtonShadowThickness and showAsDefault
These two resources interact subtly. The best way to use them is to set defaultButtonShadowThickness to the thickness of default shadow required. Use the defaultButton resource in XmBulletinBoard if this button is to be the default, and let the toolkit worry about setting showAsDefault. Using these resources on a button which does not have a XmBulletinBoard ancestor will probably not have the expected results.

3.3.2   Interesting behaviour

The XmPushButton behaves differently depending on its parent; buttons in
MenuPanes display the 3D visual when they become armed, whereas buttons not
in MenuPanes change the visual from shadow out to shadow in. XmPushButton
has special translations and actions to assist menu processing.

3.3.3   Examples of use

Figure 3.4 shows buttons which have labelType set to PIXMAP above the line;
those below the line have labelType STRING. The "Apply" button has been
specified as the defaultButton in the parent XmBulletinBoard, and so is displaying
a default border.

Figure 3.4   *Some different XmPushButtons*

3.4   XmToggleButton

The XmToggleButton appears in a number of guises, but is essentially used to
show and input Boolean values. The state of the XmToggleButton can be shown in
two ways: either by the indicator, or by a shadow which depicts the button pressed
in or out.

3.4.1   Interesting resources

**labelType, labelPixmap, selectPixmap, labelInsensitivePixmap and
selectInsensitivePixmap**
If labelType is set to PIXMAP, the XmToggleButton displays the selectPixmap or
labelPixmap according to whether or not it is set. If the widget is insensitive, then
selectInsensitivePixmap and labelInsensitivePixmap are used. There is no select-
LabelString resource comparable to selectPixmap.

indicatorOn, leftMargin and shadowThickness

These resources can be used to modify the way that the XmToggleButton presents the state information, as shown in Figure 3.5.

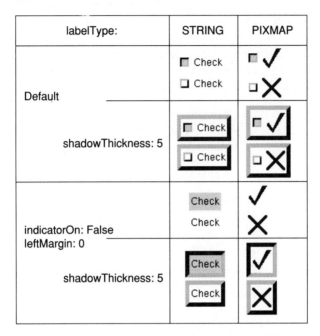

Figure 3.5   *The effect of resource settings on the appearance of XmToggleButtons*

The leftMargin resource should be set to 0 if indicatorOn is False, otherwise space is left for the indicator.

visibleWhenOff

Denotes that the indicator is visible when the toggle is set False. The resource is ignored if indicatorOn is False.

3.4.2   Interesting behaviour

Like XmPushButtons, XmToggleButtons behave slightly differently if they are in a menu system. In particular, the resource visibleWhenOff defaults to False when in a MenuPane.

XmToggleButton can display two different indicators: a diamond or a square. This is determined by the setting of indicatorType. Note that indicatorType is forced to ONE_OF_MANY if the XmToggleButton is created inside an

XmRowColumn which has radioBehavior set to True. The convenience function XmCreateRadioBox() provides an easy way of doing this.

3.4.3   Examples of use

The XmToggleButton widget is used in three main ways: to provide a check option, to specify a one of many selection or to specify a many of many selection. These three are shown in Figure 3.6.

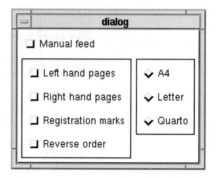

Figure 3.6   *Example XmToggleButtons*

3.4.4   Watch out for

 XmToggleButtons can also be used in PulldownMenus and PopupMenus, but not in an OptionMenu's PulldownMenu.

3.5   XmCascadeButton

XmCascadeButton is another button widget derived from XmLabel. It may only be created in an XmRowColumn parent which has its rowColumnType resource set to MENU_BAR, MENU_POPUP or MENU_PULLDOWN. Its purpose is to display an associated MenuPane when it is armed. XmCascadeButton behaviour is inextricably bound to MenuPane behaviour, which is discussed in Chapter 9.

3.5.1   Interesting resources

subMenuId

The MenuPane, usually created by XmCreatePulldownMenu(), which is to be displayed when the XmCascadeButton becomes armed.

cascadePixmap

Specifies the pixmap for the pull-right indicator if the XmCascadeButton is itself in a MenuPane.

3.5.2 Examples of use

Figure 3.7 shows XmCascadeButtons being used in a MenuBar and a PulldownMenu.

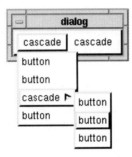

Figure 3.7   *XmCascadeButton widgets*

3.5.3 Watch out for

XmCascadeButtons can be used in PulldownMenus and PopupMenus, but not in an OptionMenu's PulldownMenu.

The activateCallback is not called if the XmCascadeButton has a PulldownMenu attached via its subMenuId resource.

The PulldownMenu must be created with the right parent. See Section 9.4.4 for details.

Accelerators on XmPushButtons in the PulldownMenu will only work if the XmPushButton is managed when the subMenuId resource is set, either by XmCreateCascadeButton() or XtSetValues(). The following example shows the correct ordering:

```
menu_bar = XmCreateMenuBar (z1, "menu_bar", al, ac);
pulldown = XmCreatePulldownMenu (menu_bar, "pulldown", al, ac);
XtSetArg (al[ac], XmNaccelerator, "Ctrl<Key>A"); ac++;
button = XmCreatePushButton (pulldown, "button", al, ac);
XtManageChild (button);
ac = 0;
XtSetArg (al[ac], XmNsubMenuId, pulldown); ac++;
```

```
cascade = XmCreateCascadeButton (menu_bar, "cascade", al, ac);
XtManageChild (cascade);
```

If the XtManageChild (button) call is made after the XmCreateCascadeButton() call, the accelerator will not work.

3.6　XmDrawnButton

XmDrawnButton is a clone of the XmPushButton widget except that, instead of drawing a label or pixmap on the button face, it provides an exposeCallback and resizeCallback to allow the application to draw on the button face.

3.6.1　Examples of use

Given that sophisticated drawings can be achieved on an XmPushButton by using pixmaps, the most likely uses of an XmDrawnButton would be either to handle drawings that resize as the button resizes, or to handle buttons where the drawing could change frequently (this may cause flicker if pixmaps are used). Figure 3.8 shows a simple XmDrawnButton that draws an ellipse scaled to fit the size of the widget. The source code for this is very simple, shown here are the expose and resize callbacks for the XmDrawnButton:

drawnbutton

```
#define LINE_WIDTH 10

void button_expose (w, client_data, call_data)
      Widget        w;
      XtPointer     client_data;
      XtPointer     call_data;
{

      Dimension   width, height, shadow, highlight;
      int             origin;
      unsigned int arc_width, arc_height;
/* Call a routine to create a Graphics Context */
      create_gc (w);
/* First get the various dimensions */
      XtVaGetValues (w,
                  XmNwidth, &width,
                  XmNheight, &height,
                  XmNshadowThickness, &shadow,
                  XmNhighlightThickness, &highlight,
                  0);
```

```
          origin = shadow + highlight + 1 + (LINE_WIDTH / 2);
/* Don't draw 0 or negatively sized circles. */
      if (width < origin * 2
      || height < origin * 2)
          return;
/*Calculate arc sizes */
      arc_width = width - origin * 2;
      arc_height = height - origin * 2;
/* Draw the Arc */
      XDrawArc (XtDisplay (w), XtWindow (w), gc, origin, origin, arc_width,
                       arc_height, 0, 360 * 64);
}

void button_resize (w, client_data, call_data)
      Widget        w;
      XtPointer     client_data;
      XtPointer     call_data;
{
      XClearArea (XtDisplay (w), XtWindow (w), 0, 0, 0, 0, True);
}
```

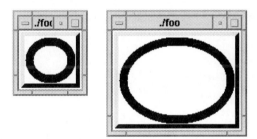

Figure 3.8   *A simple XmDrawnButton*

These callbacks take a very simplistic approach to handling the drawing. For fuller examples of drawing techniques, refer to Section 4.6.1 and Chapter 16, which also has example implementations of create_gc().

3.6.2 Watch out for

The manual notes that care should be taken not to draw into the shadow and highlight areas.

3.7 XmArrowButton

XmArrowButton is a straightforward button which can only display an arrow.

3.7.1 Examples of use

XmArrowButtons could be used to provide increment/decrement controls, as depicted in Figure 3.9.

Figure 3.9 *XmArrowButtons*

3.8 XmSeparator

XmSeparator is an output-only widget that provides several line drawing styles. It is the only widget, not derived from XmLabel, that can be put in a MenuPane.

3.8.1 Interesting resources

separatorType
Specifies what line type is drawn. It can be set to NO_LINE which will, of course, draw no line. This can be used in conjunction with the backgroundPixmap resource to tile an area.

3.8.2 Interesting behaviour

XmSeparator has no behaviour at all, traversalOn is forced to False and it has no translations.

3.8.3 Examples of use

To draw a line separating logically grouped widgets. The horizontal line in Figure 3.4 is an XmSeparator automatically created by XmMessageBox.

XmSeparator is also used in MenuPanes to provide visual separation between logically related groups of menu items.

3.8.4 Watch out for

 The orientation of an XmSeparator child of an XmRowColumn defaults to the opposite of the orientation of the XmRowColumn. This is usually desirable, but explicitly setting the XmSeparator orientation will override it.

3.9 XmScrollBar

It is intended that XmScrollBar is used as a control to specify the visible portion of a large area. There is, however, nothing inherent in the XmScrollBar widget itself that forces this behaviour. They are most commonly found incorporated in an XmScrolledWindow, but may be used to effect simply in conjunction with other widgets.

3.9.1 Interesting resources

maximum, minimum, value and sliderSize
   By convention, the XmScrollBar should have a slider whose size is proportional to the size of the XmScrollBar in the same ratio as the visible area is proportional to the size of the whole area being scrolled. The way to achieve this is to set maximum to the size of the area and sliderSize to the size of the visible area. The units used should be determined by the granularity of the scrolling required.
   For example, if you are displaying a large picture in a restricted XmDrawingArea and are using an XmScrollBar to position the drawing vertically, it would probably be appropriate to set maximum to be the height of the picture in pixels, and sliderSize to be the height of the XmDrawingArea in pixels. This will allow you to set value to be the number of pixels not drawn at the top of the picture. If, however, you were displaying lines of text in a drawing area, it might well be more appropriate to set maximum to be the total number of lines of text and sliderSize to be the number of lines visible. You would then set value to be the number of lines not displayed. See Section 7.4.2 for examples of setting these resources.

toTopCallback and toBottomCallback
   These should be named toMinCallback and toMaxCallback, respectively.

valueChangedCallback
   This is normally only called when the slider is released after a drag, but will also be called if the value is changed and there is no other callback to handle the change. The advantage of this is that normally only the valueChangedCallback need be set to handle all value changes, but it will not be called in addition if another, more specific callback is available.

3.9.2   Examples of use

As noted above, XmScrollBars are found most often as part of an XmScrolled-Window. Refer to Chapter 7 for more details.

3.9.3   Watch out for

 XmScrollBar is very picky about maximum, minimum, sliderSize and value being consistent. If, for example, you change the value resource so that it is greater than the maximum less the sliderSize, it will call XtWarning() to warn the application user.

The checks it makes are that:

- minimum < maximum.
- sliderSize > 0.
- sliderSize <= maximum - minimum.
- value >= minimum.
- value <= maximum - sliderSize.
- increment > 0.
- pageIncrement > 0.

    Changing the value resource with XtSetValues does not call the valueChanged-Callback. Use the XmScrollBarSetValues() routine and pass notify True.

3.10   XmText and XmTextField

Motif provides two text input widgets: XmText and XmTextField. The XmTextField widget is a lighter weight single line non-scrolling version of the all-powerful XmText widget. It is hard to establish exactly how much cheaper the XmTextField widget is. A simple program that creates some XmText widgets in an XmForm appears to use about 10% less heap space if XmTextField widgets are used.

The discussion below uses Text to denote XmText or XmTextField equally. XmTextField and XmText are used to indicate the particular widget type. Section 3.10.5 notes the resources of XmText that are not available in XmTextField.

3.10.1   Interesting resources

editable

Set editable to False to prevent the user from changing the text. This is better than making the widget insensitive, as the user can still use the arrow keys to move over the text, the text is not greyed out, and selections can be made from it.

source (This is not applicable to XmTextField)

The XmText widget is implemented such that the text being edited is held by an object external to the XmText widget, called the source. This idea is borrowed from the Athena widget set, where the text source is actually another widget. In Motif, however, the text source is an object which contains an opaque pointer to the data and pointers to access functions. Motif supplies a text source which supports char* and wide characters. In theory it is possible to write a specialised text source, for example to support compound strings, but in practice; the main use for this resource is to allow two XmText widgets to display the same text. This is surprisingly simple:

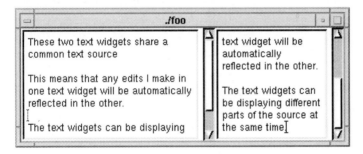

```
XtSetArg (al[ac], XmNeditMode, XmMULTI_LINE_EDIT); ac++;
XtSetArg (al[ac], XmNwordWrap, True); ac++;
XtSetArg (al[ac], XmNscrollHorizontal, False); ac++;
text1 = XmCreateScrolledText (form, "text1", al, ac);

text2 = XmCreateScrolledText (form, "text2", al, ac);

XmTextSetSource (text2, XmTextGetSource (text1), 0, 0);
```

textsources

This code creates two XmScrolledText widgets and sets the source of text2 to be that of text1. Assuming them to be in an XmForm with appropriate attachments they might appear as in Figure 3.10.

Figure 3.10 *Two XmText widgets sharing the same text source*

value and valueWcs

Internally the Text widget uses multi-byte strings to manipulate the text. However, an interface is provided to allow the programmer to use wide character strings. This interface simply calls the wide character and multi-byte conversion functions to convert to and from the internal format. Multi-byte strings code text in languages such as Japanese into a series of escape sequences, which can be stored as an array of char. The disadvantage of this is that the application cannot simply index the array to obtain a particular character. Hence wide characters, which are wide enough (perhaps two or four bytes) to encode languages such as Japanese. The Motif documentation does not mention how wide character strings should be terminated. The source code for the Text widget appears to look for a wide character where all bytes are 0.

XtSetValues() copies the supplied string (char* or wide characters) into the Text widget's internal buffer, whereas XtGetValues() returns a pointer to the internal buffer. Therefore when setting the value, the application should free any allocated memory no longer required and when getting a value the application should not alter the text returned.

This resource can also be set and fetched using XmTextSetString() and XmTextGetString(); there are alternative versions for XmTextField and wide characters. All these functions copy the string and it is the application's responsibility to free storage where appropriate.

modifyVerifyCallback and valueChangedCallback

These two callbacks work together neatly. When an attempt is made to modify the Text widget, either by the user typing in it or programmatically, the modifyVerify-Callbacks are called. This callback can make a decision about whether to allow the modification and can adjust the modification that is to take place. If the modification is allowed, the default case, then the text widget is updated and the valueChangedCallbacks are called. The callbacks can distinguish a modification programmatically from user input by examining the event field in the call_data. The event will be NULL for a programmatic modification.[1] The callback function shown below shows some techniques that might be used in a modifyVerify-Callback:

textverify

```
void modify_verify (w, client_data, call_data)
    Widget      w;
    XtPointer   client_data;
    XtPointer   call_data;
{
    XmTextVerifyCallbackStruct *cb_data =
                    (XmTextVerifyCallbackStruct *) call_data;
/* Allow programmatic changes */
    if (!cb_data->event)
        return;
/* Don't allow deletes or multiple character paste */
    if (cb_data->startPos != cb_data->endPos
    || cb_data->text->length > 1)
    {
        cb_data->doit = False;
        return;
```

---

1. However, at Motif 1.2.2 modifications caused by drop or paste operations also have a NULL event.

```
        }
    /* Only output a * */
        cb_data->text->ptr[0] = '*';
    }
```

fontList

It is important to note that although the Text widget can only handle char* strings and wide character strings and not Motif compound strings, its font resource is a full Motif font list. The Text widget selects a single font or font set from the fontList and uses it to display the text. If the fontList contains a font set, the Text widget will attempt to establish a link to an input method. See Section 20.3 for further discussion of internationalised text input.

3.10.2   Interesting behaviour

Scrolled Text

There is a convenience function XmCreateScrolledText() that creates an XmScrolledWindow and an XmText widget which combine to provide a Scrolled Text 'widget'. There is no special XmScrolledText widget; the functionality is supported by the XmText widget detecting that its parent is an XmScrolledWindow with APPLICATION_DEFINED scrollingPolicy and that the XmText widget has editMode set to MULTI_LINE_EDIT. The XmText widget then creates its own XmScrollBar widgets and sets up their callbacks to handle scrolling.

Selection operations

The Text widget supports a range of different selection operations. It uses the generic Xt selection mechanisms to provide Cut and Paste type operations via both the Primary and Secondary selections. It will also initiate a Drag operation for the Primary selection and provide some convenience routines to support moving text between the Primary selection and the Clipboard under program control. By default, the Text widget also registers itself as a drop site that will accept COMPOUND_TEXT targets. Refer to Chapters 18 and 19 for more detailed discussions of the selection and drag and drop mechanisms, respectively.

3.10.3   Examples of use

Text widgets can be used in a wide variety of ways: displaying non-editable help text, as the major component of a text editor or as a popup input control over the top of a complicated drawing. The nature of the input required will probably determine which of the Text widgets is more appropriate.

3.10.4   Watch out for

 XmCreateScrolledText() returns the XmText widget pointer. If you want to set form attachments for it you need its XmScrolledWindow parent which you can obtain by using XtParent() on the XmText widget.

    It is not possible to get a Text widget to exactly shrink wrap the text it contains. Even if you calculate the font height and the exact string length, the Text widget requires some additional space to display the I-beam cursor. You need to set marginWidth and marginHeight to some small value (2 pixels seems to be sufficient) to provide this space. If you are trying to get the Text widget to line up with some other text (perhaps displayed on an XmDrawingArea) or widget, then obtain the baseline offset from the Text widget using XmTextGetBaseline(). This will return the distance from the top of the widget to the text baseline.[1] You can use this value to adjust the y coordinate of the Text widget.

3.10.5   XmTextField differences

The following resources are available in the XmText Widget, but not in the XmTextField widget. They all relate to the use of multiple lines or scrolled text:

- autoShowCursorPosition.
- editMode.
- topCharacter.
- resizeHeight.
- rows.
- wordWrap.
- scrollHorizontal.
- scrollLeftSide.
- scrollTopSide.
- scrollVertical.

3.11   XmList

The XmList widget is a commonly used and is a very powerful widget. It is frequently used in conjunction with an XmScrolledWindow to give a scrolling list.
    The XmList widget comes with a daunting set of manipulation functions, which probably does not include the one you want.

---

1. The manual section for XmTextGetBaseline() confusingly refers to x position, when it should be y position.

3.11.1 Interesting resources

selectionPolicy
> This resource specifies the mode in which the XmList is to work. It is the setting of this resource that determines how many items can be selected, and which of the selection callbacks will be invoked. For this reason, you should, probably always explicitly set this resource to the value for which callbacks have been supplied, rather than letting the user override the selectionPolicy in a resource file, or supply callback functions for all the callbacks.

automaticSelection
> When using BROWSE or EXTENDED selection policies this resource determines when the selection callback is called. If it is set to True, the callback is called as the selection changes, i.e. as the user drags over a selection the callback is called each time the selection changes. If set to False, the callback is called only once when the selection is complete, i.e. when the mouse button is released.

items and itemCount
> These resources specify the list items. The items resource is an array of compound strings. When setting the resource, the toolkit makes a copy of the items, so the application is free to deallocate any dynamic storage it created for the array and the compound strings. When getting the items, the toolkit returns a pointer to the internal list. The application should not make any changes to the items or free them.

visibleItemCount
> This specifies the number of items that the list is going to display. This resource, though potentially useful, will be overridden by size constraints from a parent, such as an XmForm.

3.11.2 Interesting behaviour

> The correct way to set a new set of list items is to use XtSetValues() to set items and itemCount. Using the XmList functions to add all the items is costly.
> The XmList widget supports a default Drag operation. Dragging from the XmList widget will create an XmDragContext with dragOperations set to DROP_COPY and exportTargets set to COMPOUND_TEXT. If the drag is started over a selected item, the convert procedure will transfer the selected items. If the drag is started over an unselected item, the convert procedure will transfer just that item.

Scrolled List
> There is a convenience function XmCreateScrolledList() that creates an XmScrolledWindow and an XmList widget which combine to provide a Scrolled

List 'widget'. There is no special XmScrolledList widget; the functionality is supported by the XmList widget detecting that its parent is an XmScrolledWindow with APPLICATION_DEFINED scrollingPolicy. The XmList widget then creates its own XmScrollBar widgets and sets up their callbacks to correctly handle scrolling by items, etc.

3.11.3   Examples of use

Lists are used to provide a selection mechanism where the possible number of items is large. The example shows an XmList containing the X font names.

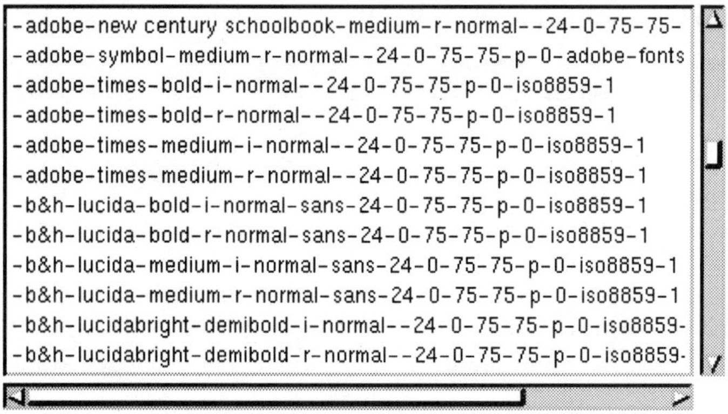

```
-adobe-new century schoolbook-medium-r-normal--24-0-75-75-
-adobe-symbol-medium-r-normal--24-0-75-75-p-0-adobe-fonts
-adobe-times-bold-i-normal--24-0-75-75-p-0-iso8859-1
-adobe-times-bold-r-normal--24-0-75-75-p-0-iso8859-1
-adobe-times-medium-i-normal--24-0-75-75-p-0-iso8859-1
-adobe-times-medium-r-normal--24-0-75-75-p-0-iso8859-1
-b&h-lucida-bold-i-normal-sans-24-0-75-75-p-0-iso8859-1
-b&h-lucida-bold-r-normal-sans-24-0-75-75-p-0-iso8859-1
-b&h-lucida-medium-i-normal-sans-24-0-75-75-p-0-iso8859-1
-b&h-lucida-medium-r-normal-sans-24-0-75-75-p-0-iso8859-1
-b&h-lucidabright-demibold-i-normal--24-0-75-75-p-0-iso8859-
-b&h-lucidabright-demibold-r-normal--24-0-75-75-p-0-iso8859-
```

Figure 3.11 *XmList widget containing X font names*

3.11.4   Watch out for

The XmList widget makes a good attempt to handle items with different vertical sizes by initialising all the items to be the same height as the largest. However, if a new largest item is inserted, the drawing gets corrupted. This unfortunately precludes using different fonts to denote 'special' list items.

Whenever individual list items are referred to, either in a callback structure or a function call, they are always indexed by position, from one to itemCount. A position of zero specifies the last element.

XmCreateScrolledList() returns the XmList widget pointer. If you want to set form attachments for it, you need its XmScrolledWindow parent which you can obtain by using XtParent() on the XmList widget.

The XmList widget has an annoying tendency to resize itself when items are added or deleted. If the user has resized the XmList, by stretching a Shell, so that more of it can be seen, the XmList will resize itself back to its initial size when the item list is modified. This is probably not what the user wants. See Section 6.4.4 for some hints on how to stop this happening.

3.12 Gadgets

Gadgets are lightweight versions of a selection of the primitive widgets. For instance, you can use an XmPushButtonGadget gadget as an alternative to an XmPushButton widget.

Gadgets achieve their lightness by not having their own window; rather, they draw directly onto, and receive events via, their XmManager parent's window. They cannot be derived from the Core widget because they do not have a window, and therefore they are not derived from XmPrimitive. Instead, a special XmGadget class is provided that is derived from the Xt RectObj class. The fact that a gadget does not have a window means that it uses fewer server resources than its widget counterpart.

The gadgets have no visual resources, but inherit their colours and pixmaps from their XmManager parent. This means that gadgets are likely to be able to share GCs with other gadgets which have the same visuals. The individual gadget classes implement GC sharing and caching between gadgets of the same type. Again this is intended to reduce the amount of server resources required.

There is some dispute as to whether gadgets really provide a significant saving of resources, given the extra work that their parents have to perform in order to support them and the extra network traffic they generate, but this is really beyond the scope of this book. For most practical purposes they can be considered as interchangeable with the corresponding widgets.

Gadget versions are provided for XmLabel, XmPushButton, XmCascadeButton, XmToggleButton, XmArrowButton and XmSeparator.

 If you do use gadgets, you must usually manipulate them using different convenience functions. For instance, you set the state of a toggle button using XmToggleButtonSetState() if it is a widget or XmToggleButtonGadgetSetState() if it is a gadget.

 If you set resources for a widget class in a resource file, this will only affect widgets, not gadgets. Any resource file entry that mentions a widget class should normally be accompanied by a corresponding entry for the gadget class if there is one:

```
*XmToggleButton.background:       pink
*XmToggleButtonGadget.background: pink
```

 Most of the Motif composite widgets (such as XmFileSelectionBox) use gadgets where they are available.

CHAPTER 4

Simple manager widgets

This chapter describes the XmManager base class and some of the simple container widgets derived from it. Manager widgets are characterised by their ability to support widget children. A number of different widget classes are derived from XmManager to provide, for instance, different sorts of child layout.

Figure 4.1 shows the hierarchy of manager widget classes. XmForm, XmScrolledWindow and the menu applications of XmRowColumn are discussed in Chapters 6, 7 and 9, respectively.

4.1 XmManager

XmManager is the base class from which the other manager widgets are derived. An XmManager widget would never be instantiated; the class exists only to provide a common base class for the Motif widgets which can have widget children.

4.1.1 Interesting resources

XmManager has resources to provide the Motif 3D visuals and to support the traversal model. The visual resources are rarely used on an XmManager or derived

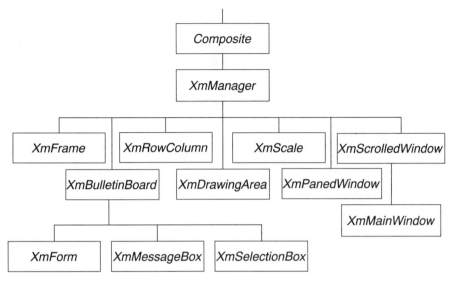

Figure 4.1 *XmManager widget class hierarchy*

widget, except to provide defaults for gadget children. The traversal resources are covered in Chapter 13.

The following resources are also pertinent to XmPrimitive and XmGadget.

helpCallback

Every Motif widget and gadget has a helpCallback. This works in conjunction with the PrimitiveHelp and ManagerGadgetHelp actions which call the helpCallback for the widget or gadget, or for the nearest ancestor which has a helpCallback.

This enables the user to press the osfHelp key at any time to get help which is sensitive to the context of the current keyboard focus. Simplistically, what happens is that the osfHelp key event is sent to the widget that currently has the keyboard focus. Every Motif widget has a translation which maps this through to the PrimitiveHelp or ManagerGadgetHelp action. These actions look up the widget hierarchy for a widget which has a helpCallback set. If one is found, it is called.

You can therefore simply attach helpCallbacks at the points where you are prepared to provide help, and rely on the toolkit to propagate help requests for widgets which do not provide help.

Obviously, applications frequently use the same help callback function throughout the system and use the widget or client_data parameters to determine the context.

unitType

Motif makes a bold attempt to provide some degree of resolution independence.The unitType resource provides the basis for this support. If this resource is set to a value other than PIXELS, any size and position resources for the widget will be interpreted as being in the specified units. This resource is inherited down the widget instance tree, so that it should only need to be set on the top widget. If an application sets any size or position resources explicitly in the code, it should either force unitType to the desired setting or be prepared to convert to and from the specified units. The drawing example in Section 3.6.1 is not resolution independent because it assumes that the width and height it fetches from the widget is in pixels; Section 4.6.1 shows a fuller example which checks for unitType settings.

userData
This resource allows the application developer to attach arbitrary data to the widget which the toolkit will not use. You might, for example, choose to store a back pointer to a C++ object in the userData of the widgets which that object owns.

4.1.2 Interesting behaviour

Gadgets cannot receive their own events, because they do not have a window. Therefore any events for them are sent to their XmManager parent. The XmManager widget has special translations and action routines to handle events and send them on to the appropriate gadget.

4.2 XmFrame

The XmFrame widget is a simple container that shrink-wraps its children and draws a frame around them. The XmFrame widget supports a single work area widget, around which it draws the frame and/or a title widget which is used to caption the frame. There is no limitation on the child types for either widget, but obviously some combinations are more useful than others.

4.2.1 Interesting resources

The XmFrame widget specifies which child has which role and the positioning of the title widget, using constraint resources.

childType
A constraint resource for each of the children in the XmFrame, it specifies which role the widget is to take. The title widget should have its childType set to FRAME_TITLE_CHILD. The other child should have its childType set to FRAME_WORKAREA_CHILD.

childHorizontalAlignment, childHorizontalSpacing and childVerticalAlignment
Although these are constraint resources and can be set for all children of the XmFrame, they are only used for the title widget.

4.2.2 Examples of use

XmFrames are used to draw 3D borders around other widgets with optional titles. Figure 4.2 shows two XmFrames. The outer one has an OptionMenu title widget and an XmForm work area. The inner one has an XmLabel title and a RadioBox work area.

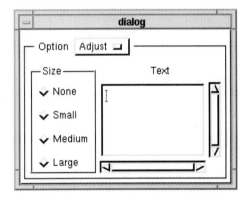

Figure 4.2 *XmFrame examples*

4.3 XmScale

The XmScale widget has a peculiar internal structure. The actual scale part is really an XmScrollbar with the arrows turned off and the title is displayed in an automatically created XmLabelGadget. This structure is not visible to programmer or user; there is no way to interrogate the widget to obtain access to its components. The application is allowed to create children of an XmScale. The intention is that these are XmLabels that can be used to indicate the value at positions along the scale. The XmScale forces the children to be equally spaced along its length. Although XmScale does not enforce any specific child type, it is hard to think of a use for an XmScale with XmFileSelectionBox children.

4.3.1 Interesting resources

Many of XmScale's resources are direct counterparts of XmScrollBars. This is not surprising, given the implementation.

decimalPoints

Instead of specifying the value resource as a floating point number, this resource is used to move the decimal point when displaying the slider value.

scaleMultiple

This resource is used in the calculation of the XmScrollBar's pageIncrement resource. It effectively allows the developer to specify how quickly the XmScale will adjust if the user clicks in the trough area. For example, consider an XmScale set to measure values between 0 and 100,000. By default, scaleMultiple will be 10,000. If the user presses and holds Button 1 in the trough area, the slider will move in increments of 10,000. If the XmScale is controlling a value that will have an effect visible to the user (say a colour value), this will probably result in the value changing too fast for the user to get helpful feedback. A scaleMultiple of 1,000 will allow the user to see the effect of the value changes more accurately.

sensitive

Setting sensitive to False make the XmScale output-only. However, it also greys out the XmScrollBar area, which does not look attractive.

4.3.2   Interesting behaviour

XmScale has helpful XmScaleSetValue() and XmScaleGetValue() routines to set and get the value resource.

4.3.3   Examples of use

XmSeparators make good check marks, but they need their width or height explicitly set. The example in Figure 4.3 shows a scale with XmLabel and XmSeparator children.

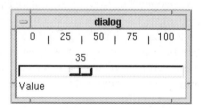

Figure 4.3   *XmScale example*

4.4 XmPanedWindow

XmPanedWindow is a Manager widget which lays out its children as tiled panes and allows the user to decide on the relative sizes of the panes. This is a useful way of handing off some of the layout decisions to the user. As of Motif 1.2.2 XmPanedWindow only handles vertical tiling.

4.4.1 Interesting resources

Most of XmPanedWindow's resources, including its constraint resources, are self-explanatory.

positionIndex
This constraint resource provides a useful way of specifying the ordering of children created out of sequence, without having to use the insertPosition procedure, which would have to take account of the sash widget children.

4.4.2 Examples of use

XmPanedWindow is really only useful where it is valid to allow the user to decide on the relative sizes of the dialog components. Figure 4.4 shows an XmPaned-Window containing help text and "see also" links. Here it is appropriate that the user can decide which section to give priority.

4.5 XmRowColumn

The XmRowColumn widget is used in so many different ways that it is surprising (and confusing) that there is only a single class. This is somewhat ameliorated by the provision of convenience routines to create XmRowColumn widgets in each of the different guises. The basic feature of the XmRowColumn widget is that it can lay out its children in rows and columns. It is also endowed with behavioural properties to implement RadioBox and menu systems.

   This section only deals with the generalities of XmRowColumn and its use as a RadioBox. Chapter 9 examines its uses in menu systems.

4.5.1 Interesting resources

There are many more interesting resources of XmRowColumn that are menu-specific. These are discussed in Chapter 9.

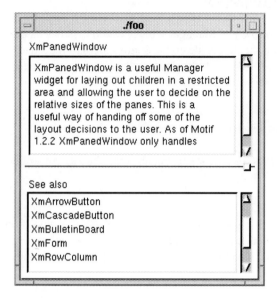

Figure 4.4 *XmPanedWindow example*

adjustLast

Setting this resource to True will cause the XmRowColumn to extend the last row or column (orientation set to HORIZONTAL or VERTICAL, respectively) to the edge of the XmRowColumn (see Figure 4.5).

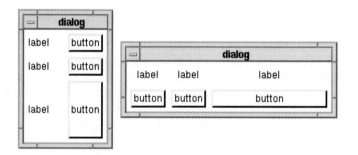

orientation set horizontal: orientation set vertical:
bottom row resizes   right column resizes

Figure 4.5 *The effect of orientation on adjustLast*

entryAlignment, isAligned and adjustMargin

The Boolean resource isAligned turns on the XmRowColumn alignment specified by entryAlignment. This overrides the alignment setting of child XmLabel and derived widgets, except for XmLabel widgets in a MenuPane, which are unaffected. The resource adjustMargin specifies whether the margin resources of XmLabel and derived widgets are to be altered, so that text lines up. Note that XmToggleButton draws its indicator in the leftMargin area, so adjustMargin is particularly useful when XmToggleButtons are mixed with other XmLabel derived widgets. Table 4.1 shows the interaction of these resources.

Table 4.1 *The effect of alignment and adjustMargin resources*

alignment	adjustMargin: True	adjustMargin: False
Beginning	Labels are aligned with XmToggle-Button indicator taken into account label button XmToggleButton	Labels aligned at beginning of widget label button XmToggleButton
Centre	Labels centred over widest label label button XmToggleButton	Labels are centred in widget label button XmToggleButton

entryCallback

Allows a single callback routine to be used as the activateCallback or valueChanged callback for all the XmPushButton, XmCascadeButton, XmDrawn-Button and XmToggleButton children. Note that if this is set on a RadioBox containing a number of XmToggleButtons, the callback is called twice, once when one XmToggleButton goes from set to unset and once when another goes from unset to set.

entryClass and isHomogeneous

The only use of these resources is so that the heavily overloaded XmRowColumn class can stop application developers building disastrous widget hierarchies, such as a MenuBar with XmToggleButtons in it.

entryVerticalAlignment

Sets the vertical alignment for XmLabel and XmText derived widgets that are arranged in rows. The effect of this resource is intriguing and is illustrated in Figure 4.6. This shows five different XmRowColumns, each with a different

setting of entryVerticalAlignment. Each XmRowColumn contains an XmLabel
with the value of entryVerticalAlignment displayed, an XmText widget with rows
set to 2 and a three-line value and an XmPushButton displaying a pixmap which
would be larger than a two-line XmText widget.

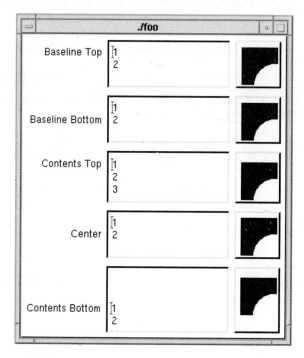

Figure 4.6   *The effect of entryVerticalAlignment*

labelString

This is only used for the OptionMenu label. The other XmRowColumn variants
ignore this resource.

orientation and numColumns

The numColumns resource is only meaningful if packing is set to COLUMN.
Some developers may feel that the layout changes caused by setting these
resources are somewhat counter-intuitive. The best way to understand it is to look
at some examples and pick the required effect (see Figure 4.7).

radioAlwaysOne and radioBehavior

These resources are used to make sure that no more than one XmToggleButton in
an XmRowColumn is set at time. Set radioAlwaysOne to True, so that there will
always be precisely one XmToggleButton set, False if is legal to have none set.

	XmRowColumn contains three label button pairs	XmRowColumn contains three labels followed by three buttons
orientation vertical — numColumns 2	label1 button2 button1 label3 label2 button3	label1 button1 label2 button2 label3 button3
orientation vertical — numColumns 3	label1 label2 label3 button1 button2 button3	label1 label3 button2 label2 button1 button3
orientation horizontal — numColumns 2	label1 button1 label2 button2 label3 button3	label1 label2 label3 button1 button2 button3
orientation horizontal — numColumns 3	label1 button1 label2 button2 label3 button3	label1 label2 label3 button1 button2 button3

Figure 4.7 *The effect of child ordering, orientation and numColumns*

XmCreateRadioBox() forces radioBehavior to True, but it can be set for any XmRowColumn which might contain XmToggleButtons, e.g. one created by XmCreatePulldownMenu().

The packing resource defaults to COLUMN if radioBehavior is set True

rowColumnType
This is the switch that sets the XmRowColumn into its particular mode.

positionIndex
Like XmPanedWindow, this constraint resource can be used to specify the logical position of children added out of order, without having to use the insertPosition procedure

4.5.2   Examples of use

As well as its extensive use in the menu system, see Chapter 9, XmRowColumn is generally useful for simple layouts. Its main drawback is the lack of intelligent resize behaviour.

4.6   XmDrawingArea

XmDrawingArea is a widget for drawing on. There is, of course, no reason why an application cannot use any widget in this way; simply add translations for Configure and Expose events that invoke actions to handle resizing and drawing, respectively. However, it is useful to have a prepackaged widget that provides simple callbacks to handle the basic functions.

4.6.1   Examples of use

This example is similar to the XmDrawnButton example in Section 3.6.1 except that it is resolution-independent. The example provides an XmText widget that allows the user to input the line width in millimetres; this widget is passed to the expose callback in the client_data. The inputCallback is used to obtain a new centre for the circle:

drawingarea

```
void da_expose (w, client_data, call_data)
        Widget       w;
        XtPointer    client_data;
        XtPointer    call_data;
{
        Arg                     al[5];
        int                     ac = 0;
        Dimension               width, height, margin_width, margin_height;
        int                     x_origin, y_origin;
        int                     arc_width, arc_height;
        int                     line_width;
        char                    *line_width_s;
        unsigned char           unit_type;
        XmTextFieldWidget       line_width_t = (XmTextFieldWidget) client_data;

/* Call a routine to create a Graphics Context */
        create_gc (w);
/* First get the various dimensions */
        XtVaGetValues (w,
                        XmNwidth, &width,
                        XmNheight, &height,
                        XmNmarginWidth, &margin_width,
                        XmNmarginHeight, &margin_height,
                        XmNunitType, &unit_type,
                        0);
/* Convert values to pixels */
        width = XmConvertUnits (w, XmHORIZONTAL, (int) unit_type,
```

```
                    width, XmPIXELS);
       height = XmConvertUnits (w, XmVERTICAL, (int) unit_type,
                       height, XmPIXELS);
       margin_width = XmConvertUnits (w, XmHORIZONTAL, (int) unit_type,
                       margin_width, XmPIXELS);
       margin_height = XmConvertUnits (w, XmVERTICAL, (int) unit_type,
                       margin_height, XmPIXELS);
/* Obtain user's required line width in millimetres */
    line_width_s = XmTextFieldGetString (line_width_t);
/* Convert to pixels */
    line_width = XmConvertUnits (w, XmHORIZONTAL,
                       Xm100TH_MILLIMETERS, 100 * atoi (line_width_s),
                       XmPIXELS);
    XtFree ((char *) line_width_s);
/*Calculate arc sizes */
    x_origin = margin_width + (line_width / 2);
    y_origin = margin_height + (line_width / 2);
    if (input_x < 0
     || input_y < 0) {
        arc_width = width - x_origin * 2;
        arc_height = height - y_origin * 2;
    } else {
        arc_width = (input_x - x_origin) * 2;
        arc_height = (input_y - y_origin) * 2;
    }
/* Don't draw 0 or negatively sized circles. */
    if (arc_width < line_width
     || arc_height < line_width)
        return;
/* Set the line width in the GC */
    XSetLineAttributes (XtDisplay (w), gc, line_width, LineSolid, CapButt,
                       JoinMiter);
/* Draw the Arc */
    XDrawArc (XtDisplay (w), XtWindow (w), gc, x_origin, y_origin, arc_width,
                       arc_height, 0, 360 * 64);
}

void da_resize (w, client_data, call_data)
    Widget      w;
    XtPointer   client_data;
    XtPointer   call_data;
{
    if (XtIsRealized (w))
        XClearArea (XtDisplay (w), XtWindow (w), 0, 0, 0, 0, True);
```

```
        }

        void da_input (w, client_data, call_data)
            Widget      w;
            XtPointer    client_data;
            XtPointer    call_data;
        {
            XEvent *event = ((XmDrawingAreaCallbackStruct *)call_data)->event;
        /* Simply set the global variables, and redraw the circle */
            if (event->type == ButtonPress
            || event->type == ButtonRelease) {
                input_x = event->xbutton.x;
                input_y = event->xbutton.y;
                XClearArea (XtDisplay (w), XtWindow (w), 0, 0, 0, 0, True);
            } else
                if (event->type == MotionNotify) {
        /* If we go negative default circle will get drawn */
                    input_x = event->xmotion.x;
                    input_y = event->xmotion.y;
                    XClearArea (XtDisplay (w), XtWindow (w), 0, 0, 0, 0, True);
                }
        }
```

When running, the program displays circles as shown in Figure 4.8. Note that the line widths reproduced here will not accurately reflect the actual lines drawn.

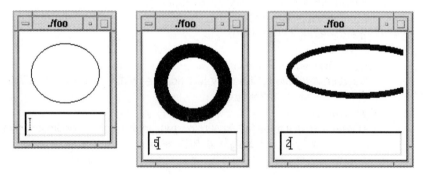

Figure 4.8   *Output from the XmDrawingArea example*

The input callback da_input() will happily handle MotionNotify events causing the circle to be redrawn as the pointer is moved. By default, the XmDrawingArea does not pass motion events to the input callback, but this is easily added. We only want Motion events when a mouse button is pressed, so the translation required is:

XtOverrideTranslations (da, XtParseTranslationTable(
"<BtnMotion>:DrawingAreaInput()"));

 However, doing this illustrates a common problem with translations. Adding this line and running the program will cause the ellipse to be animated when Button2 is pressed and dragged. If, however, Button1 is used, the ellipse will redraw on button down and up, but not during the dragging, unless the pointer is moved outside the window. This is because the translation mechanism is doing some special trickery to try and catch double button clicks. The default translation table for XmDrawingArea has a line something like <Btn1Down>(2+): DrawingAreaInput(). This can be overridden by specifying a translation for <BtnDown>:

XtOverrideTranslations (da, XtParseTranslationTable(
"<BtnDown>:DrawingAreaInput()\n\
<BtnMotion>:DrawingAreaInput()"));

Note that it is not sufficient to simply override <Btn1Down>. See Section 11.3.2 for more a more general discussion on translations and a detailed explanation of this problem.

The resolution independence is, of course, only as good as the server allows. For instance, if xdpyinfo is run on the workstation on which this book is being written it reports that the screen is 325mm wide. However, measuring it with a ruler, it looks more like 293mm. All the conversions to and from pixels use the width of the screen to calculate the size of a pixel and as a consequence all the calculations on this workstation are about 10% out.

4.7   XmBulletinBoard

XmBulletinBoard is a general purpose manager widget which has only very simple geometry management, but which is extensively subclassed to provide more generally useful layout widgets. See Chapters 5 and 6 for more detail on its subclass widgets.

XmBulletinBoard interacts heavily with the XmDialogShell widget in an attempt to hide some of the intricacies of the Shell widgets.

4.7.1   Interesting resources

autoUnmanage
This applies only to XmBulletinBoards whose parent is an XmDialogShell and must be set at create time. If it is set True, then an extra activateCallback is added to XmPushButton and XmDrawnButton children that will automatically

unmanage the XmBulletinBoard, providing the button is not the applyButton or helpButton for an XmBulletinBoard subclass. This is fine in principle and very useful for the subclasses, but for many other application-defined dialogs it is inconvenient that the default is True.

buttonFontList, labelFontList and textFontList

These resources specify the fonts to be used for descendants of the widget.

cancelButton

This resource is only used by the composite subclasses.

defaultButton

Specifies which widget is to be the default button. The XmBulletinBoard widget defines translations and installs accelerators, so that the specified button is activated when osfActivate is pressed and the keyboard focus is not in another button. Setting this resource will cause the showAsDefault resource for any button children to be set to 1, thus causing the default shadow to be drawn. The default shadow is drawn round any button that has the keyboard focus, or round the default button if another non-button widget has the keyboard focus.

⚠ The default button does not need to be an immediate child of the XmBulletinBoard, but the XmBulletinBoard will only force showAsDefault for its immediate children. Therefore if your default button is not an immediate child of the XmBulletinBoard widget, you should specify its defaultButtonShadowThickness, so that the default shadow can be drawn on it when another non-button widget has the focus.

defaultPosition

Only applies to children of XmDialogShell. If you want your dialog to be positioned automatically, set this resource to True. If you want it to be positioned where you asked for it (by setting the x and y coordinates of the child, not the shell), set this resource to False.

dialogStyle

Applies only to children of XmDialogShell. Setting this resource is a short-cut to setting the mwmInputMode resource on the parent shells (see Section 8.10.1).

dialogTitle

Applies only to children of XmDialogShell. Setting this resource is a shortcut to setting the WMShell title resource. The dialogTitle resource is a Motif compound string. As such it can contain direction, separator and font list tag segments. The string will be displayed in the font being used by the window manager, which is an X font set rather than a Motif font list. As a result, font list tags are ignored by mwm, but compound text, such as multi-byte encoded strings, is correctly displayed if the mwm font has the appropriate encodings. Note that mwm only displays the first line of a multi-line string.

mapCallback

The mapCallback callback function is called when the XmBulletinBoard is mapped, but only if the parent widget is an XmDialogShell. In particular, the mapCallback is not called if the parent is an ApplicationShell or TopLevelShell.

noResize

Applies only to children of XmDialogShell. Setting this resource is a shortcut to setting the VendorShell mwmFunctions resource. Setting this resource to False instructs mwm to add resize controls to the window's decorations. Setting it to True means that resize controls are not added (see Section 14.3.1).

resizePolicy

An XmBulletinBoard, or XmForm subclass, with its resizePolicy set to GROW is a useful container for widgets which have a tendency to snap back to their initial size.

Set the resizePolicy to NONE if the application determines the XmBulletinBoard's size and is moving its children around a lot. This will stop the XmBulletinBoard collapsing and growing as the widgets move (which will cause unnecessary Configure events).

See Section 6.4.4 for some examples of its use.

shadowType and shadowThickness

The shadowThickness for an XmBulletinBoard defaults to 0, unless its parent is an XmDialogShell.

textTranslations

This resource probably only exists to support the XmBulletinBoard-derived composite widgets.

CHAPTER 5

Composite widgets

Motif provides a number of widgets derived from XmBulletinBoard which provide specialised behaviour by combining the XmBulletinBoard with other Motif widgets. These widgets are useful in that they provide a common interface to a number of commonly used functions, such as selection from a list. These widgets are most commonly used in a shell of their own and the toolkit provides special creation routines to create an XmDialogShell with the appropriate composite child. Unlike the ScrolledText and ScrolledList composite widgets, the XmBulletinBoard derivatives are real widget classes.

Figure 5.1 illustrates the class hierarchy for these composite widgets.

5.1 XmMessageBox

The XmMessageBox widget has a simplified form (dialogType DIALOG_TEMPLATE) which provides a simple layout mechanism for dialogs consisting of a MenuBar, a work area and a number of buttons. In this mode, you must create all the component children of the XmMessageBox. Other values of the dialogType resource can be used to automatically create some default XmPushButtons and a special symbol and message area; you create any additional components you need as children of the XmMessageBox.

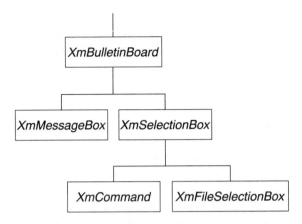

Figure 5.1 *XmBulletinBoard derived widgets*

The toolkit provides creation routines to create an XmDialogShell containing an XmMessageBox for each of the settings for dialogType. A convenience function, XmMessageBoxGetChild(), is provided which can be used to obtain the automatically created child widgets.

5.1.1 Interesting resources

dialogType, messageString and symbolPixmap

The dialogType resource specifies the type of XmMessageBox required. There are three basic types.

DIALOG_TEMPLATE creates an XmMessageBox with only an XmSeparator child. None of the other XmMessageBox resources are used in a TemplateDialog. As the name implies, this provides an empty template that can be filled in with other child widgets, giving an interface consistent with the other XmBulletinBoard derivatives.

A value of DIALOG_MESSAGE creates an XmMessageBox with an XmSeparator, a message XmLabel, a symbol XmLabel and three XmPushButtons: OK, Cancel and Help. The message XmLabel is used to display the messageString resource. The symbol XmLabel is used to display the pixmap specified in the symbolPixmap resource. If no pixmap is specified, the symbol XmLabel widget is not created.

The other values of dialogType create an XmMessageBox as for DIALOG_MESSAGE, but they set a default pixmap to be displayed in the symbol XmLabel.

defaultButtonType

Specifies which of the automatically created XmPushButtons is to be the XmBulletinBoard's defaultButton.

minimizeButtons

A simple Boolean resource which by default (False) causes all the buttons to be the same size. This usually produces the best visual appearance, unless one of the buttons has a much longer label than all the others. Setting the resource to True causes the buttons to be their natural size.

5.1.2 Examples of use

Obviously the primary intention of the XmMessageBox is to display a message or warning, but the DIALOG_TEMPLATE dialogType provides a useful layout template.

Figure 5.2 shows a familiar Motif message displayed in an XmMessageBox. The OK button has been unmanaged, as there is no appropriate action for it.

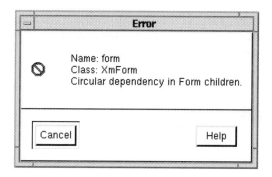

Figure 5.2 *XmMessageBox - dialogType = ERROR_DIALOG*

Figure 5.3 shows an XmMessageBox being used as a confirmation box (dialogType set to QUESTION_DIALOG). Here an extra button child has been added to allow the user to specify the No action. An XmPushButton has been used here, but other sorts of button child (XmToggleButton, XmArrowButton and XmDrawnButton) can also be used.

Figure 5.3 *XmMessageBox - dialogType = QUESTION_DIALOG*

Finally, an example of an XmMessageBox with dialogType set to DIALOG_TEMPLATE. The XmMessageBox has a MenuBar, a scrolled area and a number of button children. Figure 5.4 shows how the XmMessageBox lays out its children. It places the MenuBar at the top, the buttons at the bottom and any other child is assumed to be the work area and placed in the middle.

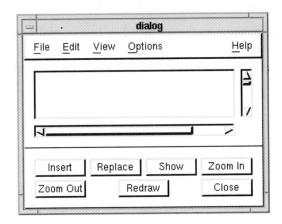

Figure 5.4 *XmMessageBox - dialogType = DIALOG_TEMPLATE*

5.2 XmSelectionBox

The XmSelectionBox widget provides a composite widget that can be used for simple list selection. It is also used as the base class for XmCommand and XmFileSelectionBox. XmSelectionBox also has a switch, dialogType, which causes the construction of the widget to alter. An XmSelectionBox may contain:

- Four XmPushButtons: OK, Apply, Cancel and Help.
- A ScrolledList.
- Two XmLabels.
- An XmSeparator.
- An XmTextField or XmText.[1]

A convenience routine, XmSelectionBoxGetChild(), is provided by the toolkit to allow the application to access the automatically created widgets.

The XmSelectionBox and its subclasses allow you to add some extra children as for XmMessageBox: a MenuBar, a work area and additional buttons.

---

1. Whether XmSelectionBox uses XmText or XmTextField depends on the setting of USE_TEXT_IN_-DIALOGS when the toolkit was built.

5.2.1   Interesting resources

The XmSelectionBox widget resources are mainly shortcuts to resources of the automatically created children. Care must be taken when setting resources on the children so that they do not conflict with the XmSelectionBox resources.

dialogType

This is a switch that alters the construction of the child widgets. There are five possible settings. Table 5.1 shows which widgets are created for the different values of dialogType. Y = created and managed, C = created but not managed, N = not created.

Table 5.1 *SelectionBox components*

Widget	Prompt	Work area	Selection	Command	File selection
OK	Y	Y	Y	N	Y
Apply	C	C	Y	N	Y
Cancel	Y	Y	Y	N	Y
Help	Y	Y	Y	N	Y
List	N	Y	Y	Y	Y
List Label	N	Y	Y	N	Y
Text	Y	Y	Y	Y	Y
Text Label	Y	Y	Y	Y	Y
Separator	Y	Y	Y	N	Y

The values DIALOG_COMMAND, and DIALOG_FILE_SELECTION need never be specified, as they are used by the subclasses. The resource defaults to DIALOG_WORK_AREA, unless the XmSelectionBox's parent is an XmDialogShell, in which case it defaults to DIALOG_SELECTION.

mustMatch and noMatchCallback

When the user presses the OK button, the okCallback will be called unless mustMatch is set to True and the value in the XmText widget does not match any of the items in the list, in which case the noMatchCallback is called.

The validation is carried out against the actual items in the list widget, not against the list set by listItems. This means that listItems cannot be used as a valid set for the DIALOG_PROMPT variant, which does not have a list widget.

childPlacement

This resource specifies where the work area child is to be placed. The various combinations are illustrated in Figure 5.5.

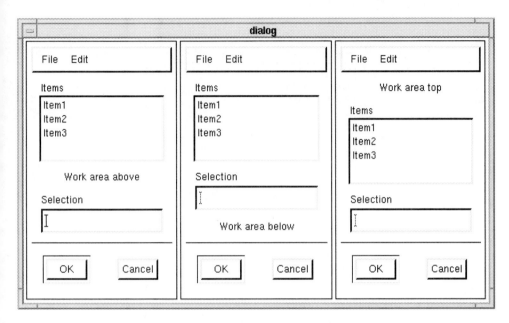

Figure 5.5 *The effect of setting childPlacement*

5.2.2 Watch out for

 Under certain circumstances (see Table 5.1), the XmSelectionBox will create the Apply button, but not manage it.

In order to maintain backwards compatibility with older versions of Motif, the first child added is always the work area, even if it is a MenuBar or button. If you do not want a work area child but do want a MenuBar, you will have to insert an invisible (XmSeparator with separatorType set to NO_LINE) or unmanaged widget first.

5.2.3 Examples of use

The DIALOG_PROMPT variant of XmSelectionBox is a hangover from earlier versions of Motif which did not have the DIALOG_TEMPLATE version of XmMessageBox to support simple dialog layout. On the limited occasions where a simple prompt is required, this may be of some use.

The selection type variants of the XmSelectionBox widget are widely used to provide a simple selection mechanism. The ability to augment the widget with an additional work area and other buttons makes it very versatile. Figure 5.6 illustrates a potential use.

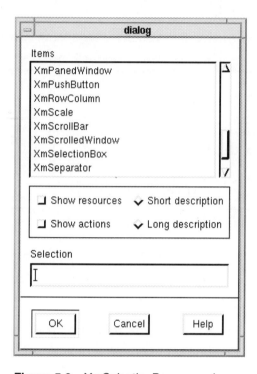

Figure 5.6   *XmSelectionBox example*

5.3   XmCommand

The XmCommand widget is a heavily stylised derivative of the XmSelectionBox widget, which is intended to be used for command-style input with the list section providing an automatic history mechanism. Although the XmCommand widget does not contain any buttons by default, they and a MenuBar and work area can be added in the same way as for an XmSelectionBox.

5.3.1   Interesting resources

Many of XmCommand's resources are simply synonyms for the equivalent XmSelectionBox resource. This seems to miss the point of deriving a subclass, but that is the way it is.

maxHistoryItems
Set this resource to stop the history list growing too big.

5.3.2 Interesting behaviour

Pressing KActivate in the text widget automatically adds the command to the history list and calls the commandEnteredCallback. Selecting an item from the list sets the text widget to contain the item text and calls the commandChanged-Callback. Double-clicking an item in the list is equivalent to doing both these actions.

Convenience routines are provided to set and append to the command string: XmCommandSetValue() and XmCommandAppendValue(), respectively. There is also a function XmCommandError() which displays the passed error string in the history list after a blank item. These extra items go away when a command is entered or an item is selected from the list. It looks a little peculiar to have an error message appear in the history list, but it probably makes it easier to port command line interfaces.

5.3.3 Examples of use

Command line interfaces are the most obvious applications to use the XmCommand widget, but most application developers who have got as far as using Motif will probably want to do something more visually appealing. Figure 5.7 shows a command line interface with the error string displayed.

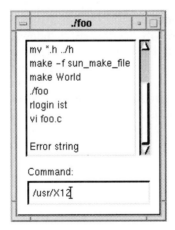

Figure 5.7 *XmCommand example*

5.4 XmFileSelectionBox

The XmFileSelectionBox is a great bonus for the Motif programmer. Even if the style of the interface is not to everyone's taste, it is a component that can be used across many different applications, thus presenting a consistent method of file selection to the user. The developer should not provide a different file selection paradigm unless it is central to the application; for instance, a source code management application might need a more graphically orientated hierarchical view of the file system.

The structure of an XmFileSelectionBox is the same as for the XmSelectionBox, but with additional widgets for the directory lists and the filter input. The apply button is used to invoke the filtering mechanism.

5.4.1 Interesting resources

Many of the XmFileSelectionBox resources are synonyms for XmSelectionBox resources. There are a number of additional resources which are used to control the searching algorithms.

The directory, dirMask, pattern and dirSpec resources are curiously specified as XmStrings. The toolkit appears to extract the text from the text segments, turning around any which are right to left and joining all the segments together.

directory, dirMask and pattern

These resources are heavily interrelated, as follows; dirMask is the filter that is to be applied to the search. The value of this resource appears in the filter Text widget. The directory resource contains the static part of the filter, i.e. the part up to the first wildcard indicator. The pattern resource contains the variable part of the filter, i.e. from the first wildcard indicator to the end. These three resources will be kept consistent. If directory and pattern are specified, then dirMask is set to be directory/pattern. If dirMask is specified, then it is split up to specify the directory and pattern resources.

Setting these resources causes the searching mechanisms to be invoked. This is a good way of setting the widget to a required state. There is a convenience routine, XmFileSelectionBoxDoSearch(), which can be used to set dirMask, but not one for setting directory or pattern.

dirSpec

The dirSpec resource contains the selected file name. The value of this resource appears in the selection Text widget.

dirSearchProc, fileSearchProc and qualifySearchDataProc

These resources can be used to specify functions which modify the search algorithm used by the toolkit. If they are not specified, the toolkit provides defaults which will suffice for most general situations. However, it is sometimes desirable to restrict the set of files and/or directories shown to the user, so that only valid choices can be made. For example, a typical fileSearchProc might check the permissions or magic number of a file before deciding whether to include it in the list. The following code illustrates a file search algorithm that only adds files to the list for which the application has write access.

To avoid having to do a lot of directory access and regular expression handling, the code uses the default fileSearchProc to build the file list, then creates a new list containing only the writeable files from the default list. This is hardly an efficient approach, but it is easy to code. Since the default fileSearchProc is not public, we have to access it by creating the XmFileSelectionBox with the default fileSearchProc and querying and saving the function pointer. We then change the fileSearchProc resource to point to our function, file_search(), and call XmFileSelectionDoSearch() to initialise the file list using our fileSearchProc:

fileselbox

```
XmSearchProc default_search_proc;
XmString     dir_mask;

fsb = XmCreateFileSelectionBox (parent, "fsb", al, ac);
/* Get and save pointer to default fileSearchProc */
ac = 0;
XtSetArg (al[ac], XmNfileSearchProc, &default_search_proc); ac++;
XtSetArg (al[ac], XmNdirMask, &dir_mask); ac++;
XtGetValues (fsb, al, ac);
/* Change fileSearchProc and refresh files list (which will have
 been initialised using the default fileSearchProc when the
 XmFileSelectionBox was created) */
ac = 0;
XtSetArg (al[ac], XmNfileSearchProc, file_search); ac++;
XtSetValues (fsb, al, ac);
XmFileSelectionDoSearch (fsb, dir_mask);
```

The new fileSearchProc function is straightforward. It calls the default one via the saved function pointer, then creates a new list. It uses this list to set the fileListItems and fileListItemCount resources of the XmFileSelectionBox. It also sets the listUpdated resource to tell the XmFileSelectionBox to redisplay the list; there is room for optimisation here:

```
void
file_search (fs, search_data)
  XmFileSelectionBoxWidget        fs;
  XmFileSelectionBoxCallbackStruct * search_data;
{
    char        *filename;
```

```
XmString    *default_files;
int         default_file_count;
XmString    *writable_files=NULL;
int         writable_file_count=0;
int         i;
Arg         args[10];
int         ac=0;

/*
Use default file search proc to do all the wildcard matching
and so on, then remove unwriteable files from its list.
Even if the default proc doesn't change the file list, we still
need to check in case permissions have changed:
*/
    (*default_search_proc) (fs, search_data);

/* Get the list of filenames */
    XtVaGetValues (fs,
                    XmNfileListItems, &default_files,
                    XmNfileListItemCount, &default_file_count,
                    NULL);
/* Run down the list, copying the names of all writeable files */
    writable_files = (XmString*) XtMalloc (default_file_count *
                    sizeof(XmString));
    for (i=0; i<default_file_count; i++)
    {
        XmStringGetLtoR (default_files[i], XmFONTLIST_DEFAULT_TAG,
                    &filename);
        if (access (filename, W_OK)==0)
            writable_files[writable_file_count++] =
                                        XmStringCopy (default_files[i]);
        XtFree (filename);
    }

    XtSetArg (args[ac], XmNfileListItems, writable_files); ac++;
    XtSetArg (args[ac], XmNfileListItemCount, writable_file_count); ac++;
    XtSetArg (args[ac], XmNlistUpdated, True); ac++;
    XtSetValues (fs, args, ac);

    for ( i=0; i < writable_file_count; i++ )
        XmStringFree (writable_files[i]);
    XtFree (writable_files);
}
```

The dirSearchProc is used in a similar fashion to build the directory list. If it decides that the directory is not valid, it can supply a new directory by updating the callback data or can set directoryValid to False to indicate that the fileSearchProc should not be called.

The qualifySearchDataProc is called to generate the directory and pattern values passed to the dirSearchProc and fileSearchProc. An application might want to specify this function, so that the user could specify regular expressions instead of shell wildcard-type expressions for the filter. The reference manual documents in some detail the exact requirements of the qualifyDataSearchProc.

5.4.2   Examples of use

The XmFileSelectionBox should be used whenever the user is asked to specify a file name. Frequently, the XmFileSelectionBox is used as the basis for a dialog which requires the specification of a file and other parameters for a function to be performed. When the user clicks on OK, or double-clicks a file, the function is

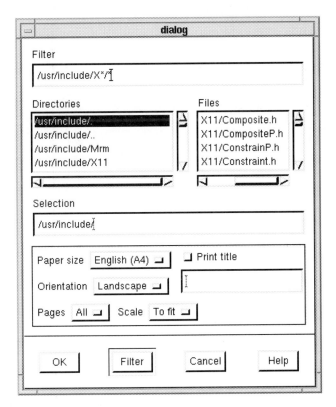

Figure 5.8   *XmFileSelectionBox example*

initiated. Figure 5.8 shows a print dialog example. This consists of an XmFileSe-lectionBox with an extra XmForm child created by the application. The XmForm in turn contains the extra dialog components used to acquire the paper size, and so on.

CHAPTER 6

Form widget

The Motif XmForm widget is a powerful manager used for controlling dialog layouts. With the XmForm widget, you can define flexible layouts which behave sensibly if the user resizes the dialog window, or if the widgets in the dialog change size. However, this flexibility is only achieved at the cost of some complexity. The layout model used by the XmForm widget is not particularly easy to understand.

The XmForm widget lets you specify the layout not by absolute positioning, but by specifying the positions of widgets relative to other widgets and the XmForm. If widget sizes change, or the user resizes the window containing the XmForm, the XmForm widget will move and possibly resize its children to keep the relative positions you have specified. This allows you to create layouts which are (to a large degree) insulated from the bad effects of font changes or user customisation.

The chapter initially looks at the XmForm's layout model and the attachment mechanism that it uses. It then discusses techniques for achieving common layouts and has a section containing hints and tips for common problems with XmForm layouts. Throughout the chapter we use a simple drawing notation to illustrate the layout definition. The basic diagram consists of a box which represents the XmForm, with a shaded box representing each of its children. Annotations representing the attachments are drawn on to the appropriate edges of the child widgets. The notation for the attachments is described in the initial section, where the different attachment types are discussed.

6.1   Attachment types

To the XmForm widget, its children are just boxes with four edges - top, bottom, left and right. The layout of the XmForm's children is specified by defining the relative position of each of the four edges. The XmForm widget defines four constraint resources for each edge of the widget - attachment, offset, position and widget. It is the attachment resource (topAttachment, bottomAttachment, leftAttachment and rightAttachment) which defines how a particular edge is treated by the XmForm. The application sets an attachment type and optionally other parameters for a given edge of a widget. The XmForm thereafter adjusts its own size and the positions and sizes of its children in order to maintain the relative position of that edge.

Obviously the effect that this has on a widget depends on the other attachments for the widget. If a widget is only attached on one edge, with the opposite edge unconstrained, its size will not be changed in that dimension, only its position. The attachments on the left and right edges affect only the horizontal position and width of the widget. The attachments on the top and bottom affect only the vertical position and height. These two dimensions can never interact and it is often helpful to consider them separately when designing layouts. The XmForm is consistent in its treatment of the vertical and horizontal dimensions. Where the examples explicitly refer to left or right attachments, the same is true for top and bottom attachments.

The remainder of this section describes each of the different attachment types.

6.1.1   No attachment *(ATTACH_NONE)*

The attachment resources for the edges of a widget default to ATTACH_NONE. This means that the XmForm will not make any adjustments to position that edge. Use this attachment type on an edge when you do not want the widget to resize and you want the position of the widget determined by the position of the opposite edge.

Edges with an attachment set to ATTACH_NONE are shown in the layout diagrams without any decoration on that edge.

6.1.2   Position attachments *(ATTACH_POSITION)*

Using a position attachment, the edge of the widget is fixed at the position specified by the matching position resource. For example, you can specify that the left edge of a child widget will always be 50% of the way across the XmForm by setting leftAttachment to ATTACH_POSITION and leftPosition to 50. If the XmForm grows larger (for whatever reason), the XmForm will move the left edge of the child widget so that it is still halfway across. Similarly, you can specify that the top of a widget will be halfway down the XmForm by setting topAttachment to ATTACH_POSITION and topPosition to 50. Whether moving the edge causes the widget to move or resize depends on the attachment type of the opposite edge. If the opposite edge has an attachment type of ATTACH_NONE, the widget will move. If it is some other attachment type, the widget will resize. Figure 6.1 shows an example where the left edge is positioned at 30%. It also shows the way it behaves when the size of the XmForm changes.

We represent a position constraint on an edge of a widget by a circle on that edge.

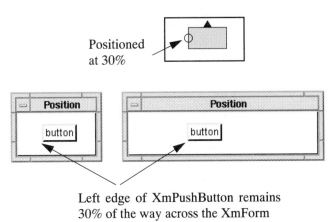

Left edge of XmPushButton remains
30% of the way across the XmForm

Figure 6.1   *Form resizing with position attachment on left edge*

Similarly setting a position attachment on the right edge of the widget causes the right position of the right edge to be maintained. If the left edge has an attachmentType of ATTACH_NONE, the whole widget will move as the XmForm resizes (Figure 6.2).

The code for a position constraint is relatively simple. To position the left edge of a widget at 30%, you need to set the attachment and position resources:

```
XtVaSetValues (mybutton,
              XmNleftAttachment, XmATTACH_POSITION,
              XmNleftPosition, 30,
              0);
```

The offset and widget resources (e.g. leftOffset and leftWidget) are not used, and should not be set.

The numbers you specify as left and right position (30) are usually, but not necessarily, percentages. The XmForm widget has a resource fractionBase and the widget position is determined by dividing the position value given by the value of the fraction base. Since the default value of fractionBase is 100, positions are given

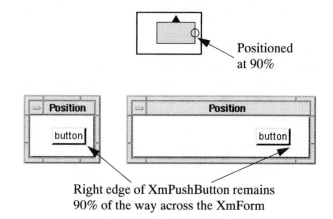

Figure 6.2   *Form resizing with position attachment on right edge*

by default as percentages. However, if you need to position a set of edges at, say, 12 evenly spaced positions across the form, it is easiest to set the fractionBase to 11 and the positions to 0, 1, 2, ..., 10, 11.

 An attempt to set the fraction base to zero is rejected (with an error message). A negative fraction base is accepted, but will usually lead to the edge synchronisation error message (see Section 6.2.3).

6.1.3   Form attachments
(ATTACH_FORM and ATTACH_OPPOSITE_FORM)

Widgets can be attached to the corresponding edge of an XmForm, using the attachment type ATTACH_FORM. Figure 6.3 shows an example where the left and top edge, are attached to the corresponding edges of the XmForm.

The attachment to the XmForm is represented as a black triangle on the edge of the widget.

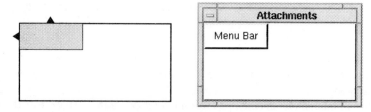

Figure 6.3   *Attachment to left and top of XmForm*

If you attach the right edge of the widget to the right edge of the XmForm and set the leftAttachment to ATTACH_NONE, then the widget will stick to the right-hand edge of the XmForm (Figure 6.4).

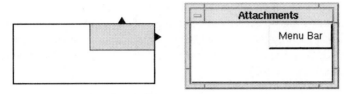

Figure 6.4 *Attachment to right side of form*

Again, the code for attaching a widget to an XmForm is straightforward:

```
XtVaSetValues (mymenubar,
               XmNtopAttachment, XmATTACH_FORM,
               XmNleftAttachment, XmATTACH_FORM,
               0);
```

If the attachment type is ATTACH_FORM, you should not set the position and widget resources for the same edge. Setting the offset is optional; if you leave it unset, the XmForm will use a default value based on the XmForm's spacing resources, as discussed in Section 6.2.5.

If you attach the left edge of a widget to the left edge of the XmForm with a non-zero offset, then there will be a gap between the edge of the XmForm and the edge of the widget, as shown in Figure 6.5.

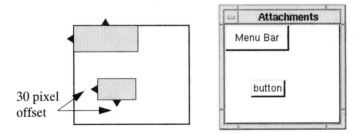

Figure 6.5 *Attachment with an offset*

To specify an offset on an attachment, you set the appropriate offset resource (left, right, top or bottom) as well as the attachment resource:

```
XtVaSetValues (mybutton,
               XmNleftAttachment, XmATTACH_FORM,
               XmNleftOffset, 30,
               0);
```

⚠ The offset is specified in units as defined by the unitType resource for the widget on which the attachment is made.

⚠ The left edge of a widget can be attached to the right edge of the XmForm. This attachment type is ATTACH_OPPOSITE_FORM. In this case, the offset must be specified as a negative amount, otherwise the XmForm will try to position the left edge of the widget beyond the right edge of the XmForm, which will cause an error. It is probably only appropriate to do this if the application knows the width of the widget and can make sure that the offset is large enough to enable the widget to fit in (see Figure 6.6).

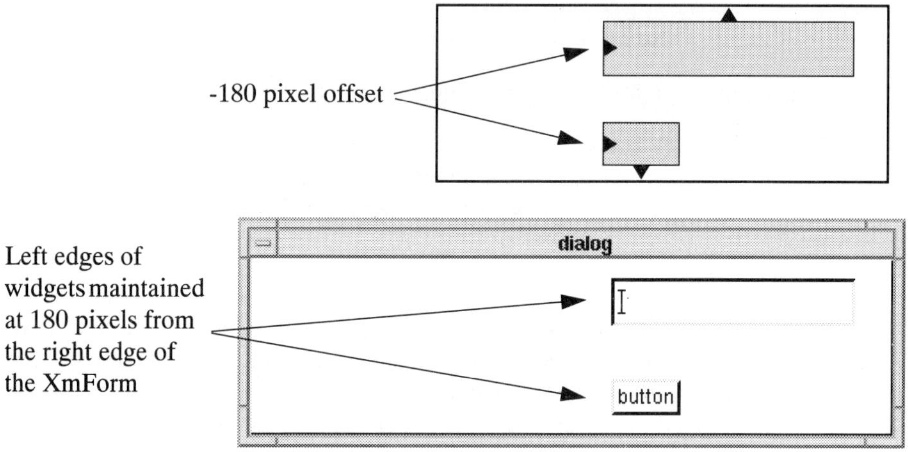

-180 pixel offset

Left edges of
widgets maintained
at 180 pixels from
the right edge of
the XmForm

Figure 6.6   *Attaching to the opposite side of the XmForm*

6.1.4   Widget attachments
(ATTACH_WIDGET and ATTACH_OPPOSITE_WIDGET)

As well as attaching the edges of a widget to the XmForm, you can also attach them to other sibling widgets. There are two sorts of attachment. To attach the left edge of one widget to the right edge of another, perhaps with an offset, use ATTACH_-WIDGET. The widgets will be positioned as shown in Figure 6.7. Here, the attachment is represented as a line starting just inside Button2 (the widget on which the attachment is set) and ending at the edge of Button1 (the widget it is attached to).

To create an attachment of one widget to another, you need to specify the attachment type, the offset (if any) and the destination widget.

```
XtVaSetValues (button2,
                XmNleftAttachment, XmATTACH_WIDGET,
                XmNleftOffset, 30,
                XmNleftWidget, button1, 0);
```

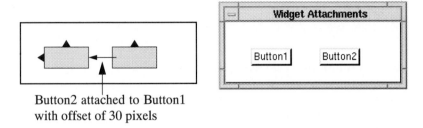

Button2 attached to Button1
with offset of 30 pixels

Figure 6.7   *Attaching widgets*

To attach the edge of one widget to the *same* edge of another, use ATTACH_OPPOSITE_WIDGET. The two widget edges will then be aligned (Figure 6.8).

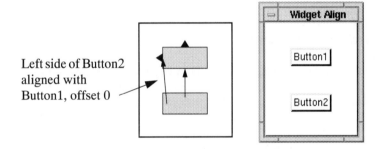

Left side of Button2
aligned with
Button1, offset 0

Figure 6.8   *Aligning widgets*

```
XtVaSetValues (button2,
               XmNleftAttachment,
               XmATTACH_OPPOSITE_WIDGET,
               XmNleftOffset, 0,
               XmNleftWidget, button1,
               0);
```

   Note the possibly confusing terminology here. If you are attaching the left edge of a widget, you use ATTACH_FORM to attach it to the *left* edge of the XmForm, and ATTACH_OPPOSITE_FORM to attach it to the *right*. However, you use ATTACH_WIDGET to attach it to the *right* of another widget, and ATTACH_-OPPOSITE_WIDGET to attach it to the *left*. The rationale for this is obscure.

The direction of an attachment is important. Attaching an edge of WidgetA to an edge of WidgetB is not the same as attaching an edge of WidgetB to an edge of WidgetA. The XmForm will resize and position the widget on which the attachment is set in order to maintain that widget's position relative to the widget to which it is attached, so attaching an edge of widgetA to an edge of WidgetB will affect only the size and position of WidgetA. WidgetB will not be moved or resized.

6.1.5   Self attachments *(ATTACH_SELF)*

This is essentially the same as a position attachment; in fact the XmForm converts self attachments into position attachments. The only difference is in the way that the initial position value is specified. For a position attachment, the position is specified in the position resource. For the self attachment, the toolkit calculates the position value from the current position of the widget and the width or height of the XmForm and uses that value. For example, if an XmForm is 200 pixels wide and a widget is added with the x resource set to 60 and the leftAttachment set to ATTACH_SELF, this is exactly the same as setting the leftAttachment to ATTACH_POSITION and the leftPosition to 30.

6.2   Interaction of attachments

In a complicated XmForm there will be many widgets, each with its own set of attachments. This section looks at some of the effects of more complicated attachment schemes and some of the problems that may arise.

6.2.1   Using attachments to resize a widget

In all the examples up to now, the attachment has always been shown opposite an edge which has no attachment. This has caused the widget to be moved to maintain its relative position. By attaching a pair of opposite edges of a widget, it can be made to resize.

Resizing with another widget

It is often useful to make two widgets the same size, or to make one of them extend up to the edge of another widget. Figure 6.9 shows an example where both edges of an XmLabel widget are aligned with a ScrolledText so that the XmLabel is centred underneath.

To achieve this layout, simply set both the leftAttachment and rightAttachment resources to ATTACH_OPPOSITE_WIDGET and both the leftWidget and rightWidget resources to the ScrolledText widget.[1]

---

1. Remembering, of course, that XmCreateScrolledText() returns the XmText widget, and XtParent() has to be used to get the XmScrolledWindow parent which is the actual child of the XmForm.

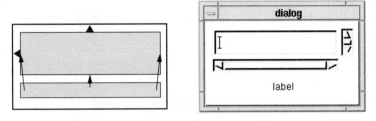

Figure 6.9 *Aligning both sides of a widget*

Resizing with the XmForm

By fixing an attachment on one edge of a widget and setting the other edge to be relative to the XmForm, either with a position attachment or a form attachment, a widget can be made to resize as the XmForm changes size. A simple example would be a MenuBar which is supposed to span the top of the dialog. By setting the top, left and right attachments to ATTACH_FORM, the desired effect can be achieved (Figure 6.10).

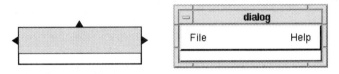

Figure 6.10 *Resizing to span the XmForm*

Resizing as a result of user action

Text widgets and all the scrolling widgets have the capacity to hide some of the information they contain if they are not large enough to display it all. You should design dialogs so that they are initially a natural and useful size, but still allow the user to see more or less information by resizing the window. An example of this can be seen in the XmFileSelectionBox. If an XmFileSelectionBox is created directly in an XmDialogShell, then the user can see more entries in the lists by resizing the window taller and can make the Directories list wider by resizing the window wider (see Figure 6.11).

Although the XmFileSelectionBox is not constructed using an XmForm, it can be simulated by using an XmMessageBox of dialogType DIALOG_TEMPLATE to handle the buttons and the separator, with an XmForm as the work area child of the XmMessageBox and the other XmTextField, XmLabel and ScrolledList widgets created as children of this form (Figure 6.12).

The attachments for the XmForm are quite straightforward, even though they look complicated; the XmTextField widgets are anchored across the XmForm, so that they resize with it. The right edge of the Files ScrolledList is attached to the right edge of the XmForm, but its left edge has no attachment. It will therefore drag

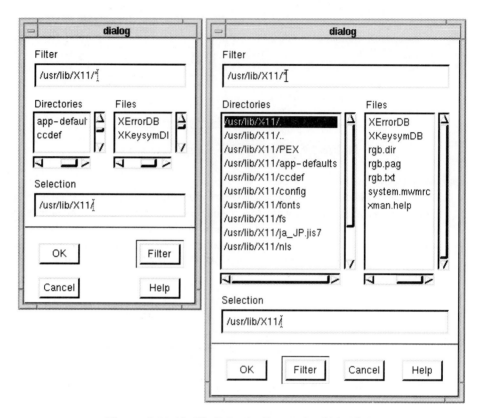

Figure 6.11 *XmFileSelectionBox resize behaviour*

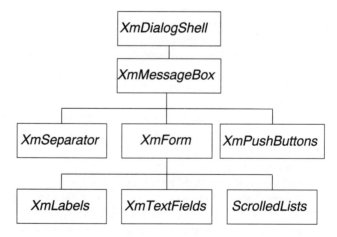

Figure 6.12 *Widget hierarchy for simulated FileSelectionBox*

across with the XmForm as it is resized. The left edge of the Directories ScrolledList is anchored to the left-hand edge of the XmForm and the right edge is attached to the Files ScrolledList so that it resizes as the XmForm resizes. The XmLabels are attached to the left edge of the XmForm as they do not need to move or resize, except for the File list's XmLabel, which is aligned with the Files ScrolledList. The XmLabel and XmTextField below the lists are attached, so that they move down as the XmForm grows. The bottoms of the list are attached to the top of the selection XmLabel, so that they resize with the XmForm (Figure 6.13).

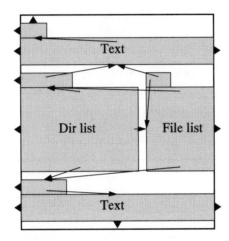

Figure 6.13 *Layout for fake FileSelectionBox*

In this layout, it is the Directories ScrolledList which gets all the additional width because it is attached on both edges, whereas the Files ScrolledList is only attached on one edge. Simply swapping the attachment around, so the left edge of the Files ScrolledList is attached to the right edge of the Directories ScrolledList, which in turn has its attachment set to ATTACH_NONE, causes the Files ScrolledList to get all the additional width.

It may be that the requirement is for both lists to share the additional width. This can be accomplished using a position attachment. Figure 6.14 illustrates a simplified case. The right edge of the Directories ScrolledList is positioned at 50% and the left edge of the Files ScrolledList is attached to it. A similar result can be achieved by setting the position attachment on the left edge of the Files ScrolledList and attaching the right edge of the Directories ScrolledList to it. Equally, both edges could have a position resource. Which solution is more appropriate will depend on the other attachments and possibly the need to avoid circularity (see Section 6.2.4).

A combination of position and widget attachments can be used to apportion additional space to several different widgets, depending on their requirements. Figure 6.15 shows some examples of this.

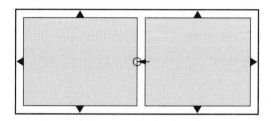

Figure 6.14 *Alternative layout where both lists resize their width*

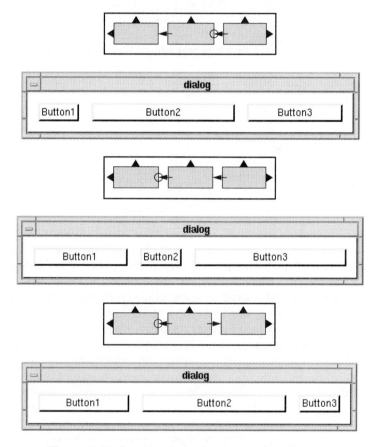

Figure 6.15 *Combined attachments and positions*

The most important point is that resize behaviour must be taken into account when designing XmForm layouts. The user is entitled to expect dialogs to display more of the hidden information when they are made bigger.

6.2.2 Default attachments

The XmForm widget cannot handle a widget which has ATTACH_NONE on two opposite edges, as it then has no control over the size or position of the widget in that particular dimension. In this case, it will change the top or left attachment to attach the edge to the XmForm. The attachment type used for the default attachment is determined by the XmForm's rubberPositioning resource. If rubber-Positioning is set False, the default attachment type becomes ATTACH_FORM with an offset set to the appropriate x or y position. If rubberPositioning is True, the default attachment becomes ATTACH_POSITION, with the position resource set to the relative position of the widget within the XmForm. Either way, the effect is that the widget remains where it is.

The difference between the two types of default attachment is that with rubberPositioning True, the widget will remain at the proportional position when the XmForm resizes. With rubberPositioning False, the widget will remain at its absolute position with respect to the top and right of the XmForm as the XmForm resizes.

6.2.3 Edge synchronisation

It is quite easy to impose contradictory constraints which the XmForm cannot resolve. Suppose the left edge off a widget is positioned at 50% and the right edge at 25%. To satisfy these constraints, the XmForm would have to give the widget a negative width, which is not possible. The XmForm will still produce a layout of some sort, but it is unlikely to be sensible.

In our simple examples, it was possible to see at a glance what the layout required to satisfy the constraints had to be. In a real example, it may not be so obvious. To work out what the layout should be, the XmForm widget uses an iterative algorithm. If there are certain sorts of contradictory constraint, this will never converge. For example, consider attaching a widget edge to the opposite edge of the XmForm but with a positive offset. This puts the widget outside the XmForm, so the XmForm grows to fit it in; the attachment is now not satisfied, so the widget is moved outside the XmForm again and so the process goes on. To avoid an infinite loop, the XmForm widget will exit from the algorithm if it has not found the right layout within a reasonable number of iterations, which is when you get the synchronisation error message:

> Bailed out of edge synchronization after 10,000 iterations.
> Check for contradictory constraints on the children of this form.

It is possible that the algorithm will reach the iteration limit even if there are no contradictory constraints, but we have never known this to happen in practice. The remedy when this message appears is to sit down with a pencil and paper and draw out the attachments. The fix will become obvious.

6.2.4 Circular attachments

If you attach WidgetA to WidgetB, the XmForm does not like it if you then attach WidgetB to WidgetA. It will also complain if you attach A to B, B to C and C to A, and so on with larger loops. You will get the error message:

Circular dependency in Form children.

There is some sense in the XmForm not allowing circular attachments, but the XmForm widget does carry it a bit far. The arrangement shown in Figure 6.16 has the bottom of a button attached to the bottom of an XmText widget and the left of the XmText attached to the right of the button.

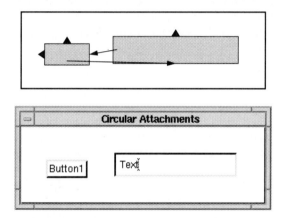

Figure 6.16 *Circular attachments*

This cannot possibly cause any problems, since the vertical and horizontal edges of a widget do not interfere with each other, but the XmForm widget still forbids it.[1] Unfortunately, this is precisely the arrangement you want when laying out an XmForm which contains, say, XmLabel and XmText widgets. You want the XmText widget to start where the XmLabel widget ends (probably offset a little), so you attach the left edge of the XmText to the right edge of the XmLabel. However, you want the vertical position to be determined by the XmText, since XmText widgets are generally taller than XmLabels. What you want to do is align the bottom and possibly the top of the XmLabel with the XmText widget, but the XmForm will not let you do this.

There are ways of getting round this, but it does make the XmForm unnecessarily awkward to use. Section 6.3 gives some examples of layout tricks you may find helpful.

---

1. An attempt to be charitable; possibly the reason this is enforced is that it ensures that attachments can be set at widget creation time, given an appropriate order of creation.

6.2.5   Offsets and XmForm spacing

When you attach one widget to another (or to the XmForm) you can specify an offset. If you do not specify an offset, the XmForm will take the value for the offset from the XmForm's spacing resources, horizontalSpacing (for attachments of left or right edges) and verticalSpacing (for attachments of top or bottom). The default value for horizontal and vertical spacing is zero, so attaching with no offset usually looks the same as attaching with an offset of zero. However, if the horizontal or vertical spacing of the XmForm is changed, it will affect only those attachments which have no offset; an explicit zero offset overrides the spacing values.

This is significant for alignments. If you try to align a column of widgets by attaching, say, their left edges with no offset, the alignment will be destroyed if the XmForm spacing is changed, as shown in Figure 6.17.

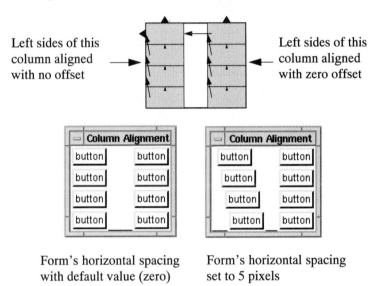

Left sides of this column aligned with no offset

Left sides of this column aligned with zero offset

Form's horizontal spacing with default value (zero)

Form's horizontal spacing set to 5 pixels

Figure 6.17 *Alignments and form spacing*

You should usually set an explicit offset of zero when aligning (i.e. when using an attachment type of ATTACH_OPPOSITE_WIDGET).

6.3   Column layouts

It is often necessary to create a column (or row) of dialog elements. This is easy if only a single column is needed, less so for multiple columns.

6.3.1   A diversion into XmRowColumn

The easy and usually the right way to create a single column layout is to use the XmRowColumn widget, rather than a XmForm. XmRowColumn will take almost any widget as a child and you can mix different sorts of widget as children of the same XmRowColumn. See Section 4.5 for some examples of how XmRowColumn lays out and sizes its children.

There are, however, occasions when an XmRowColumn is not appropriate for something that appears to have a column layout. Consider the dialog in Figure 6.18; three XmLabel and three XmText widgets are laid out in two

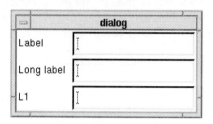

Figure 6.18 *A simple column-based dialog*

columns. We want the XmText widgets to get longer when the dialog is resized wider, but we are not concerned about what happens when it gets resized taller.

If we use a single XmRowColumn to put the XmLabel and XmText widgets in, we can get the resize behaviour by setting the packing to COLUMN, the orientation to VERTICAL and adjustLast to True. The problem is that the XmLabel widgets are initialised to be the same size as the XmText widgets. Figure 6.19 illustrates the layout.

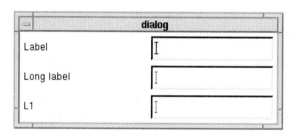

Figure 6.19 *The XmRowColumn solution*

Obviously, we could achieve the required layout by using absolute positioning on an XmBulletinBoard and handling the layout explicitly in the application by detecting when the XmBulletinBoard resizes (use a <ConfigureNotify> translation). It can also be done with XmForm attachments, although there are some difficulties.

6.3.2 The problem with attachments

If we think about the attachments that need to be made to achieve the layout, we arrive at the following list:

• Attach the left edges of the XmLabels to the (left edge of the) form.
• Attach the top of the second XmText widget to the bottom of the first and the top of the third to the bottom of the second.
• Attach the right edges of the XmText widgets to the (right edge of the) form.
• Attach the left edges of the XmText widget to the right edge of the longest XmLabel.
• Align the top and bottom of each XmLabel to the top and bottom of the corresponding XmText widget.

Figure 6.20 illustrates the required attachments and one associated difficulty: aligning the top and bottom of the middle XmLabel to its XmText widget introduces a circularity.

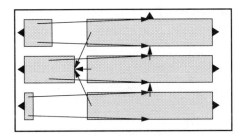

Figure 6.20 *Required layout*

Another problem not immediately apparent, is in determining which XmLabel to attach the XmText widgets to. If there is any possibility that the XmLabel's labelString will change at some point, either by the application changing it at run time, or by the user overriding the default labelString with a resource file, then it is possible that one or both of the other two XmLabels may turn out to be wider than the one we have chosen and the layout will be incorrect.

There are two ways that an XmForm can be used to provide a solution to both these problems. Both retain the alignment of the tops and bottoms of the XmLabel widgets with the XmText widgets, but change the attachment on the left of the XmText widgets to overcome the circularity and alignment problems.

6.3.3 Using a position attachment

The first solution is simply to fix the position of the left edge of the XmText widgets using a position constraint. The layout is illustrated in Figure 6.21. This

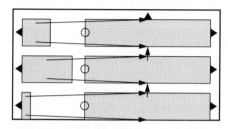

Figure 6.21 *Using position attachment to align XmText widgets*

satisfies the original layout requirements. The only remaining problem is in deciding the percentage at which the XmText widgets should be fixed, but this can probably be safely set to an approximate figure using the application defaults file. This allows the user to adapt the layout to match the local site requirements. The (somewhat verbose) code is as follows:

formposition-
attachments

```
form = XmCreateForm (appshell, "form", al, ac);
label1 = XmCreateLabel (form, "label1", al, ac);
text1 = XmCreateText (form, "text1", al, ac);
label2 = XmCreateLabel (form, "label2", al, ac);
text2 = XmCreateText (form, "text2", al, ac);
label3 = XmCreateLabel (form, "label3", al, ac);
text3 = XmCreateText (form, "text3", al, ac);

XtVaSetValues (label1,
               XmNtopAttachment,
               XmATTACH_OPPOSITE_WIDGET,
               XmNtopOffset, 0,
               XmNtopWidget, text1,
               XmNbottomAttachment,
               XmATTACH_OPPOSITE_WIDGET,
               XmNbottomOffset, 0,
               XmNbottomWidget, text1,
               XmNleftAttachment, XmATTACH_FORM,
               0);

XtVaSetValues (text1,
               XmNtopAttachment, XmATTACH_FORM,
               XmNbottomAttachment, XmATTACH_NONE,
               XmNleftAttachment, XmATTACH_POSITION,
               XmNleftPosition, 35,
               XmNrightAttachment, XmATTACH_FORM,
               0);
```

```
XtVaSetValues (label2,
                XmNtopAttachment,
                XmATTACH_OPPOSITE_WIDGET,
                XmNtopOffset, 0,
                XmNtopWidget, text2,
                XmNbottomAttachment,
                XmATTACH_OPPOSITE_WIDGET,
                XmNbottomOffset, 0,
                XmNbottomWidget, text2,
                XmNleftAttachment, XmATTACH_FORM,
                XmNrightAttachment, XmATTACH_WIDGET,
                XmNrightWidget, text2, 0);

XtVaSetValues (text2,
                XmNtopAttachment, XmATTACH_WIDGET,
                XmNtopWidget, text1,
                XmNbottomAttachment, XmATTACH_NONE,
                XmNleftAttachment, XmATTACH_POSITION,
                XmNleftPosition, 35,
                XmNrightAttachment, XmATTACH_FORM,
                0);

XtVaSetValues (label3,
                XmNtopAttachment,
                XmATTACH_OPPOSITE_WIDGET,
                XmNtopOffset, 0,
                XmNtopWidget, text3,
                XmNbottomAttachment,
                XmATTACH_OPPOSITE_WIDGET,
                XmNbottomOffset, 0,
                XmNbottomWidget, text3,
                XmNleftAttachment, XmATTACH_FORM,
                XmNrightAttachment, XmATTACH_NONE,
                0);

XtVaSetValues (text3,
                XmNtopAttachment, XmATTACH_WIDGET,
                XmNtopWidget, text2,
                XmNbottomAttachment, XmATTACH_NONE,
                XmNleftAttachment, XmATTACH_POSITION,
                XmNleftPosition, 35,
                XmNrightAttachment, XmATTACH_FORM,
                0);
```

The application defaults file might contain:

```
XApplication*form.horizontalSpacing:  12
XApplication*form.verticalSpacing:     12
XApplication*label1.labelString:       Label
XApplication*label2.labelString:       Long label
XApplication*label3.labelString:       L
XApplication*text1.leftPosition:       35
XApplication*text2.leftPosition:       35
XApplication*text3.leftPosition:       35
```

There are a couple of points worth noting. First, the constraints are set after the widgets have been created, not at creation time. This is often necessary with XmForm layout code; you cannot attach one widget to another until after the destination widget has been created, and having to reorder the widget creation code simply to alter an attachment is likely to be error prone. Some constraints can be set at widget creation time (in the XmCreate*() call), but putting them all together after the widgets have been created is probably clearer.

The second point is that the attachments of the top and bottom of the XmLabel to the XmText widgets are alignments (attachment type ATTACH_OPPO-SITE_WIDGET) and as such need an explicit zero offset. The other attachments are not alignments. The offset is allowed to default, which means that you (or the end user) can add a little space to the layout by increasing the XmForm spacing or compact it by setting the spacing to zero. This is also why the XmLabels have an explicit attachment for the left edge to the form. If it were left to default, the offset is set to zero and the horizontalSpacing overridden.

The decision of which resources to set in code and which to allow the users to override by setting in the resource file is always difficult and often a matter of personal style. The split illustrated above attempts to fix the basic layout in the code, but still give the user the ability to adjust the spacing and the relative position of the columns. It also allows the position of the left edges of the XmText widgets to be changed if necessary to allow more space for wider XmLabels. The layout can be made to adapt automatically to changes in the XmLabel widths by attaching the right edges of the XmLabels to the left edges of the XmText widgets. The XmForm will then ensure that they do not overlap, making itself wider if necessary.

This layout is probably the simplest solution, but it still has a small problem with resizing; because the left edge of the XmText widgets are set to a percentage position, when the form resizes only a proportion of the extra space is given to the XmText widgets. In practice this may not be a problem, but the next section gives a different attachment solution that overcomes this.

6.3.4 Using a form attachment

This solution fixes the left edges of the XmText widgets by attaching them to the form at an offset that is calculated at run time (Figure 6.22).

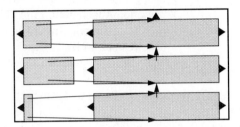

Figure 6.22 *Using form attachment to align XmText widgets*

The code for this layout is as follows:

formoffset-
attachments

```
form = XmCreateForm (appshell, "form", al, ac);
label1 = XmCreateLabel (form, "label1", al, ac);
text1 = XmCreateText (form, "text1", al, ac);
label2 = XmCreateLabel (form, "label2", al, ac);
text2 = XmCreateText (form, "text2", al, ac);
label3 = XmCreateLabel (form, "label3", al, ac);
text3 = XmCreateText (form, "text3", al, ac);

ac = 0;
XtSetArg (al[ac], XmNwidth, &width); ac++;
XtGetValues (label1, al, ac);
widest = width;
XtGetValues (label2, al, ac);
if (width > widest)
    widest = width;
XtGetValues (label1, al, ac);
if (width > widest)
    widest = width;
XtVaGetValues (form, XmNhorizontalSpacing, &spacing, 0);

XtVaSetValues (label1,
                XmNtopAttachment,
                XmATTACH_OPPOSITE_WIDGET,
                XmNtopOffset, 0,
                XmNtopWidget, text1,
                XmNbottomAttachment,
                XmATTACH_OPPOSITE_WIDGET,
```

```
                              XmNbottomOffset, 0,
                              XmNbottomWidget, text1,
                              XmNleftAttachment, XmATTACH_FORM, 0);
              XtVaSetValues (text1,
                              XmNtopAttachment, XmATTACH_FORM,
                              XmNbottomAttachment, XmATTACH_NONE,
                              XmNleftAttachment, XmATTACH_FORM,
                              XmNleftOffset, widest + spacing,
                              XmNrightAttachment, XmATTACH_FORM, 0);
```

The attachments for the other XmLabel and XmText widgets are omitted for brevity. Note that the XmForm's horizontalSpacing is added to the leftOffset of the XmText widget, as the XmLabel will be set into the XmForm by this amount. This will bring the XmText widgets hard against the right edge of the longest XmLabel. If the leftOffset of the XmText widgets includes twice the horizontalSpacing, there will be an appropriate gap between the end of the XmLabel and the start of the XmText widgets.

6.3.5   A comparison of the two approaches

Both methods have similar features.

In both cases, the right-hand edge of the XmLabels can be attached to the left-hand edge of the XmText widgets, so that the XmLabel's labelString can be centred.

Neither solution allows the XmLabel widget to be taller than the XmText widget. To work around this, the tops of both the XmLabel and the XmText widgets should be attached to the XmForm or the XmText widget above. The application can then query the widget heights to determine which of the XmLabel or XmText widget is the taller and can align the bottom of the other to it.

Using the XmForm attachment means that the application has to beware of resizing the XmLabel widgets (perhaps not very likely for XmLabels, but more probable with other widgets), as this may require a change to the leftOffset of the XmText widgets. Using the position attachment for the XmText widgets and attaching the right edge of the XmLabel to the left edge of the XmText will actually allow the layout to adjust itself if the XmLabels change size under application control.

6.4   Hints and tips

So far, this chapter has covered all the basics of the XmForm widget and ways in which it can be used to create common layouts. There are a few remaining points worth knowing.

6.4.1 Other interesting resources

resizeable

This is the one further constraint resource defined by XmForm. It allows the application to specify that an XmForm will not allow a widget to resize itself. This resource is ignored for resize requests, in a dimension where the widget has both edges attached. For instance, if a widget has the leftAttachment and rightAttachment set to something other than ATTACH_NONE, the XmForm will allow width resize requests regardless of the setting of the resizeable resource for that widget. If either leftAttachment or rightAttachment is set to ATACH_NONE, the XmForm will only allow resize requests if resizeable is set True for that widget.

6.4.2 Initial size

Many dialogs consist of a shell containing an XmForm. The initial size of such a dialog is determined by a process of negotiation between the shell, the XmForm and the widgets within the XmForm. The normal process is that the XmForm attempts to find a layout which satisfies all the constraints on its children and allows each to be at least as large as it wants to be, i.e. at least the 'natural' size. The XmForm then sizes itself to contain this layout and the shell sizes itself to contain the XmForm.

Most widgets have a sensible natural size. An XmLabel, for instance, has a natural size determined by its labelString, fontList and so on; XmText widgets normally size themselves according to the number of rows and columns they are supposed to display (as determined by their Row and Column resources).

If your dialog only contains widgets which have an acceptable natural size, then you can let the XmForm work out the initial size for you. Problems only arise where the dialog contains widgets which do not have an acceptable natural size, such as XmDrawingArea. You must then fix their size with constraints; the effect of this may be to make the initial size of the dialog too small.

If you have this problem, you should set the initial size of the dialog by setting the width and height resources of the top level XmForm (the child of the shell). You cannot set the initial size using the width and height resources of the shell, although you can set a minimum size using the appropriate shell resources.

6.4.3 Edge problems

An XmForm which is a child of an XmDialogShell will set its shadowThickness to 1 by default. The offset for ATTACH_FORM attachments is calculated from the outside of the shadow. As a result, any child widgets which are attached to the XmForm with the default offset of 0 will occlude part of this margin line. Figure 6.23 shows an XmForm with the shadowThickness set to 5 to exaggerate the problem.

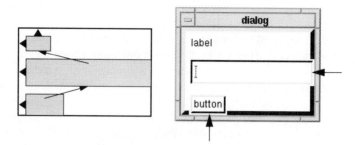

Figure 6.23 *Occluded margin*

The simplest way of dealing with this is to force the shadowThickness to 0. However, the shadow around a top level XmForm does look quite good, so it is worth investigating some techniques to stop the undesirable behaviour.

Extra attachments

The first solution is to attach the widget which overlap the margin to the edges of the XmForm, with an appropriate offset so that the margin is revealed. The drawback of this approach is that it can lead to undesirable resize behaviour (Figure 6.24).

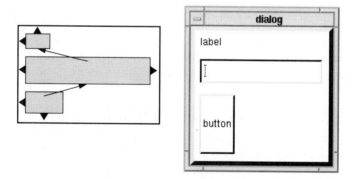

Figure 6.24 *Extra attachments and resize behaviour*

There are two other possible approaches to solving this problem, both of which involve introducing extra widgets into the design.

Invisible widgets

The problem with the simple attachment shown in Figure 6.24 is that the button resizes when the XmForm does and it looks strange. An alternative is to introduce an extra invisible widget between the button and the bottom of the XmForm. Although this will also resize with the XmForm, since it is invisible it does not look at all strange. An XmSeparator with the type resource set to NO_LINE is most suitable (Figure 6.25).

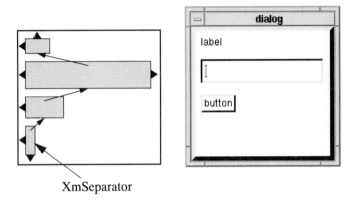

XmSeparator

Figure 6.25 *Invisible widget*

The bottom of the separator is attached to the bottom of the XmForm, with an appropriate offset so that it does not hide the margin line; the top of the separator is attached to the bottom of the button. The separator then resizes vertically with the XmForm, but the other components do not.

We could also use a second XmSeparator to keep the right edge of the XmTextField widget inset from the right edge of the XmForm (or, indeed, use the one XmSeparator for both jobs). However, the horizontal resize behaviour is appropriate for most purposes (the XmTextField widget resizes horizontally with the XmForm).

Doubled XmForms

The second technique uses an additional level in the hierarchy between the XmForm and the XmDialogShell. As the child XmForm is now not a child of the XmDialogShell, the shadowThickness will default to 0, so widgets can be attached right up to its edge. In order to retain the functions provided by having an XmBulletinBoard as a child of the XmDialogShell (see Section 4.7 for more details), the parent widget should be an XmBulletinBoard or an XmForm. If resize behaviour is required for the leaf widgets, then an XmForm is the best choice. The child XmForm is attached at all four edges to the parent XmForm, with an offset so that the shadow is visible (see Figure 6.26).

6.4.4 Jumping XmForms

In most applications the XmForm layout is fairly static. If you change the constraints when an XmForm is visible (or equivalently, manage or unmanage any

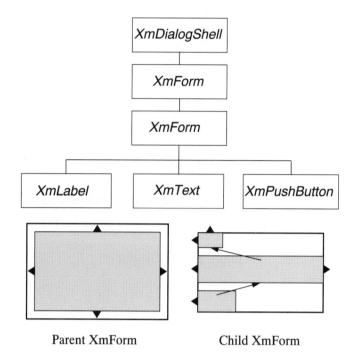

Parent XmForm   Child XmForm

Figure 6.26 *Doubled XmForms*

child widgets which have XmForm constraints set), the XmForm will recalculate the layout every time.

This can lead to some irritating behaviour. In particular, it is common for the XmForm to resize itself back to its initial size if the application changes some resources on the child widgets. This is particularly annoying to the user who has just deliberately resized the dialog.

The solution to this is simply to set the resizePolicy of the XmForm to GROW. It will then resize itself to become larger when required, but will not shrink itself at every opportunity.

The resizePolicy affects the way the XmForm behaves when its child widgets are changed in some way by the application. It does not affect the user's ability to resize the XmForm by resizing the window which contains it. You can, therefore, almost always use a resize policy of GROW in your application without any adverse affect on the user.

XmLists

Most widgets do not resize themselves when the application is running. You can, of course, write code to change widget sizes, but you have control over this and can generally make it behave sensibly.

XmList, on the other hand, resizes itself forcefully when the list items are modified. This is unfortunate, as often you will have designed your dialogs so that the user can resize the window to expand a ScrolledList. Unless it is restrained in some way, it will resize its width every time a list item is added or deleted so as to be wide enough to display the widest item in the list, but no wider. Worse, at least in some versions of the Motif toolkit, it gets confused about just how wide this is.

In particular, constraining a ScrolledList within an XmForm with attachments and positions can often give strange results. Not only will the XmForm resize frequently, but you may get 'Bailed out of edge synchronisation messages' when the application is run.

To avoid this, place the XmList or ScrolledList in its own XmForm, attaching it to the XmForm on all four edges. Set the resizePolicy of the XmForm to either GROW or NONE. You can then set the width and height of the XmForm to give the list a sensible initial size, or fix the initial size of the XmForm (and therefore the list that it contains) with attachments.

You may be tempted to control the height of a ScrolledList by setting the visible items resource on the XmList. If you do this, you may find that the ScrolledList gets confused and appears initially with the horizontal scroll bar running across the middle of the list (Figure 6.27). In this case the fix is to set the size on an enclosing XmForm. Setting the width and height of the list or the ScrolledList does not work, as the enclosing XmForm will ignore these.

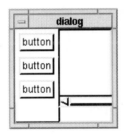

Figure 6.27 *Misbehaving ScrolledList*

6.4.5 Watch out for

Button box not possible

It is not possible to come up with a layout using attachments that will automatically layout buttons as for an XmMessageBox. The nearest you can get is to force them all to be the width of the widest determined at run time. Alternatively, set position attachments on both left and right edges to space them proportionally across the XmForm. It is much easier simply to use an XmMessageBox with dialogType set to DIALOG_TEMPLATE, which will automatically provide the button layout.

ScrolledList and ScrolledText widgets

⚠ The XmCreateScrolledList() and XmCreateScrolledText() functions return the XmList and XmText widgets, respectively. However there is an additional XmScrolledWindow widget created between the specified parent and the returned widget. When setting attachments for ScrolledText and ScrolledList, the XmScrolledWindow must have the attachments set, and should be the destination widget of any attachments. The following code fragment illustrates the significant attachments from the layout shown in Figure 6.14:

```
form = XmCreateForm (widget0, "form", al, ac);
dir_list = XmCreateScrolledList (form, "dir_list", al, ac);
dir_sw = XtParent (dir_list);
files_list = XmCreateScrolledList (form, "files_list", al, ac);
files_sw = XtParent (files_list);

XtVaSetValues (dir_sw,
                  XmNrightAttachment, XmATTACH_POSITION,
                  XmNrightPosition, 50, 0);
XtVaSetValues (files_sw,
                  XmNleftAttachment, XmATTACH_WIDGET,
                  XmNleftWidget, dir_sw, 0);
```

If the XmList widget ID is used as the destination of the attachment (the value of the leftWidget resource), the toolkit will cope with this by looking up the widget tree until it finds a widget that is an immediate child of the XmForm. That is, this code will work:

```
form = XmCreateForm (widget0, "form", al, ac);
dir_list = XmCreateScrolledList (form, "dir_list", al, ac);
files_list = XmCreateScrolledList (form, "files_list", al, ac);
files_sw = XtParent (files_list);

XtVaSetValues (files_sw,
                  XmNleftAttachment, XmATTACH_WIDGET,
                  XmNleftWidget, dir_list,
                  0);
```

However, the XmForm constraint resources must be set on the XmScrolledWindow. This will not work:

```
XtVaSetValues (files_list,
                  XmNleftAttachment, XmATTACH_WIDGET,
                  XmNleftWidget, dir_list,
                  0);
```

6.5 Conclusion

The XmForm widget is powerful and flexible, but a bit tricky. Using it effectively takes time and effort as well as skill and experience and it is often tempting to do the minimum, making little or no effort to account for resize behaviour and other run-time changes. It is a temptation to be resisted. Geometry management is one of the distinguishing features of Motif and it lets you achieve with a few lines of code results which are dauntingly expensive for developers who use other, less sophisticated toolkits. Attention to the detail of dialog layout makes a real difference to the perceived quality of your application. This book was produced using a well-known and expensive documentation tool with a Motif user interface. For all its virtues, which are many, it is irritating that few of its dialogs have sensible resize behaviour.

Many XmForm layouts use combinations of standard techniques. Consider creating a function library to handle those which you need most often (captioned text, two/three/four columns and so on). A little investment can reap big returns.

CHAPTER 7

Scrolling widgets

This chapter looks at the XmScrolledWindow widget and its derivative XmMain-Window.

The XmScrolledWindow works in two modes according to its scrollingPolicy, which can be AUTOMATIC or APPLICATION_DEFINED. These are very different; to reduce confusion they will be treated separately. A section illustrates some of the techniques required to implement scrolling.

 The visualPolicy resource is only there to confuse the developer. It is forced to CONSTANT for AUTOMATIC XmScrolledWindows and must be VARIABLE for APPLICATION_DEFINED. It can safely be ignored, as the toolkit will set it correctly.

7.1 XmScrolledWindow *(AUTOMATIC scrolling)*

An XmScrolledWindow with the scrollingPolicy set to AUTOMATIC provides a complete, configured set of components for a scrolling area. You just have to provide something for it to scroll over.

The XmScrolledWindow will create a pair of XmScrollBars and a clip widget; any work area widget that you create as a child of the XmScrolledWindow will be reparented to be a child of the clip widget. The XmScrolledWindow automatically adds callbacks to the XmScrollBars, which cause the origin of the work area to be adjusted so that the appropriate section is visible through the clip window, which provides a 'viewport' onto the work area widget.[1] When the origin is moved, a new portion of the work area is exposed and the work area widget receives an Expose event. It redraws itself in response, and the view seen through the viewport changes as if it had been scrolled. No special action is required from the work area widget; it just draws itself when exposed, something every widget does anyway.

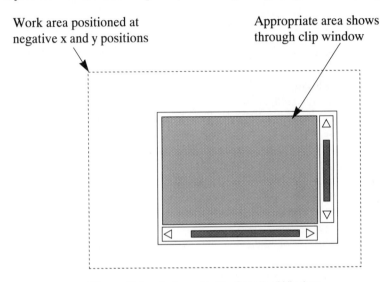

Work area positioned at negative x and y positions

Appropriate area shows through clip window

Figure 7.1   *Automatic XmScrolledWindow*

If the object that you want to scroll is small then an AUTOMATIC XmScrolledWindow is probably simplest. (The width and height resource type Dimension will usually allow a maximum widget size of 32,767 pixels, which may seem large, but may not be enough to display tabular data or a large drawing.)

 The work area widget is reparented to be the child of the clip widget. Using XtParent() on the work area yields the clip widget, not the XmScrolledWindow.

7.1.1   Interesting resources

scrollingPolicy
Set this to AUTOMATIC.

visualPolicy
This is unused for an AUTOMATIC XmScrolledWindow; it is always set to CONSTANT.

---

1. In general, widgets cannot be reparented (although windows can). The Motif toolkit reparents your work area widget by manipulating the Xt data structures directly. It is surprising that this works.

clipWindow, horizontalScrollBar and verticalScrollBar

These resources can be used to obtain the widget IDs of the widgets automatically created by the XmScrolledWindow (note that clipWindow is a widget ID, not a window ID). The clip widget happens to be an XmDrawingArea, so a resizeCallback can be added if you need to know when the size of the visible region changes.

scrollBarDisplayPolicy

Determines whether the XmScrollBars are always visible (STATIC), or if they are hidden when the work area is smaller than the clipping area (AS_NEEDED).

traverseObscuredCallback

This is an interesting callback used to inform the application that the user is trying to traverse (using the arrow keys or <Tab>) to a child widget of the work area that is obscured. The application therefore has an opportunity to scroll the view so that the widget is visible. There is a convenience routine XmScrollVisible() that can be used to effect the required scrolling:

traverse_
obscured

```
void traverse_obscured (w, client_data, call_data)
    Widget      w;
    XtPointer   client_data;
    XtPointer   call_data;
{
    XmScrollVisible (w, ((XmTraverseObscuredCallbackStruct *)
                    call_data)->traversal_destination, 0, 0);
}
```

workWindow

This resource specifies the widget that is to be scrolled. You should not need to set this resource, as the XmScrolledWindow sets it when a child widget is added.

7.2   XmScrolledWindow *(APPLICATION_DEFINED scrolling)*

You should use an APPLICATION_DEFINED XmScrolledWindow if you want to have control over how the information is scrolled. The application is responsible for all aspects of the scrolling and must create the XmScrollBars and the work area widget. The XmScrolledWindow only does the layout of the work area and the XmScrollBars. In this case the layout is simple (see Figure 7.2); the work area becomes the 'viewport' onto the data; the application has to draw the data appropriate for the XmScrollBar values.

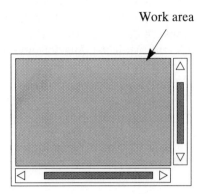

Work area

Figure 7.2 *Application_defined XmScrolledWindow*

7.2.1 Interesting resources

scrollingPolicy
Set this to APPLICATION_DEFINED.

clipWindow, visualPolicy, scrollBarDisplayPolicy and traverseObscuredCallback
These resources are not used for APPLICATION_DEFINED XmScrolled-
Windows. The visualPolicy resource must be VARIABLE (the default) and the clip
widget is never created.

horizontalScrollBar, verticalScrollBar and workWindow
These resources specify the widget IDs of the various components. The
XmScrolledWindow has a good guess at figuring out the children as they are
added, by looking at the child widget classes and the orientation of the two
XmScrollBar children, so the application should not normally need to set these.
    A convenience function, XmScrolledWindowSetAreas(), can be used to specify
the widget IDs of the children, if required. Passing NULL as an XmScrollBar ID
to XmScrolledWindowSetAreas() will unmap the corresponding XmScrollBar, so
they can be made to disappear when not needed.

7.3 XmMainWindow

The XmMainWindow widget is a container widget derived from XmScrolled-
Window that simply lays out its limited set of children. The application may add
up to four widgets to an XmMainWindow: a MenuBar, an XmCommand, a work
area and a message area. The last two can be any widget type. The work area child
is managed as the work area of the scrolling section exactly as for XmScrolled-

Window. The XmMainWindow lays out the children in a single column with the MenuBar at the top and the message area at the bottom. XmSeparators can be automatically inserted between the components. There is no requirement for the message area to provide any particular functionality, but by convention it is frequently used to provide transient messages and warnings.

XmMainWindow provides convenience routines to get the XmSeparator widgets (XmMainWindowSep1/2/3()) and to set the component areas (XmMain-WindowSetAreas()).

7.3.1 Interesting resources

showSeparator
Set to True to enable the XmSeparators between components.

commandWindowLocation
Specifies where the XmCommand widget is to be in relation to the work area.

7.3.2 Interesting behaviour

The XmMainWindow does some cunning layout on its MenuBar child which none of the other managers do. It will adjust the height of the MenuBar so that all the XmCascadeButtons are visible even if the XmMainWindow is not wide enough.

7.3.3 Examples of use

The only really useful feature of XmMainWindow that could not be achieved by using an XmForm and other child widgets is the MenuBar layout. The MenuBar layout is worth having for the main window of an application, hence the name.

If a scrolled work area is not required, then set the scrollingPolicy to APPLICATION_DEFINED, do not create any XmScrollBars and add the work area as usual. Figure 7.3 illustrates an XmMainWindow with the MenuBar being wrapped, a simple work area and a ScrolledText message area.

7.4 Handling scrolling

The remainder of this chapter describes various techniques used to handle scrolling. It starts with a very simple approach to scrolling, using an AUTOMATIC XmScrolledWindow, then progresses to a more sophisticated example using an APPLICATION_DEFINED XmScrolledWindow.

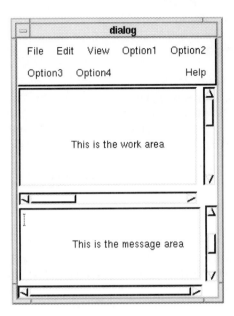

Figure 7.3 *XmMainWindow with MenuBar,
work area and message area*

7.4.1 AUTOMATIC Scrolling

Consider the following code, which consists mainly of an expose callback for an XmDrawingArea that displays a coordinate pair at 100 pixel intervals in the x direction and 20 pixel intervals in the y direction. A pointer to a canvas structure is used as client_data to identify the widgets being used. At this stage only the da and gc fields are used for the XmDrawingArea and a graphics context:

```
typedef struct canvas_s {
      Widget   da;
      Widget   hsb;
      Widget   vsb;
      int      width, height, x_offset, y_offset;
      GC       gc;
} canvas_t, *canvas_p;
```

autoscroll

Xlib drawing operations require a graphics context (see Chapter 16); this is stored in the canvas structure:

```
void create_gc (canvas)
    canvas_p      canvas;
{
    if (canvas->gc == 0)
    {
        XGCValues values;
/* Create GC with foreground taken from the XmDrawingArea */
        XtVaGetValues (canvas->da,
                    XmNforeground, &values.foreground, 0);
        canvas->gc = XCreateGC (XtDisplay (canvas->da),
                    XtWindow (canvas->da),
                    GCForeground, &values);
    }
}
```

The next function set_clip() is used simply to set the clipping region for the graphics context. Any drawing operation done with the graphics context will only affect the part of the window within the (rectangular) clipping region:

```
static void set_clip (canvas, x, y, width, height)
    canvas_p      canvas;
    int           x, y, width, height;
{
    XRectangle rect;
    rect.x = x;
    rect.y = y;
    rect.width = width;
    rect.height = height;
    XSetClipRectangles (XtDisplay (canvas->da), canvas->gc, 0, 0, &rect, 1,
                    YSorted);
}
```

Finally, the expose callback which does the drawing:

```
void expose (w, client_data, call_data)
    Widget        w;
    XtPointer     client_data;
    XtPointer     call_data;
{
    int x, y;
    XExposeEvent  *e = &((XmDrawingAreaCallbackStruct *)call_data)
                    ->event->xexpose;
    canvas_p      canvas = (canvas_p)client_data;
    Display       *display = XtDisplay (canvas->da);
```

```
      create_gc (canvas);
/* Set clipping region to be the part of the window that was exposed */
      set_clip (canvas, e->x, e->y, e->width, e->height);
/* Draw all the coordinate pairs that are (wholly or partly) within the exposed
area */
      x = (e->x / 100) * 100;
      while (x < e->x + e->width) {
          y = (e->y / 20) * 20;
          while (y < e->y + e->height + 10) {
              char buf[24];
              sprintf (buf, "%d,%d", x, y);
              XDrawString (display, XtWindow (canvas->da), canvas->gc,
                           x, y + 10, buf, strlen (buf));
              y = y + 20;
          }
          x = x + 100;
      }
}
```

An illustration is shown in Figure 7.4.

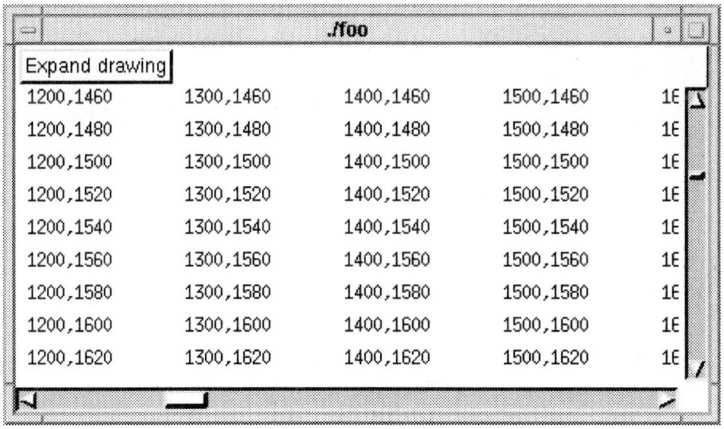

		.ffoo		
Expand drawing				
1200,1460	1300,1460	1400,1460	1500,1460	1E
1200,1480	1300,1480	1400,1480	1500,1480	1E
1200,1500	1300,1500	1400,1500	1500,1500	1E
1200,1520	1300,1520	1400,1520	1500,1520	1E
1200,1540	1300,1540	1400,1540	1500,1540	1E
1200,1560	1300,1560	1400,1560	1500,1560	1E
1200,1580	1300,1580	1400,1580	1500,1580	1E
1200,1600	1300,1600	1400,1600	1500,1600	1E
1200,1620	1300,1620	1400,1620	1500,1620	1E

Figure 7.4 *An APPLICATION_DEFINED XmScrolledWindow*

The application only needs to make the XmDrawingArea the required size. The XmScrolledWindow will adjust its origin, so that the required portion shows through the clip window and will correctly handle all the processing for the scrollbars. When the XmScrolledWindow moves the XmDrawingArea, Expose events are generated for the parts of the XmDrawingArea revealed and the callback draws in the coordinate pairs.

7.4.2 APPLICATION_DEFINED Scrolling

In the example in the previous section the scrolling is handled automatically by the XmScrolledWindow. However if the drawing is to be very large, or the application needs to control the scrolling, then an APPLICATION_DEFINED XmScrolled-Window is more appropriate. The XmScrolledWindow will manage the layout of the XmScrollBars and XmDrawingArea work area, but the XmDrawingArea will be the size of the viewport and its origin will not be moved about. The application therefore has to arrange to draw the appropriate data by itself.

Creating the XmScrollBars

For an APPLICATION_DEFINED XmScrolledWindow, the application has to create the XmScrollBars. This is straightforward, but remember to set the orientation:

jumpscroll

```
XtSetArg (al[ac], XmNscrollingPolicy, XmAPPLICATION_DEFINED); ac++;
scrollw = XmCreateScrolledWindow (form, "scrollw", al, ac);
ac = 0;
XtSetArg (al[ac], XmNorientation, XmHORIZONTAL); ac++;
canvas->hsb = XmCreateScrollBar (scrollw, "horscrollbar", al, ac);
ac = 0;
XtSetArg (al[ac], XmNorientation, XmVERTICAL); ac++;
canvas->vsb = XmCreateScrollBar (scrollw, "vertscrollbar", al, ac);
ac = 0;
canvas->da = XmCreateDrawingArea (scrollw, "da", al, ac);
XtAddCallback (canvas->hsb, XmNvalueChangedCallback, hsb_changed,
                    (XtPointer)canvas);
XtAddCallback (canvas->vsb, XmNvalueChangedCallback, vsb_changed,
                    (XtPointer)canvas);
XtAddCallback (canvas->da, XmNexposeCallback, expose,
                    (XtPointer)canvas);
```

The XmScrollBars have a single value changed callback which in the simplest case can redraw the whole XmDrawingArea. The callback stores the current value of the XmScrollBar in the canvas structure. This allows the expose callback to draw the correct portion of the image, and will be useful when we come on to the smooth scrolling example:

```
void vsb_changed (w, client_data, call_data)
    Widget      w;
    XtPointer   client_data;
    XtPointer   call_data;
{
    canvas_p canvas = (canvas_p)client_data;
```

```
        XClearArea (XtDisplay (canvas->da), XtWindow (canvas->da),
                    0, 0, 0, 0, True);
        canvas->y_offset = ((XmScrollBarCallbackStruct *)call_data)->value;
    }
```

XClearArea() causes the X server to send an Expose event for the entire XmDrawingArea every time either XmScrollBar's value is changed. This is a very inefficient way of implementing scrolling. We will describe a smooth scrolling algorithm later.

Setting the XmScrollBar values

The XmScrollBars need to have their value, sliderSize and minimum and maximum resources set appropriately so that they can be moved to scroll the image and accurately reflect the proportion of the image currently displayed. Whenever the size of the image changes, or when the XmDrawingArea resizes, the XmScrollBar resources must be recalculated. The XmScrollBar value is stored into the appropriate offset field in the canvas structure so that it accurately reflects the state of the viewport.

If the XmDrawingArea is resized to be very large (or the image becomes very small), it may be necessary to change the values of the XmScrollBars to stop wherever possible the bottom right corner of the image falling inside the XmDrawingArea. It is assumed that the required size of the image is stored in the width and height fields in the canvas structure:

```
        void adjust_scrollbar (sbar, size, visible_size, value)
            Widget      sbar;
            int         size, *value;
            Dimension   visible_size;
        {
        /* Assume that minimum is 0 */
            int     slider_size = visible_size;
            int     maximum = size;

            XtVaGetValues (sbar, XmNvalue, value, 0);
            if (slider_size > maximum)
                slider_size = maximum;
            if (*value > maximum - slider_size)
                *value = maximum - slider_size;
            XtVaSetValues (sbar, XmNvalue, *value,
                            XmNsliderSize, slider_size,
                            XmNmaximum, maximum,
                            0);
        }
```

```
void adjust_size (canvas)
    canvas_p canvas;
{
    Dimension width, height;

    XtVaGetValues (canvas->da, XmNwidth, &width,
                   XmNheight, &height,
                   0);
    adjust_scrollbar (canvas->vsb, canvas->height, height,
                      &canvas->y_offset);
    adjust_scrollbar (canvas->hsb, canvas->width, width,
                      &canvas->x_offset);
}
```

The adjust_size() function can be called by the application if the size of the image has been changed. The expose callback can call it to set up the XmScrollBars the first time through, and a resize callback is added to adjust them when the size of the XmDrawingArea is changed:

```
XtAddCallback (canvas->da, XmNresizeCallback, resize,
               (XtPointer)canvas);

void resize (w, client_data, call_data)
    Widget      w;
    XtPointer   client_data;
    XtPointer   call_data;
{
    canvas_p canvas = (canvas_p)client_data;
    adjust_size (canvas);
}
```

Expose callback for APPLICATION_DEFINED scrolling

With APPLICATION_DEFINED scrolling, the XmDrawingArea does not move. The Expose events it receives give the coordinates of the exposed area relative to the viewport, so we need to adjust the coordinates by the amount specified by the XmScrollBars, which has been stored in the canvas structure by the valueChanged-Callback. If the image is smaller than XmDrawingArea the expose callback has to be careful not to process coordinates outside the image size.

We can modify the expose callback to take account of the offsets like this:

```
void expose (w, client_data, call_data)
    Widget      w;
    XtPointer   client_data;
    XtPointer   call_data;
```

```
{
    int             x, y;
    XExposeEvent *e = &((XmDrawingAreaCallbackStruct *)call_data)
                        ->event->xexpose;
    canvas_p        canvas = (canvas_p)client_data;
    Display         *display = XtDisplay (canvas->da);

    if ( !canvas->gc )
        adjust_size ( canvas );
    create_gc (canvas);
    set_clip (canvas, e->x, e->y, e->width, e->height);
    x = ((canvas->x_offset + e->x) / 100) * 100;
    while (x < canvas->width
     && x < canvas->x_offset + e->x + e->width) {
        y = ((canvas->y_offset + e->y) / 20) * 20;
        while (y < canvas->height
         && y < canvas->y_offset + e->y + e->height + 10) {
            char buf[24];
            sprintf (buf, "%d,%d", x, y);
            XDrawString (display, XtWindow (canvas->da), canvas->gc,
                        x - canvas->x_offset, y - canvas->y_offset + 10,
                        buf, strlen (buf));
            y = y + 20;
        }
        x = x + 100;
    }
}
```

Here x and y are coordinates in the space of the image being drawn. They are mapped to the space of the XmDrawingArea by adding or subtracting the appropriate offset from the canvas structure. For the moment, we are assuming that this is simply an offset in pixels. We shall come onto adjusting the scrolling increment later.

7.4.3 Smooth scrolling

At present, the image only changes when the XmScrollBar value is changed - when the user *releases* the slider after moving it along the XmScrollBar. This section describes how to modify the application so that it will scroll the image as the XmScrollBar is dragged.

First, a dragCallback is added to adjust the offset as the slider is dragged. This can be set to the same function as the valueChangedCallback:

```
               XtAddCallback (canvas->hsb, XmNdragCallback, hsb_changed,
                            (XtPointer)canvas);
smoothscroll  XtAddCallback (canvas->vsb, XmNdragCallback, vsb_changed,
                            (XtPointer)canvas);
```

Recall that our current implementation of the valueChangedCallbacks redraws the entire XmDrawingArea every time. For some applications, if the drawing is very simple and fast, it may be appropriate to do this as the XmScrollBars are dragged. For many applications, however, the drawing will be sufficiently slow to cause an annoying flicker. In these cases, the scrolling should be done by using **XCopyArea()** to copy as much of the image as possible and only exposing the slice of the XmDrawingArea to be redrawn. Figure 7.5 illustrates how the image is redrawn when the horizontal XmScrollBar is incremented.

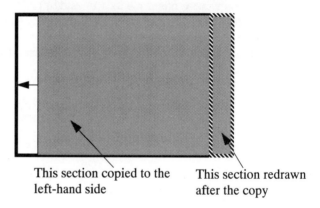

This section copied to the   This section redrawn
left-hand side   after the copy

Figure 7.5   *When the horizontal XmScrollBar is incremented,
the image moves to the left*

The following code fragment shows how this would be achieved. The callback knows how much the XmScrollBar has moved, because we remembered the old value in the adjust_size() function.

The function set_no_clip() simply removes any clipping from the graphics context by setting the clip_mask to None:

```
static void set_no_clip (canvas)
    canvas_p canvas;
{
    XSetClipMask (XtDisplay (canvas->da), canvas->gc, None);
}

void hsb_changed (w, client_data, call_data)
    Widget      w;
    XtPointer   client_data;
```

```
    XtPointer    call_data;
{
    canvas_p     canvas = (canvas_p)client_data;
    int          slider_size;
    int          pixels_to_lose;
    Boolean      positive;
    Display      *display = XtDisplay (canvas->da);
    Window       window = XtWindow (canvas->da);
    int          new_value = ((XmScrollBarCallbackStruct *)call_data)-
                     >value;

    if (canvas->x_offset == new_value)
        return;
    XtVaGetValues (canvas->hsb, XmNsliderSize, &slider_size, 0);
    /* Work out how far (and in which direction) we need to scroll */
    if (positive = (new_value > canvas->x_offset))
        pixels_to_lose = new_value - canvas->x_offset;
    else
        pixels_to_lose = canvas->x_offset - new_value;
    canvas->x_offset = new_value;
    if (pixels_to_lose >= slider_size)
        /* Scrolling more than a page, nothing worth copying */
        XClearArea (display, window, 0, 0, 0, 0, True);
    else {
        /* Copy useful section, and expose revealed section */
        Dimension width, height;
        XtVaGetValues (canvas->da, XmNwidth, &width,
                    XmNheight, &height, 0);
        set_no_clip (canvas);
        if (positive) {
            XCopyArea (display, window, window, canvas->gc,
                    pixels_to_lose, 0, width - pixels_to_lose, height, 0, 0);
            XClearArea (display, window,
                    width - pixels_to_lose, 0, pixels_to_lose, height, True);
        } else {
            XCopyArea (display, window, window, canvas->gc,
                    0, 0, width - pixels_to_lose, height, pixels_to_lose, 0);
            XClearArea (display, window, 0, 0, pixels_to_lose, height, True);
        }
    }
}
```

The code for the vertical XmScrollBar is obviously similar. There are still two further additions required that are not immediately obvious.

Handling GraphicsExpose events

If XCopyArea() attempts to copy a section of the window that is obscured (perhaps by a window belonging to another application), a GraphicsExpose event will be sent to notify the application that the server was unable to process part of the copy. Figure 7.6 illustrates how an obscured area will generate a GraphicsExpose event.

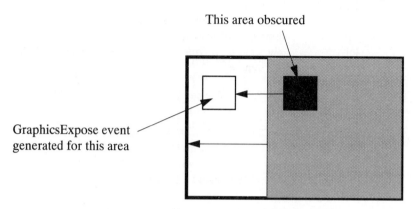

This area obscured

GraphicsExpose event
generated for this area

Figure 7.6   *When area is copied, the obscured area
cannot be drawn in the new position*

GraphicsExpose events are only generated if the graphics context used in the XCopyArea() has the graphics_exposures component set to True. This is the default when graphics contexts are created, so we will receive GraphicsExpose events when appropriate. We must respond by drawing the section of the window identified by the event.

If the XmDrawingArea used an action routine to handle Expose events and thus call the expose callback, we could add a translation to handle GraphicsExpose events in the same way. However, the XmDrawingArea handles Expose events directly via the expose method in the class. The best way of intercepting the GraphicsExpose events is therefore to use an event handler:

```
XtAddEventHandler (canvas->da, NoEventMask, True, graphics_expose,
                   NULL);
```

This can be added at any time after the widget is created. The code for the event handler is very simple: it just calls the expose callbacks for the widget:

```
void graphics_expose (w, client_data, event, continue_to_dispatch)
    Widget      w;
    XtPointer   client_data;
    XEvent      *event;
    Boolean     *continue_to_dispatch;
{
    if (event->type == GraphicsExpose) {
```

```
            XmDrawingAreaCallbackStruct cb;
            cb.reason = XmCR_EXPOSE;
            cb.event = event;
            cb.window = XtWindow (w);
            XtCallCallbacks (w, XmNexposeCallback, &cb);
        }
    }
```

Synchronising XCopyArea

Consider the following scenario. Two drag events come from the XmScrollBar in quick succession. When the first one is processed, a section of the window gets copied and a section gets cleared. Before the Expose event for the clearing gets processed another drag event is ready. If the application tries to copy a section of the window at this point, a blank area will be copied. To stop this happening, it is a good idea to make sure that any outstanding events for the XmDrawingArea have been processed before doing the XCopyArea(). This is done at the beginning of the valueChanged callback before the offset field is updated; the exposures are for the old offset:

```
    XEvent event;

    XSync (display, False);
    while (XCheckWindowEvent (display, window, ExposureMask, &event))
        XtDispatchEvent (&event);
```

7.4.4 Modifying the scrolling increment

In some situations it is desirable to have a scrolling increment expressed in units other than pixels. This will be the case where the elements being scrolled are of unequal size.

The easy way to do this is to simply set the increment resource for the XmScrollBar and to make no other changes to the code outlined above. This, however, may not be sufficient as it does not ensure that the XmScrollBar value will always be a multiple of the increment when dragging or clicking in the trough area. For instance, in the example program, lines of text are drawn at 20 pixel intervals. Simply setting the vertical XmScrollBar's increment to 20 will still allow the XmScrollBar's value to be something other than a multiple of 20.

The solution is to make the vertical XmScrollBar work in line units. The expose callback is still going to work in pixels, so there is a design decision as to the units used to store the offset and size fields in the canvas data structure. To minimise the amount of code reproduced here, we shall continue to store them in pixels and just modify the adjust_scrollbar() and vsb_changed() functions. Depending on the requirements of the application it may be more appropriate to work in lines and do the mapping in the expose() and vsb_changed() functions.

The adjust_v_scrollbar() function sets maximum to be the total number of lines which could be displayed in the image. The sliderSize is set to the number which are wholly or partially visible:

linescroll

```
void adjust_v_scrollbar (sbar, size, visible_size, offset)
    Widget       sbar;
    int          size, *offset;
    Dimension    visible_size;
{
    int slider_size = (visible_size + 19) / 20;
    int maximum = (size + 19) / 20;
    int value;

    XtVaGetValues (sbar, XmNvalue, &value, 0);
    if (slider_size > maximum)
        slider_size = maximum;
    if (value > maximum - slider_size)
        value = maximum - slider_size;
    XtVaSetValues (sbar, XmNvalue, value,
                         XmNsliderSize, slider_size,
                         XmNmaximum, maximum,
                         0);
    *offset = value * 20;
}
```

The vsb_changed() function now has to convert the XmScrollBar value to pixels:

```
void vsb_changed (w, client_data, call_data)
    Widget       w;
    XtPointer    client_data;
    XtPointer    call_data;
{
    canvas_p     canvas = (canvas_p)client_data;
    int          slider_size, value;
    Dimension    width, height;
    int          pixels_to_lose;
    Boolean      positive;
    XEvent       event;
    Display      *display = XtDisplay (canvas->da);
    Window       window = XtWindow (canvas->da);
    int          new_offset =
                     ((XmScrollBarCallbackStruct *)call_data)->value * 20;
```

```
        if (canvas->y_offset == new_offset)
            return;
        XSync (display, False);
        while (XCheckWindowEvent (display, window, ExposureMask, &event))
            XtDispatchEvent (&event);
        XtVaGetValues (canvas->vsb, XmNsliderSize, &slider_size, 0);
        if (positive = (new_offset > canvas->y_offset))
            pixels_to_lose = new_offset - canvas->y_offset;
        else
            pixels_to_lose = canvas->y_offset - new_offset;
        canvas->y_offset = new_offset;
        if (pixels_to_lose >= slider_size * 20)
            ...
    }
```

In some circumstances, the amount scrolled might be variable depending on the context. The additions required to achieve this are straightforward but messy. If our example allowed some lines to be taller than others, then:

- An offset and size in line units needs to be stored. This can be in addition to the pixel-based values.
- The adjust_v_scrollbar() function needs to calculate the number of visible lines given the offset in lines. The sliderSize is set to this value.
- The adjust_v_scrollbar() function needs to calculate the total number of lines. The maximum resource is set to this value. This need only be done when the size of the image changes.
- The vsb_changed() function calculates the number of lines being scrolled (call_data->value - canvas->y_line_offset). These are either lines that are scrolled onto or off the XmDrawingArea. The function can now calculate pixels_to_lose by adding together the heights of these lines.
- The vsb_changed() function needs to recalculate the sliderSize determined by the number of lines now visible.

The code is left as an exercise for the reader.

7.4.5   Automatic panning

If the user were allowed to select regions of the image using the mouse, it would be helpful if the image could automatically pan and scroll so that he or she can drag select over areas larger than the visible section. This is achieved by detecting when the pointer moves out of the window and adding a timer which triggers the scrolling when it times out. The example below does not add any visual behaviour or selection semantics and merely illustrates the auto-scrolling mechanism.

First, some additional fields are added to the canvas structure:

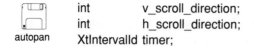

```
int           v_scroll_direction;
int           h_scroll_direction;
XtIntervalId  timer;
```

autopan

v_scroll_direction is set to -1 if the pointer is above the XmDrawingArea, 1 if it is below and 0 if it is in or parallel to the XmDrawingArea. Similarly, h_scroll_direction is set to indicate the position of the pointer in the horizontal dimension.

Translations are added to the XmDrawingArea to intercept <Btn1Down>, <Btn1Motion> and <Btn1Up> and map them to the action routines drag_start(), drag_motion() and drag_stop(), respectively. The action routines will need access to the canvas structure, so this made available to them by putting a pointer to it in the XmDrawingArea's userData resource.

The auto_scroll_bar() function decides if there is space for the XmScrollBar to be moved in the required direction. If there is and doit is True, it will actually move the XmScrollBar. This causes the valueChanged callback to be called for the XmScrollBar which will adjust the image as necessary:

```
static Boolean auto_scroll_bar (w, doit, amount)
    Widget   w;
    Boolean  doit;
    int      amount;
{
    int      min, max, value, slider_size, inc, pinc;
    Boolean  space;

    XtVaGetValues (w, XmNminimum, &min,
                   XmNmaximum, &max,
                   XmNvalue, &value,
                   XmNsliderSize, &slider_size,
                   XmNincrement, &inc,
                   XmNpageIncrement, &pinc,
                   0);
    value = value + amount;
    space = (value >= min && value + slider_size <= max);
    if (space && doit)
        XmScrollBarSetValues (w, value, slider_size, inc, pinc, True);
    return space;
}
```

The function auto_scroll() decides whether to adjust an XmScrollBar, depending on the v_scroll_direction and h_scroll_direction fields. If scrolling is required and there is space, a timer is added to continue the scrolling. If scrolling is not required (because the pointer is inside the XmDrawingArea) or there is no more space to scroll in the required direction, then any outstanding timer is removed:

```
static void timer ();

static void auto_scroll (canvas, doit)
    canvas_p    canvas;
    Boolean     doit;
{
    Boolean need_timer = False;

    if (canvas->v_scroll_direction != 0
    && auto_scroll_bar (canvas->vsb, doit, canvas->v_scroll_direction))
        need_timer = True;
    if (canvas->h_scroll_direction != 0
    && auto_scroll_bar (canvas->hsb, doit, canvas->h_scroll_direction))
        need_timer = True;
    if (need_timer)
        canvas->timer = XtAppAddTimeOut (
                        XtWidgetToApplicationContext (canvas->da),
                        100, timer, (XtPointer) canvas);
    else
        if (canvas->timer)
        {
            XtRemoveTimeOut (canvas->timer);
            canvas->timer = 0;
        }
}
```

The timer function simply sets the timer field to 0, as the timer is now inactive, and then calls auto_scroll(). The timer field is checked first in case the timer has been removed already (because dragging has been stopped, for example). There is further discussion of timers and how they work in Section 12.8.2:

```
static void timer (closure, id)
    XtPointer    closure;
    XtIntervalId *id;
{
    canvas_p canvas = (canvas_p)closure;
    if (canvas->timer)
    {
        canvas->timer = 0;
```

```
                auto_scroll (canvas, True);
        }
    }
```

The action functions are very simple. drag_start() would in any real example initiate the selection visuals, but in our simple example we shall leave it empty. The drag_motion() function determines what direction scrolling is required and calls auto_scroll() to add the timer. Note that it calls it with doit set to False, so the scrolling will not happen until the timer fires. The drag_stop() function simply removes any outstanding timer:

```
void drag_start (w, event, params, num_params)
    Widget   w;
    XEvent   *event;
    String   *params;
    Cardinal *num_params;
{
}

void drag_motion (w, event, params, num_params)
    Widget   w;
    XEvent   *event;
    String   *params;
    Cardinal *num_params;
{
    canvas_p       canvas;
    XMotionEvent   *e = (XMotionEvent *)event;
    Dimension      width, height;

    XtVaGetValues (w, XmNuserData, &canvas,
                      XmNwidth, &width,
                      XmNheight, &height, 0);
    canvas->v_scroll_direction = 0;
    canvas->h_scroll_direction = 0;
    if (e->x >= (int)width)
        canvas->h_scroll_direction = 1;
    else
        if (e->x <= 0)
            canvas->h_scroll_direction = -1;
    if (e->y >= (int)height)
        canvas->v_scroll_direction = 1;
    else
        if (e->y <= 0)
            canvas->v_scroll_direction = -1;
```

```
      auto_scroll (canvas, False);
}

void drag_stop (w, event, params, num_params)
     Widget   w;
     XEvent   *event;
     String    *params;
     Cardinal *num_params;
{
    canvas_p canvas;

    XtVaGetValues (w, XmNuserData, &canvas, 0);
    if (canvas->timer)
    {
        XtRemoveTimeOut (canvas->timer);
        canvas->timer = 0;
    }
}
```

CHAPTER 8

Shells and Xt widgets

Most of the widgets you use are provided as part of the Motif toolkit built by the OSF, but some of the most basic widgets are part of Xt. For the most part, a Motif application uses Motif widgets derived from the Xt widgets; the only Xt widget commonly used in Motif programs is ApplicationShell. However, you have to understand the base classes to get the most from the derived ones.

The first part of this chapter discusses the Xt base classes used for the Motif widgets and gadgets. This is straightforward. The second part covers shell widgets and is rather more challenging. The generalities of shell widgets are discussed, followed by a brief section on each of the different classes derived from Shell.

8.1   The Xt widget classes

Figure 8.1 shows the Xt class hierarchy and the way it relates to the Motif classes. Only the highest level of Motif classes is shown.

The Motif classes XmGadget, XmPrimitive and XmManager form the basis of all the Motif widgets and gadgets, except for XmDialogShell and XmMenuShell. They all introduce a common set of resources which support Motif-specific concepts, such as keyboard traversal and resolution independence. Ideally, these would be defined in a common Motif base class, but the class hierarchy defined by

Xt does not provide anywhere to put this. See Chapter 13 for a discussion of keyboard traversal and Section 4.6.1 for details of resolution independence.

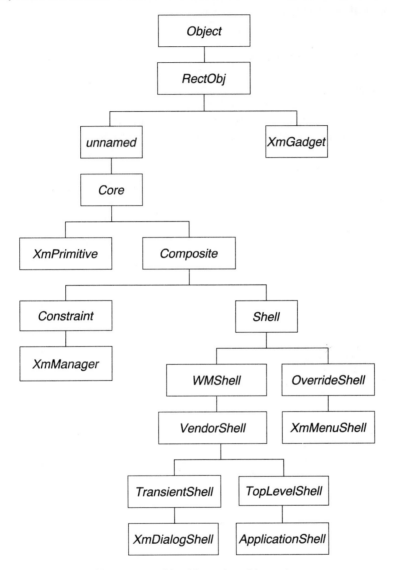

Figure 8.1 *Xt widget class hierarchy*

8.2 Object and RectObj

The root of the hierarchy is the Object class. This supports the basic features of the Xt model - subclassing and resource management.

Derived from Object is RectObj, the rectangle object. This introduces notions of geometry (it has width and height resources) and is used as the basis for the Core and XmGadget classes.

8.2.1   Interesting resources

destroyCallback

This can be used to tidy up references to the widget when it is unexpectedly destroyed, perhaps because its parent has been destroyed. For an example of this use in conjunction with C++, see Young (1992) pp 87-90.

x, y, width, height and borderWidth

Setting these (via XtSetValues()) is the only safe way for an application to change the geometry of a widget. Other Xt and Xlib functions may appear to do the job, but can cause nasty inconsistencies and failures. Figure 8.2 illustrates how the values relate to the rectangle object.

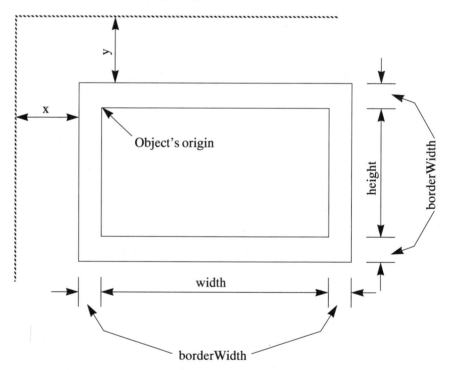

Figure 8.2   *RectObj dimensions*

sensitive and ancestorSensitive

A widget can only get the keyboard focus if it and all of its ancestors are sensitive. The ancestorSensitive resource is simply an implementation shortcut and should probably not be a resource.

You should not use XtSetValues() to set either of these resources (although there is nothing to stop you). You can set sensitive using XtSetSensitive(), which will automatically set ancestorSensitive correctly for any descendent widgets. Similarly, you should use XtIsSensitive() to query the sensitivity of a widget which will return True only if the widget and all its ancestors are sensitive.

8.2.2 Watch out for

Although Object and RectObj are shown as superclasses of Core (together with the mysterious *unnamed* class), the implementation is not completely clean. Object and RectObj were late additions to the class hierarchy. In order to introduce them without breaking existing widget code, they had to be represented not as class records containing the usual parts, but as copies of the Core class record, with the irrelevant bits ignored. This does not affect you as a developer, but it does explain why some books show Object and RectObj as parts of Core rather than superclasses.

The notional *unnamed* widget class just consists of those parts of Core which are irrelevant to RectObj. It does not really exist.

8.3 Core

Core is the base class for all widgets. It introduces the two most fundamental concepts of X - windows and events. Every widget has a window (at least potentially) and also has the ability to respond to events via the translations mechanism.

A Core widget can also be used as the parent for a popup shell (one created with XtCreatePopupShell()). It cannot be a parent for an ordinary child; for that, you need a Composite widget.

Core is used as the basis of XmPrimitive and Composite.

8.3.1 Interesting resources

mappedWhenManaged

All widgets have their windows mapped by default when they are managed. You can control the mapping of a widget by setting mappedWhenManaged, or by using XtMapWidget(). Setting mappedWhenManaged is cleaner, as it ensures that mapped widgets are all managed and so have been sensibly sized and positioned by their parents.

translations

See Chapter 11 for a description of the translations mechanism.

initialResourcesPersistent

This is only of interest if you destroy widgets while your application is running and find that memory is leaking out via resource converters. If so, there is some relevant information in Section 10.15.2, but you probably need a thicker book than this one.

background and backgroundPixmap

These resources specify how the background of the widget is to be drawn. The backgroundPixmap takes precedence; if it is not set the backgroundColor is drawn. The resource is simply copied to the appropriate window attribute and the server fills the window with the colour or pixmap when the window is exposed.

borderColor and borderPixmap

These resources specify how the border of the widget is to be drawn. The border-Pixmap takes precedence; if it is not set, the borderColor is drawn. The resource is simply copied to the appropriate window attribute and the server fills the window border with the colour or pixmap when the window is exposed.

colormap

Each widget stores a colour map which is used by the default resource converters when converting from string to pixel resources. The value of the colour map is also stored in the colormap attribute of the window belonging to the widget.

You should probably only set this resource for shell widgets, as it is propagated down the widget hierarchy. The window manager will automatically install the colour map for shell widgets when they receive the input focus. See Section 16.2.1 for further details about colour maps.

depth

Specifies the depth of the widget's window. This should probably only be set for shell widgets on a different screen (see Section 8.6.6).

screen

Specifies the screen on which the widgets window is displayed. This should probably only be set for shell widgets (see Section 8.6.6).

8.3.2   Examples of use

You are unlikely to create an instance of Core directly. However, it can be used if you need a widget that you can set up to do what you want. You will have to handle all events yourself, using event handlers or (preferably) translations and an action table, and draw and redraw the window in response to Expose events. In most cases, the Motif XmDrawingArea is easier to use.

8.3.3 Watch out for

 The Motif toolkit is implemented in such a way that it interferes with the use of the accelerators resource, so you cannot reliably use Xt accelerators in a Motif application. Note that the Core *accelerators* resource is not at all the same as the XmLabel *accelerator* resource (see Section 3.2.1).

8.4 Composite

Composite introduces support for child widgets. A composite widget can have children and Xt will handle most of the bookkeeping, ensuring that the layout is revised when children are added, removed and (un)managed.

Composite is used as the base class for Constraint, which in turn is the base class for XmManager. All the Motif widgets to which you add children are derived from XmManager.

8.4.1 Interesting resources

insertPosition

This is used to control the order of children within the parent. Some composite widgets display their children in this order. By default, the order of the children is the order in which they were created. For the Motif widgets where the child order matters (XmRowColumn and XmPanedWindow), you can set the positionIndex constraint resource on each child when you create it (or later) to get the same effect with less work.

8.4.2 Watch out for

 If you have a composite widget that is already realised, and want to manage a new composite child, you should explicitly realise the child first, so as to be sure that it appears with the right size.

The children list of a composite widget does not include popup children - those created with XtCreatePopupShell() (or XmCreateDialogShell()). Where the Xt documentation refers to a widget's children, it means only the ordinary children and not the popup ones. This means, for instance, that popup children of an ApplicationShell are not realised when the ApplicationShell is. (They will usually be realised by XtPopup().)

8.5   Constraint

Each class of widget has a predefined list of resources that can be used to store information about the widget. It is sometimes useful to be able to store extra information on a widget, typically for its parent to use in determining layout. Constraint introduces the mechanism that makes this possible.

Constraint widgets can define new resources called constraint resources for which the values are specified individually for each child. Xt takes care of storing these, so that the constraint widget can find and use them. Although the resource values are set individually on each child, a widget does not look at the resources defined by its constraint parent and does not know how to interpret them, so new constraint widgets can be introduced without affecting existing widget classes.

8.5.1   Interesting resources

Constraint itself defines no new resources.

8.5.2   Watch out for

Although all the Motif managers are constraint widgets (as XmManager is derived from Constraint) only XmForm, XmFrame, XmPanedWindow and XmRowColumn make use of the constraints mechanism.

8.6   Shell widgets

The shell widgets are a special set of composites used to encapsulate the interaction between the highest level windows of your application and the window manager and X server. Chapter 14 describes this interaction in some detail.

Shells are rather different from other widgets. There are also different sorts of shell, different ways of creating them and different ways of manipulating them. This is not a nice, orthogonal arrangement and you can mix and match creation functions and sorts of shell, but it is unlikely that the shell widget authors expected, or catered for, all combinations. There is, then, an expected way of doing things and any number of alternative approaches that may work. We cover the expected way; the others you can try for yourselves.

8.6.1   Shell widget classes

There are four shell widget classes that you would expect to instantiate in your application: ApplicationShell, TopLevelShell, XmDialogShell and XmMenuShell.

The ApplicationShell widget class is designed for the main top-level shell of an application and is usually created with no parent. It has two important characteristics:

- A parentless ApplicationShell provides context for resource database searches. That is, its class name, 'ApplicationShell', is replaced (for the purposes of searching the resource database only) by the application's class name, such as Mwm.
- Whether parentless or not, it uses its argc and argv resources to set the initial value of the WM_COMMAND property on its window (see Section 14.4). As the window manager expects that an application will only have one window with a non-null WM_COMMAND property, you should normally only have one realised ApplicationShell.

TopLevelShell is very similar to ApplicationShell, but you can have as many as you want. It creates a window that can be separately iconified, like the ApplicationShell, but it does not set the WM_COMMAND property. A TopLevelShell normally has the application's ApplicationShell as its parent.

XmDialogShell is a Motif-specific shell designed for subsidiary dialogs that cannot be iconified. Its parent is usually the application's ApplicationShell, or one of its TopLevelShells. It has an intimate relationship with XmBulletinBoard. When an XmDialogShell has an XmBulletinBoard child, you can implement some, but not all, shell-related functions by manipulating the child. This has the effect of introducing surprising side effects without making the application any simpler.

XmMenuShell is again specific to Motif. It is a customised OverrideShell designed to support the Motif menu system, and is described in Section 9.3. The remainder of this chapter ignores XmMenuShell.

8.6.2 Creating shells

Normal widgets are created by a call to XtCreateWidget() (or one of the XmCreate<widgetclass>() functions, which are mostly just wrappers for it). Shells must be created using one of the shell creation functions XtAppCreateShell() or XtCreatePopupShell().[1]

XtAppCreateShell() is designed to create a shell that is the root of a new widget hierarchy and has no widget parent; we will call this a parentless shell. The most important feature of this function is that, if the shell is an ApplicationShell, the class you pass into XtAppCreateShell() is used as the leftmost component of resource database queries. For XtCreatePopupShell(), you specify a parent widget and the resource database queries are based (as for any ordinary widget) on the class of the parent and its ancestors as well as those of the shell you create.

---

1. Some other functions, such as XtAppInitialize(), call XtAppCreateShell(). XmCreateDialogShell() calls XtCreatePopupShell().

The other major difference is that a shell created with XtCreatePopupShell() is destroyed when its parent widget is destroyed. If you start a new widget hierarchy with XtAppCreateShell(), the shell is free-standing and independent of any other widget.

8.6.3   The normal complement

An application will normally have the following complement of shells:

- One and only one parentless ApplicationShell, for resource database context.
- One and only one realised ApplicationShell to represent the application (via the WM_COMMAND property of its window) to the window manager and session manager.
- A number of TopLevelShells, corresponding to the second and subsequent iconifiable windows.
- A number of XmDialogShells, for non-iconifiable dialogs.
- A number of XmMenuShells as required by the menu system. These are usually created by the menu creation convenience functions and are invisible to the application programmer.

Usually, the parentless ApplicationShell and the realised ApplicationShell are the same and are created by XtAppInitialize(), which also performs other initialisations.

8.6.4   Multiple top-level windows

If you need only a single top-level window with a number of dependent, subsidiary dialogs you should use an ApplicationShell created by XtAppCreateShell() and a number of XmDialogShells created by XmCreateDialogShell(). If you need multiple top-level windows of apparently equal status, you need some TopLevelShells as well.

The simplest arrangement is to have a single ApplicationShell created by XtAppCreateShell() and a number of TopLevelShells created by XtCreatePopupShell(), with the ApplicationShell as their parent. The only problem with this is that the specification of resources in resource files is slightly unbalanced. Although the ApplicationShell and the TopLevelShells look the same to the user, resources for the ApplicationShell are specified using the application's name and/or class, but those for the TopLevelShells are additionally qualified by the names of those shells:

```
Myapplication.background:              pink !ApplicationShell
Myapplication.toplevel1.background:    yellow !TopLevelShell 1
Myapplication.toplevel2.background:    magenta !TopLevelShell 2
```

If this offends you, you can make it more even by having all the visible shells created as children of an unrealised parentless ApplicationShell. One of these children should be an ApplicationShell and you set its argc and argv resources so that the window manager can get the value for the **WM_COMMAND** property. The other children will be TopLevelShells, and all children (including the one that is an ApplicationShell) are created using XtCreatePopupShell(). This will allow the resources to be specified in this way:

```
Myapplication.toplevel0.background:  pink !TopLevelShell 0l
Myapplication.toplevel1.background:  yellow !TopLevelShell 1
Myapplication.toplevel2.background:  magenta !TopLevelShell 2
```

8.6.5 Multiple displays

Most applications have only one realised ApplicationShell and so have only one top-level window with the **WM_COMMAND** property set. However, if you have multiple displays (i.e. you have called XtOpenDisplay() more than once), you may be interacting with multiple window managers and should have a realised ApplicationShell for each display. As you only want to initialise the toolkit once, you have to create the second and subsequent shells with XtAppCreateShell().

To make sure that the application does not die when a user closes the ApplicationShell, you will have to handle **WM_DELETE_WINDOW** messages (see Section 14.5).

8.6.6 Multiple screens

Most applications run happily on a single screen, but there are situations where multiple screens are useful. An example might be an application which displays sophisticated drawings, but which also has extensive ancillary windows. It might be sensible to have the drawings on a high-quality screen and the other windows on another (possibly less capable but cheaper) screen. This allows the user to use the whole of the screen for the drawing and will therefore reduce the amount of redrawing as the other windows are popped up and down (see Figure 8.3).

Example code for this type of application can be found in Section 8.7.3.

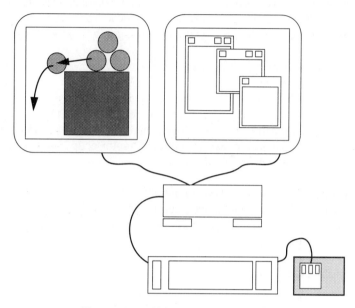

Figure 8.3 *Using multiple screens*

8.6.7 Transient shells

A transient shell is one that is only visible on screen when some other shell is; it disappears when that shell is iconified. Transient shells are typically used for popup dialogs that make no real sense if they stand alone.

The Motif XmDialogShell is designed for this purpose. When you create an XmDialogShell (using XtCreatePopupShell() or XmCreateDialogShell()), you should give an ApplicationShell or TopLevelShell as its parent. The XmDialogShell's window will then be unmapped automatically when the parent shell is iconified.

 You can choose another (non-shell) widget as the parent of an XmDialogShell, but the results may not be quite what you expect. This area of the Motif toolkit is probably imperfect and you should treat it with caution. If the toolkit support does not give you what you need, you can always hide the XmDialogShell explicitly.

8.6.8 Window and widget states

Window managers recognise three states for the window of a shell:

- Withdrawn - neither the window nor its icon is visible on the screen.

- Normal - the window is visible.
- Iconic - the icon is visible.

As you use widgets rather than windows, you also have to deal with the widget's unrealised state, where the window does not exist, and so the window manager knows nothing about it.

When a widget is realised and its window is created, it is in the withdrawn state; neither the window nor its icon is visible. When it is mapped, it moves to the normal or iconic state, according to the initial state information contained in its WM_HINTS property (for a shell widget, this is set using the initialState resource).

A parentless shell created using XtAppCreateShell() has its window created by an explicit call to XtRealizeWidget(). If the shell has mappedWhenManaged set True (the default), XtRealizeWidget() will also attempt to map the window and it moves immediately from an unrealised widget to a realised widget with a normal or iconified window, according to the value of initialState.

For a popup shell created using XtCreatePopupShell(), XtRealizeWidget() creates the window but does not map it, so it starts in the withdrawn state. However, you do not normally call XtRealizeWidget() on a popup shell; rather, the shell is realised as an effect of calling a function to pop it up.

For a TopLevelShell, XtPopup() will realise the shell (if this has not already happened) and attempt to map its window; it will then appear in the normal or iconic state. An XmDialogShell is typically realised early by the toolkit and its window is mapped by the toolkit when its child is managed. An XmDialogShell cannot (by default) be iconified, and so appears in the normal state.

Once the widget has been realised, the state of its window can be changed as shown below. There are three common possibilities.

Parentless shell

(Table 8.1): an ApplicationShell or (rarely) a TopLevelShell created by XtAppCreateShell().

 You should not use XtPopup() or XtPopdown() on a parentless shell; these are designed to work with shells created by XtCreatePopupShell() only. Note that setting the iconic resource after the shell has been realised will call XtPopup(); this should be avoided for parentless shells.

Normal popup shell

(Table 8.2): a TopLevelShell or (rarely) an ApplicationShell created by XtCreatePopupShell().

For a popup shell, you use XtPopup() to move from the unrealised or withdrawn state and XtPopdown() to move back to the withdrawn state. You should specify a grab_kind of XtGrabNone to XtPopup().

Attempting to move a popup shell from iconic to normal state by setting the iconic resource may not work if the initialState resource was set when the widget was first popped up.

Table 8.1 *Parentless shell states*

From	To	By
Unrealised	Withdrawn	XtRealizeWidget() with mappedWhenManaged False
Unrealised	Iconic	XtRealizeWidget() with initialState IconicState and mapped-WhenManaged True
Unrealised	Normal	XtRealizeWidget() with initialState NormalState and mapped-WhenManaged True
Withdrawn	Iconic	XtMapWidget() with initialState IconicState
Withdrawn	Normal	XtMapWidget() with initialState NormalState
Normal	Iconic	XIconifyWindow()
Normal	Withdrawn	XWithdrawWindow()
Iconic	Normal	XtMapWidget()
Iconic	Withdrawn	XWithdrawWindow()

Table 8.2 *Normal popup shell states*

From	To	By
Unrealised	Withdrawn	XtRealizeWidget()
Unrealised	Iconic	XtPopup() with initialState IconicState
Unrealised	Normal	XtPopup() with initialState NormalState
Withdrawn	Iconic	XtPopup() with initialState IconicState
Withdrawn	Normal	XtPopup() with initialState NormalState
Normal	Iconic	XIconifyWindow()
Normal	Withdrawn	XtPopdown()
Iconic	Normal	XtMapWidget()
Iconic	Withdrawn	XtPopdown()

    The Motif XmDialogShell cannot be (safely) iconified. From the window manager's point of view, it has only withdrawn and normal states. It is moved between these states via calls to XtPopup() and XtPopdown(), like other popup shells. However, XmDialogShell will call these functions itself when its child is managed and unmanaged and this is the preferred way of changing the state.

Motif popup dialog shell

(Table 8.3): an XmDialogShell created by XmCreateDialogShell().[1]

Table 8.3 *Motif popup dialog shell states*

From	To	By
Unrealised	Withdrawn	Done by toolkit
Withdrawn	Normal	XtManageChild() on child of shell
Normal	Withdrawn	XtUnmanageChild() on child of shell

8.7 Shell

Shell is the base class for all widgets whose windows can be children of the root
window.

8.7.1 Interesting resources

geometry

This is provided to allow the user to specify the desired geometry on the command
line:

```
xclock -geometry "300x200+100+50"
```

If the geometry is set this way, the window manager can tell that it is user-
specified and should not ask the user to position the window interactively. Setting
this from your program is not recommended.

x and y

The position of the shell's window is really for the window manager to decide. You
can set it if you wish, but the window manager may ignore the values you set.

ApplicationShells and TopLevelShells are positioned by setting their x and y
resources. For XmDialogShell, set the position on the child (which should be an
XmBulletinBoard or derivative) and set the child's defaultPosition resource to
False.

createPopupChildProc

This is a function which is called just before a shell is popped up. It is provided so
that you can create the shell at application start-up, but delay creation of its child

---

1. The fact that you use a different technique on the Motif shells is undoubtedly a mistake, resulting from an over-
enthusiastic attempt to encapsulate popup dialog behaviour. You can use XtPopup() on the XmDialogShell, but
you have to be sure that the shell's child is managed. Since, for instance, XmBulletinBoard can automatically
unmanage itself, you will probably manage the child for safety's sake, which makes any call to XtPopup()
redundant.

widgets until they are needed. Since most popups occur as a result of callback functions, you can instead create the children (and the shell) in the callback. This is not so clever, but most people find it clearer.

The createPopupChildProc is called *after* the popupCallback.

overrideRedirect

If this resource is set, the override redirect flag will be set on the shell's window; the window manager will ignore the shell and will not set its size and position or add window decorations to it. This is usually only set on shells used for menus (such as XmMenuShell), but will work on any shell.

saveUnder

Indicates that it is desirable that the contents of the screen beneath the window should be preserved because they are likely to be required again very soon. This is normally set True for shells which have a short lifetime (such as menu shells), or for shells which are going to be dragged around the screen. The resource is only a hint to the server; the server can choose to save under or not whenever it feels like it.

visual

Specifies the required visual type for this shell. Visuals are discussed further in Section 16.2.

8.7.2   Interesting behaviour

Shell encapsulates the features of a top-level window, but window manager interaction is not introduced until WMShell.

8.7.3   Examples of use

This simple example illustrates how to create a window on a different screen:

screen2

```
void create_msg_shell (parent, screen_num)
    Widget   parent;
    int      screen_num;
{
    Display  *display = XtDisplay (parent);
    Arg      al[64];
    register int ac = 0;
    Widget   msg_shell;
    Widget   msg;
```

```
        XtSetArg (al[ac], XmNallowShellResize, True); ac++;
        XtSetArg (al[ac], XmNscreen, XScreenOfDisplay (display, screen_num));
                            ac++;
        XtSetArg (al[ac], XmNvisual, XDefaultVisual (display, screen_num));
                            ac++;
        XtSetArg(al[ac], XmNcolormap, XDefaultColormap (display,
                            screen_num)); ac++;
        XtSetArg(al[ac], XmNdepth, XDefaultDepth (display, screen_num)); ac++;
        msg_shell = XmCreateDialogShell (parent, "msg_shell", al, ac);
        ac = 0;
        XtSetArg(al[ac], XmNdialogType, XmDIALOG_INFORMATION); ac++;
        msg = XmCreateMessageBox (msg_shell, "msg", al, ac);
    }
```

 The visual, colormap and depth resources should all be set explicitly for the shell on the new screen, as they will otherwise be copied from the parent and may be wrong.

8.7.4 Watch out for

 The allowShellResize resource is set False by default, so a shell will not resize itself in response to requests from its children.

 A shell can have any number of children, but only one can be managed at any time.

8.8   OverrideShell

OverrideShell is just a Shell with overrideRedirect and saveUnder set True. The window manager will ignore it, so it can control its own size and position and gets no window manager decorations. The saveUnder flag means that the server will attempt to remember what is underneath it when it pops up and restore the image when it pops down, rather than sending Expose events to applications. That is, an OverrideShell is expected to pop up only for a short period.

8.8.1 Examples of use

OverrideShell is used as a base class for XmMenuShell and anywhere else you need a window that avoids entanglement with the window manager. These are supposed to be very short-life windows and should be designed so that they stay popped up only as long as the user holds, say, a mouse button down.

8.8.2   Watch out for

The window manager is there for a reason. If your application creates OverrideShells and keeps them on screen for longer than a menu might persist, it might be wise to rethink your approach.

8.9   WMShell

WMShell has the resources needed to specify titles, icons, geometry restrictions and so on to the window manager. WMShell is generic and its resources have meaning to all window managers.

8.9.1   Interesting resources

title

This is an ordinary char* string used as the title in the window manager frame. For XmDialogShell only, you can set this by setting the dialogTitle resource of the shell's child (which should be XmBulletinBoard or a derivative).

iconPixmap

A bitmap used as the icon for the shell. This only has meaning for shells that can be iconified. It should be 1 bit deep, so icons are strictly two-colour, but mwm and many other window managers will cope with a deeper pixmap (see Section 14.2.1).

iconMask

Some window managers may use this to mask the iconPixmap, allowing non-rectangular icons. Mwm ignores it.

iconWindow

If a two-colour, rectangular icon is not good enough for you, you can create your own window and draw whatever you want in it; most window managers will use this instead (see Section 14.2.1).

initialState

Takes the values NormalState or IconicState only and defines how the window will appear when its window goes from the withdrawn state (which it can do more than once). Window state changes are described in Section 8.6.8.

transient

Indicates whether or not the shell is temporary and the sort of decorations the window manager will put on the frame. The Motif documentation warns against it, but you can use this to create an iconifiable XmDialogShell if you want.

8.9.2   Interesting behaviour

WMShell encapsulates the window manager interaction. Its behaviour is largely a reflection of what the window manager does. See Chapter 14 for details.

8.9.3   Watch out for

 The TopLevelShell iconic resource (and the flag -iconic on the command line) will override the create-time setting of initialState, but does not prevent you from changing it back with XtSetValues().

8.10   VendorShell

VendorShell is a Motif widget class, despite the absence of an Xm prefix. It provides those resources which are specific to mwm, rather than generic to all window managers, plus some other Motif-specific features.

8.10.1   Interesting resources

width and height
The shell's window is normally the same size as its managed child's. However, if an input method is used (see Section 20.3.1) the shell may have to accommodate another window for off-the-spot editing and the child's size will be reduced to fit. You should set the size on the shell or its child, depending on which you want to control.

buttonFontList, labelFontList and textFontList
Child widgets and later descendants will use these fonts as the default if they are set when the descendants are created, but descendants do not respond to changes.
The values of these resources are inherited from the shell's ancestors if they are not set.

deleteResponse
Controls the behaviour of the widget when its window receives a WM_DELETE_WINDOW message. See Section 14.4.3 for details.

mwmDecorations and mwmFunctions
Controls the decorations (resize handles and so on) displayed by mwm and the functions (f.resize, etc.) that mwm will apply. It is ignored by other window managers (see Section 14.3).

mwmMenu
Can be used to add extra items to the shell's window menu (see Section 14.3).

mwmInputMode
Can be used to make a dialog modal. For XmDialogShell, you can use the dialogStyle resource of the shell's XmBulletinBoard child instead.

⚠   Note that the toolkit relies on mwm for part of the implementation of mwmInputMode. In particular, shells with an mwmInputMode of MWM_INPUT_SYSTEM_MODAL will not in general behave as system modal under other window managers.

shellUnitType
See the discussion of resolution independence in Section 4.6.1.

8.10.2   Interesting behaviour

VendorShell is where the Motif toolkit meets the window manager protocols. This is like King Kong meets Godzilla, but rather more dangerous to the innocent bystander.

You should be very careful about using any VendorShell resources whose names start with "mwm". If you cannot guarantee that the user has mwm as his or her window manager, they are unlikely to work.

8.11   TransientShell

TransientShell is an Xt widget class designed for windows that cannot be separately iconified. It is used as a base class for XmDialogShell.

8.12   XmDialogShell

XmDialogShell should be used for all transient popup dialogs (ones that cannot be separately iconified).

8.12.1   Interesting resources

XmDialogShell introduces no new resources, but overrides the deleteResponse response of the Motif VendorShell, so that it unmaps itself by default when it receives a WM_DELETE_WINDOW message.

8.12.2 Interesting behaviour

If an XmDialogShell is created by XtCreatePopupShell() with an ApplicationShell or TopLevelShell as its parent, it will disappear and reappear as the parent shell is iconified and restored.

If the child is an XmBulletinBoard, you can manipulate the shell through its child. You can set at least x, y, width, height, mwmInputMode and title on the shell via the appropriate XmBulletinBoard resources.

Managing and unmanaging the child is the safest way to make the shell pop up and down.

8.12.3 Examples of use

This is used as the shell for any transient dialog, usually with an XmBulletinBoard as its child. The Motif dialog convenience functions, XmCreate*Dialog(), all create an XmDialogShell with an XmBulletinBoard or XmBulletinBoard derivative as its child.

8.12.4 Watch out for

 The XmDialogShell will only accept one child (where most shells will only accept one managed child).

 Beware of the defaultPosition resource on an XmBulletinBoard child. If this is set (the default), the shell will be positioned by the window manager ignoring any x and y resource settings.

 Querying the x and y resources of an XmDialogShell with an XmBulletinBoard child can give you strange numbers. Query the resources on the child widget instead.

8.13 TopLevelShell

TopLevelShell is used for iconifiable shells that do not get involved in the WM_SAVE_YOURSELF protocol. It introduces resources to support a name for the icon, but inherits those needed to define the icon or icon window.

8.13.1 Interesting resources

iconName and iconNameEncoding

These set the name used when the window is iconic. As icons are usually small, this should be shorter than the name used as the title of the window (for instance, "Myeditor" rather than "Myeditor: /home/apg/foo.c").

8.13.2   Examples of use

As the shell for any dialog that can sensibly be separately iconified, except for the first one that an application creates on a given display.

As the parent (in XtCreatePopupShell()) for XmDialogShells.

8.13.3   Watch out for

⚠ The iconic resource overrides the setting of the initialState resource and determines whether the window or the icon appears first. Changing the iconic resource after the shell is realised may call XtPopup(), even if the shell was not created as a popup shell. On the whole, you should avoid this resource.

⚠ By default, a TopLevelShell destroys itself when it gets a WM_DELETE_WINDOW message (that is, when the user selects "Close" from the window menu). This is probably not what you want and can be overridden using the deleteResponse resource and the WM_DELETE_WINDOW protocol.

8.14   ApplicationShell

ApplicationShell is intended to represent your application to the window manager, particularly in the (currently poorly supported) WM_SAVE_YOURSELF protocol. It introduces resources used to hold the command used to start the application.

ApplicationShell also provides the basic context for resource database queries, in that its effective class name (for the purposes of querying the resource database) is the application class name that you specify when you create it.

8.14.1   Interesting resources

argv and argc

If these are set, they are used to set the WM_COMMAND property on the shell's window when it is realised.

popupCallback

⚠ The popupCallback callback functions are only called when a shell is popped up using XtPopup(). They are not called when a parentless ApplicationShell appears because it has been realised.

8.14.2   Examples of use

This is used as the shell for the first dialog that an application creates on a given display and as the parent (in XtCreatePopupShell()) for XmDialogShells.

8.14.3   Watch out for

argc and argv are initialised by XtAppInitialize() to hold the command line arguments excluding the Xt specific ones (such as -geometry, -fg, ...). If you create the ApplicationShell using XtAppCreateShell() and you want it to have the WM_COMMAND property set, you should set these resources yourself.

If you use XtGetValues() to query argv, you should not free the returned value, nor the strings it points to.

Since XtAppInitialize() strips out the Xt specific arguments from argv, it is not a true record of the command used to start the application. If you need this, you should save the arguments yourself at start-up time.

Although argc and argv are used to set the initial value of WM_COMMAND, changing the resources does not update the property. Use XSetCommand().

CHAPTER 9

Menu system

The Motif toolkit provides a variety of specialised widgets and functions to support menus of various kinds. As noted in Section 4.5, these are largely based on the XmRowColumn widget, which is heavily overloaded.

This chapter first describes the various sorts of menu and the widgets used to create them. It then covers each widget class in turn, treating each different sort of XmRowColumn as though it were a separate widget class. Finally, it shows how to create shared menu panes that are accessible from a number of different places in the application.

Motif provides menu creation functions at three different levels of abstraction. The simple menu creation routines (XmCreateSimple*()) typically create a fully populated menu, including the menu items. The menu convenience functions - XmCreatePopupMenu(), XmCreatePulldownMenu(), XmCreateMenuBar() and XmCreateOptionMenu() - are less abstract; they create the menu, but do not populate it. Some of the convenience functions also create an XmMenuShell; an application can instead work at the most concrete level and call the appropriate widget creation functions to create the menu panes and XmMenuShells directly.

This chapter uses the menu convenience functions. The resources apply equally well to menus created using the simple menu creation routines or the widget creation functions.

9.1   Menu system components

The Motif menu system provides several sorts of menu. PulldownMenus are pulled down from a button. They can be cascaded, so a button in a menu can be used to access a lower level of menu; cascading menus are sometimes called pullrights.

Whereas PulldownMenus only appear associated with buttons, PopupMenus can be made to appear at any point; they typically appear at the place where the mouse is pointing, in response to a mouse button press.

Finally, OptionMenus provide a form of one-of-many selection, where the many options are displayed in and selected from a PulldownMenu. The associated button shows the current selection on its face.

In the interests of clarity we refer to MenuBar, PulldownMenu, PopupMenu and OptionMenu as if they were separate classes and refer to PulldownMenus and PopupMenus jointly as MenuPanes. These sorts of menu - pulldown (and pullright), popup and option - are implemented using three widget classes, XmRowColumn, XmMenuShell and XmCascadeButton.

The menu itself - the part that contains the menu items - is known as a MenuPane. It is an XmRowColumn widget with its rowColumnType resource set to MENU_PULLDOWN or MENU_POPUP; MENU_PULLDOWN is used for any menu that is posted (made visible) from a button, either pulled down from a MenuBar or an OptionMenu, or pulled right from the previous level of menu.

The button used to make a PulldownMenu appear is an XmCascadeButton. Its one outstanding attribute is that it knows how to make a PulldownMenu appear; it does so in response to a button press. The widget ID for the MenuPane is held as a resource of the XmCascadeButton and several XmCascadeButtons can share the same MenuPane.

A MenuPane may be so large that it needs to draw on parts of the screen that are not within the limits of the application's existing windows. To allow it to draw anywhere, each MenuPane is given its own shell, which is an XmMenuShell widget. The shell's window is a child of the root window of the screen and so is not clipped by any of the application's existing windows.

The XmRowColumn widget is used for pulldown and popup MenuPanes; it is also used in two other places in the menu system. A MenuBar is an XmRowColumn widget with its rowColumnType resource set to MENU_BAR. The job of a MenuBar is to arrange the XmCascadeButtons from which the PulldownMenus are posted. Finally, an OptionMenu is an XmRowColumn widget of rowColumnType MENU_OPTION. It automatically creates an XmCascadeButton gadget from which to post the pulldown menu containing the options and an XmLabel used to title the OptionMenu.

9.2   MenuBar

MenuBars are created with the XmCreateMenuBar() convenience function; this
creates an XmRowColumn widget and sets rowColumnType to MENU_BAR. A
MenuBar can only contain XmCascadeButton and PulldownMenu children.

9.2.1   Interesting resources

menuAccelerator

This resource specifies a key event that will force the keyboard focus to move to
the first XmCascadeButton in the MenuBar. There is no visual clue to the user what
the menuAccelerator is, so it should be set to something that is either a standard or
well known to the user. The default is <KeyUp>F10.

menuHelpWidget

This resource specifies which XmCascadeButton is to be considered the Help
button. The Help button is always placed at the bottom right of the MenuBar (see
Figure 9.1).

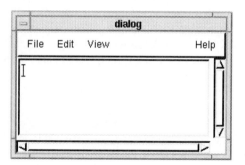

Figure 9.1   *MenuBar with Help button*

menuPost

The menuPost resource specifies (in a subset of translation table syntax) the button
event that will cause the menus to pull down from the MenuBar. This has to be a
ButtonPress event. This resource does not override the default of <Btn1Down>,
but appears to specify an additional event. That is, if <Btn3Down> is specified,
then both Button1 and Button3 can be used to pull down the menus.

9.2.2   Watch out for

 The XmMainWindow widget does special layout for its MenuBar child to keep all
the XmCascadeButtons visible, even when the XmMainWindow is made narrow,
which none of the other container widgets do.

9.3   XmMenuShell

The good thing about XmMenuShell widgets is that you need hardly ever worry about them. If you use the convenience routines XmCreatePulldownMenu() and XmCreatePopupMenu() for creating pulldown and popup menus, the XmMenuShell widget is created automatically.

XmMenuShell is derived from OverrideShell. It only allows XmRowColumn children.

9.3.1   Interesting resources

buttonFontList, labelFontList and defaultFontList
These resources can be used to set the default font of all the items in a MenuPane.

9.4   MenuPane *(PulldownMenu and PopupMenu)*

Motif provides convenience routines to create Pulldown and Popup menus. These routines create an XmMenuShell widget and an XmRowColumn child with the rowColumnType set appropriately. The XmRowColumn is returned; the application usually need not worry about the XmMenuShell.

PulldownMenus are always pulled down from XmCascadeButton regardless of whether that XmCascadeButton is in a MenuBar, an OptionMenu or a MenuPane itself. A PulldownMenu displayed from an XmCascadeButton, which is itself in a MenuPane, is often referred to as a pullright menu.

The Motif toolkit takes care of showing and hiding Pulldown menus automatically. PopupMenus are popped up from any widget directly by the application, but the toolkit takes care of hiding them. That is, the only real difference between Popup and Pulldown menus is in the way they are posted.

MenuPanes can only contain XmPushButton, XmToggleButton, XmLabel, XmSeparator and XmCascadeButton children.

9.4.1   Interesting resources

menuAccelerator *(PopupMenu only)*
Specifies a key event that will cause the menu to pop up. There is no visual clue to the user what the menuAccelerator is, so it should be set to something that is either a standard or well known to the user. The default is Shift<KeyUp>F10.

menuPost *(PopupMenu only)*
The menuPost resource specifies the button event that will cause the menu to pop up.

Setting this resource will not cause the PopupMenu to be posted when the specified button event occurs. The application has in addition to intercept the event and position and manage the PopupMenu. However, the menu system will *only* pop up the menu if an event has occurred that matches the menuPost resource.

Internally, the toolkit adds an event handler for button events on the widget from which the PopupMenu is to be posted. When a ButtonPress event is detected, it is validated against the menuPost field of the PopupMenu and, if it matches, the PopupMenu is marked as being valid and a three-second timer is added.

If the application attempts to manage the PopupMenu before the timer triggers, the toolkit allows this to go ahead and the menu pops up. If the timer triggers before the PopupMenu is managed, the PopupMenu will be marked as invalid again and later attempts to manage it will have no effect. This allows the toolkit to ensure that the menu is only popped up when the appropriate grabs are in effect.

The effect of this is that a PopupMenu can only be posted by an application in response to a ButtonPress event on the button specified by the menuPost resource, or by the toolkit in response to the key event specified in menuAccelerator; this directly manipulates the toolkit's data structures to mark the PopupMenu as valid.

mapCallback and unmapCallback

These callbacks are useful, for instance, for setting the sensitivity of the widgets in the menu. If a MenuPane has many items whose sensitivity changes depending on some context, then it may be too expensive to reset the sensitivity of all the items each time the context changes. The mapCallback can be used to set the sensitivity only if the user actually decides to look at the menu.

   If the user invokes a function using a menu accelerator, the mapCallback does not get called and the application has no opportunity to set the sensitivity of menu items to reflect the current context. See Section 9.6 for a recommended way of dealing with this.

popupEnabled *(PopupMenu only)*

Set this resource to False if the accelerators and mnemonics for the PopupMenu are to be disabled.

tearOffModel

Setting tearOffModel to TEAR_OFF_ENABLED allows the user to tear-off the MenuPane using the tear-off control.

   If you set the tearOffModel resource of a shared MenuPane to TEAR_OFF_ENABLED, you will get a run-time warning saying that this is allowed, but not recommended. See the discussion of accelerators in Section 9.6 for a possible explanation of this.

The resource representation type, XmRTearOffModel, has its own resource converter, but it is not installed by default. This prevents the user from enabling tear-off for all MenuPanes by a personal resource file entry, which could cause havoc if the application were not designed to support tear-offs. If the application is prepared to allow the user to determine which MenuPanes may be torn off, then it should add the resource converter, using the convenience routine XmRepTypeInstallTearOffModelConverter().[1]

tearOffMenuActivateCallback and tearOffMenuDeactivateCallback

These callbacks get called when a tear-off menu is torn off or closed. These callbacks would be used only in specialised circumstances, as setting of sensitivity and so on should be handled by the mapCallback and unmapCallback (in case the menu is not torn off). See the discussion of accelerators in Section 9.6 for an example of a possible use.

9.4.2 Interesting behaviour

MenuPanes have a complete set of translations to implement menu behaviour; these are mostly there to allow gadgets to be used in menus and provide very little additional behaviour.

The tear-off control used to tear-off MenuPanes is an interesting widget at first sight. It has the appearance of an XmSeparator, but the behaviour of an XmPushButton. It is in fact a special widget, XmTearOffButton, which is derived from XmPushButton, but it can only display an XmSeparator visual. The application can obtain the control using the convenience function XmGetTearOffControl().

The XmMenuShell automatically created by XmCreatePulldownMenu() or XmCreatePopupMenu() is given the same name as the MenuPane with the prefix popup_. This is useful when specifying resources for the XmMenuShell in a resource file.

The Menu panes support the use of accelerators for their XmPushButton and XmToggleButton children. This is implemented by the toolkit adding an event handler which catches the incoming accelerator event, then calls the appropriate callback function for the XmPushButton or XmToggleButton. For Popup menus, this event handler is added to the widgets for which the menu can be popped up. For Pulldown menus, the event handler is added to the highest level enclosing XmManager widget (usually the child of the dialog's shell).

9.4.3 Examples of use

Pulldown menu

Setting up a pulldown menu is very simple. For instance, the following code creates the hierarchy in Figure 9.2:

---

1. At 36 characters XmRepTypeInstallTearOffModelConverter() is the longest public function name, although _XmAllowAcceleratedInsensitiveUnmanagedMenuItem() takes the all-comers prize at 48 characters.

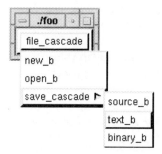

Figure 9.2   *Pulldown menu with a pullright*

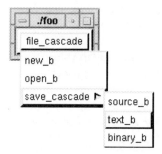
pulldown

```
ac = 0;
menubar = XmCreateMenuBar (form, "menubar", al, ac);

file_pulldown = XmCreatePulldownMenu (menubar, "file_pulldown", al, ac);
save_pulldown = XmCreatePulldownMenu (file_pulldown, "save_pulldown",
                  al, ac);

source_b = XmCreatePushButton (save_pulldown, "source_b", al, ac);
text_b = XmCreatePushButton (save_pulldown, "text_b", al, ac);
binary_b = XmCreatePushButton (save_pulldown, "binary_b", al, ac);
children[ac++] = source_b;
children[ac++] = text_b;
children[ac++] = binary_b;
XtManageChildren (children, ac);
ac = 0;

new_b = XmCreatePushButton (file_pulldown, "new_b", al, ac);
open_b = XmCreatePushButton (file_pulldown, "open_b", al, ac);
XtSetArg (al[ac], XmNsubMenuId, save_pulldown); ac++;
save_cascade = XmCreateCascadeButton (file_pulldown, "save_cascade",
                  al, ac);
ac = 0;
children[ac++] = new_b;
children[ac++] = open_b;
children[ac++] = save_cascade;
XtManageChildren (children, ac);
ac = 0;

XtSetArg (al[ac], XmNsubMenuId, file_pulldown); ac++;
file_cascade = XmCreateCascadeButton (menubar, "file_cascade", al, ac);
ac = 0;
```

```
XtManageChild (file_cascade, ac);
XtManageChild (menubar, ac);
```

Notice that the code manages all the widgets except the MenuPanes themselves. Like the XmDialogShell, the XmMenuShell pops itself up when its child is managed; this is only supposed to happen when the XmCascadeButton responds to a button press.[1]

Popup menu

Popup menus are essentially the same, except that some application code is required to make the menu post. The application has to do two things:

- Call XmMenuPosition() to set the position where the menu will pop up. XmMenuPosition() takes the MenuPane and a ButtonPress event and uses the x_root and y_root fields to work out where the menu should be positioned on the root window.
- Manage the MenuPane. This causes the XmMenuShell to pop itself up in the specified position.

The application should only do this in response to a ButtonPress on the button specified in the menuPost resource. In this example, a popup menu is created for an XmText widget, which is posted using a translation for Button3; an event handler could be used instead. As with the pulldown menu, all widgets other than the MenuPane are managed in advance.

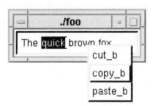

Figure 9.3 *Popup menu*

```
Widget edit_popup = (Widget) NULL;

void post_edit_menu (w, event, params, num_params)
    Widget   w;
    XEvent   *event;
    String   *params;
    Cardinal *num_params;
{
```

---

1. Managing the MenuPane is not a recommended way of posting a PulldownMenu. The XmCascadeButton does a lot of other work as well.

```
/* Position the MenuPane (which actually positions the XmMenuShell) */
XmMenuPosition (edit_popup, event);
/* Managing the MenuPane makes the XmMenuShell pop up */
XtManageChild (edit_popup);
}

/* Action table for XtAppAddActions() */
XtActionsRec my_actions[] = {
    { "PostEditMenu", post_edit_menu },
};

int main (argc, argv)
    int     argc;
    char  **argv;
{
    ...
    /* Create XmText widget (managed later) */
    ac = 0;
    text = XmCreateText (form, "text", al, ac);
    XtSetArg (al[ac], XmNmenuPost, "<Button3>"); ac++;
    /* Create but do not manage the MenuPane (and XmMenuShell) */
    edit_popup = XmCreatePopupMenu (text, "edit_popup", al, ac);
    ac = 0;
    /* Create and manage the XmPushButtons */
    cut_b = XmCreatePushButton (edit_popup, "cut_b", al, ac);
    copy_b = XmCreatePushButton (edit_popup, "copy_b", al, ac);
    paste_b = XmCreatePushButton (edit_popup, "paste_b", al, ac);
    children[ac++] = cut_b;
    children[ac++] = copy_b;
    children[ac++] = paste_b;
    XtManageChildren (children, ac);
    /* Add actions and translation to invoke post
    ** action on appropriate event */
    XtAppAddActions (app_context, my_actions, XtNumber (my_actions));
    XtOverrideTranslations (text, XtParseTranslationTable
                    ("<Btn3Down>:PostEditMenu()"));
    XtManageChild (text);
    ...
}
```

9.4.4 Watch out for

 When creating MenuPanes it is important that the correct parent is specified:

- Pulldown for XmCascadeButton in a MenuBar: specify MenuBar as parent.
- Pulldown for XmCascadeButton in a MenuPane (pullright menu): specify MenuPane as parent.
- Pulldown for an OptionMenu: specify the parent of the OptionMenu as parent.
- Popup for widget: specify the widget as parent.

9.5   OptionMenu

OptionMenus provide a convenient way of handling one-of-many choices. An OptionMenu contains an XmLabel gadget used to supply a title for the OptionMenu and an XmCascadeButton which is used both to display the current setting and as a target for pulling down the associated menu. These components can be retrieved from the OptionMenu using the convenience routines XmOptionButtonGadget() and XmOptionLabelGadget(). The application has to create a PulldownMenu containing XmPushButtons corresponding to the possible options and associate it with the OptionMenu, either by setting the subMenuId resource for the OptionMenu at create time, or by setting the subMenuId resource for the XmCascadeButton child after the OptionMenu has been created. The documentation states that the results of having pullright menus in the OptionMenu's PulldownMenu are undefined.[1]

9.5.1   Interesting resources

labelString

This is simply mapped through to the XmLabel child.

menuHistory

Use this resource to specify or determine which is the initial or current selection for the OptionMenu.

menuPost

The menuPost resource specifies the button event that will cause the menu to pull down. This has to be a ButtonPress event. This resource does not override the default of <Btn1Down> but appears to specify an additional event. That is, if <Btn3Down> is specified, then both Button1 and Button3 can be used to pull down the menu.

mnemonic and mnemonicCharset

These are mapped through to the XmLabel child to provide visual feedback for the mnemonic to the user. The mnemonic operates in a similar way as on an

---

1. This half works, but not well enough to be usable.

XmCascadeButton in a MenuBar; the user can use <Alt> and the mnemonic anywhere in the window to post the OptionMenu's PulldownMenu.

subMenuId

This is simply mapped through to the XmCascadeButton child.

9.5.2 Interesting behaviour

The toolkit attempts to post the PulldownMenu over the XmCascadeButton so that the currently selected menu item exactly overlays it. This gives the user visual feedback for the current value. If the menu cannot be so positioned, perhaps because the OptionMenu is near the bottom of the screen, the menu is posted so that it does not obscure the XmCascadeButton at all.

The XmPushButtons in the menu can have labelType STRING or PIXMAP. These can be mixed and the XmCascadeButton will display the string or pixmap according to the type of the selected button. When displaying a string, the XmCascadeButton uses the same font as the XmPushButton that was selected; this is especially useful when the XmPushButtons use different fonts with different language encodings.

9.5.3 Examples of use

The code below creates the simple OptionMenu illustrated in Figure 9.4.

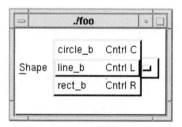

Figure 9.4 *OptionMenu*

option

```
/* Create and populate the PulldownMenu */
option_pulldown = XmCreatePulldownMenu (form, "option_pulldown", al, ac);
/* Create and manage the XmPushButtons for the menu items */
XtSetArg (al[ac], XmNaccelerator, "Ctrl<Key>C"); ac++;
tstring = XmStringCreateLocalized ("Cntrl C");
XtSetArg (al[ac], XmNacceleratorText, tstring); ac++;
circle_b = XmCreatePushButton (option_pulldown, "circle_b", al, ac);
ac = 0;
```

```
XmStringFree (tstring);
XtSetArg (al[ac], XmNaccelerator, "Ctrl<Key>L"); ac++;
tstring = XmStringCreateLocalized ("Cntrl L");
XtSetArg (al[ac], XmNacceleratorText, tstring); ac++;
line_b = XmCreatePushButton (option_pulldown, "line_b", al, ac);
ac = 0;
XmStringFree (tstring);
XtSetArg (al[ac], XmNaccelerator, "Ctrl<Key>R"); ac++;
tstring = XmStringCreateLocalized ("Cntrl R");
XtSetArg (al[ac], XmNacceleratorText, tstring); ac++;
rect_b = XmCreatePushButton (option_pulldown, "rect_b", al, ac);
ac = 0;
XmStringFree (tstring);
children[ac++] = circle_b;
children[ac++] = line_b;
children[ac++] = rect_b;
XtManageChildren (children, ac);
ac = 0;

/* A quick example of string to keysym conversion for the mnemonic... */
from_value.addr = (XtPointer) "S";
from_value.size = strlen ((char *)from_value.addr)+1;
to_value.addr = NULL;
XtConvertAndStore (form, XmRString, &from_value, XmRKeySym,
                   &to_value);
if (to_value.addr)
{
    XtSetArg (al[ac], XmNmnemonic, *(unsigned int *)to_value.addr); ac++;
}
/* Create the OptionMenu and associate the PulldownMenu with it */
tstring = XmStringCreateLocalized ("Shape");
XtSetArg (al[ac], XmNlabelString, tstring); ac++;
XtSetArg (al[ac], XmNsubMenuId, option_pulldown); ac++;
XtSetArg (al[ac], XmNmenuHistory, line_b); ac++;
option_menu = XmCreateOptionMenu (form, "option_menu", al, ac);
ac = 0;
XmStringFree (tstring);
XtManageChild (option_menu);
```

9.5.4   Watch out for

The PulldownMenu associated with an OptionMenu can only safely contain XmPushButton and XmSeparator children.

It is difficult to get several OptionMenus to look good when in the same dialog (see Figure 9.5). The most attractive way of laying them out is to align the centres.

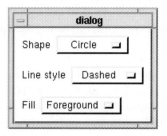

Figure 9.5   *Several unaligned OptionMenus*

Unfortunately this can only be achieved by calculating the length of the labels at run time and setting an XmForm attachment offset that will result in the OptionMenus being aligned. The following code illustrates the technique and the results are shown in Figure 9.6:

```
...
Dimension shape_width, style_width, fill_width, widest;
...
shape_option = XmCreateOptionMenu (form, "shape_option", al, ac);
style_option = XmCreateOptionMenu (form, "style_option", al, ac);
fill_option = XmCreateOptionMenu (form, "fill_option", al, ac);
...
XtVaGetValues (XmOptionLabelGadget (shape_option),
                    XmNwidth, &shape_width, 0);
XtVaGetValues (XmOptionLabelGadget (style_option),
                    XmNwidth, &style_width, 0);
XtVaGetValues (XmOptionLabelGadget (fill_option),
                    XmNwidth, &fill_width, 0);
widest = shape_width;
if (style_width > widest)
    widest = style_width;
if (fill_width > widest)
    widest = fill_width;
XtVaSetValues (shape_option, XmNleftOffset, widest - shape_width, 0);
XtVaSetValues (style_option, XmNleftOffset, widest - style_width, 0);
XtVaSetValues (fill_option, XmNleftOffset, widest - fill_width, 0);
...
```

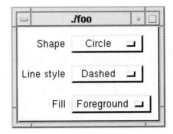

Figure 9.6 *Several aligned OptionMenus*

9.6 Shared PulldownMenus

A pulldown MenuPane has its own shell, and is no more tightly bound into the widget hierarchy than a popup dialog. In the same way that a popup dialog can be made to appear in response to events in different parts of an application, the same pulldown MenuPane can be used in more than one location by attaching it to many XmCascadeButtons. The toolkit handles setting up the accelerators on different shells transparently.

If the application requires that the sensitivity of certain menu items is different depending on how the menu has been posted, the application can call XmGetPostedFromWidget() to determine the context. Note that, as this returns the MenuBar and not the XmCascadeButton, it cannot be used for a PulldownMenu shared by a number of XmCascadeButtons in the same MenuBar.

It might be appropriate, for example, to have a single help menu that was shared by every dialog. This would ensure that the application had the same accelerators for help throughout. In the code below, the about button is only available when the help menu is accessed from the main_shell, whereas the help button is always available:

sharedmenu

```
void help_map_callback (w, client_data, call_data)
    Widget      w;
    XtPointer   client_data;
    XtPointer   call_data;
{
/* The MenuPane is being mapped. Set the about button to be
** sensitive if and only if it is being accessed from main_shell */
    Boolean got_about = (XmGetPostedFromWidget (w) == main_menubar);
    XtSetSensitive (about_b, got_about);
}

int main (argc,argv)
    int     argc;
    char **argv;
```

```
{
/* Create main window */
    ...
/* Create MenuBar and PulldownMenu in main window */
    main_menubar = XmCreateMenuBar (main_win, "main_menubar", al, ac);
    help_pulldown = XmCreatePulldownMenu (main_menubar,
                    "help_pulldown", al, ac);
    XtSetArg (al[ac], XmNaccelerator, "Ctrl<Key>A"); ac++;
    tstring = XmStringCreateLocalized ("Ctrl A");
    XtSetArg (al[ac], XmNacceleratorText, tstring); ac++;
    about_b = XmCreatePushButton (help_pulldown, "about_b", al, ac);
    ac = 0;
    XmStringFree (tstring);
    XtSetArg (al[ac], XmNaccelerator, "Ctrl<Key>H"); ac++;
    tstring = XmStringCreateLocalized ("Ctrl H");
    XtSetArg (al[ac], XmNacceleratorText, tstring); ac++;
    help_b = XmCreatePushButton (help_pulldown, "help_b", al, ac);
    ac = 0;
    XmStringFree (tstring);
/* Set up map callback to control availability of about button */
    XtAddCallback (help_pulldown, XmNmapCallback,
                    help_map_callback,NULL);
    children[ac++] = about_b;
    children[ac++] = help_b;
    XtManageChildren (children, ac);
    ac = 0;
    ...
/* Associate PulldownMenu with XmCascadeButton in main_menubar */
    XtSetArg (al[ac], XmNsubMenuId, help_pulldown); ac++;
    main_help_cascade = XmCreateCascadeButton (main_menubar,
                    "main_help_cascade", al, ac);
    ac = 0;
    XtManageChild (main_help_cascade);
/* Create print dialog */
    ...
    print_menubar = XmCreateMenuBar (print_form, "print_menubar", al, ac);
/* The print help cascade shares the help pulldown */
    XtSetArg (al[ac], XmNsubMenuId, help_pulldown); ac++;
    print_help_cascade = XmCreateCascadeButton (print_menubar,
                    "print_help_cascade", al, ac);
    ac = 0;
    XtManageChild (print_help_cascade);
    ...
}
```

The Help menu pulls down correctly in both dialogs (see Figure 9.7).

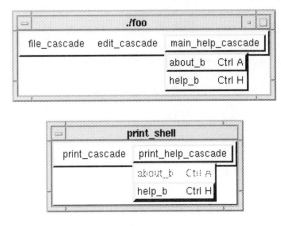

Figure 9.7　*Shared Pulldown menu*

Accelerators

Accelerators do work correctly with shared PulldownMenus, but there is a catch; when the accelerator is invoked, the toolkit checks the current sensitivity of the widget, but does not invoke the mapCallback. In the above example, this has the effect of allowing the about accelerator in both windows if the menu was last popped up from the main_menubar, or disallowing it in both windows if the menu was last popped up from the print_menubar.

To work around this problem, use the mapCallback to set the sensitivity as above. Use the unmapCallback to set all the menu items to be sensitive, then check whether the action is valid in the activateCallback or valueChangedCallback for the XmPushButton or XmToggleButton. If the menu can be torn off, then the tearOffMenuActivateCallback should also set the items sensitive, so that they can be accessed by accelerators regardless of where they were torn off from. Perhaps this is the reason for the warning about shared tear-off menus being allowed, but not recommended.

9.7　Shared PopupMenus

Sharing PopupMenus is slightly different. As the application has control over when and where the menu is popped up, a single menu can be displayed in a variety of different places under different conditions, which will give the impression of it being shared. For instance, in the example in Section 9.4.3 above (an edit popup for an XmText widget), the popup could work equally for many XmText widgets by adding the translation to every XmText widget which required the popup. Although XmGetPostedFromWidget() will always return the widget for which the menu was created, the application is in control of when the menu gets popped up, so, can handle any context-dependent menu processing in the popup routine.

This leaves only the problem of accelerators. When a PopupMenu is created for a widget, an event handler is added to process the accelerators for the XmPushButton and XmToggleButton widgets which it contains. Although the menu can be popped up by an event in another widget, there is no way of invoking the accelerators from that widget. The published API for the toolkit does not provide any mechanism for working around this.[1]

1. There are, however, two undocumented XmRowColumn resources: postFromList (an array of widgets) and postFromCount. Setting these resources for the Popup menu appears to cause the accelerators and XmGetPost-edFromWidget() to work correctly for shared Popup menus. These resources are undocumented and unsupported, by both the OSF and us and may not work as expected.

Part 2

Techniques

CHAPTER 10

Resources

Resources are fundamental to Xt. Indeed, the resource model appears in the widget class hierarchy in the most basic class - Object - whereas features like size, position and windows are only introduced later.

Resources are used in an application to control the appearance and behaviour of widgets and by the end-user to customise applications. An application can also define and use 'application resources' which are not related to any widget.

All of these uses of resources rely on common mechanisms which let the user or application writer specify the values of resources and allow the application to retrieve and use those values. This chapter describes the mechanisms and shows how they can be used to best advantage.

This chapter assumes some basic familiarity with the use of resource files.

10.1 Resource overview

A resource is just an element of data in a data structure for which Xt has certain information. This information allows Xt to set the value of the element.

The resource mechanism relies heavily on the 'resource database', which is just a data structure created when an application starts up. More precisely, when an application opens a display connection, Xt creates a resource database for the application and initialises it by reading name-value pairs from a number of text files, special properties on the root windows of the screens of the display and the arguments from the command line used to start the application.[1] Xt defines a standard set of resources which can be specified on the command line, but an application can add others. An application can also specify fallback resources, which are used if the application-specific class resource file cannot be found.

When widgets are created, Xt queries the resource database to find any entries which match the resources of the widget. The values it finds are converted by type converters from the text representation used in the resource database to whatever is appropriate to the resource (Boolean, int, pixel, font, ...) and pushed into the widget's data structure at the appropriate place. Figure 10.1 illustrates this process.

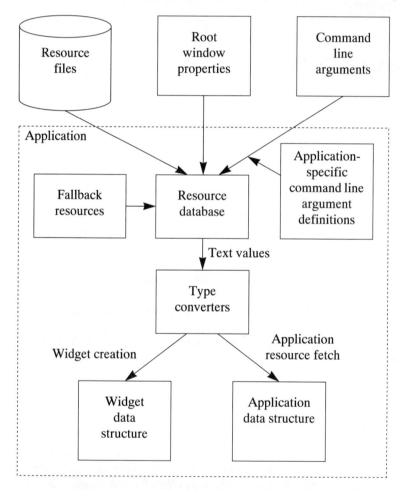

Figure 10.1 *Resource management overview*

---

1. Note that different screens on a multi-screen display can have a resource database each in X11R5.

A similar process applies for application resources. However, whereas resource values for widgets are fetched from the database automatically, application resources must be fetched explicitly.

Resource management, then, splits into two halves - the process by which the resource database is created and loaded and the way in which values are retrieved and used. The rest of this chapter covers creation first and retrieval later.

10.2   Resource database creation

The resource database has few of the features that one naively expects of a database. It is not shared; every instance of every application has its own resource database. It is not persistent; it is created when an application starts up, and destroyed when it terminates. Finally, it is organised and used in a different way from most databases; polite people say it is 'inverted'.

The resource database is just an in-core data structure used to hold details of resource values specified by the application developer and/or the user. It is an Xlib feature (although it only really makes sense in an Xt context) and can be accessed directly using the Xlib resource manager functions (which are named Xrm*()).

Resource databases are created by calls to XtAppInitialize(), XtOpenDisplay() or XtDisplayInitialize(). Each of these functions is associated with a particular display and (notionally) creates a set of resource databases, one for each screen of the display. When a widget is created, the database appropriate to its screen is used to determine the default resource values. For simplicity, the rest of this chapter assumes a single screen and a single resource database.

The resource database is initialised by taking data from a wide variety of sources, mostly text files. These sources seem to grow in number and configurability with every release and you should consult current documentation, especially if you want to use language-specific resource files. At present, the sources (and their customary names) are these:

- Application-specific class resource file,
/usr/lib/X11/app-defaults/<application_class>.
- Application-specific user resource file, $HOME/<application_class>.
- User preference file, $HOME/.Xdefaults, or the RESOURCE_MANAGER property on the root window of the default screen of the display.
- The SCREEN_RESOURCES property of each screen of the display (for the database corresponding to each screen).
- Per-host user environment file, $HOME/.Xdefaults-<hostname>.
- Command line arguments, argv and argc.

All but the last of these contain name-value pairs which are entered directly into the database. The command line arguments are translated into name-value pairs using a mapping table, as described in Section 10.9.

A later entry with the same name as one already in the database just overwrites the earlier one, so the sources later in the list take precedence over the earlier ones. However, this does not mean that the list is loaded in first-to-last order. The places where Xt looks for the application-specific class and user resource files can be configured by setting resources (the language and customization resources), so Xt checks all the other sources of resource setting first and uses the values derived from these to locate these resource files.

The files used to load the resource database also depend on the *application class*. The entries made in the resource database as a result of parsing the command line arguments use the *application name* as their first element. Before we can discuss the way in which the resource database is loaded, we need to define these.

10.3   Application class and application name

The application name and application class are easily confused with the widget name and resource class string specified when an application's ApplicationShell widget is created. They are not the same, although they probably should be and XtAppInitialize() forces the two classes and the two names to the same values. The application name and application class are used in creating the resource database and the ApplicationShell's widget name and resource class string are used in resource database queries.

This portion of this chapter is concerned with resource database creation, so we define (clearly and unambiguously, we hope) the application class and application name here and leave the ApplicationShell for later (see Section 10.12.1).

10.3.1   Application class

The application class is defined by the string passed as a parameter to XtAppInitialize(), XtOpenDisplay() or XtDisplayInitialize(). It is used to locate the resource files used to load the resource database (such as /usr/lib/X11/app-defaults/ <application_class>). It is an attribute of the display connection, not of the application, so an application that uses multiple displays can use different resource files for each.

By convention, the application class starts with a capital letter: Bitmap, Mwm, Xwnmo.

To add to the confusion, the application class is sometimes called the application class name.

10.3.2   Application name

The application name is also set when the display is initialized, but the three available functions do it differently.

XtDisplayInitialize() sets the application name to the string passed in as a parameter.

XtOpenDisplay() sets the application name to the first of these that it finds:

- The name specified by the -name argument on the command line.
- The application name passed in as a parameter, unless a null pointer is passed.
- The value of the environment variable $RESOURCE_NAME.
- argv[0].
- The string 'main'.

XtAppInitialize() just calls XtOpenDisplay(), passing a null pointer for the application name, so uses -name, $RESOURCE_NAME, argv[0] or 'main'.

The application name is used to create resource database entries from command line arguments. This process is described in Section 10.9.

Now that we know the application name and class, we can go looking for resource files to load the resource database.

10.4   Application-specific class resource file

This is usually referred to as the 'application defaults file'. It is the customary place for the application developer to put the resource definitions which are needed by an application, but which can sensibly be overridden by the user.[1]

Xt searches for the file in a number of places, based on a template string. It makes a number of substitutions in the template, based on the local language, application class and so on.

The precise content of the template string is not (any more) defined by the Xt specification, so different vendors may use different templates. Furthermore, the user can override the template by setting the environment variable $XFILESEARCHPATH. This is not something to lose sleep over; if you ensure that the application can find its resource file in each vendor's default environment (with appropriate language versions, if you have them), then you have done all that can reasonably be expected.

In the MIT X11R5 distribution, the default file search path contains the following components (separated by colons in the path, but shown here on separate lines for clarity):

```
/usr/lib/X11/%L/%T/%N%C%S
/usr/lib/X11/%l/%T/%N%C%S
/usr/lib/X11/%T/%N%C%S
/usr/lib/X11/%L/%T/%N%S
```

---

1. Resources that cannot sensibly be overridden should be hard-coded.

```
/usr/lib/X11/%l/%T/%N%S
/usr/lib/X11/%T/%N%S
```

To find the application-specific class resource file, Xt makes the following substitutions, then tests for each file in turn, stopping at the first one found:

- %L is replaced by the language string of the display. This is set using the xnlLanguage resource or the $LANG environment variable.
- %l is replaced by the language part of the language string, which is the part up to the first underscore ('_').[1]
- %T is the type, and is replaced by 'app-defaults'.
- %N is replaced by the application class, as defined in Section 10.3.1. To all intents and purposes, the class identifies the application - Xedit, XCalc and so on - not a related 'class' of applications.
- %C is replaced by the customization string. The user can set this (via the customization resource) to specify, for instance, different resource files for colour and mono screens.
- %S is the suffix, and is replaced by NULL.

The substitutions are actually performed by XtResolvePathname().

As an example, suppose that the application language string is 'ja_JP.jis7', the customization is '-color' and the application class is 'App_class'. Xt will then look for the following files in order:

```
/usr/lib/X11/ja_JP.jis7/app-defaults/App_class-color
/usr/lib/X11/ja/app-defaults/App_class-color
/usr/lib/X11/app-defaults/App_class-color
/usr/lib/X11/ja_JP.jis7/app-defaults/App_class
/usr/lib/X11/ja/app-defaults/App_class
/usr/lib/X11/app-defaults/App_class
```

Xt will load into the resource database the first of these which it finds. If it finds none of them, it will load the fallback resources, if any (see Section 10.10).

10.5 Application-specific user resource file

Each user can have an application-specific user resource file for each (class of) application, describing the user's preferences for that application. As with the application-specific class resource file, a complex search path template is used to locate it. Again, the precise content of the template string is not defined by the Xt

---

1. A typical language string has the form language_territory.codeset, to cope with differences in, say, the French language between France and Belgium (which are regarded as territories!). The third part of a language string defines the way characters are represented internally.

specification; the default can be overridden by the environment variable $XUSERFILESEARCHPATH (rather than $XFILESEARCHPATH).

The default behaviour is to look in the user's home directory, unless the environment variable $XAPPLRESDIR is set, in which case that directory is searched first.

Suppose first that $XAPPLRESDIR is not set, but that the user's home directory is '/u/apg', the application language string is 'ja_JP.jis7', the customization is '-color' and the application class is 'App_class'. The MIT X11R5 distribution of Xt will then look for the following files in order:

```
/u/apg/ja_JP.jis7/App_class-color
/u/apg/ja/App_class-color
/u/apg/App_class-color
/u/apg/ja_JP.jis7/App_class
/u/apg/ja/App_class
/u/apg/App_class"
```

This is, in essence, the same set as for the application-specific class resource file, but with a different root directory.

If the environment variable $XAPPLRESDIR is set (to /test/resources, say), the search covers the following files:

```
/test/resources/ja_JP.jis7/App_class-color
/test/resources/ja/App_class-color
/test/resources/App_class-color
/u/apg/App_class-color
/test/resources/ja_JP.jis7/App_class
/test/resources/ja/App_class
/test/resources/App_class
/u/apg/App_class
```

This list includes all the default names for the application-specific class resource file, but rooted on /test/resources rather than /usr/lib/X11/app-defaults, so setting $XAPPLRESDIR is one way of testing out a new application resource file at the cost of losing any application-specific preferences from your home directory.

10.6 User preferences

The user preferences apply to all applications, regardless of application class and are loaded into the resource database for every application.

Xt first looks for a property named RESOURCE_MANAGER on the root window of the default screen of the display. If this is found, it uses the value of the property. If it is not found, it looks for a file '.Xdefaults' in the user's home directory. Neither the property name nor the resource name can be configured.

The idea of the RESOURCE_MANAGER property is that it allows the user to specify preferences once on the server, rather than having to maintain a '.Xdefaults' file on every host. The utility xrdb can be used to create and set the value of the RESOURCE_MANAGER property (and also the screen-specific SCREEN_RESOURCES properties). This would normally be run from the user's X start-up file.

Xt will use either the RESOURCE_MANAGER property or the '.Xdefaults' file, not both. If you do run xrdb at start-up, applications will ignore the '.Xdefaults' file, and editing it will have no effect. It seems that xrdb is nowadays preferred over the '.Xdefaults' file.[1]

10.7   Screen resources

Screen resources are similar to user preferences, in that they apply to all applications, but they are specific to a particular screen. Screen resources are held in the SCREEN_RESOURCES property of the root window of each screen.

As with the RESOURCE_MANAGER property, the SCREEN_RESOURCES properties are usually set up with xrdb. The RESOURCE_MANAGER property (or the '.Xdefaults' file) will contain preferences that apply to all screens and the SCREEN_RESOURCES properties will contain entries that override or augment these general settings. To set these, xrdb allows you to specify entries in a file that are conditionally applied to the SCREEN_RESOURCES properties according to the characteristics of the corresponding screen. This is achieved by passing the file through cpp once for each screen, with certain symbols predefined. The -symbols flag to xrdb will tell you which symbols are defined for a screen and what their values are.

A typical use is to set different defaults for colour and mono screens. If the screen can support colour, xrdb defines the symbol COLOR, so you can set up entries like this:

```
#ifdef COLOR
*Background:      light steel blue
*customization:   -color
#else
*customization:   -mono
#endif
```

Note that the setting for the customization resource will affect the places that Xt searches to find the application-specific resource files (the '%C' substitution).

---

1. It is not, therefore, very sensible to xrdb application defaults files (as some users have been known to do), as there is then almost no chance of overriding the defaults.

Although the screen resources take precedence over the application-specific defaults files, they are read in earlier.

 You can specify resources based on screen resolution, but xrdb gives the resolution in pixels per metre, rather than dots per inch.[1]

10.8 Per host user environment file

This file is specific to the user and the host on which the application is running. The name is specified by the environment variable $XENVIRONMENT if this is set, otherwise the file '.Xdefaults-<hostname>' in the user's home directory. Clearly, this should be used to specify preferences for the host (like *autoSave: True on an unreliable host machine).

10.9 Command line arguments

All of the Xt functions that create resource databases (XtAppInitialize(), XtOpenDisplay() and XtDisplayInitialize()) take the command line arguments and count, argv and argc and scan them for entries that they recognise. Any recognised entry is removed from argv and a corresponding entry is made in the resource database.

Where the resource specifications in the resource files consist of name-value pairs that can be loaded into the resource database directly, a command line argument (like -expert or -fg red) needs to be converted into a name-value pair (.expert: True or *foreground: red). Xt does this using an option description record that you must provide; in other words, Xt provides a table-driven argument cracker and you provide the table. Xt has a predefined option description for arguments like -display; anything in your description augments this.

10.9.1 Defining command line arguments

A number of different kinds of command line argument are supported:

```
typedef enum {
    XrmoptionNoArg,      /* Value is specified in OptionDescRec.value */
    XrmoptionIsArg,      /* Value is the option string itself */
    XrmoptionStickyArg,  /* Value is characters immediately after option */
    XrmoptionSepArg,     /* Value is next argument in argv */
    XrmoptionResArg,     /* Resource and value in next argument in argv */
    XrmoptionSkipArg,    /* Ignore this option and the next argument in argv */
    XrmoptionSkipLine,   /* Ignore this option and the rest of argv */
```

---

1. This exemplifies a general trend: the X window system is inching towards metrication.

XrmoptionSkipNArgs   /* Ignore this option and the next
                                OptionDescRes.value arguments in argv */
} XrmOptionKind;

For each argument that you want to be recognised, you have to specify its name, its kind (or style), the form of the resource database entry to be made and possibly a value for the resource database entry. This is done in an XrmOptionDescRec structure:

```
typedef struct {
    char            *option;     /* Option abbreviation in argv */
    char            *specifier;  /* Resource specifier */
    XrmOptionKind argKind;       /* Which style of option it is */
    XPointer        value;       /* Value to provide if XrmoptionNoArg */
} XrmOptionDescRec, *XrmOptionDescList;
```

Note that the value is usually a character string. The type XPointer is a char*, so no cast is usually needed.

10.9.2   Command line argument example

This example shows the important features; it builds the resource database from the command line arguments, then writes it out to a file using XrmPutFileDatabase() (see Section 10.11):

command
line

```
#include <X11/Intrinsic.h>

static XrmOptionDescRec options[] = {
    { "-noarg", ".noArg", XrmoptionNoArg, "Use this value if arg is found" },
    { "-isarg", ".isarg", XrmoptionIsArg, NULL},
    { "-stickyarg", ".stickyarg", XrmoptionStickyArg, NULL },
    { "-separg", ".separg", XrmoptionSepArg, NULL },
    { "-resarg", NULL, XrmoptionResArg, NULL },
    { "-skiparg", NULL, XrmoptionSkipArg, NULL },
    { "-skipline", NULL, XrmoptionSkipLine, NULL },
    { "-skipnargs", NULL, XrmoptionSkipNArgs, (XPointer)2 }
};

int main (argc,argv)
    int     argc;
    char   **argv;
{
    XtAppContext   app_context;
```

```
Display          *display;

XtToolkitInitialize ();
app_context = XtCreateApplicationContext ();

/* XtOpenDisplay() builds the resource database */
display = XtOpenDisplay (app_context, NULL, "app_name",
               "App_class_name", options, XtNumber (options),
               &argc, argv);

/* Use XtScreenDatabase() for multi-screen displays */
XrmPutFileDatabase (XtDatabase (display), ",tmp");
exit (0);
}
```

Inspecting the contents of the database dump file shows how the arguments are parsed. The command is shown first (after the prompt 'iscurry>') and the database dump after.

XrmoptionNoArg means that there is no value on the command line; the value is taken from the option description record. This is useful for a novice/expert switch, say:

```
iscurry> xmain -noarg
app_name.noArg: Use this value if arg is found
```

For XrmoptionIsArg the value in the database is the argument itself:

```
iscurry> xmain -isarg
app_name.isarg: -isarg
```

XrmoptionStickyArg is followed immediately by the value, with no intervening whitespace:

```
iscurry> xmain -stickyargvalue_follows_immediately
app_name.stickyarg: value_follows_immediately
```

XrmOptionSepArg allows and insists on some whitespace between the option flag and the value:

```
iscurry> xmain -separg value_follows_after_whitespace
app_name.separg: value_follows_after_whitespace
```

Note that all of the above form the name part of the name-value pair from the name of the application (see Section 10.3.2) and the specifier given in the option description - the '.noArg' field. The specifier need not bear any relation to the argument (see the Xt example below).

XrmoptionResArg allows you to specify both the name and value as the next argument. It is used for the standard Xt option, -xrm:

```
iscurry> xmain -resarg "foo: name and value given as next argument"
foo: name and value given as next argument
```

XrmoptionSkipArg will skip the next argument:

```
iscurry> xmain -skiparg -isarg -noarg -stickyargskips_one_arg

app_name.noArg: Use this value if arg is found
app_name.stickyarg: skips_one_arg
```

XrmoptionSkipLine skips all remaining arguments. In this example, this means that the resource database is left empty:

```
iscurry> xmain -skipline -isarg -noarg -stickyargskips_rest_of_line
```

XrmoptionSkipNArgs skips the number of arguments specified in the option description record:

```
iscurry> xmain -skipnargs -isarg -noarg -stickyargskips_two_args
app_name.stickyarg: skips_two_args
```

10.9.3 Standard Xt command line arguments

Xt has a standard set of command line arguments that it recognises and uses to load the resource database. This is best documented by its own option description record:

```
static XrmOptionDescRec Const opTable[] = {
    {"+rv", "*reverseVideo", XrmoptionNoArg, (XtPointer) "off"},
    {"+synchronous", "*synchronous", XrmoptionNoArg, (XtPointer) "off"},
    {"-background", "*background", XrmoptionSepArg, (XtPointer) NULL},
    {"-bd", "*borderColor", XrmoptionSepArg, (XtPointer) NULL},
    {"-bg", "*background", XrmoptionSepArg, (XtPointer) NULL},
    {"-bordercolor", "*borderColor", XrmoptionSepArg, (XtPointer) NULL},
    {"-borderwidth", ".borderWidth", XrmoptionSepArg, (XtPointer) NULL},
    {"-bw", ".borderWidth", XrmoptionSepArg, (XtPointer) NULL},
    {"-display", ".display", XrmoptionSepArg, (XtPointer) NULL},
    {"-fg", "*foreground", XrmoptionSepArg, (XtPointer) NULL},
```

```
    {"-fn", "*font", XrmoptionSepArg, (XtPointer) NULL},
    {"-font", "*font", XrmoptionSepArg, (XtPointer) NULL},
    {"-foreground", "*foreground", XrmoptionSepArg, (XtPointer) NULL},
    {"-geometry", ".geometry", XrmoptionSepArg, (XtPointer) NULL},
    {"-iconic", ".iconic", XrmoptionNoArg, (XtPointer) "on"},
    {"-name", ".name", XrmoptionSepArg, (XtPointer) NULL},
    {"-reverse", "*reverseVideo", XrmoptionNoArg, (XtPointer) "on"},
    {"-rv", "*reverseVideo", XrmoptionNoArg, (XtPointer) "on"},
    {"-selectionTimeout", ".selectionTimeout", XrmoptionSepArg, (XtPointer)
                    NULL},
    {"-synchronous", "*synchronous", XrmoptionNoArg, (XtPointer) "on"},
    {"-title", ".title", XrmoptionSepArg, (XtPointer) NULL},
    {"-xnllanguage", ".xnlLanguage", XrmoptionSepArg, (XtPointer) NULL},
    {"-xrm", NULL, XrmoptionResArg, (XtPointer) NULL},
};
```

Notice how different argument names can be used with the same resource specifier, so that -fg and -foreground both correspond to *foreground. This is the way to implement aliases.

Note also that some of the specifiers have loose bindings (*foreground) whereas others are tightly bound (.selectionTimeout). The former lead to a resource database entry which matches any widget, whereas the latter will only match the ApplicationShell widget. In fact, most of the tightly bound resources are considered to be resources of the application itself, or at least its display connection, rather than resources of the ApplicationShell.

10.10   Fallback resources

An application usually has most of its resource values, in particular the values of text strings, defined in the application-specific class resource file. If this is missing when the application starts up, the application cannot usefully run.

The fallback resources provide a way of specifying in the code a (presumably small) core set of resource values which are loaded into the resource database if the application-specific class resource file, /usr/lib/X11/app-defaults/<class> cannot be opened. There are two possible uses: to provide a set of resource values sufficient to run the application, or to display a message explaining the problem to the user. The former is expensive to do and maintain, especially in a substantial or growing application.

A typical set of fallback resources is declared and used as follows:

```
    ...
    static String fallback_resources[] = {
        "*labelString: Application class res file cannot be opened - contact support",
```

```
            NULL,
    };
    ...

    XtToolkitInitialize ();
    app_context = XtCreateApplicationContext ();

    /* Set fallback resources - usually done via XtAppInitialize() */
    XtAppSetFallbackResources (app_context, fallback_resources);
    /* XtOpenDisplay() builds the resource database */
    display = XtOpenDisplay (app_context, NULL, "app_name", "App_class",
                    NULL, 0, &argc, argv);
```

The fallback resources must be set up as a static array, as XtSetFallbackRe-
sources() does not take a copy and the final entry must be null.

XtAppInitialize() takes a fallback resources parameter which it passes to
XtSetFallbackResources(), so it is unusual for an application to use XtSetFallback-
Resources() directly.

10.11   Contents of the resource database

The easiest way to understand what is in the resource database is to dump its
contents and inspect them. In this example, the resource database is built by the call
to XtOpenDisplay(). The application class and application name are explicitly
given as 'mwm' and 'Mwm', so the application loads into its resource database the
same information as mwm does. Once loaded, the resource database is dumped to
a file by the call to XrmPutFileDatabase(). XtDatabase() is used to locate the
database for the default screen of the display; XtScreenDatabase() will do the
same for an individual screen database on a multi-screen display:

```
            #include <X11/Intrinsic.h>

mwm_resdb   int main (argc,argv)
                int     argc;
                char    **argv;
            {
                XtAppContext    app_context;
                Display         *display;

                XtToolkitInitialize ();
                app_context = XtCreateApplicationContext ();
                /* XtOpenDisplay() builds the resource database */
                display = XtOpenDisplay (app_context, NULL, "mwm", "Mwm", NULL, 0,
                                &argc, argv);
```

```
    /* Use XtScreenDatabase() for multi-screen displays */
    XrmPutFileDatabase (XtDatabase(display), ",tmp");
    exit (0);
}
```

Because the application class is given as 'Mwm', the resource database will be built using mwm's application-specific resource files. For example, suppose that these are as follows.

Application-specific class resource file:

```
!/usr/lib/X11/app-defaults/Mwm
Mwm*fontList:               variable
Mwm*icon*fontList:          fixed
```

Application-specific user resource file:

```
!/u/apg//Mwm
Mwm*activeBackground:       White
Mwm*activeBackgroundPixmap: 50_foreground
Mwm*icon*fontList:          variable
*activeBottomShadowPixmap:  background
*activeTopShadowPixmap:     foreground
```

User preferences file:

```
!.Xdefaults
XDesigner.c++BaseClassHeader:
Mwm*keyboardFocusPolicy:    pointer
Mwm*focusAutoRaise:         False
*foreground:                blue
```

Finally, suppose that the program is invoked with command line arguments:

```
mwm -display iscurry:0 -fg red
```

The contents of the resource database will be dumped to the file and can be inspected. The comments are not part of the database, but identify the source of each database entry:

```
! From standard command line arguments
mwm.display: iscurry:0
mwm*foreground: red
! From user preferences
```

```
XDesigner.c++BaseClassHeader:
! Application-specific user resource file (overrides class resource file)
Mwm*icon*fontList: variable
! Application-specific class resource file
Mwm*fontList: variable
! Application-specific user resource file
Mwm*activeBackgroundPixmap: 50_foreground
! User preferences file
Mwm*focusAutoRaise: False
! Application-specific user resource file
Mwm*activeBackground: White
! User preferences file
Mwm*keyboardFocusPolicy: pointer
*foreground: blue
! Application-specific user resource file
*activeBottomShadowPixmap: background
*activeTopShadowPixmap: foreground
```

There are a number of points worth noting:

* Entries are copied from the resource files to the database unchanged.
* Command line arguments are converted into resource file entries, using the application name, 'mwm'.
* The resource database is loaded with all the entries from the relevant files even if, like the XDesigner resource, they have no possible relevance to the application.
* The resource database holds only one entry for a given name (such as Mwm*icon*fontList). Where the files contain more than one entry, the most significant one overrides all others.
* Wildcards ('*' and '?') are allowed in database entry names. The database will quite happily hold multiple entries that might match the same widget, such as mwm*foreground: red and *foreground: blue.

10.11.1   Quarks

The database dump above makes it look as though the resource database stores information as text strings. In fact, it uses things called quarks.

A quark is an integer that represents a text string. Within an application, there is a one-to-one correspondence between strings and quarks. Given a string, it can be converted to a quark using XrmStringToQuark() and back again using XrmQuarkToString(). Quarks are very similar to atoms, except that quarks exist within the client, whereas atoms are generated by the server and so can be shared by all of a server's clients.

Most application programmers never deal with quarks directly. However, they are widely used in type converters and internally in widgets and a passing familiarity is useful.

10.12   Database retrieval

Resource database retrieval in an Xt program happens under two circumstance: automatically when a widget is created, or explicitly when an application fetches its application resources.

Where the resource database is loaded using the application name and application class, retrievals use the names and classes of widgets. Specifically, given a resource and a widget both of which have both a name and a class, Xt forms a list of names by putting together the name of the resource, the name of the widget and the names of all the widget's ancestors. This list of names is sometimes called the *fully specified name*. The fully specified class is formed similarly and both the name and class are used to query the resource database.

10.12.1   Database retrieval for ApplicationShell widgets

Consider the simple widget hierarchy shown in Figure 10.2.

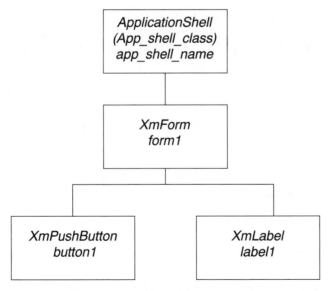

Figure 10.2 *Widget hierarchy example*

Each widget has a fixed class and a name which is specified when it is created. However, the widget at the root of the tree - the ApplicationShell - also has a class specified at creation time:

```
...
/* Creation specifies both name and class */
appshell = XtAppCreateShell ( "app_shell_name", "App_shell_class",
                    applicationShellWidgetClass, display, al, ac );
/* Creation specifies name only */
form1 = XmCreateForm (appshell, "form1", al, ac);
button1 = XmCreatePushButton (form1, "button1", al, ac);
label1 = XmCreateLabel (form1, "label1", al, ac);
...
```

When Xt creates the XmPushButton widget, say and wants to determine the value for the foreground resource (class Foreground), it builds the names into half of a database query:

app_shell_name.form1.button1.foreground

The other half of the query is the list of classes of the resource, the widget and all its ancestors. However, if the ultimate ancestor - the widget at the root of the tree - is an ApplicationShell widget, the application class passed to XtAppCreateShell() is used for the first element of the list of class names, rather than the class of the ApplicationShell widget, which is, of course, ApplicationShell. In other words, the class passed to XtAppCreateShell() becomes the effective class of the ApplicationShell widget for the purpose of querying the resource database and so is the name used at the start of a resource specification in, say, the user preference resource file.[1] Here, the class name list would be:

App_shell_class.XmForm.XmPushButton.Foreground

Note that this only happens if the root of the widget tree is a widget of class ApplicationShell, or a subclass. If you use some other class of shell, such as TopLevelShell, in the call to XtAppCreateShell(), the class used in that call is not used when querying the resource database and the list of class names used in the query might (unhelpfully) be:

TopLevelShell.XmForm.XmPushButton.Foreground

In this example, then, Xt will take the list of names and the list of classes as the key for a database query and find the closest match in the database. The class name

---

1. The obsolete function XtCreateApplicationShell() does not take a class parameter; it uses the application class - the one that is used to locate resource files.

used as the first element of the query on the database is that specified when the ApplicationShell is created. It need not be the same as the application class used to find the resource files, but XtAppInitialize() will ensure that they are the same.

The value found in the database is used for the foreground resource when the widget is created. If there is no matching entry in the database, Xt will use a default value defined by the widget author. These values are overridden by resource values specified in the code. The easiest way to think of this is that the widget author provides default values and the resource database modifies the defaults on a per-widget basis. If you do not specify a value in the code, Xt will use the default value.

10.12.2   Database retrieval for popup shells

The same naming scheme is carried through to popup shells such as an XmDialogShell. If an XmDialogShell is created with the ApplicationShell as its parent, the name and class used to query the resource database starts with the application shell name and the class passed to XtAppCreateShell():

```
appshell = XtAppCreateShell ("app_shell_name", "App_shell_class",
                    applicationShellWidgetClass, display, al, ac);
dialogshell = XmCreateDialogShell (appshell, "dialogshell", al, ac);
form2 = XmCreateForm (dialogshell, "form2", al, ac);
button2 = XmCreatePushButton (form2, "button2", al, ac);
```

The name and class used to find the foreground resource for button 2 will be:

```
app_shell_name.dialogshell.form2.button2.foreground
App_shell_class.XmDialogShell.XmForm.XmPushButton.Foreground
```

10.12.3   Database retrieval for menus

Menus are implemented using popup shells and again the naming passes up through the popup shell. However, if you use the Motif convenience functions to create menus, you should be aware that they create the XmMenuShell widgets for you. Consider this code, which create a pulldown menu containing one item (an XmPushButton) and an XmCascadeButton with a pullright menu:

```
appshell = XtAppCreateShell ("app_shell_name", "App_shell_class",
                    applicationShellWidgetClass, display, al, ac);
form1 = XmCreateForm (appshell, "form1", al, ac);

/* Create menu bar and pulldown menu */
menubar = XmCreateMenuBar (form1, "menubar", al, ac);
```

```
menubutton = XmCreateCascadeButton (menubar, "menubutton", al, ac);
pulldown = XmCreatePulldownMenu (menubar, "pulldown", al, ac);
ac = 0;
XtSetArg (al[ac], XmNsubMenuId, pulldown); ac++;
XtSetValues (menubutton, al, ac);


/* An item in the pulldown menu */
menuitem = XmCreatePushButton (pulldown, "menuitem", al, ac);


/* Create cascade button in pulldown menu, and its pullright menu */
cascadebutton = XmCreateCascadeButton (pulldown, "cascadebutton",
                    al, ac);
pullright = XmCreatePulldownMenu (pulldown, "pullright", al, ac);
ac = 0;
XtSetArg (al[ac], XmNsubMenuId, pullright); ac++;
XtSetValues (cascadebutton, al, ac);


/* An item in the pullright menu */
pullrightitem = XmCreatePushButton (pullright, "pullrightitem", al, ac);
```

For the XmPushButton in the pulldown menu, the name and class (again for the foreground resource) will be:

> app_shell_name.form1.menubar.popup_pulldown.pulldown.menuitem.fore ground
> App_shell_class.XmForm.XmRowColumn.XmMenuShell.XmRowColumn. XmPushButton.Foreground

Note that Motif has created an XmMenuShell widget named popup_pulldown as the parent of the menu pane, pulldown.

At the next level down, the XmPushButton in the pullright benefits from two XmMenuShell widgets. Motif calls these popup_pulldown and popup_pullright:

> app_shell_name.form1.menubar.popup_pulldown.popup_pullright.pullright. pullrightitem.foreground
> App_shell_class.XmForm.XmRowColumn.XmMenuShell.XmMenuShell.X mRowColumn.XmPushButton.Foreground

Of course, you would normally use a loose binding in specifying the resources, so that the extra widgets created by Motif would be handled in the matching process.

10.13 Database matching

When a widget is created (or application resources are fetched) Xt queries the resource database using the fully qualified name and class. There are no wildcards ('*' or '?') in the query; the wildcards are in the data stored in the resource database. This is very different from most databases, where the data stored is fully specified and the query is inexact. A typical query involves matching a name and class like:

```
app.form1.button1.foreground
App.XmForm.XmPushButton.Foreground
```

against a set of database entries like:

```
app*foreground:                      red
XDesigner.c++BaseClassHeader:
App*fontList:                        variable
app*Foreground:                      green
App.?.foreground:                    blue
app.XmForm.*.Foregrond:              yellow
```

The object is to find the closest match, if any. If there is more than one match, precedence rules are used to select one. However, the first step is to find if there is a match at all.

A database entry matches the fully qualified name and class in the query at a given level, if the string in the entry is the same as the name or class at that level, but '*' matches any names and classes at any number of levels, and '?' matches any single name or class. This will eliminate, in particular:

```
app.XmForm.*.Foregrond:              yellow
```

From the point of view of Xt, this is just another entry in the database which happens not to match. It is not that Xt ignores database entries that are misspelt; it just has no way of distinguishing these from other irrelevant entries.

The precedence rules for multiple matches are detailed in the Xlib documentation. Very approximately, names matter more than classes, which are better matches than the '?' wildcard, and the '*' loose binding matches least well of all.

10.14 Application resources

The values in the resource database are used automatically as defaults when widgets are created, but it is also possible for you to retrieve them for other purposes.

The usual use of this is to define application resource, resources which apply to the application as a whole, rather than to any of its widgets. However, the mechanism is just the same as that used to retrieve resource values during widget creation and you can use it to inspect the resource database for the default values that apply to a particular widget if you want.

10.14.1   Defining application resources

In order to retrieve an application resource value from the resource database, you have to tell the toolkit:

- The name and class of the resource. These are used as the final parts of the name and class used to query the database.
- The representation type that you want the value expressed as (Boolean, string, pixel and so on), and the size of the representation type. Xt will automatically convert from the string held in the resource database to the type you request.
- An address offset telling Xt where to put the result.
- A default value to use if the resource database has no matching value and the representation type of the default, again allowing Xt to convert the default to the type you asked for.

This is done using instances of the XtResource structure:

```
typedef struct _XtResource {
    String      resource_name;    /* Resource name */
    String      resource_class;   /* Resource class */
    String      resource_type;    /* Representation type desired */
    Cardinal    resource_size;    /* Size in bytes of representation */
    Cardinal    resource_offset;  /* Offset from base to put resource
                                      value */
    String      default_type;     /* Representation type of specified
                                      default */
    XtPointer   default_addr;     /* Address of default resource */
} XtResource, *XtResourceList;
```

The resource name is a string, and for widget resources is usually represented by an 'XmN' or 'XtN' symbol. For application resources, there will not usually be a suitable predefined symbol and it is not worth defining your own, so string literals are often used.

The resource class is also a string. In widget resources, a class is represented by an 'XmC' or 'XtC' symbol, and there may be a suitable one (such as XmCBoolean or XmCString) already defined. The class can be used to set a group of related resource using a resource specification like:

*ResourceClass: value

In theory, then, you choose a class for an application resource by finding some existing resources of that class and asking yourself if it makes sense for your new resource and the existing ones to be set as a group. In practice, the existence of classes like XtCBoolean make a nonsense of this; there is no reason why the user should want to set all the Boolean flags True, using a single resource specification.

The XtResource structure tells Xt to retrieve a resource value from the resource database, convert it to the correct representation and put the result at an address for which the offset is given. The base address to be added to the offset and the information needed to determine the database retrieval query are specified in the function call that retrieves the resources. Normally, the base address is the address of a structure instance and the offset is the offset of a field within that structure, calculated using the macros XtOffset() or, more portably, XtOffsetOf().[1]

The XtResource records effectively define what application resources the application has. They are usually declared in a single static array and all application resources are retrieved from the resource database during application initialisation. However, there is no reason (other than efficiency) why application resources should not be retrieved one by one, as and when needed.

10.14.2   Application resource example

In an application, the first coding step is to declare a structure to receive the information retrieved from the resource database, say:

app_res

```
typedef struct {
        Boolean auto_save;
        short    auto_save_threshold;
        String   auto_save_ext;
        Pixel    form_fill_colour;
} app_res_rec;
```

Next, statically initialise the XtResource records that tell Xt how to map information from the database onto the structure:

```
static XtResource resources[] = {
    {
```

---

1. The mechanism is designed to retrieve information from the database to initialise widget data structures. The offset is fixed by the widget class, but the base is different for each widget instance. This is rather unnatural for application resources, as they are usually only retrieved once.

```
            "autoSave", XtCBoolean, XmRBoolean, sizeof (Boolean),
                         XtOffsetOf (app_res_rec, auto_save ), XmRImmediate,
                         (XtPointer) False
    },
    {
        "autoSaveThreshold", "AutoSaveThreshold", XmRShort, sizeof (short),
                         XtOffsetOf (app_res_rec, auto_save_threshold ),
                         XmRImmediate, (XtPointer) 20
    },
    {
        "autoSaveExt", XtCString, XtRString, sizeof (String),
                         XtOffsetOf (app_res_rec, auto_save_ext ),
                         XtRString, ".sav"
    },
    {
        "formFillColor", XmCColor, XmRPixel, sizeof (Pixel),
                         XtOffsetOf (app_res_rec, form_fill_colour),
                         XmRString, "White"
    },
};
```

The default value - the final field in the XtResource structure - is usually given as a string (representation type XmRString or XtRString), or an immediate value (representation type XmRImmediate or XtRImmediate). The resource manager understands how to convert from string to other representation, as the information in the resource database is held as strings. The immediate value representation, which is not converted, is often but not invariably used when the resource is a Boolean or integer value. An alternative to the first resource specification above is:

```
static XtResource resources[] = {
    {
    "autoSave", XtCBoolean, XmRBoolean, sizeof (Boolean),
                     XtOffsetOf(app_res_rec, auto_save ), XmRString,
                     "False"
    },
```

There are many other possible representation types, most of which are rarely used by application programmers. See the Xt documentation for details.

10.14.3   Retrieving the application resource values

In the start-up process (at any time after we have created the first widget), we can query the resource database, which copies the information it finds into our application resources data structure. It can then be printed out or, more likely, used in other parts of the application:

```
app_res_rec app_res;
/* Create an application shell */
appshell = XtAppCreateShell ("app_shell_name", "App_shell_class",
                    applicationShellWidgetClass, display, NULL, 0);
/* Use the application shell to provide context for the query */
XtGetApplicationResources (appshell, &app_res, resources,
                    XtNumber (resources), NULL, 0);
fprintf (stderr, "Autosave %s\n", app_res.auto_save?"True":"False");
fprintf (stderr, "Autosave threshold %d\n", app_res.auto_save_threshold);
fprintf (stderr, "Autosave extension %s\n", app_res.auto_save_ext);
fprintf (stderr, "Form fill colour %d\n", app_res.form_fill_colour);
```

The ApplicationShell widget is used in the call to XtGetApplicationResources() to allow Xt to build the full name and class for the database query. For instance, the auto_save_threshold resource has the name and class (in the resources record) 'autoSaveThreshold' and 'AutoSaveThreshold'. These are combined with the name and class of the ApplicationShell to give the name and class for the database query:

```
app_shell_name.autoSaveThreshold
App_shell_class.AutoSaveThreshold
```

The user can configure the values of these application resources with resource file entries like:

```
App_shell_class.AutoSaveThreshold:  10
App_shell_class.autoSaveThreshold:  10
app_shell_name.AutoSaveThreshold:  10
app_shell_name.autoSaveThreshold:  10
```

If a different widget is used, the name and class used in the database query will include the fully qualified name and class of the widget and so it might be:

```
app_shell_name.form2.autoSaveThreshold
App_shell_class.XmForm.AutoSaveThreshold
```

This is not particularly useful, but is allowed.

10.15 Resource type conversion

Type converters, or resource converters, are functions whose job is to convert a resource value in one representation, usually a string, into the corresponding value in another - int, Pixel, Dimension or whatever. Type converters are registered with the resource manager and invoked by Xt whenever there is any conversion work to be done.

Xt provides many predefined type converters; these are listed in the Xt documentation. Motif also provides others for the types that it defines: compound string, font list, all the Motif enumeration types and so on. Many of these type converters have side-effects. For instance, converting a string to a Pixel value will also allocate a read-only colour cell for the named colour. Using the side-effects of a type converter in this way is sometimes the easiest way to create and allocate toolkit data structures and it is common practice to do this directly.

The supplied type converters may not have the behaviour you need, so we also show how to write and register a simple type converter procedure.

10.15.1 Direct type conversion

An application can invoke a type converter directly (rather than as a consequence of, say, fetching application resources) by calling XtConvertAndStore() (although older code using XtConvert() is still common and still works):

```
Boolean XtConvertAndStore (object, from_type, from_value, to_type,
                  to_value)
    Widget          object;
    String          from_type;
    XrmValuePtr     from_value;
    String          to_type;
    XrmValuePtr     to_value;
```

The widget is used for two purposes. First, a type converter can be registered so that, when it is invoked, it is passed some of the resource values from the widget, as well as the from_value and to_value. For instance, the String to Pixel converter needs a screen and colour map and takes these from the widget resources. The second use of the widget is in maintaining the reference count in Xt's resource conversion cache (described below). Xt arranges for the reference count to be decremented when the widget is destroyed, so it is not safe to use the converted value after destroying the widget.

The from_type and to_type are the representation type names used to find the correct converter; these will usually be represented by XmR symbols - XmRString, XmRPixel and so on.

The value to be converted is passed in from_value and the converted value is returned via to_value. These are both pointers to XrmValue structures:

```
typedef struct {
    unsigned int    size;
    XPointer        addr;
} XrmValue, *XrmValuePtr;
```

This structure is usually used to pass a pointer to the value to be converted, and its size. For instance, to convert from a Pixel value to an XColor structure, use this code:

```
XrmValue    from_value, to_value;
Pixel       pixel;
XColor      colour;
Boolean     status;
/* Set value of pixel */
...
/* Convert to XColor (RGB triple) value */
from_value.size = sizeof (Pixel);
from_value.addr = (XPointer) &pixel;
to_value.size = sizeof (XColor);
to_value.addr = (XPointer) &colour;
status = XtConvertAndStore (appshell, XmRPixel, &from_value,
                    XmRColor, &to_value);
```

The type String (which is just a typedef for char*) is treated differently. Rather than using the XrmValue to pass the address of the String (that is, the address of the char*, a char**), the String itself is passed and the size is the length of the character string, including the terminating NULL. To convert a String to a Pixel value, the code looks like this:

```
XrmValue    from_value, to_value;
Pixel       pixel;
Boolean     status;

from_value.addr = "red";
from_value.size = strlen (from_value.addr) + 1;
to_value.size = sizeof (Pixel);
to_value.addr = (XPointer) &pixel;
status = XtConvertAndStore (appshell, XmRString, &from_value,
                    XmRPixel, &to_value);
```

This unique treatment of the String type should also apply to to_value. The only example of a type converter that converts to a String is the String-to-Geometry converter. This is not part of the Xt specification and the MIT sample code appears to be incorrect.

There are two ways of using the to_value:

• Allocate storage before calling the converter and pass its size and address in via to_value. Provided the storage is large enough, the converter will copy the converted value into it and return True. If the converted value is too large to fit the storage, the converter will put the size of the converted value in to_value.size and return False. The application can then allocate more storage and try again.
• Pass in a NULL address in to_value, in which case the converter will allocate some (possibly temporary) storage for the converted value and return its address and size in to_value. The application must then copy the converted value, as it may well get overwritten the next time the converter is called.

The first is probably easiest for dealing with fixed-size types. String to Pixel conversion using the second method looks like this:

```
XrmValue    from_value, to_value;
Pixel       pixel;
XColor      colour;
Boolean     status;

from_value.addr = "red";
from_value.size = strlen (from_value.addr) + 1;
to_value.addr = NULL;
status = XtConvertAndStore (appshell, XmRString, &from_value,
                XmRPixel, &to_value);
pixel = *(Pixel*) to_value.addr;
```

10.15.2   Writing a type converter

Writing and registering a type converter is a serious business and you would do well to look at some existing type converters in the Xt code before getting too deeply involved. However, there is no reason why you cannot write and install a simple type converter. One particularly simple case is the string to enumeration converter. Motif needs so many of these itself that the toolkit includes a single table-driven converter and a way of registering new tables for new enumeration types (XmRepTypeRegister()). This is very simple to use and can save significant work.

If you have a more complex conversion requirement, you will have to write a type converter. There are then two features of the type converter system that you should bear in mind: the conversion cache, and destructors.

Conversion cache

Type converters are used when a resource database entry is converted to a resource value on widget creation. Because resource database entries can have wildcards, the same entry may match many widgets and the exact same resource conversion may be done many times. Xt provides a caching mechanism which can be used to avoid unnecessary calls to type converters. If the type converter is registered to use the cache, Xt checks to see if the parameters being passed to the type converter are the same as in a previous call. If not, it calls the type converter and places a copy of the returned value in its cache. If the conversion is the same, it returns the cached value from the previous conversion and does not call the type converter at all.

Use of the cache is specified by the XtCacheType argument when the converter is registered. The basic values are XtCacheNone and XtCacheAll.

XtCacheNone means that the Xt cache mechanism is not used at all; the type converter is called for every conversion. This is the simplest option and is safe even if the result of the conversion is a pointer to some data structure that can be modified.

XtCacheAll means that Xt will reuse the results of any previous conversion of the same value. This is useful for converters to simple types, such as integer, but unsafe if the result of the conversion is something that can be modified. The converted values will remain in the cache indefinitely. If XtCacheByDisplay is used instead of XtCacheAll, the values are removed from the cache (and the destructor is called) when the display connection is closed. This is appropriate if the returned value is something that is bound to a particular display, such as a cursor or font.

Destructors

Consider the string to compound string converter. This takes a String and creates and returns an XmString. Having created it, it also needs to make sure that it gets destroyed at an appropriate time. The XmString will be destroyed by the converters associated destructor, which is called by Xt when the widget that references the XmString is destroyed.

Because converted values may be cached, Xt arranges for reference counting if required and only calls the destructor when the last reference is removed. You request reference counting by specifying XtCacheRefCount in the XtCacheType mask when the type converter is registered. If the converter is registered with XtCacheType XtCacheByDisplay, the destructor will also be called when the display connection is closed.

Destructors are usually very simple, one-line functions which free memory allocated by the corresponding converter. They receive the to_value that was returned by the converter and the converter can, if necessary, save additional information at the time of the conversion which is passed to the destructor as client data.

10.16   String to compound string converter

The standard string to compound string converter calls XmStringCreateLtoR(). It can therefore only handle left-to-right strings. This section shows a slightly different converter; this starts in left-to-right mode, but changes direction every time it encounters a # in the text (unlike the default converter, it cannot handle \n in text, so this is strictly a one-line converter).

First, we need a utility function to concatenate compound strings. This is similar to the one given in Section 15.2.2:

resconvert

```
static XmString string_append(s1, s2)
    XmString   s1;
    XmString   s2;
{
    XmString   s3;
    if (s1==NULL)
        return NULL;
    s3 = XmStringConcat (s1, s2);
    XmStringFree (s1);
    XmStringFree (s2);
    return s3;
}
```

The converter itself is straightforward. The prototype procedure for a type converter is XtTypeConverter. The most important parameters are the from_value and to_value:

```
static Boolean string_to_xmstring(display, args, num_args, from_value,
                    to_value, converter_data)
    Display      *display;
    XrmValue     *args;
    Cardinal     *num_args;
    XrmValue     *from_value;
    XrmValue     *to_value;
    XtPointer    *converter_data;
{
    static XmString     string;
    char                *instring;
    char                *p;
    XmStringDirection dir = XmSTRING_DIRECTION_L_TO_R;
/* Complain if nothing to convert */
    if (from_value->addr==NULL)
    {
        XtDisplayStringConversionWarning (display, from_value->addr,
```

```
                XmRXmString);
        return False;
    }
/* If the caller has allocated storage for the converted value, check that it is
big enough */
    if ((to_value->addr != NULL) && (to_value->size < sizeof (XmString))) {
        to_value->size = sizeof(XmString);
        return False;
    }
/* Take a copy of the from_value, parse it into segments and create the
compound string*/
    string = XmStringCreateLtoR ("", XmFONTLIST_DEFAULT_TAG);
    instring = strdup (from_value->addr);
    if (instring != NULL) {
        for (p = strtok (instring, "#"); p != NULL; p = strtok (NULL, "#")) {
            string = string_append (string,
                        XmStringCreateLocalized (p));
            if (dir == XmSTRING_DIRECTION_L_TO_R)
                dir= XmSTRING_DIRECTION_R_TO_L;
            else
                dir = XmSTRING_DIRECTION_L_TO_R;
            string = string_append (string, XmStringDirectionCreate(dir));
        }
        free (instring);
    }
/* Failed to create compound string... */
    if (string == NULL) {
        XtDisplayStringConversionWarning (display, from_value->addr,
                        XmRXmString);
        return False;
    }

/* Successful conversion, return value to caller */
    if (to_value->addr)
        *(XmString *) to_value->addr = string;
    else
        to_value->addr = (XPointer) &string;
    to_value->size = sizeof (XmString);
    return True;
}
```

Most type converters are written using a macro to provide most of the code. This makes it easy to write type converters, but hard to understand them, so we have expanded this one and rearranged it for readability.

The type converter creates one more XmString than it frees. We have to ensure that this is freed eventually, by providing a destructor procedure. The prototype procedure for this is XtDestructor. Its most important parameter is a copy of the to_value returned by the converter for this particular conversion:

```
static void string_to_xmstring_destroy (app, to_value, converter_data, args,
                         num_args)
    XtAppContext  app;
    XrmValue      *to_value;
    XtPointer     converter_data;
    XrmValue      *args;
    Cardinal      *num_args;
{
    XmStringFree (*(XmString *) to_value->addr);
}
```

All the destructor has to do is recover the memory allocated for the compound string by destroying it.

10.16.1   Registering a type converter

Registering a simple type converter is straightforward. Xt needs to know the types it converts between, the address of the type converter and the corresponding destructor, if any, information about the cache support required and information about the extra parameters required by the converter (which we do not use and do not cover).

If multiple type converters are registered for the same conversion, the last one registered is used. This means that we must register our new one after Motif registers its own (that is, after the first VendorShell is created):

```
appshell = XtAppCreateShell ( "name", "Class",
                 applicationShellWidgetClass, display, NULL, 0);
XtSetTypeConverter (XmRString, XmRXmString, string_to_xmstring,
                 NULL, 0, XtCacheNone | XtCacheRefCount,
                 string_to_xmstring_destroy);
```

Notice that the converter is registered not to use the Xt converter cache (XtCacheNone). An application is unlikely to use the same compound string in many places, so there is little to be gained from the cache and something to be lost in fruitless cache searches. Reference counting is enabled, so the destructor will be called when the widget using the compound string is destroyed.

CHAPTER 11

Translations and accelerators

The mapping between events and a widget's action in response is not hard-coded in the widget, but defined by a table known as a translation table. Most of the functions that make the Motif widgets behave as they do are in fact invoked via the translations mechanism. An application can modify or replace a widget's translation table, thus changing or extending the behaviour of that widget. This can be done successfully with Motif widgets, although a little care is needed.

Xt supports a similar mapping, known as an accelerator, between events occurring on one widget and actions taken by another. This was intended to support keyboard accelerators for buttons and so on. However, the Motif toolkit is implemented in such a way that it makes use of the Xt accelerators at best uncertain. We show you a way of implementing keyboard accelerators using passive grabs, based on the way that Motif implements its menu accelerators.

11.1   Translations and predefined action routines

A translation is a specification of an event, or a sequence of events, followed by the name of the action to take when the event (sequence) occurs:

    <Btn1Down>:Arm()

187

Every Motif widget instance has a table containing many translations, initialised when the widget instance is created. You can add translations to a widget's table, modify existing translations, or replace the entire table. As translations are heavily used by the internals of widgets, replacing the entire table is likely to stop a widget working.

Actions are given as text names, so that translation tables (or additions to them) can be specified in resource files. When the translation manager finds an event sequence that matches the left-hand side of a translation, it then has to find a function to perform the action named on the right-hand side. It does this by looking at two action tables, one for the widget class and one global to all widgets. Action tables contain entries like this:

```
    ...
{"MultiActivate",      MultiActivate },
{"ArmAndActivate",     ArmAndActivate },
{"Disarm",             Disarm },
    ...
```

The first element of each entry is an action name and the second is a function pointer. Convention and common sense dictate that their names should be the same, or at least systematically related.

This explains why translations are rather less efficient than event handlers. Not only does the translation manager have to scan the event stream looking for event sequences that match the translations in the translation table, but when it finds a match, it has to scan the action table to find the function to call. Of course, the implementation is cunningly optimised and tuned, but it still has to do a fair amount of work on each event.

You can use a translation in two ways. First, you can add an entry to a widget's translation table, so that it invokes an action that is already in the widget class action table - one that the widget writer provided for you. This just makes the widget display some of its usual behaviour, but in response to a new event sequence. Second, you can add a translation that invokes a new action and add that action to the global action table. This can add completely new behaviour to the widget.

11.1.1   Modifying a translation table

Translations in code

In code, you can modify a widget's translation table in three ways.

First, you can remove it using XtUninstallTranslations() or replace it using XtSetValues() on the translations resource. As explained above, this will probably leave the widget completely crippled.

Second, you can augment the translation table by calling XtAugmentTrans-lations(). This takes a (compiled) list of translations, which are added to the existing translations. Where the existing translation table and the new list of translations both have an entry for the same event sequence, the one that is already in the translation table takes precedence. Augmenting translations is a nice, safe, non-destructive merge.

Finally, you can override the translations using XtOverrideTranslations(). This is virtually identical to XtAugmentTranslations(), except that the translations in the new list take precedence over those already in the translation table.

In every case you must parse the text representation of the translation table with XtParseTranslations() before passing it to the Xt function. A typical code fragment is:

```
XtAugmentTranslations (pushb, XtParseTranslationTable(
                "Ctrl<KeyPress>Q:   ArmAndActivate()\n\
                Meta<KeyPress>P:   Activate()"));
```

Note the '\n' between the translations in the table. The actions used here are predefined for XmPushButton, so this single statement is enough to change the behaviour of the widget. If you want to use an action which is not predefined, you have to write the action routine and register it; this is covered in Section 11.2.

Since this augments the translation table, it is relatively safe. Overriding is less safe, although the Motif widgets are surprisingly robust. This translation causes no obvious problems (but has no obvious purpose):

```
XtOverrideTranslations (pushbutton,
                XtParseTranslationTable ("<EnterWindow>: Arm()"));
```

This, on the other hand, is asking for trouble:

```
XtOverrideTranslations (pushbutton,
                XtParseTranslationTable (
                "<EnterWindow>: ProcessDrag()"));
```

 The point is simply this: although translations let you invoke a widget's inbuilt actions in response to any event sequence, many such actions were written on the assumption that they are only invoked as a result of certain events, or under certain circumstances. These restrictions are completely undocumented and may of course change between releases of the widget. Caution is advised.

Translations in resource files

The translation table for a widget can be set or modified in a resource file, like most other resources. The form of the translation table is the same as in code, but starts with an optional directive that indicates whether you want to replace, augment or override (you can also have this directive in a translation table that you use in code, but it will be ignored). For the XtAugmentTranslations() example above, the resource file entry is:

```
Myapplication*pushbutton.translations: #augment\
Ctrl<KeyPress>Q:      ArmAndActivate()\n\
Meta<KeyPress>P:   Activate()
```

⚠ If you have a space at the end of a line in your translation definition (after the final '\') it will be taken as terminating the table, and entries on subsequent lines will be ignored.

To override translations, use the directive #override; to replace, use #replace (the default if no directive is given).

⚠ In versions of Motif up to and including Motif 1.1, the directive was ignored and any translations specified in a resource file replaced the entire widget translation table. The only way to override or augment was in the code, after the widget had been created. This appears to have been fixed in Motif 1.2.

As an application developer you may, with appropriate caution, want to specify translations for a widget in your application in an application defaults file. The user may want to do the same in his or her defaults file. Xt will find two definitions of the translations resource and the user's one will take precedence. The result is that your application default translations are ignored altogether and the widget ends up with the default translations specified by the widget author, modified by the user-specified translations, but not yours.

To get round this problem, Xt defines a pseudo-resource called baseTranslations. The general idea is that the application writer specifies the baseTranslations resource, the user specifies the translations resource and Xt makes sure that they are both applied in the right order. As an application writer, you would specify a translation table in an application defaults file as:

```
Myapplication*pushbutton.baseTranslations: #augment\
Ctrl<KeyPress>Q:      ArmAndActivate()\n\
Meta<KeyPress>P:   Activate()
```

The user might change this in the '.Xdefaults' file with:

```
Myapplication*pushbutton.translations: #override\
Ctrl<KeyPress>Q:      Activate()\n\
Meta<KeyPress>P:   ArmAndActivate()
```

11.2   Defining new actions

Thus far we have only specified translation tables which use actions that are predefined by the widget writer. You can also specify new actions in the same way, but you have to write and register the action code. The steps are very similar to those needed to register an event handler.

11.2.1 Registering an action routine

You register new action routines using XtAppAddActions().

```
void XtAppAddActions (app_context, actions, num_actions)
    XtAppContext   app_context;
    XtActionList   actions;
    Cardinal       num_actions;
```

An XtActionList is an array of XtActionsRec entries, each of which contains an action name and a pointer to the function that implements the action. This is usually defined as a statically initialised array:

```
extern void action1();
extern void action2();
...
static XtActionsRec my_actions[]={
    {"action1",   action1},
    {"action2",   action2},
    ...
};
```

XtAppAddActions() needs a count of the elements in the array; the macro XtNumber() comes in handy:

```
XtAppAddActions (app_context, my_actions, XtNumber (my_actions));
```

Adding an action places it in an action table in the application context - one that is global to all widgets. The action you add is therefore available for use in any widget's translation table. When the translation manager finds a match between the event stream and a widget's translation table, it looks for the action first in the widget class's action table, then in the global one; in other words, if you register an action with the same name as an inbuilt action of a widget class, the widget class one takes precedence (for widgets of that class).

You can call XtAppAddActions() repeatedly. If you register more than one action with the same name, adding the second one overwrites the entry for the first.

Notice that you do not specify an event, widget or client data when you register an action. Actions are global to the application. You use the translation tables of individual widgets to specify when the actions are invoked and what extra information is passed on a particular invocation.

11.2.2 Action routines

An action routine is similar to a callback function or event handler, but again takes different parameters:

```
typedef void (*XtActionProc) (Widget, XEvent *, String *, Cardinal *)
    Widget      widget;
    XEvent      *event;
    String      *params;
    Cardinal    *num_params;
```

The widget and event arguments are as for the event handler. The params and num_params arguments are the action routine's version of client data. When you specify an action in a translation table, you can also specify strings to be passed in when the action routine is invoked:

```
Ctrl<KeyPress>A:    action1(a)
Ctrl<KeyPress>B:    action1(b)
<KeyPress>x:        handle_exit(confirm, pink, tuesday)
```

The number of strings in the translation table entry is passed to the action routine via num_params and the strings themselves are in params. As translation tables have to be specifiable in a resource file, only string-valued parameters are possible.

11.2.3 Action routine example

This example shows how to use an action routine to let the user drag an XmLabel widget round its parent XmDrawingArea using Button1. A similar (and slightly simpler) example using an event handler is given in Section 12.6.3.The first step is to create a widget hierarchy of ApplicationShell, XmDrawingArea and XmLabel:

actroutine

```
    ...
    ac = 0;
    XtSetArg (al[ac], XmNallowShellResize, TRUE); ac++;
    shell = XtAppCreateShell (app_name, "XApplication",
                        applicationShellWidgetClass, display, al, ac);
    ac = 0;
    XtSetArg (al[ac], XmNwidth, 400); ac++;
    XtSetArg (al[ac], XmNheight, 400); ac++;
    XtSetArg (al[ac], XmNresizePolicy, XmRESIZE_GROW); ac++;
    drawarea = XmCreateDrawingArea (shell, "drawarea", al, ac);
    ac = 0;
```

```
xmstring = XmStringCreateLtoR ( "Drag me!",
                 (XmStringCharSet) XmFONTLIST_DEFAULT_TAG);
XtSetArg (al[ac], XmNlabelString, xmstring); ac++;
drag_label = XmCreateLabel (drawarea, "drag_label", al, ac);
XmStringFree (xmstring);
XtManageChild (drag_label);
XtManageChild (drawarea);
```

The action routine has to be registered:

```
extern void handle_drag();

static XtActionsRec drag_actions[]={
    {"handle_drag", handle_drag}
};
...
XtAppAddActions (app_context, drag_actions, XtNumber (drag_actions));
```

This can be done at any time before the translations are added to the XmLabel widget; if the action is not known when the action table is parsed, the translation will be ignored (with an error message).

Setting the translations on the XmLabel is straightforward:

```
XtAugmentTranslations(drag_label, XtParseTranslationTable(
"<Btn1Down>:  handle_drag(start)\n\
<Btn1Motion>:  handle_drag(move)"));
```

The translations will invoke the action handle_drag on Button1 down or pointer motion with Button1 down. However, different text arguments are passed in for the two different sorts of event. The action routine can inspect these to work out what it should do:

```
#include <Xm/Label.h>

void handle_drag (widget, event, params, num_params)
    Widget   widget;
    XEvent   *event;
    String   *params;
    Cardinal *num_params;
{
/* Handle dragging of a label in a drawing area */

    static int  x_offset, y_offset;
    Position  x, y;
```

```
        if (*num_params != 1)
            return;
        if (!strcmp (params[0], "start"))
        {
/* Work out the offset used to translate between root window coordinates
(available in the event structures) and the position of top/left of the label and
remember it */
            if (event->type != ButtonPress)
                return;
            XtVaGetValues (widget, XmNx, &x, XmNy, &y, NULL);
            x_offset = (int) x - event->xbutton.x_root;
            y_offset = (int) y - event->xbutton.y_root;
            return;
        }
        if (!strcmp (params[0], "move"))
        {
/* Mouse has moved, move the label in response */
            if (event->type != MotionNotify)
                return;
            x = event->xbutton.x_root + x_offset;
            y = event->xbutton.y_root + y_offset;
            XtVaSetValues (widget, XmNx, x, XmNy, y, NULL);
            return;
        }
        return;
}
```

This code is *almost* identical to the event handler code. It uses the string argument passed in via params to work out what to do, where an event handler might use the event type. The action routine has to do extra work to check that it has the right number of strings and that their values are consistent with the event type; remember that the user can change the translations in a resource file to invoke handle_drag() with the wrong number of parameters at the wrong times.

11.3   Translation table syntax

The examples above use only the simplest form of translation: single events invoking single actions. Translation tables can be a good deal more complex. For a complete definition of the translation table syntax, you should consult the Xt reference documentation. This section gives an outline description that describes the major features.

Each entry in a translation table has the form:

[modifier_list]<event>[(count)][detail][,[modifier_list]<event>[(count)][detail]]
...: [action([arguments])...]

Square brackets ([]) indicate that an item is optional and an ellipsis (...) indicates that the item may be repeated. Some items are only meaningful with certain types of event.

The section up to the colon is an event (or event sequence) specification; the colon is followed by a list of action names.

The translation syntax usually offers about six different ways to describe the same event. In particular, the <event> portion may be:

- An X event name such as <KeyPress> or <ButtonPress>, or a synonym such as <Key> or <BtnDown>.
- A combination of an event name and a modifier: <Ctrl> is the same as Ctrl<KeyPress>.
- A combination of an event name and a detail: <Btn1Down> is (supposedly) the same as <ButtonPress>Button1.

This flexibility and variability means that translations are easier to read than to describe. Rather than defining the generic meaning of each part of the translation specification, we treat the different event types separately and use copious examples as a substitute for lucid description.

11.3.1   Key events

Key events are probably the most complex. The modifier list, event and detail fields can all be used. The count can also be used to detect multiple presses (or releases) of the same key, but this is unusual. A typical translation to detect key events is:

Ctrl <KeyPress>a:act-up()

Modifier list

The modifier list represents the state (pressed or not pressed, except for the shift lock key where 'state' means in effect or not) of the modifier keys and the mouse buttons. An X server may know about up to eight modifier keys (Ctrl, Shift, Lock and Mod1 to Mod5) and five mouse buttons (Button1 to Button5). The defining characteristic of a modifier key is that the X server can tell whether or not it is being held down (that is, it generates a hardware signal when it is released). As not all keys on all keyboards behave this way, the number of modifier keys actually supported may be less than the eight possible. Similar hardware limitations may mean that the server only supports a few of the five possible mouse buttons.

The translation manager knows about all the modifiers that the server supports, and understands some aliases (Alt, Meta, Hyper and Super) for the keys Mod1 to

Mod5. The aliases will not be the same for all servers, nor will they all be supported. You can find out which modifier keys a server supports and the corresponding aliases by running xmodmap:

xmodmap: up to 2 keys per modifier, (keycodes in parentheses):

shift Shift_L (0x6a), Shift_R (0x75)
lock Caps_Lock (0x7e)
control Control_L (0x53)
mod1 Meta_L (0x7f), Meta_R (0x81)
mod2
mod3
mod4
mod5

In this case, the server supports Shift, Lock, Ctrl and Mod1 as modifier keys. The translation manager will cope with these four and understands Meta as an alias for Mod1.

The physical keys corresponding to the different modifiers can usually only be determined by experimentation. Run xev and press each key in turn until you have found the ones that produce the keysyms Meta_R, Meta_L and so on.[1]

If you need to write code that will run on any common server, you should use only a restricted set of modifier keys and mouse buttons. Ctrl, Shift and Lock are safe and you can expect to have one of Alt or Meta available. Since you do not know which, you should have matched pairs of translations for Alt and Meta:

```
...
Ctrl Alt <KeyPress>osfDelete: cut-primary()
Ctrl Meta <KeyPress>osfDelete: cut-primary()
...
```

You should not use Mod1 to Mod5, as the user cannot easily identify the corresponding physical keys (whereas there is usually someone around who knows which the Meta key is).

The translation manager also understands some special modifier names which do not correspond to keys, but alter the interpretation of the rest of the modifier list.

Table 11.1 shows the safest modifiers, as understood by the translation manager. The translation manager lets you abbreviate the modifier names as shown.

The modifier list consists of a space-separated list of modifier names. The named modifiers must be down at the time of the key event for the translation to take effect.

---

1. Even in an IBM environment, it is usually straightforward to identify Shift, Lock and Ctrl.

Table 11.1 *Modifier names*

Modifier name	Abbreviation	Description
Ctrl	c	Key held down
Lock	l	Caps lock is in effect
Shift	s	Key held down
Alt	a	Key (if any) held down
Meta	m	Key (if any) held down
Button1		Button held down
Button2		Button held down
Button3		Button held down
~		Next modifier in the list must not be pressed
!		Modifiers not in the list must not be pressed
:		Case of keysyms matters
None		No modifiers are allowed

If the modifier list is omitted, the state of the modifiers is unimportant:

> <KeyPress>Q matches 'Q', 'Ctrl-Q', 'Shift-Meta-Q', etc.

If a particular modifier is not mentioned in the list, its state is unimportant:

> Ctrl<KeyPress>Q matches 'Ctrl-Q', 'Ctrl-Meta-Q', 'Ctrl-Alt-Meta-Q',...

You can specify multiple modifiers in the modifier list:

> Ctrl Meta <KeyPress>Q matches 'Ctrl-Meta-Q', but not 'Ctrl-Q' or 'Meta-Q'

To specify that a modifier must not be pressed, precede it with a tilde (~):

> Ctrl ~Meta<KeyPress>Q matches 'Ctrl-Q', but not 'Ctrl-Meta-Q'

To specify that the modifiers pressed must exactly match what you specify, start the modifier list with an exclamation mark (!):

> !Ctrl<KeyPress>Q matches 'Ctrl-Q', but not 'Ctrl-Meta-Q' or 'Ctrl-Q' with a mouse button pressed.

The modifier 'None' means that there must be no modifiers in effect at all:

None<KeyPress>Q matches 'Q', but not 'Ctrl-Q' or 'Alt-Meta-Q', etc.

Normally, translations are not case-sensitive. <KeyPress>Q matches both 'Q' and 'q'. You can specify that a translation is case-sensitive by preceding it with a colon (:):

:<KeyPress>Q matches 'Q', but not 'q'.

Key events

Key events in a translation table use the event names given in Table 11.2.

Table 11.2 *Key event names in translation tables*

Event name	Event type	Description
KeyPress	KeyPress	
Key	KeyPress	
KeyDown	KeyPress	
Ctrl	KeyPress	Same as Ctrl <KeyPress>
Meta	KeyPress	Same as Meta<KeyPress> (but may be buggy)
Shift	KeyPress	Same as Shift <KeyPress>
KeyRelease	KeyRelease	
KeyUp	KeyRelease	

 Most of these are aliases for the X event names <KeyPress> and <KeyRelease>. The event names Ctrl, Shift and Meta are unreliable aliases for 'KeyPress with a modifier key'.

Detail in key events

The detail field after a key event is optional. It is normally used to specify a particular key; if it is omitted, the translation will match irrespective of the key pressed.

The detail should be a keysym or an OSF keysym. Keysyms are defined in <X11/keysymdef.h> and represent the symbols you might find engraved on the keys of a keyboard:

```
#define XK_ampersand  0x026
#define XK_plus       0x02b
#define XK_A          0x041
#define XK_a          0x061
```

```
#define XK_agrave      0x0e0
#define XK_aogonek     0x1b1
#define XK_approximate 0x8c8
#define XK_fivesixths     0xab7
```

There are keysyms for the usual alphanumeric characters and punctuation, for function keys, for languages other than English and for special symbols used in technical contexts and publishing. Fortunately (unless you are writing an application for technical publishing in Hebrew) you only deal with a restricted subset.

When you use a keysym as the detail for a translation you omit the prefix 'XK_'. As the keysym for, say, 'a' is XK_a, this leads to the translation <KeyPress>a (or just <Key>a) as a way of detecting a press on the 'a' key. Similarly, you can detect a press on the '+' key (keysym XK_plus) with the translation <Key>plus.

There are also keysyms defined for function keys and for keys that are labelled with words, like XK_Delete. Unfortunately, some of the standard keysyms, like XK_Delete, cannot be used in Motif applications; you have to use the equivalent OSF keysyms instead. Rather than the translation:

```
<Key>Delete:      do-my-delete-action()
```

you need:

```
<Key>osfDelete:  do-my-delete-action()
```

The only trick is knowing where to use an OSF keysym rather than a real one. Table 11.3 shows all the OSF keysyms (at the time of writing). Section 12.7.3 describes the OSF keysyms in more detail.

Table 11.3 *OSF keysyms*

osfActivate	osfAddMode	osfBackSpace	osfBeginLine
osfCancel	osfClear	osfCopy	osfCut
osfDelete	osfDown	osfEndLine	osfHelp
osfInsert	osfLeft	osfMenu	osfMenuBar
osfPageDown	osfPageLeft	osfPageRight	osfPageUp
osfPaste	osfPrimaryPaste	osfQuickPaste	osfRight
osfSelect	osfUndo	osfUp	

11.3.2   Button events

In button events, the modifier list, event, detail and count can all be used. A typical translation might be:

Shift<Btn1Down>(2): do-double-shifted()

Modifier list

The modifier list for button events is identical to that for key events:

Ctrl Shift <Btn1Down> matches a press of Button1 when the Ctrl and Shift keys are both being held down.

Mouse buttons can be specified in the modifier. This gives a reasonably neat way of detecting combinations of buttons:

Button1 <Btn2Down>: both-buttons()
Button2 <Btn1Down>: both-buttons()

will invoke the action when both mouse buttons are pressed, in whatever order.

If you use modifier keys in the modifier list, you should restrict these to the common subset and have duplicate entries for Alt and Meta, as for key events.

Button events

The event field in a button event is usually used to define both the event (ButtonPress or ButtonRelease) and the detail - the particular button you are interested in. Table 11.4 gives a complete list of the event names usually used to detect button events.

Detail in button events

The detail in button events can be used with the event names BtnDown and BtnUp to specify a particular mouse button. That is, you can write <BtnDown>Button1 instead of <Btn1Down>.

 Button event detail is not reliable; it is safer (and easier) to use the event names in Table 11.4.

Count

The count field is used to detect multiple mouse clicks. It interacts in various non-obvious ways with single mouse clicks and pointer motion, so has to be used with care.

Table 11.4 *Button event names in translation tables*

Event name	Event type	Description
BtnDown	ButtonPress	Any button
Btn1Down	ButtonPress	Button1 pressed
Btn2Down	ButtonPress	Button2 pressed
Btn3Down	ButtonPress	Button3 pressed
Btn4Down	ButtonPress	Button4 pressed
Btn5Down	ButtonPress	Button5 pressed
BtnUp	ButtonRelease	Any button
Btn1Up	ButtonRelease	Button1 released
Btn2Up	ButtonRelease	Button2 released
Btn3Up	ButtonRelease	Button3 released
Btn4Up	ButtonRelease	Button4 released
Btn5Up	ButtonRelease	Button5 released

The event specification:

    `<Btn1Up>(2)`

is equivalent to:

    `<Btn1Down>,<Btn1Up>,<Btn1Down>,<Btn1Up>`

The event specification:

    `<Btn1Down>(2)`

is equivalent to:

    `<Btn1Down>,<Btn1Up>,<Btn1Down>`

In other words, the first matches the second button up of a double click and the second matches the second button down. The interval between clicks must be less than the multi-click time of the display (set using XtSetMultiClickTime() and defaulted to 200 ms).

You can specify a larger count (up to nine), and a count like (3+) means three or more clicks.

Multi-click examples

Suppose we have registered an action routine hello(), which just prints out its single text parameter (this is two lines of code, and worth doing yourself if you want to understand button translations). We can then use it to test the translations needed to detect multiple clicks. For instance, suppose the translations for a widget are replaced with this set:

```
<Btn1Down>,<Btn1Up>:  hello(one)
<Btn1Up>(2):          hello(two)
<Btn1Up>(3+):         hello(three)
```

The widget will then respond to multiple clicks (on the button up), as follows:

*   One click: one.
*   Two clicks: one two.
*   Three clicks: one two three.
*   Four clicks: one two three three.

The first point to note is that a double click also invokes the single click action and three (or more) invoke the single, double and triple click actions. There is no way that the translation manager can be persuaded not to invoke the single click action if the user is intending to click again; its crystal ball is sadly defective. If you need separate single and double click actions, you should design them so that the single click action is some subset of the double click one.

The second point is that the event specification for the single click has to be as shown: <Btn1Up>: hello(one) does not work. This is because of the way the translation manager treats translations which share a common event sequence. If a translation's event sequence is also a *non-initial* part of the event sequence of another translation, it is not taken if it occurs in the context of the second translation. The double click translation event sequence, <Btn1Up>(2), is expanded to:

```
<Btn1Down>,<Btn1Up>,<Btn1Down>,<Btn1Up>
```

The single click event sequence <Btn1Up> will not be taken if the <Btn1Up> event occurs immediately after a <Btn1Down> event (the usual case), as this matches the first part of the double click event sequence. However, <Btn1Down>,<Btn1Up> does work as a single click event sequence, because it is the same as the *initial* part of the double click event sequence; in this case, the translation manager invokes the single click action on the first button up, but remembers that it has matched the first half of the double click event sequence and needs only a second single click to complete the match.

A similar set of translations to trigger the action on the button down event is:

```
<Btn1Down>:      hello(one)
<Btn1Down>(2):   hello(two)
<Btn1Down>(3+): hello(three)
```

In this case, the single click event specification is uniform with the others.

Button clicks and motion events

The user is quite likely to jiggle the mouse while clicking a button, so the translation manager will often receive an event sequence <ButtonPress>, <Motion-Notify>, <ButtonRelease> instead of just the ButtonPress and ButtonRelease events. To cope with this, the translation manager will ignore MotionNotify events if it thinks that it may be in the middle of receiving a sequence of events (usually, but not necessarily, a sequence of button events). If a widget has translations for, say, two or more clicks on Button1 and you add an additional translation for button motion, the resulting translation table might look like this:

```
<Btn1Down>(2+): do-some-widget-action()
<BtnMotion>:       do-my-action()
```

This will detect pointer motion when Button2 or Button3 is pressed. However, if Button1 is pressed, the translation manager thinks that it might be the start of a double click and starts ignoring MotionNotify events. It will stay in this state until it is thoroughly well convinced that the next non-motion event is not going to match the double click on Button1; for instance, it will start to take note of MotionNotify events again if it receives a ButtonPress on Button2 or Button3.

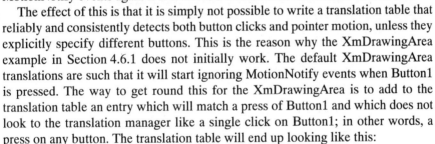 The effect of this is that it is simply not possible to write a translation table that reliably and consistently detects both button clicks and pointer motion, unless they explicitly specify different buttons. This is the reason why the XmDrawingArea example in Section 4.6.1 does not initially work. The default XmDrawingArea translations are such that it will start ignoring MotionNotify events when Button1 is pressed. The way to get round this for the XmDrawingArea is to add to the translation table an entry which will match a press of Button1 and which does not look to the translation manager like a single click on Button1; in other words, a press on any button. The translation table will end up looking like this:

```
<BtnDown>:        noop()
<Btn1Down>(2+): do-some-widget-action()
<BtnMotion>:       do-my-action()
```

In this case, the translation on <BtnDown> swallows the Button1 presses and effectively disables the translation on <Btn1Down>(2+). The double click will no longer be detected, but the MotionNotify events will not be ignored.

If you need to respond to both button clicks and pointer motion with the same or no buttons, the easiest solution is to use translations for the button clicks and an event handler for the pointer motion. You can check the state of the modifiers in an event handler by inspecting the state field of the XButtonEvent structure.

11.3.3 Motion events

Motion events in translations are relatively simple. The modifier list and event are commonly used. The count can be used, but has little meaning. If the event is MotionNotify or one of its aliases, the detail field can be used to distinguish pointer motion hints from ordinary pointer motion events;[1] if the event is BtnMotion or Btn[1-5]Motion, no detail field is allowed. A typical translation is:

> Ctrl <Btn3Motion>: drag-sideways()

Modifier list

The modifier list is the same as for key and button events and can specify both key and mouse button modifiers. However, it is more common (and perhaps clearer) to use the modifier list for key modifiers and the event for the button modifiers: Meta <Btn1Motion> rather than Meta Button1 <Motion>.

Motion events

The motion event field can specify motion with no, any or one particular mouse button pressed. Table 11.5 shows the event names.

Table 11.5 *Motion event names in translation tables*

Event name	Description
MotionNotify Motion PtrMoved MouseMoved	Motion with any or no buttons pressed. Can specify detail field as 'Normal' or 'Hint'
BtnMotion	Motion with any button pressed
Btn1Motion	Motion with button 1 pressed
Btn2Motion	Motion with button 2 pressed
Btn3Motion	Motion with button 3 pressed
Btn4Motion	Motion with button 4 pressed
Btn5Motion	Motion with button 5 pressed

---

1. See PointerMotionHintMask in any good Xlib book.

11.3.4 Translations for other event types

Translations for other types of event are mostly straightforward.

You can only use the modifier fields with EnterNotify and LeaveNotify events (as only those events and the device events report the modifier state on the event structure).

A few of the event types can be used with detail fields. These are described in Table 11.6.

Table 11.6 *Other event names in translation tables*

Event name	Event type	Notes
CirculateNotify Circ	CirculateNotify	
CirculateRequest CircReq	CirculateRequest	
ClientMessage Message	ClientMessage	Detail is name of an atom to match against event.xclient.message_type.
ColormapNotify Clrmap	ColormapNotify	
ConfigureNotify Configure	ConfigureNotify	
ConfigureRequest ConfigureReq	ConfigureRequest	
CreateNotify Create	CreateNotify	
DestroyNotify Destroy	DestroyNotify	
EnterNotify Enter EnterWindow	EnterNotify	Can use modifier field. Detail can be 'Normal', 'Grab', 'Ungrab' or 'WhileGrabbed'.
Expose	Expose	
FocusIn	FocusIn	Detail can be 'Normal', 'Grab', 'Ungrab' or 'WhileGrabbed'.
FocusOut	FocusOut	Detail can be 'Normal', 'Grab', 'Ungrab' or 'WhileGrabbed'.
GraphicsExpose GrExp	GraphicsExpose	

Table 11.6 (cont.) *Other event names in translation tables*

Event name	Event type	Notes
GravityNotify Grav	GravityNotify	
KeymapNotify Keymap	KeymapNotify	
LeaveNotify Leave LeaveWindow	LeaveNotify	Can use modifier field. Detail can be 'Normal', 'Grab', Ungrab' or 'WhileGrabbed'.
MapNotify Map	MapNotify	
MappingNotify Mapping	MappingNotify	Detail can be 'Modifier', 'Keyboard' or 'Pointer'.
MapRequest MapReq	MapRequest	
NoExpose NoExp	NoExpose	
PropertyNotify Prop	PropertyNotify	Detail is name of an atom to match against event.xproperty.atom.
ReparentNotify Reparent	ReparentNotify	
ResizeRequest ResReq	ResizeRequest	
SelectionClear SelClr	SelectionClear	Detail is name of an atom to match against event.xselectionclear.selection.
SelectionNotify Select	SelectionNotify	Detail is name of an atom to match against event.xselection.selection.
SelectionRequest SelReq	SelectionRequest	Detail is name of an atom to match against event.xselectionrequest.selection.
UnmapNotify UnMap	UnmapNotify	
VisibilityNotify Visible	VisibilityNotify	

11.4 Accelerators

Translations allow you to specify that an action will be invoked when a given sequence of events occurs on a widget. The translation manager searches for the action routine in the widget's action table and, if necessary, the global action table and passes as a parameter to the action routine the widget on which the event occurred. Loosely, the action happens on the same widget as the events which invoked it.

Xt provides accelerators that allow you to specify that an action should occur on one widget in response to a sequence of events on some other widget. The Xt accelerator mechanism uses accelerator tables that have an identical format to translation tables and are parsed in a similar way.

It is important to distinguish between the Xt accelerators and the Motif toolkit menu accelerators. The Motif menu accelerator is set in the accelerator resource of a button widget (XmPushButton or XmToggleButton) whose parent is a pulldown or popup MenuPane. It specifies a string that represents a key event used to invoke the menu item from anywhere in the application. Xt accelerators are set using the accelerators resource. They are much more general and can be used on any widget. Where the Motif menu accelerator is a key event, the Xt accelerator can be any event sequence, just like a translation.

Even though the Xt accelerators offer a superset of the Motif menu accelerator functionality, the Motif menu accelerators are actually implemented by the toolkit installing passive grabs and event handlers in all sorts of places. This is because the Xt accelerators interact with translations and other event handling mechanisms and their behaviour is, in general, hard to predict. In a particular, known application it is possible to use the Xt accelerators profitably, but there are many pitfalls.

The following two sections describe some of the known problems. They should be enough to convince you that Xt accelerators and Motif do not mix well, so we do not give an example. You can find examples in most Xt books, but be aware that you are likely to have to modify them substantially before they will work with recent versions of Motif.

11.4.1 Accelerators and translations

Accelerators are specified using the same syntax as translations. The accelerator table is parsed and used to set the accelerators resource on the widget whose actions are to be invoked. The accelerators must then be installed onto all the widgets which are to detect the events. This is illustrated by Figure 11.1.

Accelerators work by adding extra entries to the translation tables of the widgets which are to detect the events. The terminology is based on this; the widget whose actions are to be invoked (the one on which XmNaccelerators is set) is called the source widget and the widgets which detect the events are called destination

Source widget   Destination widget

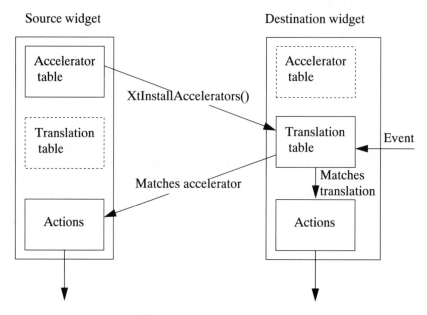

Figure 11.1 *Xt accelerators*

widgets. The source widget's accelerator table is used to modify the destination widgets' translation tables.

When an event arrives, the translation manager looks at the translation table of the widget whose window is specified. If it matches an ordinary entry, the action specified in that widget's action table is invoked. If it matches an accelerator entry, the action belonging to the source widget is invoked. The translation manager uses its normal algorithm to determine which translation table entry matches, so only one action routine (either local or on the source widget) will be invoked and all the problems of translation table ordering and interaction still apply. However, where it may be tricky to find a way of augmenting a single widget's translation table so as to add extra behaviour without disturbing its normal operation, it can be virtually impossible to find an accelerator table that can safely and effectively be installed on multiple destination widgets, each with a different translation table already in place.

11.4.2   Accelerators and event propagation

An accelerator table has to be installed on every widget that is to detect the events. Most accelerators are intended to detect device events - keyboard and mouse events - and, with most toolkits, can rely on device event propagation to reduce the number of destination widgets that the application needs to deal with.

When a device event occurs on a window, the X server checks to see if any client process has selected for that event on the window. If so, it reports the event to the client (possibly many clients). If not, it checks to see if the do_not_propagate mask attribute of the window includes the event type, discarding the event if this is so. If it has not found a client for the event and has not been told not to propagate it, it then moves up to the parent window and tries the same procedure. It repeats this all the way up the hierarchy until it finds a taker for the event or a window with the do_not_propagate mask set.

If an application wants to detect, say, 'Ctrl-A' happening somewhere in a dialog, it can set up the appropriate accelerator table and install it on a single widget - the one at the root of the dialog's hierarchy. If a key event occurs anywhere in the hierarchy, it will normally be propagated up to the root, and the accelerator will invoke the action required. Of course, if the event happens in, say, a text entry widget which selects for key events, it will not be propagated to the root, but will be reported to the text entry widget instead. The application may have to install the accelerator on such widgets explicitly, but can still use the event propagation for most of them.

In the Motif toolkit, alas, things are not so simple. Many widgets - even those that do not respond to keyboard input themselves - have translations to detect certain key events. For instance, all primitive widgets have translations for KActivate. The translation manager will select for KeyPress events (at least) on the windows of all such widgets and the X server will never propagate them (Motif propagates them up the widget hierarchy instead, using a private, undocumented, toolkit-specific technique).

There is a similar problem with mouse events. As if this were not enough, some of the Motif widgets set the do_not_propagate mask to disable all device event propagation. In effect, Motif disables much of the X event propagation which is used to simplify the installation of accelerators; an application has to install most accelerators on every widget, which is awkward and error-prone.

11.4.3 General keyboard accelerators

The Xt accelerator mechanism and Motif do not mix well. However, it is possible to use Xlib grabs and event handlers to detect and respond to device events that occur anywhere in a widget hierarchy. As an example, this section describes how to implement keyboard accelerators for XmPushButton widgets. This is a simplified form of the technique used by Motif for menu accelerators. Although the techniques needed to implement this are not described until later (Section 12.6 and Section 17.1), we present the code here in a form that can be used without having to understand the mechanisms.

The Motif toolkit allows you to specify keyboard accelerators for items in menus. When the user presses the appropriate keyboard combination (provided the

MenuBar's shell has the input focus), the ArmAndActivate action for the menu item button is invoked.

Motif only supports this behaviour for menu items, not for XmPushButtons in general. If you need a keyboard accelerator for a XmPushButton in a form, say, the usual recipe is to have a copy of the XmPushButton hidden in a menu somewhere. This is expensive as well as inelegant.

You can get round this problem by using a passive grab. When the keyboard event occurs, the X server first searches from the root window down to try and find a passive grab to activate. If there is a suitable passive grab, the keyboard event is reported to the grabbing window (rather than some descendant Motif widget's window), so the Motif toolkit never gets a chance to interfere with the event propagation. The passive grab should be on the highest appropriate window; the window belonging to the XmPushButton's shell ancestor is usually appropriate.

The passive grab will ensure that the keyboard event is reported to the shell widget even if it happens over some distant descendant. The final part of the trick is to invoke the XmPushButton's ArmAndActivate action in response. This could be done with an Xt accelerator, but this mechanism needs the event specified in translation table syntax, whereas the passive grab is defined in terms of keycodes and modifiers. Translating one to the other is tedious and it is easier to use a single low-level description and use an event handler to test incoming keyboard events against the keycode and modifiers, invoking the XmPushButton's actions when appropriate. As keycodes are device-dependent, the appropriate description is in terms of keysyms and modifiers.

To set up the passive grab and event handler on the shell requires little code:

accelerators

```
#include <Xm/Xm.h>

/* Structure used to pass details of the accelerator to the event handler */
typedef struct {
    KeyCode     keycode;
    Modifiers   modifiers;
    Widget      pushbutton;
} accel_key_t, *accel_key_p;

void handle_accel();

void install_accelerator (shell, keysym, modifiers, pushbutton)
    Widget      shell;
    KeySym      keysym;
    Modifiers   modifiers;
    Widget      pushbutton;
{
    KeyCode         keycode;
    accel_key_p     accel;
```

```
/* Convert keysym to keycode and set up passive grab on shell */
    keycode = XKeysymToKeycode (XtDisplay (shell), keysym);
    if (keycode == 0)
        return; /* with error message */
    XtGrabKey (shell, keycode, modifiers, False, GrabModeAsync,
                    GrabModeAsync);


/* Set up event handler on shell */
    accel = (accel_key_p) XtMalloc (sizeof (accel_key_t));
    accel->keycode = keycode;
    accel->modifiers = modifiers;
    accel->pushbutton = pushbutton;
    XtAddEventHandler (shell, KeyPressMask, False, handle_accel,
                    (XtPointer) accel);
}
```

Notice that we use XKeysymToKeycode() to convert from the keysym specified to the keycode required for the passive grab and the event handler. This is something of a shortcut, as the default X server keycode to keysym mapping may be overridden by Motif's key translator. However, it will work for keysyms that are known to the X server. Like the Motif menu accelerators, it does not work with the OSF keysyms. We have also assumed that there is only one keycode for a given keysym, which is not always true. Again, this example is consistent with the Motif toolkit; it works with alphabetic accelerators. A more general mechanism would use XtKeysymToKeycodeList(), adding a grab for each keycode that corresponds to the keysym.

The event handler just checks to see if the KeyPress event corresponds to the accelerator key combination and invokes the XmPushButton's action if this is so. Note the use of the client data to pass in the accelerator details:

```
void handle_accel (widget, client_data, event, cont)
    Widget      widget;
    XtPointer   client_data;
    XEvent      *event;
    Boolean     *cont;
{
/* Check that we have the right key combination */
    accel_key_p accel=(accel_key_p)client_data;
    if ((event->xkey.state == accel->modifiers)
      && (event->xkey.keycode == accel->keycode))
        XtCallActionProc(accel->pushbutton, "ArmAndActivate", event,
                    NULL, 0);
}
```

The accelerator is installed by a call to install_accelerator():

```
install_accelerator (shell, XK_q, ControlMask | ShiftMask, quitb);
```

The XmPushButton quitb will then have its ArmAndActivate action invoked when the user types 'Ctrl-Shift-q'. Multiple calls to install_accelerator() can be used to add multiple accelerators to a single button.

Note that, unlike translations (but like the Motif menu accelerator), an exact match of the modifiers is required; the action will not trigger on 'Ctrl-Shift-Meta-q'. Some further work would be required to make the accelerators case-insensitive; the grab needs to activate irrespective of the state of the Shift and Lock modifiers (which means adding four passive grabs) and the event handler needs to mask Shift and Lock out of the event's modifier state; this is left as an exercise for the reader.

CHAPTER 12

Event handling

A Motif program works with an event-driven programming model; the program responds to events representing actions of the user. As an application programmer, you normally deal with these events in callback functions invoked by the Xt intrinsics. Sometimes it is useful to drop down a level and handle the raw X events. Even if you do all event handling in callbacks, the information in the X event (which you can access via the call data) can often be useful to you and it helps to know how it should be interpreted.

This chapter contains a great deal of information about event processing. Some of this and in particular the early sections, is background information. The latter part of the chapter gives many examples of ways to detect, interpret, respond to and generate events.

Two topics are not covered here; we assume that you know how to write a callback function and we cover translations in Chapter 11.

12.1 The XEvent data structure

The key to X event handling from the programmer's point of view is the XEvent data structure:

```
typedef union _XEvent {
    int                 type;
    XAnyEvent           xany;
    XKeyEvent           xkey;
    XButtonEvent        xbutton;
    XMotionEvent        xmotion;
    XCrossingEvent      xcrossing;
    ...
} XEvent;
```

Every event returns the information needed to complete an instance of this union. You should access the member of the union appropriate to the type of the event. For instance, if the type of event is ButtonPress or ButtonRelease, you should look at event.xbutton, which has this structure:

```
typedef struct {
    int                 type;
    unsigned long   serial;
    ...
    int                 x, y;
    int                 x_root, y_root;
    unsigned int    state;
    unsigned int    button;    /* detail */
    ...
} XButtonEvent;
```

You can extract useful information from this, like the button that was pressed:

```
if (event.type == ButtonPress)
            printf ("Button %d pressed\n", event.xbutton.button);
```

The interpretation of the fields in each structure is usually straightforward, helped by the comments in <X11/Xlib.h>. For the more arcane events, you should check the Xlib reference documentation.

Notice that the first field in the XButtonEvent structure is the event type, as it must be given that it is overlaid with event.type. In fact, event structures for all types of event have the same first few fields:

```
typedef struct {
    int                 type;
    unsigned long   serial;
    Bool                send_event;
    Display             *display;
    Window              window;
} XAnyEvent;
```

⚠ If you have any event, you can always look at the structure event.xany. However, you must be a bit careful, as there are some event types that do not fill in all the fields of the XAnyEvent structure. Furthermore, any client can create a fake event and send it via XSendEvent(); such events will always have send_event set true, but the rest of the event may be nonsense.

12.2 Event types

There are 33 different types of event, each representing a different user action or other important occurrence. These are (very approximately) described in Table 12.1. The event type is a symbol (defined in <X11/X.h>) that you use to test the type member of the XEvent union. From the type, you can determine the particular member to look at; the name of the relevant member is given in the third column and its structure in the fourth.

Table 12.1 *Event types*

Event type	Description	Member name	Member structure
KeyPress	User has pressed a key	xkey	XKeyEvent
KeyRelease	User has released a key	xkey	XKeyEvent
ButtonPress	User has pressed a mouse button	xbutton	XButtonEvent
ButtonRelease	User has released a mouse button	xbutton	XButtonEvent
MotionNotify	Mouse has moved	xmotion	XMotionEvent
EnterNotify	Mouse has entered a window	xcrossing	XCrossingEvent
LeaveNotify	Mouse has left a window	xcrossing	XCrossingEvent
FocusIn	Window has gained keyboard focus	xfocus	XFocusChangeEvent
FocusOut	Window has lost keyboard focus	xfocus	XFocusChangeEvent
KeymapNotify	Gives state of keys after EnterNotify and FocusIn	xkeymap	XKeymapEvent
Expose	Part of window has become visible	xexpose	XExposeEvent
GraphicsExpose	Part of source area missing when copying area	xgraphicsexpose	XGraphicsExposeEvent
NoExpose	All of source area available when copying area	xnoexpose	XNoExposeEvent

Table 12.1 (cont.) *Event types*

Event type	Description	Member name	Member structure
CirculateNotify	Window has been raised or lowered	xcirculate	XCirculateEvent
ConfigureNotify	Change of size, position, etc., of window	xconfigure	XConfigureEvent
CreateNotify	Subwindow has been created	xcreatewindow	XCreateWindowEvent
DestroyNotify	Window has been destroyed	xdestroywindow	XDestroyWindowEvent
GravityNotify	Child window has moved because parent was resized	xgravity	XGravityEvent
MapNotify	Window has become mapped	xmap	XMapEvent
MappingNotify	Keyboard has been reconfigured	xmapping	XMappingEvent
ReparentNotify	Window has been reparented	xreparent	XReparentEvent
UnmapNotify	Window has become unmapped	xunmap	XUnmapEvent
VisibilityNotify	Window has changed visibility state	xvisibility	XVisibilityEvent
ColormapNotify	Window's colourmap has been changed or (un)installed	xcolormap	XColormapEvent
ClientMessage	Only generated by another client using XSendEvent()	xclient	XClientMessageEvent
PropertyNotify	Property has changed	xproperty	XPropertyEvent
SelectionClear	Application has lost selection ownership	xselectionclear	XSelectionClearEvent
SelectionRequest	Client wants selection conversion	xselectionrequest	XSelectionRequestEvent
SelectionNotify	Selection conversion complete	xselection	XSelectionEvent
CirculateRequest	Attempt to raise or lower a window	xcirculaterequest	XCirculateRequestEvent
ConfigureRequest	Attempt to change size, position, etc., of window	xconfigurerequest	XConfigureRequestEvent
MapRequest	Attempt to map a window	xmaprequest	XMapRequestEvent

Table 12.1 (cont.) *Event types*

Event type	Description	Member name	Member structure
ResizeRequest	Attempt to change size of window	xresizerequest	XResizeRequestEvent

For instance, you might test an event like this:

```
switch (event.type)
{
    case KeyPress:
        code=event.xkey.keycode;   /*keycode is in XKeyEvent structure*/
        break;
    case MotionNotify:
        pos_x=event.xmotion.x;     /*x, y are in XMotionEvent structure*/
        pos_y=event.xmotion.y;
        break;
    ...
}
```

In practice, you usually find Xlib programmers pass a pointer to the XEvent structure, rather than the structure itself. Rather than accessing a member of the union, they may sometimes cast the event pointer to a pointer to the member structure:

```
if (event->type == MappingNotify)
    XRefreshKeyboardMapping ((XMappingEvent *) event);
```

This is not best practice; all the MIT sources do it properly and with fewer keystrokes:

```
if (event->type == MappingNotify)
    XRefreshKeyboardMapping (&event->xmapping);
```

Some events report actions of the user, such as moving the mouse. Others can be generated as an effect of requests to the server. If you map a window using XMapWindow(), you will get back a MapNotify event. If another client unmaps one of its windows, you may get an Expose event on one of yours.

If you develop applications using Motif, the toolkit takes care of responding to many types of event, perhaps invoking callback functions as part of this response. In particular, you do not have to get involved in tedious processing of Expose events on buttons, labels and so on, nor with boilerplate code to handle events like MappingNotify. However, the toolkit is limited; its support for graphical input and output is restricted to a few simple widgets like XmScrollBar. If you need to draw pictures, you may need to get involved in Expose event processing. If you want the user to be able to manipulate the pictures, drawing new bits or dragging things with the mouse, you will have to process pointer events.

12.3   Event masks

An application does not get told about all events on all its windows; this would involve so many events that any affordable network would grind to a halt. Rather, an application must tell the X server in advance that it is interested in certain sorts of event on certain windows under certain circumstances, by selecting for those events. This is done by specifying an event mask for each window. The event mask is set when the window is created, but can be changed at any time.

Table 12.2 shows the event masks that can be used to select for certain types of events, ordered by event type.

Table 12.2 *Event types and event masks*

Event type	Event mask	Notes
No events	NoEventMask	
ButtonPress	ButtonPressMask	
ButtonRelease	ButtonReleaseMask	
CirculateNotify	StructureNotifyMask	
CirculateNotify	SubstructureNotifyMask	Selects for event on any child
CirculateRequest	SubstructureRedirectMask	For use by window managers
ClientMessage	Non-maskable	
ColormapNotify	ColormapChangeMask	
ConfigureNotify	StructureNotifyMask	
ConfigureNotify	SubstructureNotifyMask	Selects for event on any child
ConfigureRequest	SubstructureRedirectMask	For use by window managers
CreateNotify	SubstructureNotifyMask	Selects for event on any child
DestroyNotify	StructureNotifyMask	
DestroyNotify	SubstructureNotifyMask	Selects for event on any child
EnterNotify	EnterWindowMask	
Expose	ExposureMask	
FocusIn	FocusChangeMask	

Table 12.2 (cont.) *Event types and event masks*

Event type	Event mask	Notes
FocusOut	FocusChangeMask	
GraphicsExpose	GCGraphicsExposures in GC	
GravityNotify	StructureNotifyMask	
GravityNotify	SubstructureNotifyMask	Selects for event on any child
KeyPress	KeyPressMask	
KeyRelease	KeyReleaseMask	
KeymapNotify	KeymapStateMask	
LeaveNotify	LeaveWindowMask	
MapNotify	StructureNotifyMask	
MapNotify	SubstructureNotifyMask	Selects for event on any child
MapRequest	SubstructureRedirectMask	For use by window managers
MappingNotify	Non-maskable	
MotionNotify	Button1MotionMask	When button 1 pressed
MotionNotify	Button2MotionMask	When button 2 pressed
MotionNotify	Button3MotionMask	When button 3 pressed
MotionNotify	Button4MotionMask	When button 4 pressed
MotionNotify	Button5MotionMask	When button 5 pressed
MotionNotify	ButtonMotionMask	When any button pressed
MotionNotify	PointerMotionMask	When any or no buttons pressed
MotionNotify	PointerMotionHintMask	Used to discard uninteresting pointer motion events
NoExpose	GCGraphicsExposures in GC	
PropertyNotify	PropertyChangeMask	
ReparentNotify	StructureNotifyMask	
ReparentNotify	SubstructureNotifyMask	Selects for event on any child
ResizeRequest	ResizeRedirectMask	
SelectionClear	Non-maskable	
SelectionNotify	Non-maskable	
SelectionRequest	Non-maskable	

Table 12.2 (cont.) *Event types and event masks*

Event type	Event mask	Notes
UnmapNotify	StructureNotifyMask	
UnmapNotify	SubstructureNotifyMask	Selects for event on any child
VisibilityNotify	VisibilityChangeMask	
VisibilityNotify	OwnerGrabButtonMask	Affects event processing during automatic grabs

A single event mask (e.g. StructureNotifyMask) may select for a number of different event types. Similarly, a single event type (e.g. MotionNotify) can be selected by a number of different event masks; the different masks report the events under different circumstances. If you OR two event masks together, you select for all the event types selected for by either.

Most event masks select for events on a particular window. The SubstructureNotifyMask selects for events that happen on any child of a given window (even if the children do not exist at the time the event mask is set).

The SubstructureRedirect mask is mostly used by window managers. It is briefly described in Section 14.1.1.

The PointerMotionHintMask does not select for any event, but can be used with other pointer motion masks. It reduces network traffic by discarding many of the motion events, reporting only 'interesting' ones. It is useful if you do not need to know all the intermediate positions of the mouse, but only the position where it comes to rest and positions when the user presses or releases buttons or keys.

For a discussion of the OwnerGrabButtonMask see Section 17.1.3.

GraphicsExpose and NoExpose events are only produced during certain operations that copy an area from one window to another. You select for these by setting a flag in the graphics context you use in the copy operation. This is covered in Section 7.4.3.

Finally, there are some events that are non-maskable; the X server will always tell you about them, even if you have selected for no events. These are mostly used for handling selections (a sort of cut and paste mechanism), described in Chapter 18.

12.4 Toolkit event processing

If you write applications using Motif (or another Xt-based toolkit), events are processed by a call to XtAppMainLoop() or equivalently by an infinite loop that calls XtAppNextEvent() to get each event and XtDispatchEvent() to send the events on to the functions that handle them:

```
for (;;) {
    XtAppNextEvent (app_context, &event);
    XtDispatchEvent (&event);
}
```

XtAppNextEvent() is similar to the Xlib function XNextEvent(), but it can handle input from multiple displays as well as alternate input sources, timers and workprocs (these are described below). The list of displays from which it will handle events is in the application context.

XtDispatchEvent() passes events on to event handlers that have been registered for particular events and to the translation manager (this description is conceptual; the implementation may be completely different and the order in which things happen is not guaranteed).

Figure 12.1 shows the Xt event processing in outline.

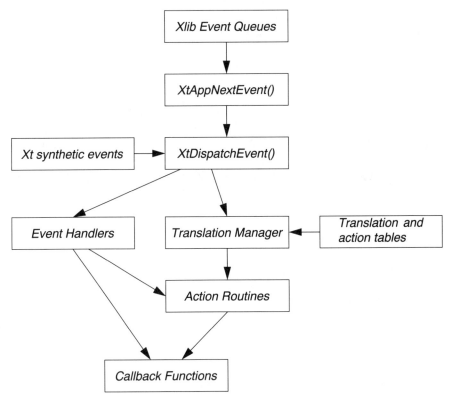

Figure 12.1 *X toolkit event processing*

 Note that, as well as events received from the Xlib event queues, Xt itself generates some fake (or synthetic) events, and pushes them into the event dispatching mechanism. This is mainly of interest when dealing with FocusIn and FocusOut events, as described in Section 13.3.

Events are passed to event handlers and the translation manager. Event handlers are functions which receive events that occur on a given window and match a particular event mask. Event handlers are widely used by widget writers, but can also be used by application writers. An event handler is invoked every time an event that matches the mask occurs on the window.

Sometimes you want to respond, not to any event that matches a mask, but to an event with some particular detail value (KeyPress on key 'a', rather than any KeyPress) or to a sequence of such events (double click on Button1). You can do this with suitable event handlers, but the requirement is so common that Xt provides support in the form of translations. A translation is simply a definition of a sequence of events, including detail like the key on a KeyPress, together with the name of an action to perform when the event sequence is detected. Most widgets have a number of predefined actions which are commonly used in translations. The translation manager monitors the incoming event stream and invokes action routines when it finds an event sequence that matches a widget's translation table. This is described in Chapter 11.

What an event handler or action routine does is entirely up to its author. Event handlers in a widget may call action routines and both may call the functions on a widget's callback lists.

With few exceptions, Xt does not invoke callback functions itself. They are invoked by widget code and the widget code is invoked in response to events via event handlers or (more usually) action routines. Of course, invoking the convenience functions for a widget may also call some callbacks. For instance, calling XmScrollBarSetValues() invokes the scroll bar's callbacks. This is done directly by Motif; the Xt event processing mechanisms are not involved.

12.5   Responding to events

There are a number of places that you can respond to events. This does not mean (in general) that you stop them going any further, just that you have a chance to act on them. For instance, registering an event handler for an event does not stop the translation manager (or other event handlers) from seeing it.

You can put code to respond to an event:

- In an event handler.
- In an action routine called via a translation.
- In a callback.

The choice is part of your design freedom, which is to say it is yet one more thing to think about. Some points to consider:

• Event handlers are the most efficient and may be necessary for handling high-volume events.

• It is easy to remove an event handler, but not so easy to disable or remove the translation table entry that calls an action routine. Event handlers that remove themselves are useful for initialising things on the first occurrence of an event.

• Event handlers are non-invasive. Registering an event handler does not change a widget in any way, whereas changing a widget's translation table to use new actions may disable some of its existing behaviour.

• You cannot use a translation table to detect both general pointer motion and multiple button clicks.

• Translation tables can be customised in a resource file; event handlers are hard-coded.

• The call data provided by a widget to a callback function can be much more informative than the event information.

• Everyone understands callbacks.

You can also put event handling code between XtAppNextEvent() and XtDispatchEvent(). If the code is just responding to an event, this is unnecessary; an event handler will do the job more cleanly. The usual reason for doing this is to prevent some events ever reaching XtDispatchEvent() so as to make the behaviour of your application modal in some way. This is described in Section 12.9.

12.6 Event handlers

Event handlers provide an efficient, unobtrusive way of responding to events and are particularly well suited to high-volume events. On the other hand, a translation and associated action routine can do almost anything that an event handler can and may be easier to maintain.

12.6.1 Registering an event handler

An event handler is a function like a callback function, but it receives slightly different parameters. Where a callback function is registered for a widget using XtAddCallback(), you register an event handler with XtAddEventHandler():

```
void XtAddEventHandler(widget, event_mask, nonmaskable, handler,
                       client_data)
Widget            widget;
EventMask         event_mask;
Boolean           nonmaskable;
XtEventHandler    handler;
XtPointer         client_data;
```

The widget is the widget whose events are wanted. Those events that would be selected for by event_mask will be reported to the event handler function handler. The event mask is formed by ORing together the mask symbols in Table 12.2.

If nonmaskable is true, the event handler will also get the non-maskable events: ClientMessage, GraphicsExpose, MappingNotify, NoExpose, SelectionClear, SelectionNotify and SelectionRequest. This is almost always set False, as these events are rarely wanted.

The client_data is a pointer just like the client data for a callback function. As with callback functions, you can use the same event handler on many widgets (with different event masks) and use the client data to pass in extra context so that it can work out what to do.

If there are multiple event handlers on a widget, the order in which they are called is undefined. The function XtInsertEventHandler() allows you to add an event handler that becomes the first or last to be called for a widget. However, there is no guarantee that it will remain the first or last; the Motif toolkit adds and inserts event handlers whenever the spirit moves it.

Adding an event handler will normally cause Xt to select for the events in the event mask on the widget's window. It is possible to add an event handler without changing the selected events using XtAddRawEventHandler(). This will not get called until something happens that does select for the events (like adding another event handler) and so will initially lie dormant. It can be used, for instance, to install an event handler that shadows another, logging all the events that it receives. The shadow event handler can be added at any time, but only receives events when the primary event handler is added.

 Because toolkits and applications may take actions that change the event mask at any time, adding a raw event handler is a chancy business and should be avoided in normal code.

12.6.2   Event handler functions

A typical event handler looks like this:

```
void event_handler (widget, client_data, event, continue_to_dispatch)
Widget      widget;
XtPointer   client_data;
XEvent      *event;
Boolean     *continue_to_dispatch;
```

The widget and client_data parameters are as for a callback function. Instead of call data, an event handler receives a pointer to the XEvent structure for the event.

The Boolean *continue_to_dispatch is set true before the event handler is invoked. If the event handler sets it to be False, no more event handlers will be called for this particular event and it will not be passed to the translation manager;

in other words, there will be no further processing for this particular event. However, since an unknown number of toolkit event handlers may already have been invoked to deal with the event, setting this flag False may leave things in an inconsistent state.

12.6.3   Event handler example

This simple event handler example is essentially the same as the action routine example in Section 11.2.3 (moving a label round a drawing area by dragging with the mouse), but uses an event handler rather than an action routine.

The code to create the widget hierarchy is essentially the same as before. Instead of adding an action routine, we have to register an event handler:

The event handler can be registered as soon as the XmLabel widget is created:

```
extern void handle_drag();
...
```

eventhdlr

```
XtAddEventHandler (drag_label, ButtonPressMask|Button1MotionMask,
                   False, handle_drag, NULL);
```

The event mask ensures that we will get all ButtonPress events and any MotionNotify events when Button1 is pressed.

The event handler function is remarkably simple:

```
#include <Xm/Label.h>

void handle_drag (widget, client_data, event, cont)
    Widget      widget;
    XtPointer   client_data;
    XEvent      *event;
    Boolean     *cont;
{
/* Handle dragging of a label in a drawing area */

    static int  x_offset, y_offset;
    Position  x, y;

    switch (event->type)
    {
        case ButtonPress:
/* Work out the offset used to translate between root window coordinates
(available in the event structures) and the position of top/left of the label and
remember it */
            if (event->xbutton.button != Button1)
```

```
            break;
        XtVaGetValues (widget, XmNx, &x, XmNy, &y, NULL);
        x_offset = (int) x - event->xbutton.x_root;
        y_offset = (int) y - event->xbutton.y_root;
        break;

        case MotionNotify:
/* Mouse has moved, move the label in response */
        x = event->xbutton.x_root + x_offset;
        y = event->xbutton.y_root + y_offset;
        XtVaSetValues (widget, XmNx, x, XmNy, y, NULL);
        break;
    }
    return;
}
```

The event handler relies on the fact that the ButtonPress and MotionNotify events have both the coordinates of the pointer relative to the XmLabel's window (which are no good to us at all, as we keep moving the XmLabel in an attempt to keep these constant) and the coordinates relative to the root window. Provided the parent XmDrawingArea does not move around, we can use the root window coordinates to calculate the x and y position of the XmLabel quite simply. In a real example, you might check on the current position of the parent in root coordinates (using XtTranslateCoords()) before calculating the new position of the XmLabel.

12.7 Keyboard events

Most events are easy to interpret. Interpreting KeyPress and KeyRelease events is more complicated than might reasonably be expected. There are two reasons for this:

- The X keyboard model is designed to support all manner of keyboards, but its flexibility comes at the cost of some complexity.
- Some vendors used the flexibility of the X model unwisely, so the OSF added an extra layer - OSF keysyms - to reassert some basic consistency between vendors.

This section describes the X keyboard model, its use by Xt and the OSF keysyms.

12.7.1   X keyboard model

To enable your program to work with a wide variety of keyboards, X provides three layers of keyboard mapping:

• A *keycode* is an integer that represents a particular key on a keyboard. Keycodes are hardware-dependent and vary between vendors and between different types of keyboard from the same vendor. The KeyPress and KeyRelease events report the keycode; this has to be translated into a hardware-independent form, known as a keysym, before an application can interpret it.
• A *keysym* is an integer representing a symbol engraved on a key - 'a', 'b', 'A', 'B' and so on, but also '+', 'F12', 'Shift', 'PageDn', 'Delete' and the rest. Keysyms are represented by symbolic constants with an 'XK_' prefix. A keycode is mapped to a keysym using a server-wide mapping that takes into account the state of the Shift and Lock modifiers. The default mapping is hard-wired into the server; it can be changed, although it rarely is.
• Those keysyms that represent printable (ASCII) characters can be further translated to yield a *keystring*. The default mapping (hardwired into Xlib) translates, for instance, the keysym XK_a to the keystring 'a'. Any client can change the mapping from keysyms to keystrings. For instance, you can bind the keysym XK_F12 to the keystring 'help'.

An application interprets a key event by translating the keycode in the event into a keysym; if the keysym represents a printable character, it can be translated into a keystring.

In an Xlib program both translations are done using XLookupString(). This uses the keycode and the state of the modifier keys to index into the keyboard mapping table and so derives a keysym. It then translates any printable keysym into the corresponding keystring and returns both the keysym and keystring. If the keysym does not represent a printable character, no keystring is returned.

The mapping from keycodes to keysyms is global to the server. However, to avoid a server round trip for every key event, each client holds a cached copy of this keyboard mapping. If the global server mapping is changed, each client receives a MappingNotifyEvent and must update its cache by calling XRefreshKeyboardMapping(). There is code in XtAppNextEvent() to handle this for you.

The mapping from keysym to keystring is local to an application and can be changed using XRebindKeysym().

Figure 12.2 shows this event processing in outline.

12.7.2   Keyboard events in Xt

Keycodes are hardware-dependent, and therefore essentially useless to application writers. Any X application that makes even a pretence of portability will convert

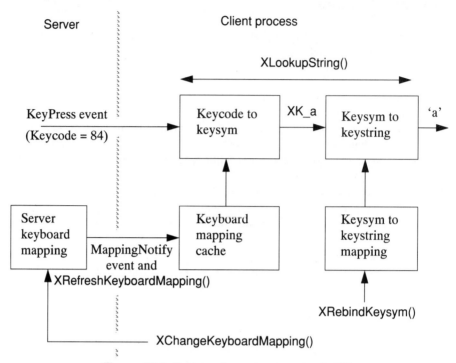

Figure 12.2 *Keyboard event processing in Xlib*

the keycodes in incoming key events to keysyms before deciding how to respond to the event. In particular, Xt translates keycodes to keysyms before attempting to match the incoming events against translation tables, which express key events in terms of keysyms. This is done by a key translator function. The default translator is XtTranslateKey(), which just mimics the operation of XLookupString(). However, an application (or, more pertinently, a toolkit used by an application) can install its own key translator by calling XtSetKeyTranslator().

The key translator is used by Xt to determine the keysym from a key event so that it can be matched against the keysym given in the detail field of a key event in a translation. This adds an extra element to the event-processing mechanism described in Figure 12.3.

An action routine called as a result of a key event does not receive the keysym as a parameter; it gets the event and can determine the keysym from this by calling XtGetActionKeySym(). An application can also (rather less efficiently) translate a keycode to a keysym using XtTranslateKeycode().

Xt does not provide a keysym to keystring translation mechanism. If an Xt application needs a keystring, it uses XLookupString(), just as an Xlib application would.

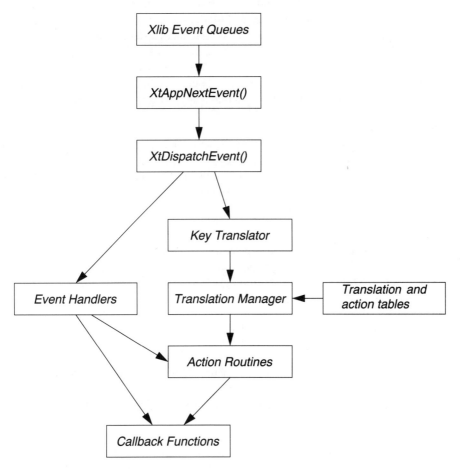

Figure 12.3 *Keyboard event processing in Xt*

12.7.3 OSF keysyms

The X keyboard model is very flexible and allows the server vendor to choose the mapping of physical keys onto keysyms. In a perfect world, all the server vendors would have mapped keys with similar positions and markings onto the same keysyms. For instance, many keyboards have a key at the top right with a left pointing arrow engraved on it and the default server keyboard mapping for most servers maps this key to the keysym XK_BackSpace. However, some vendors map the similarly positioned and marked key to the keysym XK_Delete. The result of this is that a user has to learn a new set of finger mappings to use a server from one of those vendors; this can be annoying.

To get round this, Motif installs a key translator XmTranslateKey() that finesses the default keyboard mapping defined by the server vendor, fixing up the parts of the mapping which different vendors treat inconsistently. It translates certain keycodes on particular servers into a special set of keysyms - the OSF keysyms, also known as the OSF virtual keysyms. This could also have been done by Motif modifying the server's keyboard mapping, but this would have affected other (non-Motif) applications and could have led to a keyboard mapping war.

Virtual modifiers, keys and buttons

As well as the OSF (virtual) keysyms, OSF documentation talks about virtual modifiers, keys and buttons. These really are virtual, in the sense that they are purely used for documentation. For instance, the translations for the XmList widget (as documented) include the following:

```
KActivate: ListKbdActivate()
```

KActivate is a virtual key. It is a documentation shorthand for one or more key events, in this case any one of <Key>Return, Ctrl<Key>Return or <Key>osfActivate (see VirtualBindings(3X)). The translation table for XmList actually includes the following entries:

```
<Key>osfActivate:        ListKbdActivate()\n\
~s ~m ~a <Key>Return:  ListKbdActivate()\n\
```

These translations implement the documented behaviour of the XmList widget in terms of keysyms that the toolkit knows about.

Virtual keys, modifiers and buttons have no significance to the toolkit. They cannot be used in translations and have no purpose other than to reduce (or increase) the amount of paper used to document the toolkit. OSF virtual keysyms, on the other hand, are real, and the toolkit does understand them. To try and reduce the confusion, the OSF no longer talks about *virtual* keysyms in the documentation, but calls them "osf" keysyms. The toolkit source and common usage have yet to catch up with this change.

Effect of OSF keysyms

The Motif key translator is installed when a VendorShell (or subclass) widget is created, so it will be in place by the time any widget events arrive. It is used to translate all key events before the translation manager sees them, so all translations have to be expressed in terms of the OSF keysyms. A full and current list of OSF keysyms can be found in VirtualBindings(3X).

Apart from the effect on translations, the key translator affects the Xt mechanisms used to translate keycodes to keysyms, but not the Xlib ones (Xlib does not use the key translator mechanism). You can see the effect of this by installing an action routine that translates key events, using both Xt and Xlib mechanisms:

keysyms

```
void keys (widget, event, params, num_params)
    Widget   widget;
    XEvent   *event;
    String   *params;
    Cardinal *num_params;
{
    char             strbuf[128];
    int              num_bytes;
    KeySym           ks;
    XComposeStatus   stat;
    Modifiers        mods;

    printf ("Keycode 0x%x modifiers 0x%x\n", event->xkey.keycode,
                    event->xkey.state);
    num_bytes = XLookupString (&(event->xkey), strbuf, 127, &ks, &stat);
    printf ("X keysym 0x%x (%s)\n", ks, XKeysymToString(ks));
    strbuf[num_bytes] = '\0';
    printf ("X keystring %s\n", strbuf);
    XtTranslateKeycode (XtDisplay (widget), event->xkey.keycode,
                    event->xkey.state, &mods, &ks);
    printf ("Xt keysym 0x%x (%s)\n", ks, XKeysymToString (ks));
    printf ("\n");
}
```

Here, XLookupString() is used to translate the keycode to a keysym and keystring using the server keyboard mapping and the default keysym to keystring mapping.[1] XtTranslateKeycode() does the keycode to keysym translation, using the key translator installed by Motif. To print the results, XKeysymToString() is used to convert the keysyms back to their symbolic names (these are not the same as the keystrings).

Typical output from this (suitably annotated) is:

```
Keycode 0x54 modifiers 0x0
X keysym 0x61 (a)          /* Keysym name with XK_ prefix removed */
X keystring a              /* Use this to interpret the key as typed text */
Xt keysym 0x61 (a)         /* Motif key translator gives same keysym as
                              XLookupString() for most keys */


Keycode 0x6a modifiers 0x0
X keysym 0xffe1 (Shift_L)
X keystring                /* Non-printing keysym, so no string */
Xt keysym 0xffe1 (Shift_L)
```

_____

1. The Motif XmText widget uses XLookupString() or its internationalised cousin, XmbLookupString() to convert keystrokes to text characters, so it should be safe for you to do the same.

Keycode 0x54 modifiers 0x1 /* 0x1 is Shift modifier, changes case for same
keycode */
X keysym 0x41 (A)
X keystring A
Xt keysym 0x41 (A)

Keycode 0x7e modifiers 0x0
X keysym 0xffe5 (Caps_Lock)
X keystring
Xt keysym 0xffe5 (Caps_Lock)

Keycode 0x54 modifiers 0x2 /* 0x2 is Lock modifier, also changes case */
X keysym 0x41 (A)
X keystring A
Xt keysym 0x41 (A)

Keycode 0x32 modifiers 0x0
X keysym 0xff08 (BackSpace)
X keystring
Xt keysym 0x1004ff08 (osfBackSpace) /* OSF keysym used in translations */

Keycode 0x49 modifiers 0x0
X keysym 0xffff (Delete)
X keystring
Xt keysym 0x1004ffff (osfDelete)

Keycode 0x19 modifiers 0x0
X keysym 0xffc6 (F9)
X keystring
Xt keysym 0xffc6 (F9)

Keycode 0xe modifiers 0x0
X keysym 0xffc7 (F10)
X keystring
Xt keysym 0x1004ff45 (osfMenuBar) /* OSF treat some function keys specially
*/

Keycode 0x30 modifiers 0x0
X keysym 0x3d (equal)
X keystring =   /* Note keystring is not the same as keysym
name */
Xt keysym 0x3d (equal)

Keycode 0x6a modifiers 0x0
X keysym 0xffe1 (Shift_L)
X keystring
Xt keysym 0xffe1 (Shift_L)

Keycode 0x30 modifiers 0x1
X keysym 0x2b (plus)
X keystring +
Xt keysym 0x2b (plus)

The basic keysym names and values are contained in the file /usr/include/X11/ keysymdef.h. The OSF keysyms and other additional keysyms are in /usr/lib/X11/ XKeysymDB. If this is missing or incomplete, Xt will not be able to parse translation tables that use the OSF keysyms.

12.8 Alternate event sources

An Xt application normally waits for events from the X server; when it receives an event, it feeds this into the dispatch mechanism and some application code may be executed. If there is no event pending, it just waits. This model has two consequences:

- An Xt application can only respond when an event arrives. If there are no events (because the user is at lunch or comatose), the application does nothing.
- Xt applications spend most of their time waiting for events and may leave a great deal of valuable processor time unused (or worse, allow it to be used by someone else).

Xt addresses this by allowing the application to add extra 'event sources' and providing a mechanism for an application to perform background work when there are no events waiting to be processed.

In an Xt application input sources and timers can be treated as though they are sources of events. The 'event' indicates that the input source (usually a pipe or similar asynchronous byte stream) is available for reading (or writing), or that the timeout has expired and the timer has triggered. These 'events' are not the same as Xlib events and the Xlib event processing functions know nothing about them.

Xt also allows you to define a background work procedure. If there are no events pending, XtAppNextEvent() will call the work procedure. Any events that arrive while the work procedure is executing are queued, ready for processing when the work procedure returns. A work procedure will be called repeatedly until it indicates that it is done.

12.8.1   File input

The function XtAppAddInput() sets up a file as a source of events for Xt, with a function to be called when the file is ready for reading (or writing): an input callback. Xt then checks for input and calls the input callback from within both XtAppNextEvent() and XtAppProcessEvent(), so you have to call one of these functions to have the input processed at all.

For instance, to add stdin as a source of input, call:

```
XtAppAddInput(app_context, fileno(stdin), XtInputReadMask,
                my_input_callback, client_data);
```

 The major defect of XtAppAddInput() is that (on some operating systems) a file or pipe may always be reported as ready for reading, even if there is no new input to be read. This causes the input callback to be called unnecessarily. To get round this, you can remove the input callback when the end of file is reached, adding a timer to reinstate it after a decent interval. See Section 12.8.3 for an example.

12.8.2   Timeouts

Timeouts are set up using XtAppAddTimeOut(). A timeout function is called once only, at or after the expiry of the timeout. As with file input, Xt checks for and calls timeout functions from XtAppNextEvent() and XtAppProcessEvent(); a timeout function will not be called until the timer has expired and control has passed to one of these functions and may not be called then if there are other events waiting to be processed.

Since timeouts trigger once only, polling is achieved by having the timeout function call XtAppAddTimeOut() again. Timeout intervals are specified in milliseconds, but the actual achievable resolution will depend on the platform and is likely to be rather less.

 As timers may trigger late, if you want a function to execute at (on the whole) regular intervals, you should calculate the interval until the next execution with reference to the current time. If you use a fixed interval, the timer will gradually slip:

```
void tick (client_data, id)
     XtPointer       client_data;
     XtIntervalId    *id;
{
    /* Get current time into tim */
    ...

       /* Set timer to go at end of minute */
       XtAppAddTimeOut (app_context, (60 - tim->tm_sec) * 1000, tick,
```

```
                          client_data);
        }
```

A timeout added with an interval of zero will presumably be called quite soon.

12.8.3 Tailing a file in Motif

To tail a file (that is, display the end of it and update the display as more is appended to the file) requires only a few lines of code. We use the file as an Xt input source, reading up to the end of the file whenever Xt invokes the input callback. When the end of the file is reached, we remove the input callback and replace it with a timeout and reinstate the input callback when the timeout triggers. This is so that we do not attempt to read past the end of file too often:

tail

```
...
void timer (cdata, id)
        XtPointer    cdata;
        XtIntervalId *id;
{
    /* Reinstate the input callback */
    XtAppAddInput (app_context, infid, XtInputReadMask, input, NULL);
}

void input (cdata, source, id)
        XtPointer    cdata;
        int          *source;
        XtInputId    *id;
{
    char     inbuf[256];
    int      i;
    static int textlength=0;

    i = read (*source, inbuf, 255);
    if (i == 0) {
        /* At EOF - remove input callback and replace with timer */
        XtRemoveInput (*id);
        XtAppAddTimeOut (app_context, 250, timer, NULL);
    } else {
        /* Append input to text widget */
        inbuf[i] = '\0';
        XmTextInsert (text_widget, textlength, inbuf);
        textlength += i;
        XmTextShowPosition (text_widget, textlength);
```

```
        }
    }
```

To start the process off, all, you need to do is open the file and set up the input callback:

```
infid = open (argv[1], O_RDONLY);
XtAppAddInput (app_context, infid, XtInputReadMask, input, NULL);
```

Of course, a real application would pay a good deal more attention to portability and error checking than we have done.

12.8.4   Work procedures

A work procedure, added via XtAppAddWorkProc(), gives Xt something to do if there are no events (X events, timers or alternate input) to process. As with the other Xt events, work procedures are called from XtAppNextEvent() and XtAppProcessEvent().

Xt maintains an ordered list of work procedures and, if there is nothing more urgent to do, always calls the first one on the list. Work procedures which are later on the list do not execute until the earlier ones are removed. A work procedure is removed from the list by a call to XtRemoveWorkProc(), or when the work procedure itself returns true. An application cannot respond to events while a work procedure is executing, so it is usual for a work procedure to do a little bit of work at a time, returning after each tranche to give Xt a chance to deal with urgent input.

 Work procedures are added at the head of the list, so that the latest one added is the one that gets called, but if a work procedure adds another work procedure, the new one is placed after the existing one on the list. This behaviour is sufficiently arcane that it may be worth your while to write a single scheduler work procedure and use this to control background processing.

The classic use of work procedures is in program initialisation. There are many widgets in an application which do not have to be created at start-up time, but are likely to be needed during execution. These can be created in work procedures, so that the application is able to respond to user actions almost immediately, but can also use the processor idle time to complete its initialisation. Of course there has to be a synchronisation mechanism so that, if a widget is needed before it has been created, the application does not embarrass itself.

12.9   Event loops

There is one further place where you can change the way in which events are processed: in the event loop itself. At any time, an application can decide to execute a private event loop, one that only processes certain types of event or events on certain windows, say.

This approach seems to exert a terrible power over some developers, perhaps because it gives a clearly visible thread of control and is used far more often than is justified. A private event loop is sometimes necessary, but there are comparatively few requirements that cannot be met by a suitable combination of Xlib grabs (see Section 17.1) and modal dialogs (see Section 8.10.1).

The basic Xt event loop is this:

```
for (;;) {
    XtAppNextEvent (app_context, &event);
    XtDispatchEvent (&event);
}
```

This loop will process all events from any number of displays, as well as timers and file input. The X events will be passed into XtDispatchEvent(); timers and file input are handled entirely within XtAppNextEvent().

A typical private event loop will alter this in several ways:

• It will usually have a termination condition. When the private event loop terminates, the application drops back to using the main event loop.
• It may discard certain types of event, or events on certain windows, rather than passing them to XtDispatchEvent().
• It may only take certain types of event, or events on certain windows, off the event queue, leaving others to be processed in the main event loop after the private one has terminated.
• It may look at other sources of input, or perform other processing not associated with the user interface.

Some of these features can be achieved using the Xt event handling. However, it is often easier to drop down to the Xlib level to poll for events.

Most private event loops process certain events out of order, or not at all, so widgets may not see the events they expect when they expect them; it is reasonable to ask if this is safe. The theoretical answer is that it is not: it is straightforward to write a widget that takes some drastic action on a KeyPress and tidies up on the corresponding KeyRelease. If a private event loop discards this second event (where XtAppMainLoop() would dispatch it), the widget will misbehave, but the author might legitimately deny responsibility.

In practice, Xt and the Motif widgets are quite robust and a mangled event stream rarely causes problems. However, you need to be aware of the possibility. Most problems are caused by a failure to dispatch the release event for a button or key and a cautious main loop will dispatch all KeyRelease and ButtonRelease events, even if it discards some KeyPress and ButtonPress events.

12.9.1   Motif event loop functions

Motif provides only a few event-processing functions: XmUpdateDisplay() and XmTrackingEvent().

XmUpdateDisplay() synchronises the application and server; it sends any queued requests to the server, and waits until the server has processed them, then processes any Expose events that the server has sent back before returning control to the caller.

Often, an application will create and show a 'busy' dialog before plunging off into some calculation that will keep it from responding to events for a while. XmUpdateDisplay() is typically used to make sure that this dialog has been completely drawn before the non-interactive processing starts. However, because the window manager is involved in any requests to map a top-level window, the mapping and consequent Expose events may not happen until some time after the server processes the map request. A call to XmUpdateDisplay() immediately after creating the busy dialog may not succeed in drawing it, as the Expose events have yet to be generated.

There are two ways of dealing with this. The first and preferred is to arrange to call XmUpdateDisplay() periodically during any non-interactive computing. The second is to wait until the dialog's shell window becomes mapped before calling XmUpdateDisplay(). Section 14.2.4 shows ways of tracking when the window becomes mapped. Remember that the window may never become mapped if the dialog (or its nearest iconifiable ancestor) is iconified; you must check for this.

XmTrackingEvent() is a private event loop that is intended to support context help. The general idea is that you call this function when the user asks for context help, then the user clicks Button1 or presses a key on some widget in a dialog. XmTrackingEvent() returns that widget's ID and your application can use this to select and display the help relevant to that widget (perhaps by calling its action procedures). No other events are processed while XmTrackingEvent() is active.

XmTrackingEvent() returns the event that caused it to return (either a ButtonRelease or a KeyRelease).

12.9.2   Xt event processing

As well as the usual Xt event processing functions (XtAppMainLoop(), XtApp-NextEvent() and XtDispatchEvent()) there are a few less often used.

XtAppPending() checks to see if there is any input waiting to be processed. Its usual use is to check for pending input during a long calculation, say. It always returns immediately; a non-zero return value indicates that there is something to be processed (this may be an X event, or a timer or file input).

If there is pending input, XtAppPeekEvent() will return a copy of the first event on the queue without removing it from the queue. It returns True if the input is an X event, otherwise (for timer or file input) it returns False and sets the type, window and display elements of the event structure to zero. XtAppPeekEvent() blocks if there is no X event, timer or file input to process.

XtAppProcessEvent() processes a single event; it is approximately equivalent to XtAppNextEvent() followed by XtDispatchEvent(), but you can restrict it to process only an X event, a timer or file input. Like XtAppPeekEvent(), it blocks if there is nothing to process.

A common sort of Xt event loop performs application processing interspersed with event processing:

```
for (;;) {
    if (XtAppPending (app_context))
        XtAppProcessEvent (app_context, XtIMAll);
    /* Do application processing... */
}
```

This loop performs a similar job to XtAppMainLoop() with a work procedure, but gives the application writer more control over the division of processing resources; the application code is called after each event, whereas a work procedure is only called when there are no events pending at all.

12.9.3 Xlib event processing

Event polling

Xt offers relatively few functions for polling events. By dropping down to the Xlib level, you can get far more flexibility. The Xlib event polling functions are summarised in Table 12.3:

- Blocking: the function only returns when there is an event on the queue; it blocks if the queue is empty.
- Leave: the function leaves the event on the queue, but returns a copy to the caller.
- Predicate: the function takes a predicate procedure as a parameter. The procedure is called for each event, and must return a Boolean value.
- Window: the function only considers events on a particular window.
- Mask: the function only considers events that match an event mask.
- Type: the function only considers events of a given type.

For an example of a couple of the Xlib functions in use, see Section 7.4.3.

Timer and input events in Xlib event loops

Whereas XtAppNextEvent() can handle multiple displays, timers and alternate input sources, the Xlib functions will only take X events from a single display. Most applications use only a single display and do not use timers or alternate input,

Table 12.3 *X Event polling functions*

Function	Blocking	Leave	Predicate	Window	Mask	Type
XNextEvent()	✓					
XPeekEvent()	✓	✓				
XIfEvent()	✓		✓			
XCheckIfEvent()			✓			
XPeekIfEvent()	✓	✓	✓			
XWindowEvent()	✓			✓	✓	
XCheckWindowEvent()				✓	✓	
XMaskEvent()	✓				✓	
XCheckMaskEvent()					✓	
XCheckTypedEvent()						✓
XCheckTypedWindowEvent()				✓		✓

but a number of the Motif widgets set timers and you may need to make sure that timer events are processed even if you are using the Xlib functions to handle the X events. In particular, XmScrollBar relies on timers to implement its auto-repeat behaviour. This code fragment uses XtAppProcessEvent() to handle a single timer or input event, if there is one pending:

```
XtInputMask mask;
if (mask = (XtAppPending (app_context) &~XtIMXEvent))
    XtAppProcessEvent (app_context, mask);
```

This code does not block, so you can call it at any time. The difficulty is knowing when to call it; you have to combine this, or similar, code with code that calls the Xlib functions to poll the X event queue and it is very easy to end up with a loop that spends all its time testing the event sources alternately, even when there is nothing to do.

Putting events back on the queue

Xlib provides the function XPutBackEvent(), which pushes an event back onto the head of the event queue. Its normal use is to put back an event that you are not able to deal with, such as a KeyPress event that, translated to a keystring and appended to the other pending input, causes input buffer overflow.

You can call it repeatedly and, despite the name, there is no assumption that the event is one that was ever taken off the queue. You can use XPutBackEvent() to send a fake event to your application, or a modified version of one that really arrived. For instance, a common need is to have a graphical display (in an XmDrawingArea, say) where the user can edit textual annotations of the drawn objects. This can be done by creating an XmText widget child of the drawing area; when the user clicks on Button1, say, the XmText widget is moved to the position where the mouse click occurred and the user can start editing the text. If the user double clicks, we would want the text to be selected as normally happens in an XmText widget. To make sure that this happens, we modify the first ButtonPress event so that it is dispatched to the XmText widget and put it back on the event queue. Normal event processing then takes over:

```
void da_input (w, client_data, call_data )
    Widget      w;
    XtPointer    client_data;
    XtPointer    call_data;
{
    XEvent *event = ((XmDrawingAreaCallbackStruct *)call_data)->event;

    if (event->type == ButtonPress && event->xbutton.button == 1)
    {
        Dimension height;
        XtVaGetValues text, XmNheight, &height, 0);
        XtVaSetValues (text,
                XmNx, event->xbutton.x,
                XmNy, event->xbutton.y - height / 2,
                0);
        event->xbutton.x = 0;
        event->xbutton.y = height / 2;
        event->xbutton.window = XtWindow (text);
        XPutBackEvent (XtDisplay (text), event);
    }
}
```

Notice how the event is modified before being put back: the window becomes that of the XmText widget and the coordinates are changed to the XmText widget's coordinate system. When the event is taken off the queue for the second time, it is delivered to the XmText widget, which treats it just like any other ButtonPress. It could, of course, have been dispatched directly to the XmText widget by calling XtDispatchEvent() here rather than XPutBackEvent(), but this assumes that normal delivery is required (there may be a private event loop which will mangle the event further when it is taken off the queue for the second time).

12.10   Sending events

XPutBackEvent() allows you to put an event onto the event queue of the calling application. You can also send events to other applications using XSendEvent(). This is often used by window managers, as the ICCCM requires them to send synthetic (that is, fake) events. It is unlikely that you will need to use this directly, but you should not be too nervous if you do. Xlib event handling is basically straightforward and widgets are quite good at ignoring events that appear when they should not.

CHAPTER 13

Focus and traversal

Pointer events - ButtonPress, ButtonRelease and MotionNotify - are generally reported to the window that the pointer is in and dispatched by Xt to the corresponding widget. For keyboard events, this approach is a little too simplistic. Although it is possible to arrange for KeyPress and KeyRelease events to follow the pointer, this requires the user to move the mouse every time the key input is to be directed to a new window; worse, the input moves every time the mouse is knocked.

X, Xt and Motif provide a more usable model for keyboard input, based on a notion of 'focus'. Key events are dispatched to the widget that has the keyboard focus, regardless of the pointer position and various mechanisms are provided to let the user move the focus between widgets. In particular, if the user chooses to operate with an explicit (click-to-type) focus policy, the focus can be moved using keyboard keys (such as <Tab>), as well as by clicking the mouse.

The Motif toolkit provides a number of features that let an application define the way in which focus moves between the component widgets of a dialog in response to keyboard input. These only have an effect with an explicit focus policy and only when the keyboard - rather than the mouse - is used to change the focus. Also, they can only be used to control the movement of focus within a dialog; movement of focus between dialogs is the responsibility of the window manager and cannot be controlled using toolkit facilities.

This chapter describes the focus control facilities of the Motif toolkit. It shows you how to control the order in which the focus visits the widgets in a dialog and how to prevent and force focus changes.

13.1 Focus policies and mechanisms

The Motif focus model uses mechanisms provided by Xlib and Xt. This section describes how these are related to the resources used to configure the Motif focus policy.

The focus model is applied at two different levels, using two different mechanisms. The window manager is responsible for directing the X *input focus* to the windows belonging to shell widgets and the Xt *keyboard focus* is used within a widget hierarchy whose shell has the input focus to direct key events to some chosen widget descendant of the shell.

A keyboard focus policy can be specified at both of these levels. There are two policies: implicit (pointer-driven) and explicit (click-to-type) and the policies at the two levels can be, and often are, different.

The X input focus policy is specified by mwm's keyboardFocusPolicy resource. According to the setting of this resource, mwm moves the X input focus between shells' windows either when the pointer moves, or only when the user clicks in a window; it highlights the border of the window that has the input focus to give the user a visual cue.[1] This policy, being a window manager resource, applies to all the windows managed by a given instance of the window manager, which usually means that the user regards it as a feature of his or her environment.

The Xt keyboard focus policy is determined by the keyboardFocusPolicy resource on each shell. The Motif toolkit will move the Xt keyboard focus between widgets, either to follow the pointer or when the user clicks in a widget's window, according to the keyboardFocusPolicy of the shell. Motif also provides visual cues in the form of a highlight rectangle drawn around the widget that has the keyboard focus. If (and only if) the shell's window also has the X input focus, the descendant widget that has the Xt keyboard focus will receive keyboard input. Since this is a shell resource, different policies can be set for different applications, or even for different dialogs within the same application. However, this policy is usually also regarded as a feature of the user's personal environment and it is rare and probably wrong for an application to set it.

If the user selects a pointer-driven policy at either level, then changes in focus at that level only occur as a result of pointer motion and the widget that has the focus is determined by the layout and position of the windows on the screen and the position of the pointer. If, however, the policy is explicit (click-to-type), there is no necessary connection between the pointer position and the focus and the focus can be moved using the keyboard as well as by point-and-click. Within a Motif

---

1. Window managers other than mwm may behave somewhat differently, but they will all set the X input focus to the shells' windows in response to the appropriate user actions.

widget hierarchy, movement of the Xt keyboard focus as a response to keystrokes is rather grandly called 'keyboard traversal' and can be controlled using tab groups, or explicitly by the application.

13.2   Tab group traversal

Much of Motif's keyboard traversal is based on the concept of *tab groups*. A tab group is just a collection of traversable elements; the user can move (traverse) from one to the next using the cursor keys. For instance, a group of button widgets might constitute a tab group, allowing the user to arrow between them before selecting one by pressing the space bar. Equally, the characters displayed in an XmText widget are a tab group, so the user can move about the text in the usual way.

The focus moves between elements of a tab group in response to the cursor keys. It moves between tab groups when the user presses the <Tab> key, or <Shift><Tab> to go backwards.

Every tab group is represented by a widget. If the elements of the tab group are widgets, the corresponding *tab group widget* will be a manager widget which is their common ancestor. If the tab group consists of non-widget elements (like the characters in an XmText widget) the tab group widget will be the widget that contains the elements; the widget writer then has to ensure that it supports traversal over its internal elements. That is, only certain primitive widget classes (XmText, XmTextField and XmList) will behave sensibly as one-widget tab groups. However, any manager widget can be designated as representing a tab group by setting its navigationType resource.

13.2.1   Tab group types

A given widget can represent any one of three different types of tab group - normal, exclusive or sticky - or may not be a tab group at all. This is represented by the four possible values of the navigationType resource:

- NONE - The widget does not represent a tab group.
- TAB_GROUP - The widget represents a normal tab group, unless there is another widget in the hierarchy that represents an exclusive tab group, in which case normal tab groups are ignored.
- STICKY_TAB_GROUP - The widget represents a sticky tab group. Sticky tab groups behave like normal tab groups, but they are not disabled by exclusive tab groups.
- EXCLUSIVE_TAB_GROUP - The widget represents an exclusive tab group. Exclusive tab groups change the order in which the focus moves between widgets and also disable all the normal tab groups in the same widget hierarchy.

In this context, the term 'widget hierarchy' means the tree of widgets used to create a single dialog, up to and including the shell widget, but not including the shell's ancestors.

A widget is a tab group widget if its navigationType resource is set to STICKY_TAB_GROUP or EXCLUSIVE_TAB_GROUP, or its navigationType is TAB_GROUP and there are no exclusive tab group widgets in the same hierarchy. Within a widget hierarchy, then, there may be a mixture of normal and sticky tab groups or a mixture of sticky and exclusive ones, but exclusive and normal tab groups cannot coexist.

Note that the child of a shell always behaves as a tab group, whatever its navigationType. If a leaf widget has no ancestor that is a tab group widget, it will behave as an element of the tab group defined by its shell's child.

13.2.2   Tab group elements

A tab group is defined by a widget whose navigationType is not NONE.[1] By default, manager widgets (except menus) are created with navigationType TAB_GROUP, so every manager usually defines a new normal tab group. The elements of the tab group will be the descendant widgets that are not themselves tab groups and where there is no intervening tab group widget (see Figure 13.1).

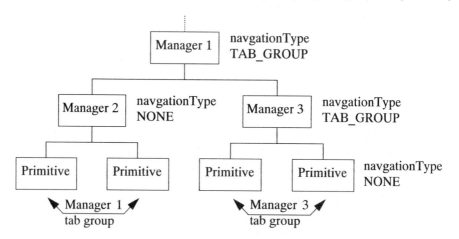

Figure 13.1 *Tab groups*

A manager widget of navigationType NONE, such as Manager 2 in the figure, does not define a new tab group. Moreover, since manager widgets do not usually accept the focus themselves, non-tab group managers play no part in keyboard traversal. The widget hierarchy is effectively flattened to two levels: tab group

---

1. The function XmAddTabGroup() is now obsolete.

manager widgets containing tab group elements (primitive widgets with navigationType NONE).[1]

Primitive widgets can also define tab groups, although most do not. The default navigationType for primitive widgets is NONE, except for XmList, XmText, XmTextField and XmScrollbar, so most primitives respond to the cursor keys by passing the focus to another element of the same tab group. The exceptions are those widgets that expect to use the cursor keys for internal traversal or internal navigation.

13.2.3 Traversal order

If a widget hierarchy contains only widgets of navigationType NONE, TAB_GROUP and STICKY_TAB_GROUP, the cursor keys will move the focus between widgets in the tab groups in a left-to-right, top-to-bottom order.[2] That is, the order of traversal within a normal or sticky tab group is determined by the locations of widgets on the screen. Similarly, the order of traversal between tab groups (using the <Tab> key) is also determined by screen position. If this is not appropriate, an application can define the traversal order. The easiest way to do this is to use exclusive tab groups.

Traversal order within tab groups

In a normal tab group or a sticky tab group, the traversal order is based on screen position. In an exclusive tab group, traversal depends on the order of the children that constitute the tab group in their parents' child lists. By default, this is the same as the order in which the children were created. Figure 13.2 shows the traversal order for a tab group consisting of an XmForm containing four XmPushButton widgets. The buttons are labelled 1, 2, 3 and 4 in the order they were created; with an exclusive tab group, traversal follows this creation order, as shown.

Traversal order between tab groups

If a widget hierarchy contains any exclusive tab groups, that is, any widget in the hierarchy has a navigationType of EXCLUSIVE_TAB_GROUP, the order of traversal between tab groups is changed. Instead of using an order defined by screen positions, the traversal mechanism uses the order in which the tab groups were created; that is, the order in which the navigationType resources were set. If the navigationType is set for each appropriate widget when it is created, this is the same as the creation order, but it is possible to create all the widgets with default navigationType, then use XtSetValues() to set the navigationType of the relevant managers to EXCLUSIVE_TAB_GROUP (for child order traversal within the group) or STICKY_TAB_GROUP (for position order traversal within the group).

---

1. Nesting of tab group widgets is significant for determining initial focus, as described below.
2. This may be different in a right-to-left language environment.

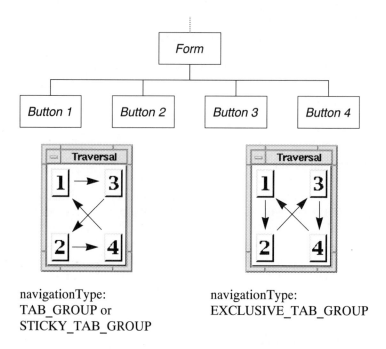

navigationType:
TAB_GROUP or
STICKY_TAB_GROUP

navigationType:
EXCLUSIVE_TAB_GROUP

Figure 13.2 *Traversal order within a tab group*

13.2.4 Initial focus

The initialFocus resource can be used to specify the widget that will receive the focus under two circumstances:

- When the shell first receives the X input focus.
- When the user traverses into a tab group and the toolkit has to decide which element of the tab group gets the focus.

First focus on a shell

When a shell hierarchy first receives the input focus, the toolkit has to decide which widget receives the keyboard focus. By default, it goes to the first widget in the first tab group, where 'first' is determined by the tab group types, as described in Section 13.2.3.

To set the initial focus to a widget which is a member of the tab group defined by the shell's child, simply set the initialFocus resource on that child to point to the appropriate widget. If the initial focus widget is not an element of that tab group (because there are one or more other tab group widgets between the initial focus widget and the shell's child), set the initialFocus resource on the shell's child and all the tab group widgets between it and the initial focus widget, so that there is a chain of pointers from shell's child to initial focus widget.

Note that if a shell has the X input focus, but loses then regains it, the Xt keyboard focus remains where it was at the time focus was lost; the keyboard focus location is remembered. Setting the initialFocus resource only has effect the very first time that the shell gets the X input focus.

Focus traversing into a tab group

The initialFocus resource is also used to determine the widget that receives focus every time the user traverses into a tab group, not just the first time. The default behaviour is to give the focus to the first widget, as determined by the tab group type. The initialFocus resource can be set to point to a widget element of the tab group, or to a descendant widget which itself defines a tab group, in which case the initialFocus widget chain is followed until a widget is found to accept the focus.

If a tab group loses focus by traversal to another tab group then regains it, the previous focus widget in the tab group is ignored and the keyboard focus widget is determined afresh by the initialFocus resource (which can successfully be changed dynamically).

13.2.5   Traversal to obscured widgets

It is not normally possible to traverse to a widget unless some part of it is viewable. The exception is that it may be possible to traverse to an obscured widget which is a descendant of an XmScrolledWindow widget with AUTOMATIC scrolling-Policy. This is achieved using the traverseObscuredCallback of the XmScrolled-Window, as described in Section 7.1.1.

13.2.6   Preventing traversal to a widget

A widget can be kept out of the traversal order altogether by setting its traversalOn resource to False. If the keyboard focus policy is explicit, this will prevent the toolkit giving the widget the keyboard focus in response to the users actions. With an implicit focus policy, this has no effect.

If traversalOn is set False on a manager widget (whether or not it is a tab group), all its descendant widgets become ineligible to receive focus through keyboard traversal.

A widget that does not have the keyboard focus can still receive input from the mouse. To prevent a widget from receiving input, you should set it to be insensitive using XtSetSensitive(), which will also disbar it from receiving the keyboard focus.

If none of the widgets in a tab group are able to accept the keyboard focus, the entire group is skipped when moving between tab groups. If a widget which has the keyboard focus is made ineligible to receive focus, the focus is passed to the next eligible widget in the tab group if there is one, or the first eligible widget in a subsequent tab group. If no widget can accept the keyboard focus, it will end up nowhere and no widget will receive keyboard events until one becomes eligible.

It is not possible to reject the focus, although it is possible to force the focus onto another widget (perhaps the one that last had the focus) by calling XmProcessTraversal() (see Section 13.4).

13.2.7 Preventing traversal from a widget

There is only one circumstance where the toolkit allows you to prevent the focus leaving a widget, which is an attempt to traverse out of an XmText or XmTextField widget using the keyboard. There is no way of preventing the focus moving out of a widget in response to a mouse click (or mouse movement, if the focus policy is pointer-driven).

Traversal out of an XmText or XmTextField widget is disallowed in the losingFocus callback in the same way that an edit can be disallowed in the modifyVerify callback. The call data structure includes a Boolean flag, doit. If this flag is set False, the action, which in this case is the focus change, is prevented, so the focus stays put:

```
#include <Xm/Xm.h>

void keep_focus (w, client_data, call_data)
Widget      w;
XtPointer   client_data;
XtPointer   call_data;
{
    /* Prevent loss of focus from XmText or XmTextField */
    ((XmTextVerifyCallbackStruct *)call_data)->doit=False;
}
```

If this callback is called because the keyboard focus is leaving the widget in response to a mouse click or mouse movement, or because the X input focus is moving to some other shell, the focus change will go ahead, but the widget will generate an indignant beep.

Although it is not possible to prevent loss of focus in the general case, it is possible to use XmProcessTraversal() to force the focus to return immediately (see Section 13.4.3).

13.3 Detecting focus changes

The X server generates focus events of types FocusIn and FocusOut when the X input focus moves to and from a window. A single change of input focus can cause the X server to send a number of focus events to different windows; the precise description of the windows involved is long and complex.

In a Motif application, the X input focus will be set to the shell's window and the Xt keyboard focus is then used to dispatch keyboard input to the shell's descendants. Although the Xt keyboard focus may move between descendant widgets and the user perceives that the focus has changed, the X input focus does not move, so the X server does not generate focus change events.

So that an application can detect changes of the keyboard focus, XtSetKeyboardFocus() generates fake FocusIn and FocusOut events and pushes them into the event dispatching process at a level below XtDispatchEvent(), so they never pass through XtAppNextEvent() and cannot be intercepted. These events can be detected using translations and event handlers and through the focus and losingFocus callbacks on XmText, XmTextField and XmBulletinBoard[1] widgets.

FocusIn and FocusOut events, then, may come from the X server or from XtSetKeyboardFocus(). In a Motif application, XtSetKeyboardFocus() will be called via the Motif keyboard focus traversal function XmProcessTraversal(), not directly. The fake focus events it creates are dispatched and processed immediately, so any application code that is invoked (callbacks, event handlers and so on) is, in effect, called from XmProcessTraversal(). Recursive traversal calls are not allowed; if XmProcessTraversal() is called from this application code, it will fail.[2]

The result of this is that it is not safe to change the keyboard focus from within code invoked as an immediate result of a focus change, other than to prevent keyboard traversal out of an XmText or XmTextField widget, as described above. A focus or losingFocus callback can be used to change the appearance of a widget, perhaps to provide a strong visual focus cue to the user, but cannot itself be used to manipulate focus. This is sometimes too restrictive. A common requirement is to keep the focus fixed on a certain input widget until it contains a valid value and the next section describes the way in which an application can take effective control of the focus.

13.4 Application-defined traversal

Tab groups give keyboard traversal behaviour that is appropriate for most circumstances. The traversal order can be changed by using exclusive tab groups and the initial focus widget is easily configured. However, tab groups are largely static, and cannot take account of any requirement to force the focus dynamically to a particular widget.

A Motif application can move the Xt keyboard focus between widgets by calling the function XmProcessTraversal(). This calls XtSetKeyboardFocus() to move the keyboard focus and generate FocusIn and FocusOut events, but also does

---

1. XmBulletinBoard has no losingFocus callback, although the code to provide it is in the toolkit.
2. In some (early) versions of Motif, it will cause a segmentation fault.

a lot of other housekeeping. If you call the Xt function directly, you may confuse the Motif traversal mechanisms and suffer strange keyboard behaviour at inconvenient moments.

XmProcessTraversal() can be used to move the keyboard focus within a widget hierarchy, even if its shell does not currently have the input focus. In this case, the FocusIn and FocusOut events are delayed and will only occur when the shell regains the input focus.

13.4.1   The XmProcessTraversal() function

XmProcessTraversal() is a straightforward function made complex by its documentation. It takes two parameters:

```
void XmProcessTraversal(widget, direction)
    Widget                  widget;
    XmTraversalDirection  direction;
```

There are three sorts of traversal operation that can be invoked using different values for the direction:

• Traversal within a tab group.
• Traversal between tab groups.
• Traversal to a particular widget.

In the first two cases, the widget parameter is used only to identify the widget hierarchy of interest. The widget that receives the focus is then determined by the widget within that hierarchy that currently has the focus, plus the direction. Only in the last case does it matter which widget in the hierarchy is specified.

Traversal within a tab group

Traversal within a tab group occurs if the direction is XmTRAVERSE_RIGHT, XmTRAVERSE_LEFT, XmTRAVERSE_UP, XmTRAVERSE_DOWN, XmTRAVERSE_NEXT, XmTRAVERSE_PREV or XmTRAVERSE_HOME. The effect is to move the keyboard focus for the widget hierarchy containing the specified widget to another widget in the same tab group as the widget that currently has the focus, as if the user had pressed a cursor key.

As with cursor key traversal, the meaning of the directions right, left, up and down depends on the type of the tab group; exclusive tab groups use child order traversal, where sticky and normal tab groups use an order defined by screen positions. XmTRAVERSE_HOME also behaves differently according to the tab group type, but XmTRAVERSE_NEXT and XmTRAVERSE_PREV always use the child order.

If the focus is within a primitive widget such as XmText that is itself a tab group, XmProcessTraversal() will not move the focus between the tab group elements (the characters in the XmText widget). Under these circumstances, XmProcessTraversal() returns False and there is no focus change.

Traversal between tab groups

There are only two possible directions for traversal between tab groups, XmTRAVERSE_NEXT_TAB_GROUP (corresponding to the user pressing <Tab>) and XmTRAVERSE_PREV_TAB_GROUP (corresponding to <Shift><Tab>).

Again, the action of the function depends on the tab group types, just as it does if the user instigates the traversal.

Traversal to a widget

The traversal direction XmTRAVERSE_CURRENT attempts to give the keyboard focus to the specified widget. This will fail if the widget is not eligible to receive the focus.

This is the useful one.

13.4.2   Modifying a widget's keyboard traversal

Most widgets implement their keyboard traversal behaviour through hard-coded translation tables. In particular, most primitive widgets have translation table entries like this:

```
<Key>osfBeginLine:  PrimitiveTraverseHome()
<Key>osfUp:         PrimitiveTraverseUp()
<Key>osfDown:       PrimitiveTraverseDown()
<Key>osfLeft:       PrimitiveTraverseLeft()
<Key>osfRight:      PrimitiveTraverseRight()
s ~m ~a <Key>Tab:   PrimitivePrevTabGroup()
~m ~a <Key>Tab:     PrimitiveNextTabGroup()
```

The default traversal behaviour can be changed by overriding these parts of the translation table and providing new action routines which use XmProcessTraversal() to move the focus when and where needed. If the action routines do nothing, the focus remains where it is.

This simple example only permits keyboard traversal away from a toggle button if it is set. The behaviour is set up by calling set_toggle_traversal(), which modifies the toggle button's translation table and registers the action routine, toggleb_traverse(). A single action routine is used; it determines the direction of traversal from the parameter given in the translation table:

modify_
traversal

```
#include <Xm/Xm.h>
#include <Xm/ToggleB.h>
```

```
void toggleb_traverse();

static XtActionsRec toggleb_actions[]={
    {"toggleb_traverse", toggleb_traverse}
};

static char toggleb_translations[]={
    "<Key>osfBeginLine:  toggleb_traverse(home)\n\
    <Key>osfUp:          toggleb_traverse(up)\n\
    <Key>osfDown:        toggleb_traverse(down)\n\
    <Key>osfLeft:        toggleb_traverse(left)\n\
    <Key>osfRight:       toggleb_traverse(right)\n\
    s ~m ~a <Key>Tab:    toggleb_traverse(next_tab)\n\
    ~m ~a <Key>Tab:      toggleb_traverse(prev_tab)"
};

void set_toggle_traversal (toggle_button)
    Widget toggle_button;
{
    XtAppAddActions (XtWidgetToApplicationContext (toggle_button),
                    toggleb_actions, XtNumber (toggleb_actions));
    XtOverrideTranslations (toggle_button, XtParseTranslationTable
                    (toggleb_translations));
}

void toggleb_traverse (toggle_button, event, params, num_params)
    Widget   toggle_button;
    XEvent   *event;
    String   *params;
    Cardinal *num_params;
{
/* Prevent keyboard traversal from an unset toggle button */
    if ((*num_params!=1) || !XmToggleButtonGetState (toggle_button))
        return;

/* Use XmProcessTraversal() to move focus */
    if (!strcmp (params[0], "home"))
        XmProcessTraversal (toggle_button, XmTRAVERSE_HOME);
    else if (!strcmp(params[0], "up"))
        XmProcessTraversal (toggle_button, XmTRAVERSE_UP);
    ...
/* Similarly for down, left, right and next_tab */
    ...
    else if (!strcmp(params[0], "prev_tab"))
```

```
        XmProcessTraversal (toggle_button,
                    XmTRAVERSE_PREV_TAB_GROUP);

}
```

This example is trivial, but can obviously be extended to other widget classes and other criteria. There are certain widget classes where some changes are needed:

- XmText and XmTextField, where the focus callback (rather than actions on the <Tab> key) should be used to prevent traversal away and which use the cursor keys for internal traversal between characters.
- XmList and XmScrollBar again use the cursor keys for internal traversal or navigation and these parts of the translation table should not be disturbed. Overriding the actions on the <Tab> key is possible.
- Any widget in a menu system has a different translation table. It is unwise to try and change the menu traversal behaviour.

XmText widgets have a slightly peculiar translation table:

```
s ~m ~a <Key>Tab:prev-tab-group()
c ~m ~a <Key>Tab:next-tab-group()
~m ~a <Key>Tab:process-tab()
```

The process-tab action will move to the next tab group if the XmText widget has editMode set to SINGLE_LINE_EDIT. If editMode is MULTI_LINE_EDIT process-tab will simply insert a tab character. The user should type <Control><Tab> to move to the next tab group.

13.4.3 Focus control

Changing a widget's translation table can alter its keyboard traversal behaviour, but it does not give full control of the focus. In particular, the focus can still be moved with the mouse.

If the user has chosen a pointer-driven focus policy, the focus will always follow the mouse pointer and the application has no control. If, however, the focus policy is explicit (click-to-type), the application can control the focus position to a degree; it cannot prevent the user changing the focus, but it can detect this and force it back.

An application detects the change of focus as a focus event, typically FocusOut on the current focus widget. XmProcessTraversal() cannot be used immediately, as the event is received while the focus change is still in progress and recursive focus changes do not work. Instead, the application queues a focus change by establishing a zero-interval timer. The timer triggers as soon as control is returned to the event processing loop, by which time the traversal processing is complete and XmProcessTraversal() can safely be called.

The previous example can be recast in this form. The function set_toggle_traversal() sets up an event handler to watch for focus events and the event handler, toggleb_traverse_back(), sets up a timer to force the focus back there after traversal processing is complete:

focus_
control

```
#include <Xm/Xm.h>
#include <Xm/ToggleB.h>
void toggleb_traverse_back();

void set_focus (toggle_button, id)
    XtPointer    toggle_button;
    XtIntervalId *id;
{
    /* Traverse back to the toggle button */
    XmProcessTraversal ((Widget)toggle_button,
                    XmTRAVERSE_CURRENT);
}

void set_toggle_traversal (toggle_button)
    Widget toggle_button;
{
    XtAddEventHandler (toggle_button, FocusChangeMask, False,
                    toggleb_traverse_back, NULL);
}

void toggleb_traverse_back (toggle_button, client_data, event, cont)
    Widget        toggle_button;
    XtPointer     client_data;
    XEvent        *event;
    Boolean       *cont;
{
    /* Force focus back to an unset toggle button */
    /* Set zero interval timer to force focus back after XmProcessTraversal()
has finished its processing */
    if (event->type==FocusOut && !XmToggleButtonGetState
                    (toggle_button))
            XtAppAddTimeOut(XtWidgetToApplicationContext(toggle_button),0,
                    set_focus, (XtPointer) toggle_button);
}
```

An event handler is used in preference to a translation so as to leave the widget's existing response to FocusIn and FocusOut events unaltered. The toolkit makes extensive use of focus (and EnterNotify and LeaveNotify) events to maintain its internal traversal state.

CHAPTER 14

Window managers

In X, control of the interaction between windows belonging to different applications is not built into the core system, but is provided by a separate client, the window manager. The Motif window manager mwm is only one example, but it is the one of most interest to developers of Motif applications. This chapter describes a number of features that are specific to mwm, as well as generic window manager features. You should assume that anything with 'mwm' (or 'MWM') in the name is specific to Motif and provides a facility or feature that will not necessarily be honoured by other window managers.

In an attempt to help you understand what is going on, this chapter first describes the way a window manager typically works. This description is somewhat simplified and should not be taken as a guide for window manager implementers. If you want to write a window manager, get the source code for an existing one and dissect it.

The remainder of the chapter covers the major interactions between an application and a window manager: icons and iconified windows, window manager decorations and the window manager protocols, including the WM_DELETE_WINDOW protocol (which is useful and important) and the WM_SAVE_YOURSELF protocol (which will become so in future).

14.1   Window manager basics

Window managers work with windows, not widgets. That is, they work at the X level and are full of calls to obscure Xlib functions. To understand them, you need to know a little about windows, events and the way an X server treats them. At this point, you should review Section 2.1.

14.1.1   Window managers and events

Window managers use all the same types of event as normal clients, but they also make use of one particular event mask to gain control of the root window: the SubstructureRedirect event mask.

For the most part, selecting for events on a window will cause the server to report things that happen to that window. However, if a client selects for events on a window using the SubstructureRedirect event mask, the server will tell it whenever another client makes a request that would change the size or position of any child of that window, map or unmap any child, or change a child's position in the stacking order. What is more, the server does not act on the request, it only generates a *request event* to tell the client what the request was and sends it off. The event contains all the information needed to reproduce the request.

The SubstructureRedirect event mask is the key to the way a window manager works, as it lets it intercept requests that your program makes. This is described below.

14.1.2   The role of the shell

The window manager works with windows. You work with widgets. The shell widgets occupy the border territory. A shell is just a widget which has been written so that it understands how to deal with window managers and the X server, rather than with a parent widget.

A shell is a composite widget with only one (managed) child. It has very simple geometry management that ensures that the shell's window and its child's window are the same size and precisely overlaid.[1] The shell's window is never therefore visible on the screen and the shell is said to shrink-wrap its child.

Shells have numerous resources that specify to the window manager how it wants its window to be treated. Most of these are used to set properties on the shell's window, as described below.

The widgets in your application are restricted to using those parts of the screen that are occupied by their ancestor shell's windows. This means that every time you need to use a new portion of the screen, you need a new shell. In particular,

---

1. The shell may be larger than the child to accommodate an off-the-spot input method (see Section 20.3.1).

popup dialogs need shells and so do popup and pulldown menus. You need the window manager to treat different sorts of window in different ways - you do not want resize handles on a menu - so there are different classes of shell for different purposes (described in Chapter 8). From the window manager's point of view, these differ only in the values they set for certain properties and attributes of their window, but they also treat their children differently. The widget writer's job is to make sure that the way a window manager treats a shell's window and the way a shell treats its children are consistent so that, for instance, a popup menu does not have a window menu with a close item, but pops down when an item is selected.

14.1.3   Inside the window manager

This section describes (approximately) how a window manager works. This is not a how-to guide; there is a lot more happening than we have space to discuss.

Typically, a window manager will control the top-level windows of your application - the shells' windows - and let the user manipulate them with the mouse and keyboard. To do this, it has first to find out about them.

When it starts up, the window manager will first select for events on the root window using the SubstructureRedirect event mask. Only one client can select for this mask on a given window, so if the selection fails, it will assume that another window manager is already running and exit. The window manager will then query the X server to find existing children of the root window; we will assume that there are none (see Figure 14.1).

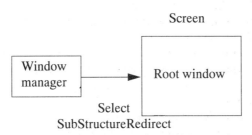

Figure 14.1 *Window manager start-up*

From this point on, the window manager will receive events from the server related to top-level windows. Since SubstructureRedirect reports map requests, the window manager will certainly get to hear of such windows when their owners first try to map them, before they first become visible to the user. The window manager gets the window ID of the top-level window in the request event and can use this to manipulate the window (see Figure 14.2).

Sometimes, the only thing that is required is that the window manager should keep out of the way. In particular, you do not want the window manager to add

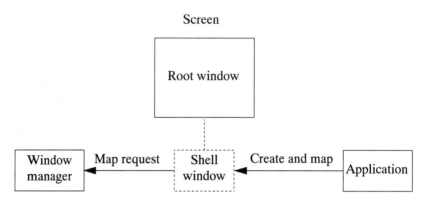

Figure 14.2 *Application start-up*

borders and decorations to a menu, nor reposition it. Every window has an override redirect flag; if this is set, the window manager will ignore the window.

Most window managers draw some form of frame round the window, with a system menu, resize handles and so on. To give itself somewhere to draw the frame without interference, it will create a new frame window as a child of the root window and make the application's top-level window a child of the frame window (see Figure 14.3). This is known as reparenting; it can be done to windows, but not widgets.[1]

To enable the window manager to display the window appropriately, it must get information (like the title to be displayed in the title bar of the frame) from the application. It does this by inspecting certain properties that the client places on the top-level window when it creates it. Once it has all the information it needs, the window manager maps the application's top-level window and its frame window parent and the window appears on the screen. When the window manager gets the expose events for the frame window, it draws the decorations round the edge, as shown in Figure 14.4.

Note that the border of the application's top-level window is considered fair game for the window manager, and it may well force the width of the window border down to zero.

If the user grabs one of the resize handles in the frame and moves it, the window manager just resizes the application's window accordingly, via a request to the X server. The application gets notified of the change of size by way of an event and does whatever is appropriate (perhaps changing its layout).

If the user iconifies the window, the window manager will typically unmap the frame window and map an icon window. The window manager normally takes care of creating the icon window, but an application can create its own and pass the window ID to the window manager.

---

1. You can query the window tree using XQueryTree(), starting from the root window. If you do this with and without a window manager running, you will see the effect of reparenting.

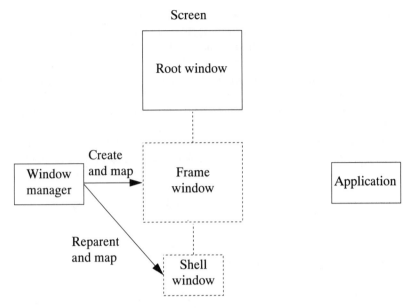

Figure 14.3 *Reparenting*

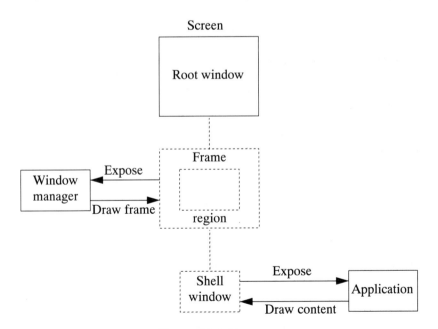

Figure 14.4 *Exposure*

One of the properties that a client can create on its top-level windows tells the window manager that the application is willing to participate in some conversations, using predefined protocols. In this case, the window manager may send messages (as fake events) to the window, the server passes them on to the application and it should respond appropriately.

To make all this work, the client, window manager and X server engage in a complex three-handed game, whose rules are defined in the Inter-Client Communication Conventions Manual, or ICCCM (Scheifler and Gettys, 1992 pp. 629-666). This is not a particularly easy document and it is hard to write a compliant application from first principles. Fortunately, the shell widgets hide almost all inter-client communication. All you need to do is set resources to the right values and the shell takes care of ICCCM compliance.

There are some facilities that are not enveloped by the shell. For those and in particular for the window manager protocols, you have to get involved in nasty, low-level interactions. The Motif toolkit makes this easy for you.

14.1.4   Window manager properties

A window manager queries various properties to get extra information from the application about how it wants to be displayed and may also set other properties to tell applications about how it is prepared to display them. Although most of this is hidden from you, a little explanation of the properties and their use does clarify just what a window manager can do for you. In Table 14.1 some, though not all, of the properties are listed. These are mainly *hints* to the window manager; the window manager is free to ignore them.

Direct involvement with these is not recommended; you should work with the Xt widget resources and the Motif convenience functions described here and in Chapter 8.

14.2   Icons and iconified windows

Only certain windows on the screen can be iconified. In Motif terms, if you create an ApplicationShell or TopLevelShell, the window will be iconifiable; if you create an XmDialogShell, it will not; if you create an XmMenuShell, it will be ignored altogether by the window manager, as it sets the override redirect flag.

You can only sensibly set the icon on an iconifiable window, even though the XmDialogShell does have icon-related resources.

14.2.1   Setting the icon

An icon may typically display both a picture and a text string. The text string is the icon name and is set as the iconName resource on the shell.

Table 14.1 *Window manager properties*

Property name	Set by	Used by	Contains
WM_NAME	Application	Any WM	Name to be used in title bar
WM_ICON_NAME	Application	Any WM	Name to be used in icon
WM_NORMAL_HINTS	Application	Any WM	Minimum and maximum sizes, size increments, aspect ratio restrictions
WM_HINTS	Application	Any WM	Input model, initial state (iconic or not), icon pixmap and position
WM_CLASS	Application	Any WM	Name and class to be used by WM to retrieve resources related to the application
WM_PROTOCOLS	Application	Any WM	List of protocols that the application is prepared to participate in
WM_COMMAND	Application	Any WM	Command needed to restart the application
WM_ICON_SIZE	Any WM	Application	Restrictions on the sizes of icons the window manager will display
WM_STATE	Any WM	Session manager	Unspecified, but actually reflects the state of the window (iconised, normal or withdrawn)
_MOTIF_WM_HINTS	Application	Mwm only	Desired window decorations, etc.
_MOTIF_WM_MENU	Application	Mwm only	Extra items for window menu
_MOTIF_WM_INFO	Mwm only	Application	Used to check if mwm is running (via XmIsMotifWMRunning())

There are two ways to set the picture: the easy way and the hard way.

Setting the icon pixmap

The easy way is to set the iconPixmap resource on the shell. This will cause the shell to change the WM_HINTS property on the top-level window; the window manager detects the change, extracts the pixmap and uses it to draw the icon.

In the application, setting the icon pixmap is easy:

```
#include <Xm/Xm.h>

void set_icon_pixmap (shell)
    Widget shell;
```

icon_pixmap

```
{
    Pixmap new_pixmap;

    new_pixmap=XmGetPixmapByDepth (XtScreen (shell),
                    "/usr/include/X11/bitmaps/mailfull",
                    1, 0, 1);
    XtVaSetValues (shell, XmNiconPixmap, new_pixmap, NULL);
}
```

In theory, at least, the icon pixmap must be a bitmap (a pixmap of depth 1), so we create a pixmap using XmGetPixmapByDepth() and specify depth 1. Most window managers, including mwm, seem happy to work with pixmaps of other depths; they take the first bit from each pixel and use that to create a bitmap from the pixmap.

The ICCCM says that the icon size should conform to the width and height restrictions given in the WM_ICON_SIZE property on the root window, if this property exists. By default, mwm sets this to limit icons to a minimum of 16 x 16 pixels, and a maximum of 50 x 50 in increments of 1 pixel. The user can configure this in the mwm application defaults.

Fortunately, mwm is quite sensible about oversized and undersized icon pixmaps and they will work well enough. If you are concerned about this, you can query the WM_ICON_SIZE property using XGetIconSizes(), then generate something of an appropriate size.

Window managers use the bitmap to mask foreground and background colours which can be specified for each application. If not specified, mwm will use some rather muddy defaults. The user can specify icon colours in mwm's resource files like this:

```
Mwm*Myapplication*iconImageForeground:  hotpink
Mwm*Myapplication*iconImageBackground:  blue
```

There is no way for your application to indicate its preferred icon colours to mwm (other than by editing mwm's resource files).

As a final step in configuring an application's icon, you can set the iconMask resource on the shell. This may be used by the window manager to mask the icon pixmap, giving you a non-rectangular icon. On the other hand, it may be ignored, which is what mwm does.

Setting the icon window

If you set the icon pixmap, mwm will create a two-colour icon and display this in an icon window that it creates and manages. If two colours are not enough, or you want to change the icon frequently without excessive flicker, you can supply an icon window rather than an icon pixmap. Having created it, you set the iconWindow resource on the shell and this is communicated to the window manager via the WM_HINTS property, as with the icon pixmap. The window manager will use this window as the icon and ignore any pixmap that you may have specified.

The window is just a raw X window and Motif and Xt give you no help with it. You have to use the drawing techniques described in Chapter 16 to create visual appearance and handle Expose events as normal.

Obviously, since you are getting involved in low-level event processing, this is harder than just setting the icon pixmap. However, if all you want is a multi-coloured icon (perhaps your sister-in-law sells X terminal memory), it is not too much work.

This code sets an icon window for a shell and installs a pixmap as its background pixmap. The background pixmap is automatically drawn in to any exposed areas of a window by the X server, so we do not have to handle Expose events:

icon_
window

```
#include <Xm/Xm.h>

void set_icon_window (shell, pixmap)
    Widget    shell;
    Pixmap    pixmap;
{
    Window          icon_win, root_win;
    int             x, y;
    unsigned int    width, height;
    unsigned int    border_width;
    unsigned int    depth;
    /* Get width, height etc. from the pixmap */
    XGetGeometry (XtDisplay (shell), pixmap,
                        &root_win,&x, &y,
                        &width, &height, &border_width, &depth);
    /* Create window and set background pixmap */
    icon_win = XCreateSimpleWindow (XtDisplay (shell),
                        root_win, 0, 0, width, height, 0, 0, 0);
    XSetWindowBackgroundPixmap (XtDisplay (shell), icon_win, pixmap);
    XtVaSetValues (shell, XmNiconWindow, icon_win, NULL);
}
```

As with icon pixmaps, the icon window should be one of the sizes specified by the WM_ICON_SIZE property on the root. Again, mwm treats incorrectly sized windows sensibly.

⚠ The icon window needs to be set before the shell is realised (if an ApplicationShell) or popped up (if a TopLevelShell).

The ICCCM restricts what you are allowed to do with an icon window. In particular, you should not map or unmap it, change its size or position or expect to be able to receive input events from it. About the most you can sensibly do is to select for, and respond to, Expose events.

14.2.2 Initial icon state

The window manager recognises three states for windows: normal, iconic and withdrawn. A withdrawn window is not visible either as a window or as an icon. All newly created top-level windows start in the withdrawn state and move to the normal or iconic state, when they are made visible. This happens when the shell is realised, popped up or has its child managed, according to the type of shell (see Chapter 8).

The window manager uses one field of the WM_HINTS property on the window to determine whether to show the window or just its icon. You can set this field by setting the initialState resource of the shell to NormalState (the default) or IconicState. Equally, the user can start the application as iconic by specifying the flag -iconic on the command line; if this is set, all TopLevelShells will have their initialState forced to IconicState.

If you want a shell's window to appear initially as iconic, just set the initialState resource. If you want to know if it is going to appear initially as iconic, use XtGetValues() to check the value of initialState just before it is realised or popped up.

14.2.3 Iconifying windows

If a window has the appropriate decorations, a user can iconify it by clicking on the "minimize" button and restore it with a double click. You can also iconify and restore windows under program control.

The way in which you do this depends on the class of the shell and the function you used to create it. Section 8.6.8 describes the full set of state transitions for shells and ways of inducing them.

14.2.4 Determining icon state

There is no easy, clean way to check if the window of a shell is currently iconic. If you need this information, you have several choices. You can track changes to the map state, query the map state or inspect the WM_STATE property on the window.

Tracking state changes

The ICCCM guarantees that a top-level window is unmapped when it goes from normal to iconic state and mapped again when it goes from iconic to normal. This is not strictly necessary, as the window manager will also map and unmap the parent frame window, which is enough to make the top-level window appear and disappear; the window manager does it only as a conventional courtesy.

This technique tracks MapNotify and UnmapNotify events to determine if the window is mapped or not. It is especially suitable if you want to take some action when the state changes. If the window contains a large, complex and time-varying picture, you might stop updating it when the window is iconified and start again when it is restored to normal state.

The easiest way to track the events is with an event handler. You install the event handler in this way:

icon_state

```
#include <Xm/Xm.h>
extern void watch_maps();

void set_handler (shell)
    Widget shell;
{
    XtAddEventHandler (shell, StructureNotifyMask,
                        False, watch_maps, (XtPointer) NULL);
}
```

The event handler function, watch_maps(), will be called whenever the shell's window is mapped or unmapped, or under a number of other circumstances we do not need to worry about. The event handler can inspect the event to find out what has happened:

```
#include <Xm/Xm.h>

void watch_maps (shell, client_data, event, cont)
    Widget      shell;
    XtPointer   client_data;
    XEvent      *event;
    Boolean     *cont;
{
    if (event->type == MapNotify)
        printf ("Map state changed, window is Normal\n");
    else if (event->type == UnmapNotify)
        printf ("Map state changed, window is Iconified\n");
}
```

The event handler will see a number of events which are neither MapNotify nor UnmapNotify. It just ignores them.

Inspecting the map state

Rather than tracking changes to the map state, you can query the window to find out if it is currently mapped, perhaps to determine if the user can see the big red warning notice you are about to draw in it. Widgets do not hold information about the map state of their windows, so you have to query the attributes of the window directly:

```
#include <Xm/Xm.h>
#include <stdio.h>

void check_map_state (shell)
    Widget shell;
{
    Display                 *display;
    Window                  window;
    XWindowAttributes       win_attr;

    printf("Map state is ");
    display=XtDisplay (shell);
    window=XtWindow (shell);
    XGetWindowAttributes (display, window, &win_attr);
    if (win_attr.map_state==IsUnmapped)
        printf ("Unmapped\n");
    else if (win_attr.map_state==IsUnviewable)
        printf ("Unviewable\n");
    if (win_attr.map_state==IsViewable)
        printf ("Viewable\n");
}
```

The map state IsViewable means that the window and all its ancestors are mapped, but it may still be invisible because its window is hidden behind another window. IsUnviewable means that it is mapped, but one of its ancestors is not. This should never happen for a shell's window.

Inspecting the WM_STATE property

Inspecting or tracking the map state will tell you whether a window is mapped or not, but there are three window states (from the window manager's point of view): Normal, Iconic and Withdrawn. A shell's window will be unmapped in both the Iconic and Withdrawn states and you have to be sure that you can distinguish between these two.

The WM_STATE property is intended to be used for communication between window managers and session managers and ordinary applications are not supposed to look at its content.[1] However, if you are prepared to cheat, it will tell you precisely what the state of a top-level window is:

---

1. It is considered legitimate to check if it exists.

```
#include <Xm/Xm.h>
#include <stdio.h>

void check_wm_state (shell)
   Widget shell;
{
   Display          *display;
   Window           window;
   Atom             xa_WM_STATE;
   unsigned long    *property = NULL;
   unsigned long    nitems;
   unsigned long    leftover;
   Atom             actual_type;
   int              actual_format;

   printf("WM state is ");
   display=XtDisplay (shell);
   window=XtWindow (shell);
/* Get WM_STATE property from window */
   xa_WM_STATE = XInternAtom (display, "WM_STATE", False);
   XGetWindowProperty (display, window,xa_WM_STATE, OL, 1, False,
                   xa_WM_STATE, &actual_type, &actual_format,
                   &nitems, &leftover, (unsigned char **) &property);
   if (property==NULL)
       printf ("Unknown\n");
   else if (*property==IconicState)
       printf ("Iconic\n");
   else if (*property==NormalState)
       printf ("Normal\n");
   else if (*property==WithdrawnState)
       printf ("Withdrawn\n");
/* Tidy up */
   if (property!=NULL)
        XFree ((char *) property);
}
```

This code takes you into the depths of X, where any number of things can go wrong; you should be more careful about checking return status and returned values than the example shows.

14.3 MWM decorations and menus

The Motif window manager puts decorations, resize handles, maximize button and so on, on the frames of top-level windows. The menu decoration in the top left of the mwm frame pops up a window menu. The user can manipulate these windows by selecting items from the menu, invoking menu items via keyboard accelerators or clicking on the decorations.

You can control the contents of the menu and the decorations that mwm puts on a window by setting the VendorShell resources mwmFunctions, mwmDecorations and mwmMenu.

The mwmFunctions resource controls what functions are applied to the window. mwmDecorations controls the visibility of decorations to invoke these functions if they are available. The default contents of the window menu are specified in the user's Mwm application defaults file in conjunction with the mwmrc file, not by the resources of the shell. However, items will only appear in the menu if the corresponding functions are available and you can add extra items to the default menu via mwmMenu.

As the names suggest, these resources are specific to mwm. Setting these resources affects the _MOTIF_WM_HINTS and _MOTIF_WM_MENU properties on the top-level window and only mwm is likely to take any notice.

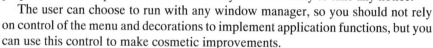 The user can choose to run with any window manager, so you should not rely on control of the menu and decorations to implement application functions, but you can use this control to make cosmetic improvements.

14.3.1   Setting the applicable functions

The functions that can be applied to a window are set on the VendorShell resource mwmFunctions. This is a bitwise OR of the symbols given in Table 14.2.

Table 14.2 *Mwm functions*

Symbol	Function
MWM_FUNC_RESIZE	f.resize
MWM_FUNC_MOVE	f.move
MWM_FUNC_MINIMIZE	f.minimize
MWM_FUNC_MAXIMIZE	f.maximize
MWM_FUNC_CLOSE	f.kill

The special symbol MWM_FUNC_ALL means that all these functions are applied, except for those specified in the rest of mwmFunctions.

If mwmFunctions is not set, mwm will take the functions on a shell to be those specified by mwm's clientFunctions resource (for ApplicationShell and TopLevelShell) or transientFunctions resources (for XmDialogShell). The clientFunctions can be set on a per application basis; the default is all functions. The transientFunctions resource has the same setting for all applications, and defaults to all functions except f.maximize and f.minimize.

If the shell's child is an XmBulletinBoard (or derivative) with noResize set True, the XmBulletinBoard will itself alter the setting of mwmFunctions on its parent shell. It attempts to give you the functions you have set in mwmFunctions plus a standard set, but excluding f.resize. However, if you set mwmFunctions using MWM_FUNC_ALL, it may get confused and give you only f.resize.

Whatever functions mwm eventually applies to a window can be invoked from the window menu or the decorations. If a function has not been applied to a window, mwm will remove it from the menu and not show the decorations that would invoke it. For instance, the default window menu is defined (in the system.mwmrc start-up file) as:

```
Menu DefaultWindowMenu
{
    Restore     _R    Alt<Key>F5      f.restore
    Move        _M    Alt<Key>F7      f.move
    Size        _S    Alt<Key>F8      f.resize
    Minimize    _n    Alt<Key>F9      f.minimize
    Maximize    _x    Alt<Key>F10     f.maximize
    Lower       _L    Alt<Key>F3      f.lower
    no-label                          f.separator
    Close       _C    Alt<Key>F4      f.kill
}
```

All of these items will, by default, be available from the window menu.

Mwm provides decorations for f.resize (resize handles) and f.minimize and f.maximize (minimize and maximize buttons); all of these are shown by default for an ApplicationShell or TopLevelShell.

The following function set_funcs() sets the available functions to just f.kill and f.resize and so will reduce the default window menu to Restore, Size, Lower and Close and remove the maximize and minimize buttons:

```
#include <Xm/Xm.h>
#include <Xm/MwmUtil.h>

void set_funcs (shell)
    Widget shell;
{
    XtVaSetValues (shell, XmNmwmFunctions,
                    MWM_FUNC_CLOSE|MWM_FUNC_RESIZE, NULL);
}
```

If you want to remove, say, the Close item from the menu, this code will do it:

                    XtVaSetValues (shell, XmNmwmFunctions,
                              MWM_FUNC_ALL | MWM_FUNC_CLOSE, NULL);

Note that removing the move function (MWM_FUNC_ALL | MWM_FUNC_MOVE) will remove the Move item from the window menu, but will not stop the user moving the window by dragging the title bar with the mouse.

14.3.2   Setting the MWM decorations

Decorations are controlled by mwmDecorations. This is a bitwise OR of some of the symbols illustrated in Figure 14.5.

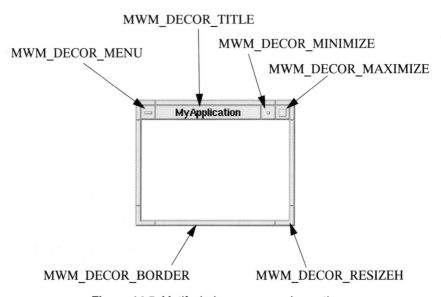

Figure 14.5 *Motif window manager decorations*

The special symbol MWM_DECOR_ALL means that all decorations, except those specified by the rest of mwmDecorations, are to be applied.

The decorations are also affected by the setting of the mwm clientDecorations resource (for ApplicationShell and TopLevelShell) or transientDecorations resource (for XmDialogShell). For a decoration to be visible, it must be specified both by the mwmDecorations resource on the shell and the clientDecorations or transientDecorations resource of mwm (if mwmDecorations is left unset, as is usual, all the decorations specified in the mwm resource will be shown). The function invoked by the decoration must also be included in mwmFunctions.

For instance, this function will give the window minimize and maximize buttons, but no menu button or resize handles:

```
#include <Xm/Xm.h>
#include <Xm/MwmUtil.h>

void set_decor (shell)
    Widget shell;
{
    XtVaSetValues (shell, XmNmwmDecorations,
                   MWM_DECOR_MINIMIZE
                   | MWM_DECOR_MAXIMIZE,
                   NULL);
}
```

If you want everything except the minimize and maximize buttons, use MWM_DECOR_ALL:

```
XtVaSetValues (shell, XmNmwmDecorations,
               MWM_DECOR_ALL
               | MWM_DECOR_MINIMIZE
               | MWM_DECOR_MAXIMIZE, NULL);
```

The settings are not orthogonal, so if you ask for buttons, you will also get a title bar. The behaviour (for an ApplicationShell) is as in Table 14.3.

Table 14.3 *MWM decorations*

mwmDecorations	*Visible decorations*
MWM_DECOR_BORDER	None (not even a border)
MWM_DECOR_RESIZEH	Border and resize handles
MWM_DECOR_TITLE	Title bar only
MWM_DECOR_MENU	Menu button and title bar
MWM_DECOR_MINIMIZE	Minimize button and title bar
MWM_DECOR_MAXIMIZE	Maximize button and title bar

Unlike mwmFunctions, mwmDecorations does not affect the contents of the window menu.

14.3.3   Setting the window menu

The default window menu is defined by the mwm resource windowMenu and can be changed in mwm's resource files. The value is a string which points to a menu definition in a mwmrc file, /usr/lib/X11/system.mwmrc or $HOME/.mwmrc. The menu definition gives the names of the menu items, mnemonics and accelerators for them and the mwm function that they invoke.

You can disbar the user from invoking certain functions and remove the corresponding entries from the window menu by setting mwmFunctions on the shell, but be careful, as XmBulletinBoard may decide to change this if it has noResize set True. You can also add extra items to the menu by setting the mwmMenu resource.

This resource is a text string; each line of the text string contains the name of the menu item, the mnemonic character, the accelerator key combination and the function to invoke. This code adds Big and Little items to the window menu for the shell, which can be invoked via Ctrl-b and Ctrl-l:

```
#include <Xm/Xm.h>
#include <Xm/MwmUtil.h>

void set_menu (shell)
    Widget shell;
{
    XtVaSetValues (shell, XmNmwmMenu,
                "Big      _B    Ctrl<Key>b  f.maximize\n\
                Little    _L    Ctrl<Key>l  f.minimize",
                NULL);
}
```

  The mnemonic is case sensitive, and must be preceded by the underscore. The accelerator specification is a simplified form of that used in translation tables. See the documentation in mwm(1X) for details.

14.4 Window manager protocols

So far, we have looked at ways in which you can persuade a window manager and mwm in particular to display your windows in particular ways. The traffic has been all one way, with the application telling mwm what it wants mwm to do.

There are some circumstances where mwm needs the application to cooperate to achieve the best result. In these cases, mwm has to ask the application to do something and it is the application's job to respond appropriately. This is done via the window manager protocols.

Window manager protocols sound difficult, but they are actually quite straightforward and made more so by the fact that Motif provides convenience functions you can use to detect messages from the window manager. Programming the response to a message is no more difficult than writing a callback function.

There are only three sorts of message used by window managers in general. These are listed in Table 14.4.

Table 14.4 *Window manager protocol messages*

Protocol name	Purpose
WM_TAKE_FOCUS	Used to tell an application that it should take keyboard input.
WM_DELETE_WINDOW	Used to tell an application to delete one of its windows.
WM_SAVE_YOURSELF	Used to tell an application to save itself (presumably because something is contemplating killing it).

In addition to these, mwm has a mechanism for defining extra protocols; this is described in Section 14.7.

An application does not have to participate in any of these protocols; in this case, the window manager may do something rather drastic. The Motif toolkit ensures that an application avoids this sort of outcome, primarily by ensuring that every window participates in the WM_DELETE_WINDOW protocol.

An application indicates to the window manager that it is willing to participate in a protocol by putting the message name (as an atom) onto the list in the WM_PROTOCOLS property of the shell's window. The Motif convenience functions hide this from you and you do not need to understand the messy details.

14.4.1   Protocol summary

If an application has indicated that it wants to participate in the window manager protocols, the window manager will send it ClientMessage events from time to time. The ClientMessage event contains the following information:

```
typedef struct {
    int         type;
    unsigned    long serial;   /* # of last request processed by server */
    Bool        send_event; /* True if this came from a SendEvent request */
    Display     *display;      /* Display the event was read from */
    Window      window;
    Atom        message_type;
    int         format;
    union {
        char  b[20];
        short s[10];
        long  l[5];
    } data;
} XClientMessageEvent;
```

The type will always be ClientMessage (as opposed to, say, KeyPress or Expose). The message_type tells you the protocol. For messages from the window manager, this will always be WM_PROTOCOLS (as an atom, of course). The data union has room for 20 bytes of data; the first four bytes, data.l[0], are the type of the message - WM_DELETE_WINDOW, say. This is confusing; the type of the message (the field that tells you what you need to do) is not event.type, nor even event.message_type, but event.data.l[0].

You will never actually have to look at the event structure (except when debugging), as the Motif protocol manager will take care of sorting out the protocol and the type of the message and the window and will then invoke a callback function that you provide. The callback function has to respond appropriately, according to the type of the message.

WM_TAKE_FOCUS protocol

The window manager sends a WM_TAKE_FOCUS message to an application's top-level window when it thinks that the application should start taking keyboard input. It gives the application an opportunity to direct this input to a particular one of its subwindows by setting the X input focus to the subwindow.

In a Motif application, you should let the toolkit handle this. Motif (and Xt-based toolkits in general) use the Xt keyboard focus rather than the X input focus to control the destination of keyboard input. Motif then layers a keyboard traversal model on top and you should use XmProcessTraversal() to work with this model (see Chapter 13 for some examples). If you set the focus using Xlib or Xt mechanisms, you risk confusing the toolkit. The advice is, do not get involved in this protocol.

WM_DELETE_WINDOW protocol

This is the useful one. A window manager sends a WM_DELETE_WINDOW message to an application's top-level window when the user indicates that he or she wants to close or delete the window, typically by selecting the Close menu item from the window menu. The application then decides how to respond. Usually, the response will involve making the window disappear, but the application does not have to do this. It can ignore the message altogether (in which case the Close menu item is effectively disabled and the user may be unable to halt the application), or it can hold a confirmation dialog with the user, then decide what to do.

If *any* top-level window is not participating in this protocol, then mwm will kill the entire application (using XKillClient()) when the user selects Close from that window's menu. Not all window managers are so forceful, but this is legitimate window manager behaviour; closing a popup dialog box can potentially terminate the application. To avoid this, the Motif toolkit makes sure that every top-level window takes part in this protocol and responds to the messages. How a shell responds to a WM_DELETE_WINDOW message is defined by the deleteResponse resource that all shells (except XmMenuShell) inherit from VendorShell. There are a number of possible responses, as described in Section 14.4.3.

In addition to the toolkit's response, you can define your own response by adding a protocol callback. You typically do this on an application's main window shell, so that the user can be asked to confirm exit from the application when the main window is closed.

WM_SAVE_YOURSELF protocol

When the window manager thinks that an application should prepare itself for sudden death, it sends it a WM_SAVE_YOURSELF message. This is the only window manager protocol that really looks like a protocol, in that the application has to make a timely response that the window manager can detect.

The application should save its internal state (to disk files, say) and update the WM_COMMAND property on its top-level window so that it holds the command needed to restart the application in its current state. The application is not allowed to interact with the user in any way after it receives the WM_SAVE_YOURSELF message and will not receive any user input. The window manager detects the change to WM_COMMAND and (presumably) saves the command somewhere, so that it can restart the application later.

WM_SAVE_YOURSELF is a warning that an application may be about to be killed, but the threat may go away. An application can assume that the danger has passed if it receives any mouse or keyboard event after the WM_SAVE_YOURSELF message.

WM_SAVE_YOURSELF is provided to support 'session managers'. The idea of a session manager is that it can save the state of a user's session when the user logs out and restart all the applications in their checkpointed state when the user logs in again. The session manager can be separate from the window manager.

There are a limited number of these in common use, but their use is likely to grow. The Motif window manager itself does send WM_SAVE_YOURSELF messages to applications that are participating in the protocol, but it does not yet have (and may never have) real session manager functionality. With an eye to the future, we give an example of a handler for the WM_SAVE_YOURSELF message.

14.4.2 Motif window manager and WM protocols

The Motif window manager sends WM_DELETE_WINDOW and WM_SAVE_YOURSELF messages when the user selects "Close" from the window menu (or otherwise invokes the f.kill function):

- If the window does not participate in either protocol, mwm simply kills the application.
- If it participates only in WM_DELETE_WINDOW, mwm sends a WM_DELETE_WINDOW message.

• If it participates only in WM_SAVE_YOURSELF, mwm sends a WM_SAVE_YOURSELF message and sets a timer. The timeout period is configurable (resource quitTimeout) and defaults to 1000 milliseconds. If the window's WM_COMMAND property is updated before the timer triggers, it removes the timer and kills the application; otherwise, it waits for the timer to trigger before it kills the application. In other words, it kills the application anyway, irrespective of the application's behaviour.

• If a window participates in both protocols, mwm will send both messages. In some versions, it will kill the client as part of the WM_SAVE_YOURSELF protocol, as above. In later (Motif 1.2.2 on) versions, it does not kill the client.

 The default toolkit behaviour for most shells is such that their window is destroyed when they receive WM_DELETE_WINDOW. Since mwm sends WM_DELETE_WINDOW first, a window that is hoping for a WM_SAVE_YOURSELF message will not be around to see it, unless it changes the shell delete response.

14.4.3   Motif shell delete response

The Motif VendorShell widget defines default behaviour for shells that receive a WM_DELETE_WINDOW message. You can change the default behaviour by setting the deleteResponse resource. This has three possible value: UNMAP, DESTROY and DO_NOTHING. The default value and the action taken for each value depend on the class of shell, as shown in Table 14.5.

Table 14.5 *Motif shell delete responses*

Shell class	Default deleteResponse	UNMAP action	DESTROY action
ApplicationShell	DESTROY	Calls XtPopDown()	Calls XtDestroyApplication-Context() and exit()
TopLevelShell	DESTROY	Calls XtPopdown()	Calls XtDestroyWidget()
XmDialogShell	UNMAP	Unmanages child	Calls XtDestroyWidget()

DO_NOTHING does nothing in all cases.

The default behaviour is such that closing an XmDialogShell just causes the window to popdown, closing a TopLevelShell destroys the widget and closing an ApplicationShell terminates the application.

If this is not what you want, you have to change the deleteResponse to disable or modify the toolkit's inbuilt response and add a protocol callback for WM_DELETE_WINDOW to add the behaviour you need.

14.5 Handling WM_DELETE_WINDOW

When the user selects Close off the window menu, mwm will send a WM_DELETE_WINDOW message to the shell's window. At this point, you can do whatever you want. Typical behaviour might be to popup a "Save work before exiting..." dialog when the user closes the application's main window.

We specify the behaviour by adding a protocol callback, using XmAddWMProtocolCallback(). The callback behaves just like any other callback, in that it is invoked when the server reports an event on the window belonging to the widget. In this case, the callback is invoked on an event whose type is ClientMessage, message_type is WM_PROTOCOLS and data.l[0] is WM_DELETE_WINDOW.

By way of example, consider this function:

wm_delete_
window

```
#include <Xm/Xm.h>
#include <Xm/Protocols.h>

extern void cb_handle_delete();

void set_delete_cb (app_shell)
   Widget app_shell;
{
   Atom xa_WM_DELETE_WINDOW;
   /* Disable default deleteResponse */
   XtVaSetValues (app_shell, XmNdeleteResponse, XmDO_NOTHING,
                   NULL);
   /* Convert message name to atom */
   xa_WM_DELETE_WINDOW = XmInternAtom (XtDisplay (app_shell),
                   "WM_DELETE_WINDOW", False);
   /* Add protocol callback */
   XmAddWMProtocolCallback (app_shell, xa_WM_DELETE_WINDOW,
                   cb_handle_delete, (XtPointer) NULL);

}
```

This sets the deleteResponse on the applicationShell to DO_NOTHING, which stops the toolkit destroying the application automatically. It then adds a protocol callback using XmAddWMProtocolCallback(). This is similar to XtAddCallback(), except that you give it the name of a type of message rather than a callback name. The message name has to be converted to an atom first; XmInternAtom() is just XInternAtom() with some fancy caching.

The callback function cb_handle_delete() is like any other. The call data is a pointer to an XmAnyCallbackStruct which in turn has a pointer to the event. The sample code here just prints out the details; in a real callback you would probably do precisely what you would if the user selected Exit from your application's File menu. Indeed, provided you do not make assumptions about the widget or call data parameters, you can use the same function:

```
#include <Xm/Xm.h>
#include <Xm/Protocols.h>
#include <Xm/AtomMgr.h>
#include <stdio.h>

void cb_handle_delete (w, client_data, call_data)
    Widget      w;
    XtPointer   client_data;
    XtPointer   call_data;
{
    int                     type;
    Atom                    message_type;
    Atom                    protocol_message;
    char                    *s;
    XmAnyCallbackStruct *   cd;
    XClientMessageEvent *   cm;

    cd = (XmAnyCallbackStruct *) call_data;
    fprintf (stderr, "Callback reason is %d\n", cd->reason);
    if (cd->event->type==ClientMessage)
    {
        fprintf (stderr, "type is ClientMessage\n");
        cm = &(cd->event->xclient);
        s = XmGetAtomName (XtDisplay (w), cm->message_type);
        fprintf (stderr, "message_type is %s\n", s);
        XFree (s);
        s = XmGetAtomName (XtDisplay (w), cm->data.l[0]);
        fprintf (stderr, "message is %s\n", s);
        XFree (s);
    }
    else
        fprintf (stderr, "Message type is %d\n", cd->event->type);
                        /* Won't happen */
}
```

XmGetAtomName() is the reverse of XmInternAtom(). It converts the atoms in the event data structure back into strings.

The output from this function looks like this:

```
Callback reason is 6666
type is ClientMessage
```

message_type is WM_PROTOCOLS
message is WM_DELETE_WINDOW

You will get this output whenever the user attempts to close the window. Note that the callback reason has the value 6666 (XmCR_PROTOCOLS). This value is not made public by the OSF, so it might change at any time.

14.6 Handling WM_SAVE_YOURSELF

WM_SAVE_YOURSELF is similar to WM_DELETE_WINDOW, in that mwm sends this message under the same circumstances and you detect it in much the same way. However, while you can do anything you want when you get WM_DELETE_WINDOW, the ICCCM specifies how you must respond to WM_SAVE_YOURSELF. You must save the application's state and update the WM_COMMAND property to contain the command needed to restart. You must not attempt any interaction with the user and you have to be quick.

Registering the callback is almost the same as for WM_DELETE_WINDOW:

wm_
saveyrself

```
#include <Xm/Xm.h>
#include <Xm/Protocols.h>

extern void cb_handle_saveyrself();

void set_saveyrself_cb (app_shell)
    Widget app_shell;
{
    Atom xa_WM_SAVE_YOURSELF;
    /* Disable default deleteResponse */
    XtVaSetValues (app_shell, XmNdeleteResponse, XmDO_NOTHING,
                    NULL);
    /* Convert message name to atom */
    xa_WM_SAVE_YOURSELF = XmInternAtom (
                    XtDisplay (app_shell), "WM_SAVE_YOURSELF",
                    False);
    /* Add protocol callback */
    XmAddWMProtocolCallback ( app_shell, xa_WM_SAVE_YOURSELF,
                    cb_handle_saveyrself, (XtPointer)NULL);
}
```

You still have to change the delete response of the applicationShell to DO_NOTHING, otherwise the application will exit, because it receives a WM_DELETE_WINDOW message just before the WM_SAVE_YOURSELF message.

What you do in the callback depends on the application, but you must update the WM_COMMAND property on the window so that the window (or session) manager knows the command to use to restart:

```
#include <Xm/Xm.h>
#include <Xm/Protocols.h>

void cb_handle_saveyrself (w, client_data, call_data)
    Widget      w;
    XtPointer   client_data;
    XtPointer   call_data;
{
    char **restart_argv;
    int   restart_argc;
    /* Save internal state and work out restart command */
    ...
    /* Update WM_COMMAND property */
    XSetCommand (XtDisplay(w), XtWindow(w), restart_argv, restart_argc);
}
```

 The applicationShell resource argv is set (by XtAppInitialize()) to contain the command and arguments originally used to start the application, but with the Xt-specific arguments (-display, -geometry, ...) removed. If you want to include these in the restart command you must save argv at start-up time, before Xt has had a chance to mangle it.

 The application should not exit when it gets a WM_SAVE_YOURSELF message. The message is supposed to indicate that the application may be about to be killed, not that it should kill itself. After it updates the WM_COMMAND property, the application can do anything that does not invalidate the restart command. If the application receives a mouse or keyboard event after WM_SAVE_YOURSELF, it means that there is no longer a danger of sudden death and it can resume normal operation (the window manager or session manager is supposed to keep these events away from the application until it is safe to continue). As most applications only change their state in response to user input, this means that they can continue normally.

At the time of writing, mwm's support for this protocol is inadequate.

14.7   Additional message types

The standard window manager protocols defined by the ICCCM follow a clear pattern. An application indicates that it wants to receive a given sort of message by putting the message name (such as WM_DELETE_WINDOW) into a certain property, WM_PROTOCOLS. When the corresponding message is sent, the property name is in the message_type field and the first four bytes of the data field contain the message name. All names are represented as atoms.

The Motif window manager has a private set of protocols built on a similar pattern. Instead of WM_PROTOCOLS, they use the _MOTIF_WM_MESSAGES property. There are no predefined message names; you can make them up as you go along. Mwm has a f.send_msg function that sends messages to your application, just as f.kill sends a WM_DELETE_WINDOW message.

These protocols are private only in the sense that they are not standard. Your applications are free to use them. For instance, consider this function:

wm_special

```
#include <Xm/Xm.h>
#include <Xm/Protocols.h>
#include <Xm/AtomMgr.h>

extern void cb_handle_mwmspecial();

void set_mwmspecial_cb (app_shell)
    Widget app_shell;
{
    char  buf[64];

    Atom xa__MOTIF_WM_MESSAGES;
    Atom xa__MYAPPLICATION_SPECIAL;
    /* Convert protocol and message name to atom */
    xa__MOTIF_WM_MESSAGES = XmInternAtom(XtDisplay(app_shell),
                    "_MOTIF_WM_MESSAGES", False);
    xa__MYAPPLICATION_SPECIAL=XmInternAtom(XtDisplay(app_shell),
                    "_MYAPPLICATION_SPECIAL", False);
    /* Add protocol callback */
    XmAddProtocolCallback(app_shell, xa__MOTIF_WM_MESSAGES,
                    xa__MYAPPLICATION_SPECIAL,
                    cb_handle_mwmspecial, (XtPointer)NULL);

    /* Set mwmMenu to add extra item to window menu */
    sprintf(buf, "Special _S Ctrl<Key>s f.send_msg %d",
                    xa__MYAPPLICATION_SPECIAL);
    XtVaSetValues(app_shell, XmNmwmMenu, buf, NULL);
}
```

This is very similar to the function to register a callback for the standard window manager protocols. However, we add the callback using XmAddProtocol-Callback(), rather than XmAddWMProtocolCallback(). This allows us to specify the name of the property, _MOTIF_WM_MESSAGES, as well as the message name, _MYAPPLICATION_SPECIAL.

We then add an extra item to the menu via mwmMenu. This has to be done from the application code, as it includes as a parameter the atom (an integer) for the string '_MYAPPLICATION_SPECIAL'. This will vary between different server invocations, so the actual value of mwmMenu might be:

```
Special _S Ctrl<Key>s f.send_msg 179
```

today and

```
Special _S Ctrl<Key>s f.send_msg 168
```

tomorrow.

When the user selects this special item, it invokes f.send_msg and mwm sends a ClientMessage event, appropriately filled in. The Motif protocol manager checks the message_type and data.l[0] fields and invokes the callback we specified. If the callback prints out the message details as for the WM_DELETE_WINDOW message, we will see this:

```
Callback reason is 6666
type is ClientMessage
message_type is _MOTIF_WM_MESSAGES
message is _MYAPPLICATION_SPECIAL
```

As a final note, you can use these mechanisms to exchange arbitrary messages between applications. You can use the Motif protocol manager to handle receipt, provided you use the customary pattern for message content, but you will need to do some Xlib programming to find all application top-level windows (XQueryTree()), find their properties and the message names they contain (XGetWindowProperty()) and send the ClientMessage events (XSendEvent()).

CHAPTER 15

Compound strings and font lists

Motif supports an additional level of mapping between fonts and strings to be displayed in that font. The original intention was that this would provide support for internationalisation, but much of this is now provided by the internationalisation facilities of X11R5. There is, as a result, some confusion of terms which makes compound strings less easy to understand than is really necessary.[1] This chapter attempts to explain simply the way that compound strings can be used in an application. For further information on internationalisation, see Chapter 20.

Motif defines two new types: compound strings and font lists, which are used extensively by the rest of the toolkit.

15.1 Basic concepts

Any attempt to describe compound strings and font lists and their use is going to be severely hampered by their interdependency. This is not a problem for the toolkit - indeed it is a benefit - but for literary style it is less helpful.

The combination of compound strings and font lists enable the application to specify a string that displays text in more than one font, on more than one line and

---

1. To get this straight from the beginning: compound strings and font lists are Motif-only concepts; compound text and font sets are X concepts. They are all addressing the same problems and there are ways of converting between the pairs, but they should not be confused. Chapter 20 looks in more detail at internationalisation and the toolkit mechanisms supplied. Chapter 18 also contains some example uses of compound text.

in both left-to-right and right-to-left directions. Most applications do not require this level of flexibility, but it can be used to some effect, both in providing interesting visuals and in supporting the internationalisation of applications.

At the heart of the relationship is the font list entry tag and it is appropriate to look briefly at this concept before discussing compound strings and font lists themselves in any detail.

15.1.1   Font list entry tags

A font list entry tag (hereafter referred to as a tag) is simply a char* string used to match text segments of a compound string with entries in a font list. When the toolkit displays a compound string, it chooses the font from the font list which has a tag that matches the tag for the text. In Motif 1.1 these tags were known as charsets. However, except in a very particular case, they do not convey any information about the character set encoding of the text itself. The name has been changed in most of the Motif documentation, although charsets persist in the code and headers and in functions provided for backward compatibility.

There is a predefined tag that can be used to match entries in a font list depending on the current locale setting: XmFONTLIST_DEFAULT_TAG. This is used as a default by the resource converters in the absence of an explicit tag in both compound strings and font lists.

15.1.2   Compound strings

Compound strings consist of string segments joined together in order. A segment can be:

- text, consisting of the text characters and a tag,
- a direction change indicator or
- a separator indicator (new line).

To display a compound string, the toolkit starts at the beginning of the list of segments and works through displaying the text segments and using the direction and separator segments to control the layout. The text segments that are on the same line are all displayed with their baselines aligned.

15.1.3   Font lists

A font list, as the name suggests, is a list of fonts. Each entry (or element) in the list consists of two components: the font itself (of which more later) and a tag. As described above, the tag is used to identify a particular entry, so that it can be matched by a tag from a compound string.

Each entry in a font list contains a font. Unfortunately for the OSF, X11R5 added a whole new level of font control called font sets, used for international-isation. As a result, a font list entry now contains either a single font (XFontStruct *) or a font set (XFontSet).[1] Chapter 20 contains a much fuller discussion of font sets. For the purposes of this chapter, we will not distinguish between fonts and font sets, except where necessary.

15.1.4 Matching compound string segments with font list entries

When the toolkit performs some operation on a text segment in a compound string, it may need to choose a particular font from an associated font list. To do so, it searches the font list for an entry which has a tag that matches the tag of the text segment. There is, however, a slight complication if the text tag is the default tag, XmFONTLIST_DEFAULT_TAG. We shall consider the two cases separately. Examples where these different searches are used are considered in Section 15.2.3.

Explicit tag

- The font list is searched for an entry that has a tag that exactly matches the text tag. If one is found, this is used.
- If no entry is found, the first entry in the list is used.

XmFONTLIST_DEFAULT_TAG

- The font list is searched for an entry that has a tag that exactly matches the text tag (that is, an entry that has the default tag). If one is found, this is used.
- If no entry is found, the font list is searched for an entry that has a tag that matches the character set for the current locale setting.
- If an entry is still not found, the first entry in the list is used.

15.2 Creating compound strings and font lists

Most applications will only need to create very simple compound strings and font lists with a single entry and they will probably do this via the resource file. A resource file for a typical application might include entries such as:

```
Application.labelFontList: -*-helvetica-medium-r-normal--12-*-*-*-*-*-*-*
Application*apply_button.labelString:  Apply
Application*cancel_button.labelString: Close
Application*undo_button.labelString:   Undo
Application*help_button.labelString:   Help
```

---

1. XFontStruct is a data structure. XFontSet is a pointer. Font lists always use pointers.

```
Application*add_button.labelString:    Add
Application*open_button.labelString:   Open...
```

The font list here contains a single entry with the default tag. All the labels also simply use the default tag and will therefore match the specified font.

However, in some applications it might be desirable to support more sophisticated strings and fonts.

15.2.1   Creating font lists

There are two basic ways or creating a font list: either programmatically, or from a string resource.

Converting strings to font lists

The syntax for a font list string that can be converted by the default string to font list converter is slightly messy. It is basically a comma-separated list of font entries:

```
font_list ::= font_list_entry[,font_list_entry]+
```

Each font_list_entry identifies either a single font or a font set and may have an optional tag. A font set includes a list of fonts:

```
font_list_entry ::= <font_entry|font_set_entry>
font_entry ::= font_name ['=' tag]
font_set_entry ::= font_name [';' font_name ]+ ':' [ tag ]
```

 Note that a font set is always terminated by a colon to indicate that it is a font set and that an equals sign is required in a single font entry to separate a single font name from the tag. Also note that font set entries are separated by semicolons rather than with commas, as they would be for string to font set conversion.

Here are some examples:

*   A single font with the default tag:

    fontList: --lucidabright-*-*-*-*-24-*-*-*-*-*-*-*

*   Two fonts, one with the default tag:

    fontList: --helvetica-*-*-*-*-24-*-*-*-*-*-*-*,\
                      -*-lucidabright-demibold-*-*-*-24-*-*-*-*-*-*-*=bold

- Two fonts, one tagged italic, one tagged bold:

```
*fontList: -*-lucidabright-demibold-*-*-*-24-*-*-*-*-*-*-*=bold,\
                 -*-lucidabright-*-i-*-*-24-*-*-*-*-*-*-*=italic
```

- A font set with Xlib selecting the fonts. Xlib will select fonts with different character set encodings to satisfy the requirements of the current locale, so the font set may contain more than one font in a single font list entry:

```
*fontList: -*-*-*-*-*-*-24-*-*-*-*-*-*-*:
```

- A font set with the fonts explicitly listed. The three fonts have different character set encodings and together satisfy the requirements of the locale ja_JP.jis7 (a Japanese locale):

```
*fontList: -*-fixed-medium-r-*-*-24-*-*-*-*-*-jisx0208.1983-*;\
                  -*-fixed-medium-r-*-*-24-*-*-*-*-*-jisx0201.1976-*;\
                  -*-fixed-medium-r-*-*-24-*-*-*-*-*-iso8859-*:
```

- Two font sets with tags:

```
*fontList: -*-fixed-*-*-*-*-24-*-*-*-*-*-*-*:large,\
                  -*-fixed-*-*-*-*-14-*-*-*-*-*-*-*:small
```

- A single font and a font set. Again, Xlib will create a font set that satisfies the current locale. The font list tag 'japanese' is significant only to the application and does not mean that the font set selected by Xlib will be suitable for displaying Japanese characters:

```
*fontList: -*-lucidabright-*-*-*-*-24-*-*-*-*-*-*-*=simple,\
                  -*-fixed-*-*-*-*-24-*-*-*-*-*-*-*:japanese
```

The application program can use this resource format to create a font list using the resource converter mechanisms. Calling a converter is very simple:

```
XrmValue from_value, to_value;

from_value.addr = "-*-lucidabright-*-*-*-*-24-*-*-*-*-*-*-*=simple,\
                  -*-fixed-*-*-*-*-24-*-*-*-*-*-*-*:japanese";
from_value.size = strlen (from_value.addr) + 1;
to_value.addr = NULL;
XtConvert (parent, XmRString, &from_value, XmRFontList, &to_value);
if (to_value.addr)
{
```

```
            XtSetArg (al[ac], XmNfontList, *(XmFontList *) to_value.addr); ac++;
        }
```

Creating font lists programmatically

The Motif functions XmFontListAppendEntry(), XmFontListEntryCreate() and
XmFontListEntryLoad() can be used to build up a list programmatically.

XmFontListEntryLoad() takes a font or font set name and automatically loads
the appropriate font or creates the font set structure. It then creates a font list entry
from the structure it has created.

Note that the entries in the font set are separated by commas here, not by
semicolons as for string to font list conversion:

```
        XmFontListEntry   entry1, entry2;
        XmFontList        fontlist;

        entry1 = XmFontListEntryLoad (display,
                            "-*-lucidabright-*-*-*-*-24-*-*-*-*-*-*",
                            XmFONT_IS_FONT, "simple");
        entry2 = XmFontListEntryLoad (display,
                            "-*-fixed-medium-r-*-*-24-*-*-*-*-*-jisx0208.1983-*,\
                            -*-fixed-medium-r-*-*-24-*-*-*-*-*-jisx0201.1976-*,\
                            -*-fixed-medium-r-*-*-24-*-*-*-*-*-iso8859-*",
                            XmFONT_IS_FONTSET, "japanese");
        fontlist = XmFontListAppendEntry (NULL, entry1);
        fontlist = XmFontListAppendEntry (fontlist, entry2);
        XmFontListEntryFree (&entry1);
        XmFontListEntryFree (&entry2);
```

If you have already loaded the font (using XLoadQueryFont()) or created the
font set (using XCreateFontSet()), XmFontListEntryCreate() will create a font list
entry containing the font or font set. You are only likely to do this if you need the
font or font set to do, say, Xlib drawing operations elsewhere in your application.

This example shows how to build up a font list from scratch, creating all the
Xlib intermediate structures on the way:

```
        XmFontListEntry   entry1, entry2;
        XmFontList        fontlist;
        XFontSet          fontset;
        XFontStruct       *font;
        char              **missing_charsets;
        int               num_missing_charsets = 0;
        char              *default_string;

        fontlist = NULL;
        font = XLoadQueryFont (display, "-*-lucidabright-*-*-*-*-24-*-*-*-*-*-*");
```

```
if (font)
{
    entry1 = XmFontListEntryCreate ("simple", XmFONT_IS_FONT, font);
    fontlist = XmFontListAppendEntry (fontlist, entry1);
    XmFontListEntryFree (&entry1);
}
else
    XtWarning ("Cannot load font");
fontset = XCreateFontSet (display,
                        "-*-fixed-medium-r-*-*-24-*-*-*-*-*-jisx0208.1983-*,\
                        -*-fixed-medium-r-*-*-24-*-*-*-*-*-jisx0201.1976-*,\
                        -*-fixed-medium-r-*-*-24-*-*-*-*-*-iso8859-*",
                        &missing_charsets, &num_missing_charsets,
                        &default_string);
if (num_missing_charsets > 0)
{
    XtWarning ("Font set does not satisfy current locale");
    XFreeStringList (missing_charsets);
}
else
{
    entry2 = XmFontListEntryCreate ("japanese", XmFONT_IS_FONTSET,
                        fontset);
    fontlist = XmFontListAppendEntry (fontlist, entry2);
    XmFontListEntryFree (&entry2);
}
```

15.2.2   Creating compound strings

Unlike font lists, compound strings with non-default tags cannot be represented in
resource files.

Creating compound strings in code is a somewhat laborious process. In order to
create a compound string consisting of several segments, you have to create one
compound string for each segment. These compound strings are then concatenated
one at a time to form a new compound string using XmStringConcat(). This
function copies both of the input strings, so they should be freed unless they are
used again later. If you are doing a lot of this, you might want to use a function that
will do the concatenation, then free the two input strings:

```
static XmString string_append (s1, s2)
    XmString s1, s2;
{
    XmString s3 = XmStringConcat (s1, s2);
    XmStringFree (s1);
    XmStringFree (s2);
```

```
        return (s3);
    }
```

Text segments

Suppose that you have already created a font list with italic and bold tag. You could create a compatible compound string with two text segments as follows:

```
xmstring = XmStringCreate ("The", "italic");
xmstring = string_append (xmstring, XmStringCreate ("Guardian", "bold"));
```

If this is applied to an XmPushButton with an appropriate fontList resource, the button will appear as in Figure 15.1.

Figure 15.1 *XmPushButton with two segment compound string*

Separator segments

Separator segments are added using XmSeparatorCreate():

```
xmstring = string_append (xmstring, XmStringSeparatorCreate ());
xmstring = string_append (xmstring, XmStringCreate ("Angel", "bold"));
```

This would display as shown in Figure 15.2.

Figure 15.2 *Compound string with separator segment*

Direction segments

A direction segment is created using XmStringDirectionCreate():

```
xmstring = string_append (xmstring, XmStringDirectionCreate
                (XmSTRING_DIRECTION_R_TO_L));
xmstring = string_append (xmstring, XmStringCreate ("Islington", "italic"));
```

This would display as shown in Figure 15.3.

Figure 15.3 *Compound string with direction segment*

 The default direction for compound strings is left-to-right and the supplied converters for reading XmString and XmStringTable (for XmList items) values from resource files both use XmStringCreateLtoR(). The most obvious way to work around this would be to provide an application resource that specified the default string direction and if necessary install a new type converter to handle right-to-left as the default string direction. See Section 10.15 for examples of how to do this.

15.2.3 Using the default tags

Compound strings created by the resource converters contain text segments with the default tag. To create a compound string consisting of a single text component with the default tag from within the application, the toolkit provides a special function XmStringCreateLocalized().[1] The default tag can be used to match an entry in the font list that is tagged to match the setting of the current locale:

```
Arg         al[64];
register    int ac = 0;
XrmValue    from_value, to_value;
XmString    xmstring;
XmFontList  fontlist = (XmFontList)NULL;
Widget      button = (Widget)NULL;

to_value.addr = NULL;
from_value.addr = (XtPointer)
                "-*-lucidabright-demibold-r-*-*-24-*-*-*-*-*-*=bold,\
                -*-lucidabright-medium-i-*-*-24-*-*-*-*-*-*=italic,\
                -*-helvetica-medium-r-*-*-24-*-*-*-*-*-*=jis7";
from_value.size = strlen((char *)from_value.addr) + 1;
XtConvert (shell, XmRString, &from_value, XmRFontList, &to_value);
if (to_value.addr)
{
```

---

1. This is exactly like calling XmStringCreate() and specifying XmFONTLIST_DEFAULT_TAG for the tag.

```
        fontlist = *(XmFontList *)to_value.addr;
        XtSetArg (al[ac], XmNfontList, fontlist); ac++;
}
xmstring = XmStringCreate ("The", "italic");
xmstring = xd_string_append (xmstring, XmStringCreateLocalized
                    ("Guardian"));
XtSetArg (al[ac], XmNlabelString, xmstring); ac++;
button = XmCreatePushButton (shell, "button", al, ac);
XmStringFree (xmstring);
if (fontlist)
    XmFontListFree (fontlist);
XtManageChild (button);
```

The font list has three entries: the first is a bold lucida font with the tag bold. The second is an italic lucida font with the tag italic. And the third is a bold helvetica font with the tag jis7. The XmPushButton displays a compound string with two text segments. The first has an explicit tag of italic, so it will always match the italic tagged font list entry. The second text component has a tag of XmFONTLIST_DEFAULT_TAG. If the locale is set to anything other than a locale with a jis7 character set, then this will match the first entry in the list, which is the one tagged bold. The string will be displayed as shown in Figure 15.1.

If the LANG environment variable is set to ja_JP.jis7, the second text component will match the font list entry tagged jis7 and will display as in Figure 15.4.

Figure 15.4 *Compound string with localised segment*

   Note that if the font list has any entries which do not have an explicit tag, these will match any default tags in the compound string before the font list is searched for entries with character set tags (see Section 15.1.4).

For further examples and discussion of the locale and its uses, see Chapter 20.

15.3   Manipulating compound strings and font lists

15.3.1   Extracting fonts from font lists

In some applications you might want to extract a font from a font list. For example, if the user is able to set the font for an application using an application resource, you may want to extract a font to use when rendering strings directly onto an XmDrawingArea.

The following fragment of code contains a function that could be called to create a graphics context and set the single font to be one of those used by the widgets in the application. It assumes that the given widget's parent is either a shell or an XmBulletinBoard. It gets a font list from the parent's labelFontList resource and searches it for an entry which is tagged "Drawing". If no such entry is found, the first entry in the list is used. The font or font set is then extracted from the selected entry; if it is a font set then the set of fonts is extracted and the first font in this list is used.

```
static GC gc = 0;

void create_gc (w)
    Widget w;
{
    XmFontList          fontlist;
    XGCValues           values;
    XFontStruct         *font, **font_struct_list;
    XFontSet            fontset;
    char                **font_name_list, *tag;
    XtPointer           t;
    XmFontContext       context;
    XmFontListEntry     first_entry, entry;
    XmFontType          font_type;
    int                 font_count;

    if (gc)
        return;

    /* Assume parent is Shell or BulletinBoard */
    XtVaGetValues (XtParent(w), XmNlabelFontList, &fontlist, 0);
    if (fontlist)
        if (XmFontListInitFontContext (&context, fontlist)) {
            /* Get first entry */
            entry = XmFontListNextEntry (context);
            first_entry = entry;
            /* Walk down list looking for "Drawing" */
            while (entry) {
                tag = XmFontListEntryGetTag (entry);
                if (strcmp (tag, "Drawing") == 0) {
                    XtFree (tag);
                    break;
                }
                XtFree (tag);
                entry = XmFontListNextEntry (context);
```

```
          }
          XmFontListFreeFontContext (context);
          /* If we didn't find it use first entry */
          if (! entry)
                entry = first_entry;
          /* Get the font */
          t = XmFontListEntryGetFont (entry, &font_type);
          if (font_type == XmFONT_IS_FONT)
                font = (XFontStruct *)t;
          else {
                /* It's a font set - use the first one in the set */
                fontset = (XFontSet) t;
                font_count = XFontsOfFontSet (fontset, &font_struct_list,
                            &font_name_list);
                font = font_struct_list[0];
          }
          values.font = font->fid;
          values.foreground = BlackPixelOfScreen(XtScreen(w));
          gc = XCreateGC (XtDisplay(w), XtWindow(w),
                      GCFont|GCForeground, &values);
    }
}
```

15.3.2   Manipulating compound strings

The compound string is an opaque data type and can only be manipulated using functions provided by the Motif toolkit. However, it is possible to extract the text from a compound string as a char* and manipulate it in this more familiar form.

Comparing

Use the function XmStringCompare() to compare two compound strings.

The toolkit provides another comparison function, XmStringByteCompare(), but the documentation notes that a compound string with redundant information may not match a semantically equivalent string. Use this at your peril.

The function XmStringHasSubstring() can be used to search for one string within another. The algorithm is fairly simple. The first text segment is extracted from the substring and each of the text segments in the source string is searched to see if the substring occurs in it. Text direction and the tag are not considered.

Drawing

There are three explicit drawing routines that handle compound strings: XmStringDraw(), XmStringDrawImage() and XmStringDrawUnderline().

XmStringDrawUnderline() takes a main string and a substring. The whole of the main string is drawn with the matching substring underlined for its first occurrence in the main string.

There are also functions to obtain size information about compound strings: XmStringExtent(), XmStringHeight() and XmStringWidth().

The following code fragment illustrates an expose callback for an XmDrawingArea that displays all the items from an XmList and underlines the selected one. The items are joined together to make a single compound string with separators where required to fit them into the XmDrawingArea. The create_gc() function is as illustrated in Section 15.3.1.

drawlist

```
void da_expose (w, client_data, call_data)
    Widget      w;
    XtPointer    client_data;
    XtPointer    call_data;
{
    XExposeEvent *e = &((XmDrawingAreaCallbackStruct *)call_data)
                        ->event->xexpose;
    XmString     *items, *selected_items, out_string, tmp_string;
    Boolean      underline;
    int          item_count, selected_count;
    Widget       list = (Widget)client_data;
    Dimension    width, height, extent, item_extent, string_height;
    int          i;
    XmFontList   font_list;
    XRectangle   clip;

/* Extract items, selected items and font from XmList */
    XtVaGetValues (list, XmNitems, &items, XmNitemCount, &item_count,
                        XmNselectedItems, &selected_items,
                        XmNselectedItemCount, &selected_count,
                        XmNfontList, &font_list,
                        0);
    XtVaGetValues (w, XmNwidth, &width, XmNheight, &height, 0);
    underline = (selected_count > 0);
    create_gc (w, font_list);
    extent = 0;
    out_string = NULL;
/* Form list items into a single compound string, inserting separators where
needed to avoid drawing outside the XmDrawingArea */
    for (i = 0; i < item_count; i++)
    {
        item_extent = XmStringWidth (font_list, items[i]);
        if (out_string != NULL && (extent + item_extent > width))
        {
            extent = 0;
            out_string = string_append (out_string,
                        XmStringSeparatorCreate());
        }
```

```
                        tmp_string = XmStringConcat (out_string, items[i]);
                        XmStringFree (out_string);
                        out_string = tmp_string;
                        extent = extent + item_extent;
                   }
                   string_height = XmStringHeight (font_list, out_string);
                   clip.x = e->x;
                   clip.y = e->y;
                   clip.width = e->width;
                   clip.height = e->height;
                   XSetClipRectangles (XtDisplay (w), gc, 0, 0, clip, 1, YXBanded);
              /* Draw compound string, underlining the selected item if any */
                   if (underline)
                        XmStringDrawUnderline (XtDisplay (w), XtWindow (w), font_list,
                                  out_string, gc, 0, (height - string_height) / 2, width,
                                  XmALIGNMENT_CENTER,
                                  XmSTRING_DIRECTION_L_TO_R, NULL,
                                  selected_items[0]);
                   else
                        XmStringDraw (XtDisplay (w), XtWindow (w), font_list, out_string, gc,
                                  0, (height - string_height) / 2, width,
                                  XmALIGNMENT_CENTER,
                                  XmSTRING_DIRECTION_L_TO_R, NULL);
                   XmStringFree (out_string);
              }
```

The results are shown in Figure 15.5.

Figure 15.5 *Drawing a compound string on a drawing area*

The XmString drawing routines require that the graphics context passed in has a valid font member. This is overwritten by fonts from the font list during the drawing operation, but the graphics context is restored to its initial state before the drawing routine returns.

 The drawing routines all take a clipping rectangle, but it is not optimally used (that is, drawing will take place outside the specified rectangle). Instead of using this, simply set the clipping rectangle in the graphics context as shown above and pass NULL as the clip parameter to the drawing routines to stop the routine from removing the clipping for the gc when it returns.

 The y position specified refers to the top of the bounding box and not the baseline of the text as for XDrawString(). XmStringBaseline() can be used to return the offset from the top of the bounding box to the baseline of the first line of text if you need to align the text baseline with something else in the drawing.

Traversing

Occasionally it is necessary for the application to traverse the segments in a compound string. The toolkit supports this by providing the functions XmStringIn-itContext(), XmStringGetNextSegment() and XmStringFreeContext(). The following function uses these to extract the text with a given tag from a compound string:

```
char *find_tag (s, in_tag)
    XmString    s;
    char        *in_tag;
{
    XmStringContext   context;
    char              *text, *tag;
    XmStringDirection direction;
    Boolean           separator;

    if (XmStringInitContext (&context, s))
    {
        while (XmStringGetNextSegment (context, &text, &tag, &direction,
                    &separator))
        {
            if (strcmp (in_tag, tag) == 0)
            {
                XtFree (tag);
                XmStringFreeContext (context);
                return text;
            }
            XtFree (text);
            XtFree (tag);
        }
        XmStringFreeContext (context);
```

```
        }
      return NULL;
   }
```

The alert reader will have noticed that Motif already provides a function that does a similar job. XmStringGetLtoR() returns the text for the first segment which has the specified tag. It also checks that the direction of the segment is left-to-right.

There are two further functions - XmStringGetNextComponent() and XmString-PeekNextComponent() - which can also be used to traverse the string. These provide a slightly different view of the compound string (actually the internal representation). Instead of returning each text component with a tag, a tag component is returned each time the tag changes. Treat these functions with caution.

Converting to and from compound text

As noted at the beginning of this chapter, X supports the concept of compound text, which addresses some of the same issues as compound strings. The most important use of compound text, as far as Motif programs are concerned, is within drag and drop and other selection transfers; by using this format Motif programs can exchange data with non-Motif programs. Fortunately there are simple functions to convert between the formats: XmCvtXmStringToCT() and XmCvtCTToXmString(). For examples of their use in drag and drop transfers, see Chapter 19.

CHAPTER 16

Drawing

Drawing with X is a large subject and deserves much more coverage than we have space for here. However, in many Motif applications, there is only a relatively small amount of drawing to be done. This chapter is for developers of these applications; it is a whistle stop tour of the drawing concepts and facilities, with examples of how to achieve the most common effects.

16.1   Drawables, pixmaps and bitmaps

This is simply to clear up a bit of terminology. A window is a server side data structure which is displayed by the server. A pixmap is simply an 'off-screen' window. It can be drawn on in exactly the same way as an ordinary window, except that the result is not visible. It can be useful, for example, to have a pixmap that contains a frequently used drawing, which is then drawn in a number of different windows using XCopyArea() when they are exposed. Windows and pixmaps are referred to collectively as drawables.

Drawables have three dimensions: width, height and depth. The width and height are obvious; the depth refers to the number of bits used to store the colour for each pixel. So, if a hardware display can display 256 different colours at the same time (this is usually independent of the number of distinct colours that it can display), it is said to have a depth of 8 bits. Each pixel, indexed by an x and y position, consists of 8 bits which specify a colour index from 0 to 255.

A bitmap is a pixmap that is only one bit deep. That is, each pixel is either a zero or a one. Bitmaps are often used as masks, or stencils, where the drawing will "go through" the one bits, but not the zero bits. This is indeed how fonts are specified, each character in the font is a little bitmap stencil through which colour can be drawn.

16.2   Colours and visuals

When building display hardware (as with most of the rest of life) there are trade-offs to be made between cost and effectiveness. The display being used to write this can display an enormous number of distinct colours, but only a maximum of 256 different colours at the same time. This is because its display memory (the memory which it uses as the source to refresh the screen every few milliseconds) is only 8 bits deep. For it to display all the different colours at the same time, the display memory would have to be 24 bits deep. This would be much more expensive and would only be useful for a few, specialist applications.

In an attempt to shield applications from the design of the hardware and to give the developer a fighting chance of his or her application running on different types of display, X introduces a number of abstraction mechanisms to support the use of colour.

The underlying support for colours in X uses RGB (red, green, blue) values. That is, a colour value consists of a red, green and blue triple which indicates the relative strength of each primary component. Because different devices use phosphors with different characteristics, the same RGB values will probably not display exactly the same colour on two different devices. X therefore supports additional device-independent colour spaces and allows applications to map from device-independent colour representations to device specific RGB values, so that they can be used in drawing routines. The whole subject of device-independent colour spaces is unfortunately beyond the scope of this book. We shall be looking only at routines that use the RGB colour space and named colours. RGB colour values can be specified in a number of different ways, as described in Section 16.2.2.

16.2.1   Colour maps

The server holds a limited number of bits of data (perhaps eight) for each pixel on the screen. When it draws the pixel it has to convert the bit pattern in the pixel to RGB values to drive the hardware. It does so by treating the bit pattern as an index into a colour map. The way in which the server uses the pixel value and indexes the colour map is determined by the visual type; different visual types are discussed in Section 16.2.3.

A colour map is a server side data structure which consists of a table of colour cells, where each colour cell is (notionally) a triple of unsigned short red, green and blue values. A colour map is indexed using a pixel value which is actually an unsigned long. Pixel values are used in drawing operations.

An application typically needs to do the following four things:

- Allocate colour cells in a colour map, thus obtaining valid pixel values.
- Optionally store RGB values in those cells, depending on how they were allocated.
- Use the pixel values to do drawing.
- Deallocate the colour cells.

Colour maps are created with respect to a particular screen of the display. The actual hardware device connected to the screen determines how many entries the colour map needs and how many bits of the RGB values are significant.

Private colour maps

A screen can have many colour maps associated with it and will always have a default colour map. An application can use the default colour map, or create one for its exclusive use. Whether an application should allocate its own colour map depends on how many colours it wants to use (and how much irritation the user is prepared to put up with). Most applications use only a few colours and so use the default colour map. If an application wants to use lots of different colours, it may find that there is not enough room in the default colour map to allocate the required number of cells. The application can then create its own colour map, attach it to the required window and use it as required.

There is always an installed colour map, which is used by the server to convert from pixel to RGB values.[1] When one particular colour map is installed, any pixels drawn with pixel values from a different colour map will be rendered in random colours. The window manager is responsible for making sure that the appropriate colour map is installed; the ICCCM forbids applications from installing colour maps themselves.

If an application uses a private colour map, it should set the colormap resource on its shells and allow it to be inherited down the widget hierarchy. The window manager will then (by default) automatically install the correct colour map depending on the position of the pointer. This can cause every pixel on the screen to change colour as the pointer is moved from one window to another. Some users may find this irritating and applications should allow users to specify that they only want to use the default colour map and will suffer the consequences if it does not have sufficient room.

---

1. Some hardware can support multiple concurrently installed colour maps.

Allocating colour cells

Colour cells can be allocated as read/write or read-only. If a colour cell is allocated as read/write, the application has to initialise the RGB value. For read-only colour cells, the required RGB value is specified when the cell is allocated. Read-only cells are shared among multiple clients, so it is not polite (or possible) to change the RGB value of such a cell.

Depending on the visual type, a colour map will be either fixed or variable. If it is fixed, the values in the cells will be predetermined and the application can only allocate read-only cells. If the colour map is variable, the application can additionally allocate read/write cells and store colour values in them.

Read-only colour cells

To allocate a read-only (or shared) colour cell use XAllocColor() or XAlloc-NamedColor(), depending on how you wish to specify the required colour value. For example, if you want a pixel value that corresponds to the colour red, you can use the following code (which stores the colour into a graphics context ready for use in a drawing operation):

*shared_*
colour

```
create_gc (w)
    Widget w;
{
    XGCValues values;
    XColor      screen_def, exact_def;
    Display     *display = XtDisplay (w);
    Colormap    cmap = XDefaultColormapOfScreen (XtScreen (w));
    int         mask = 0;

    if (gc != 0)
        return;
    /* Allocate read-only colour cell for colour 'red' */
    if (XAllocNamedColor (display, cmap, "red", &screen_def, &exact_def)
            != 0) {
        /* Put the pixel value for red into the GC, ready for drawing
            operations */
        values.foreground = screen_def.pixel;
        mask = GCForeground;
    }
    gc = XCreateGC (display, XtWindow (w), mask, &values);
}
```

XAllocNamedColor() first looks up the colour 'red' in the colour database (/usr/lib/X11/rgb.* by default), and returns in exact_def (an XColor structure) the exact RGB values given there. The closest RGB mix that the hardware can provide is determined and the colour map is searched for a read-only cell that already contains these actual RGB values. If one is not found a new cell is allocated. The actual RGB values and the index of the cell containing these values are returned in screen_def. The exact and actual RGB values may differ drastically if, for instance, the display device can only handle a very small number of colours.

The application should free the colour cell when it has finished with it, using XFreeColors(). The cells are reference counted and will remain allocated until the reference count goes to 0.

Read/write colour cells

Read/write colour cells, also called private colour cells, give the application much more control. The following code fragment is essentially the same as for the read-only colour cell, except that the application can now store new colour values in the colour cell when it needs to:

```
static GC gc = 0;

create_gc (w)
    Widget w;
{
    XGCValues values;
    XColor      screen_def, exact_def;
    Pixel       pixel;
    Display     *display = XtDisplay (w);
    Colormap    cmap = XDefaultColormapOfScreen (XtScreen (w));
    int         mask = 0;

    if (gc != 0)
        return;
    /* Allocate private colour cell */
    if (XAllocColorCells (display, cmap, False, NULL, 0, &pixel, 1)) {
        /* Lookup RGB values for 'red' */
        if (XLookupColor (display, cmap, "red", &screen_def, &exact_def)
                    != 0) {
            /* Store RGB values into the allocated cell */
            screen_def.pixel = pixel;
            screen_def.flags = DoRed | DoGreen | DoBlue;
            XStoreColor (display, cmap, &screen_def);
            /* Set the GC to use pixel as foreground */
            values.foreground = pixel;
            mask = GCForeground;
        }
    }
    /* Create the GC, ready for drawing operations */
    gc = XCreateGC (display, XtWindow (w), mask, &values);
}
```

Private colour cells can only be allocated in a writable colour map - one created for a visual type of GrayScale, PseudoColor or DirectColor (visual types are discussed in Section 16.2.3).

Again the application should free the colour cell when it has finished with it, using XFreeColors(). Section 16.2.2 has more details on converting a string to a colour value.

Any drawing that the application does with the graphics context will display red pixels. If it requires this, the application can change all those red pixels to a different colour simply by storing the new colour in the colour cell. It does not have to redo the drawing. Doing this will not interfere with any red pixels drawn from a different colour cell; the colour map is providing the extra level of indirection.

The other advantage of using read/write colour cells is that certain drawing modes set in the graphics context (such as xor) combine the source colour cell with the graphics context's foreground value to give a new colour cell. This will produce random effects if the colour cells are read-only. Using read/write colour cells the application can determine the effect exactly. More on this in Section 16.4.1.

16.2.2   Obtaining colour values from a string

There are several ways of specifying a colour in a string and several ways of determining the required colour from a string.

Using a converter
Using the default String to Pixel converter will simply call XAllocNamedColor() for the supplied string, thus returning a shared colour cell index.

Looking up a colour name
XLookupColor() looks up the supplied name in the colour database (by default /usr/lib/X11/rgb.*) and fills in the colour values with the exact and the nearest possible RGB values.

Parsing a colour specification
XParseColor() parses the supplied colour specification string. Colour specification strings consist of a colour space name followed by a colon (:) followed by a set of slash (/) separated values, such as CIELuv:50.0/0.0/0.0 or rgb:00/ff/00. For backward compatibility, RGB values can also be specified as, for instance, #00ff00. See the Xlib documentation for a complete description and examples.

16.2.3   Visuals

There are six visual types which specify the way in which colour map is used. A visual also specifies red, green and blue masks, bits per RGB and the size of the colour map.

A screen can support many different visuals simultaneously. The required visual type is specified when a window or colour map is created. Most applications are content to use the default visual of the screen for all their windows.

The visual types can be considered in three pairs. Each pair use the colour map in a particular way, but one of the pair has a fixed colour map, where the other has a variable colour map. The different visual types are:

StaticGray and GrayScale

A pixel value is used as an index into the colour map. The colour map entries have red, green and blue values, all set to the same value (in other words, these visuals only support shades of grey) (see Figure 16.1).

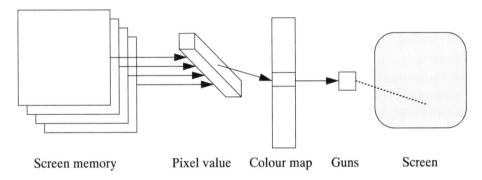

| Screen memory | Pixel value | Colour map | Guns | Screen |

Figure 16.1 *Visual type StaticGray and GrayScale*

StaticGray colour maps are fixed and the application cannot allocate private cells. Each pixel always represents the same shade of grey. The shades are arranged such that they provide linear increments from white to black (or from black to white).

GrayScale colour maps are variable. The application can allocate private colour cells and store colours in them. The red, green and blue components should be set to the same value in the call to XStoreColor().

A StaticGray colour map with a depth of 1 (that is, a colour map with only two entries) is called monochrome and supports only black and white.

StaticGray and GrayScale visuals usually have a small number of bits per pixel (8 or fewer).

StaticColor and PseudoColor

A pixel value is used as an index into the colour map. The colour map entries have red, green and blue values all set to arbitrary values (see Figure 16.2).

StaticColor colour maps are fixed and the application cannot allocate private cells. Each pixel always represents the same colour.

PseudoColor colour maps are variable. The application can allocate private colour cells and store colours in them.

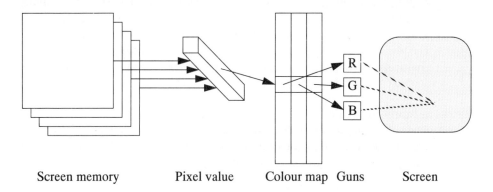

Figure 16.2 *Visual type StaticColor and PseudoColor*

StaticColor and PseudoColor visuals usually have a relatively small number of bits per pixel (4 to 8). They provide a cost-effective way of implementing colour hardware. PseudoColor is probably the most common visual.

TrueColor and DirectColor

A pixel value is decomposed into red, green and blue fields which are used to index three separate colour maps (see Figure 16.3).

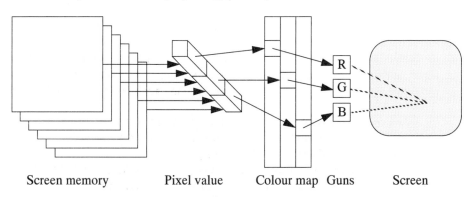

Figure 16.3 *Visual type TrueColor and DirectColor*

TrueColor colour maps are fixed and the application cannot allocate private cells. Each pixel always represents the same colour. The colour maps are arranged such that they provide linear increments in colour. There is therefore a direct correlation between pixel value and colour. This enables applications to perform calculations directly on pixel values to determine contrasting or matching colours.

DirectColor colour maps are variable. The application can allocate private colour cells and store colours in them.

TrueColor and DirectColor visuals usually have a larger number of bits per pixel (24 or 32). These visuals are used on high-quality, expensive hardware.

16.3 Drawing primitives

Xlib provides a fairly simple set of drawing functions, which are clearly described in the X documentation and many of the books listed in the bibliography.

The drawing primitives, with cross-references to where they are used elsewhere in the book, are:

- XClearArea(), Section 4.6.1.
- XCopyArea(), Section 7.4.3.
- XCopyPlane().
- XDrawPoint() and XDrawPoints().
- XDrawLine() and XDrawLines().
- XDrawSegments().
- XDrawRectangle() and XDrawRectangles(), Section 16.4.2.
- XDrawArc() and XDrawArcs(), Section 4.6.1.
- XFillRectangle() and XFillRectangles(), Section 16.4.2.
- XFillPolygon().
- XFillArc() and XFillArcs().

These drawing primitives are combined with a set of attributes, known as a graphics context, to provide a large number of drawing operations. There are additional primitives for drawing text: XDrawText(), XDrawString() and XDrawImageString(). These are described in Section 16.5.2.

16.4 Graphics contexts and drawing

Graphics contexts (GCs) are server side data structures used to communicate parameters between a client and the server when performing graphics operations. The client creates a GC using XCreateGC() and can subsequently update the components using XChangeGC() or one of many convenience functions such as XSetForeground(). It should be freed when no longer wanted, using XFreeGC().

If the GC is never going to be changed, an Xt application can obtain a shared, read-only GC using XtGetGC(); it must release it when it is no longer wanted, using XtReleaseGC(). It is a decided mistake to apply XFreeGC() to a GC obtained from XtGetGC().

A GC has a large number of attributes or components, represented by the elements of the XGCValues structure used to create and modify GCs. Not all of the drawing operations use all of the components of the GC passed as a parameter (see Table 16.1).

The remainder of this section shows how the most important components can be used in conjunction with basic drawing operations. Where a particular component is discussed, it is named in a bold heading.

Table 16.1 *X drawing functions and GC components*

Function	function	foreground	background	Line drawing	cap_style	join_style	Tiling and stippling	fill_rule	arc_mode	graphics_exposures	font
XDrawPoint(s)	✓	✓									
XDrawLine & XDrawSegments	✓	✓	✓	✓	✓		✓				
XDrawLines	✓	✓	✓	✓	✓	✓	✓				
XDrawArc(s)	✓	✓	✓	✓	✓	✓	✓				
XDrawRectangle(s)	✓	✓	✓	✓	✓	✓	✓				
XFillRectangle(s)	✓	✓	✓				✓				
XFillPolygon	✓	✓	✓				✓	✓			
XFillArc(s)	✓	✓	✓				✓		✓		
XCopyArea	✓									✓	
XCopyPlane	✓	✓	✓							✓	
XDrawText and XDrawString	✓	✓	✓				✓				✓
XDrawImageString		✓	✓								✓

The line drawing components are line_width, line_style, dash_offset and dashes. If the line_style is LineDoubleDash, the background is also used by these functions.

The tiling and stippling components are fill_style, tile, stipple, ts_x_origin and ts_y_origin. If the fill_style is FillOpaqueStippled, the background is also used.

All functions use plane_mask, subwindow_mode, clip_x_origin, clip_y_origin and clip_mask.

16.4.1 Basic drawing

The most basic drawing relies on the function and foreground components of the GC.

function and foreground

The function component specifies how the server will modify the destination pixels when it does the drawing. The default value, GXcopy, is the most useful. Exactly what is copied depends on the actual operation being performed. For example, when drawing a line using XDrawLine(), the foreground value is copied to the drawable. Alternatively when copying an area from one drawable to another, using XCopyArea(), the pixels in the source drawable are copied to the destination drawable.

16.4.2 Rubber-band drawing

Although the most commonly used function is GXcopy, GXxor is also useful, in that drawing the same thing twice with function GXxor will leave the window unchanged. This is frequently used for implementing simple rubber-band animation.

For example, consider an application that draws a red, green and blue striped background, and drags out a rectangle using button 2. To implement this, we first need to create some GCs. In this example, we use only two GCs, one for the background and one for the dragged rectangle. This code assumes that the colour map is variable:

rubberband

```
static GC    gc = (GC)0;
static GC    drag_gc = (GC)0;
static Pixel  pixels[3];

static void create_gc (w)
    Widget w;
{
    XGCValues  values;
    XColor      screen_def, exact_def;
    Display     *display = XtDisplay (w);
/* We use the default colour map */
    Colormap    cmap = XDefaultColormapOfScreen (XtScreen (w));

    if (gc != 0)
        return;
/* Allocate three private colour cells (although we could use shared ones)*/
    if (XAllocColorCells (display, cmap, False, NULL, 0, pixels, 3)) {
```

```
/* Store the RGB values for red, green and blue in the colour cells */
      screen_def.flags = DoRed | DoGreen | DoBlue;
      if (XLookupColor (display, cmap, "red", &screen_def, &exact_def)
                 != 0) {
          screen_def.pixel = pixels[0];
          XStoreColor (display, cmap, &screen_def);
      }
      if (XLookupColor (display, cmap, "green", &screen_def, &exact_def)
                 != 0) {
          screen_def.pixel = pixels[1];
          XStoreColor (display, cmap, &screen_def);
      }
      if (XLookupColor (display, cmap, "blue", &screen_def, &exact_def)
                 != 0) {
          screen_def.pixel = pixels[2];
          XStoreColor (display, cmap, &screen_def);
      }
  }
/* Create a GC for drawing the background. The default values are suitable,
** so pass in a null value mask */
    gc = XCreateGC (display, XtWindow (w), 0, &values);

/* Create a GC for drawing the rectangle - with some non-default values */
    values.foreground = pixels[0];
    values.function = GXxor;
    values.line_width = 10;
    drag_gc = XCreateGC (display, XtWindow (w),
                GCFunction | GCLineWidth | GCForeground, &values);
}
```

The background GC has all default values. These are suitable for our purposes, except for the foreground component, which we will set to the red, green and blue pixel values when drawing the background. This is done in the expose callback of the XmDrawingArea:

```
void do_expose (w, client_data, call_data)
    Widget      w;
    XtPointer   client_data;
    XtPointer   call_data;
{
    Dimension   width, height;
    int         i;
    Pixel       pixel;

    create_gc (w);
```

```
/* Get width and height of XmDrawingArea */
    XtVaGetValues (w, XmNwidth, &width, XmNheight, &height, 0);
    pixel = 0;
    for (i = 0; i < height; i += 20) {
/* Foreground colour runs over the three pixel values as we draw successive
** horizontal stripes using XFillRectangle() */
        XSetForeground (XtDisplay (w), gc, pixels [pixel]);
        XFillRectangle (XtDisplay (w), XtWindow (w), gc, 0, i, width, 20);
        pixel = (pixel + 1)% 3;
    }
}
```

The basic algorithm for drawing the rectangle is to obtain the origin and draw the initial rectangle on button down, undraw the last rectangle and draw a new one for each motion event, then undraw the final rectangle on button up. Since the function in the dragging GC is GXxor, we undraw the rectangle by drawing it a second time:

```
static int x, y, width, height;

void start_drag (w, event, params, num_params)
    Widget    w;
    XEvent    *event;
    String    *params;
    Cardinal  num_params;
{
/* Save start position and draw initial rectangle */
    x = event->xbutton.x;
    y = event->xbutton.y;
    width = 0;
    height = 0;
    XDrawRectangle  (XtDisplay (w), XtWindow (w), drag_gc,
                        x, y, width, height);
}

void continue_drag (w, event, params, num_params)
    Widget    w;
    XEvent    *event;
    String    *params;
    Cardinal  num_params;
{
/* Undraw existing rectangle */
    XDrawRectangle (XtDisplay (w), XtWindow (w), drag_gc,
                        x, y, width, height);
    width = event->xbutton.x - x;
    height = event->xbutton.y - y;
```

```
        /* Draw new one */
           XDrawRectangle (XtDisplay (w), XtWindow (w), drag_gc,
                           x, y, width, height);
        }

        void stop_drag (w, event, params, num_params)
           Widget   w;
           XEvent   *event;
           String   *params;
           Cardinal num_params;
        {
        /* Undraw rectangle */
           XDrawRectangle (XtDisplay (w), XtWindow (w), drag_gc, x, y, width,
                           height);
        }
```

Finally, we need to set up the callbacks, translation table and action routines:

```
        static XtActionsRec drag_actions[ ] = {
           { "start_drag",      start_drag},
           { "continue_drag",   continue_drag },
           { "stop_drag",       stop_drag },
        };


           ...
           da = XmCreateDrawingArea (appshell, "da", al, ac);
           XtAddCallback (da, XmNexposeCallback, do_expose,NULL);
           XtAppAddActions (app_context, drag_actions, XtNumber (drag_actions));
           XtOverrideTranslations (da, XtParseTranslationTable (
                           "<Btn2Down>: start_drag()\n\
                           <Btn2Motion>:continue_drag()\n\
                           <Btn2Up>:     stop_drag()"));
           ...
```

Further explanation on the use of translations and actions can be found in Chapter 11.

The display is shown in Figure 16.4; you will have to use a little imagination for the colours. The actual colours produced for the rectangle are random: the value of a pixel, say 4, is exclusively ORed with the foreground of the GC, say 8. This gives an index into the colour map, 12, which may, or may not, have been allocated by this application or another. The colour corresponding to that colour map cell is not under our control

Obviously, if we had control of the whole colour map, we could guarantee what would be in the colour cell produced by XOR. X provides a better way of doing this within the default colour map. We can request a set of private colour cells

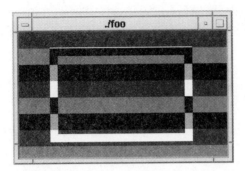

Figure 16.4 *XORing random colours*

whose indices are related in a particular way. If we specify that we want a single colour plane and three colour cells, six colour cells are actually allocated. Three cell numbers and a plane mask are returned and it is guaranteed that the plane mask will have no bits set in common with any of the pixels. The other three cell numbers allocated are obtained by ORing the plane mask with the three cell numbers returned by the function.

For instance, suppose that we request 3 cells and 1 plane. We might get cell values 18, 19 and 26, and the mask value 4. We then know that we have been allocated these 3 cells, and also cells 18 | 4 = 22, 19 | 4 = 23 and 26 | 4 = 30.

We can then store, say, red in cell 18 and blue in cell 22. If we draw the rectangle using GXxor, with the foreground value set to the plane mask, 4, any red area (with pixel value 18) we draw over will turn a predictable blue. Redrawing will turn it red again.

In other words, the plane mask value is used as the foreground value in the GC and we store in the value of cell | plane the complementary colour required when XORing. This sounds complicated, but the example shows that it is relatively straightforward. The only change is in the way the colour cells are allocated:

nicerubber

```
static void create_gc (w)
    Widget w;
{
    XGCValues      values;
    XColor         screen_def, exact_def;
    Display        *display = XtDisplay (w);
    Colormap       cmap = XDefaultColormapOfScreen (XtScreen (w));
    unsigned long  plane;

    if (gc != 0)
        return;

    if (XAllocColorCells (display, cmap, False, &plane, 1, pixels, 3))
```

```
{
    screen_def.flags = DoRed | DoGreen | DoBlue;
    if (XLookupColor (display, cmap, "red", &screen_def, &exact_def)
                != 0) {
        screen_def.pixel = pixels[0];
        XStoreColor (display, cmap, &screen_def);
        screen_def.pixel = pixels[1] | plane;
        XStoreColor (display, cmap, &screen_def);
    }
    if (XLookupColor (display, cmap, "green", &screen_def, &exact_def)
                != 0) {
        screen_def.pixel = pixels[1];
        XStoreColor (display, cmap, &screen_def);
        screen_def.pixel = pixels[2] | plane;
        XStoreColor (display, cmap, &screen_def);
    }
    if (XLookupColor (display, cmap, "blue", &screen_def, &exact_def)
                != 0) {
        screen_def.pixel = pixels[2];
        XStoreColor (display, cmap, &screen_def);
        screen_def.pixel = pixels[0] | plane;
        XStoreColor (display, cmap, &screen_def);
    }
}
gc = XCreateGC (display, XtWindow (w), 0, &values);

values.foreground = plane;
values.function = GXxor;
values.line_width = 10;
drag_gc = XCreateGC (display, XtWindow (w),
                GCFunction | GCLineWidth | GCForeground, &values);
}
```

The application will now display red over the green stripe, green over the blue and blue over the red. Figure 16.5 shows the new display (which really does look great in colour).

16.4.3 Plane_mask

plane_mask

This is a mask that determines which bits of the destination pixel can be changed by drawing operations. Those bits of the destination pixel not set in the plane_mask will not have their values changed; those bits that are will be combined with the corresponding bit of the source pixel using the GC function.

In the GXxor example above, we draw with the foreground set to the mask returned by XAllocColorCells() and leave plane_mask set to all ones (the default).

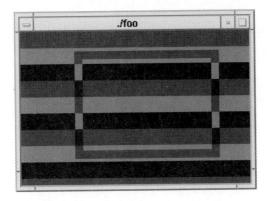

Figure 16.5 *XORing known colours*

We could have equivalently set foreground to all ones and set plane_mask to the mask returned by XAllocColorCells(). On certain hardware where the Pixel value is in fact a complicated structured index into different colour maps for different screen overlays, it may be more appropriate to use this latter technique. This level of complexity is beyond the scope of this book and probably the majority of X/ Motif applications.

16.4.4 Line drawing

line_width, line_style, dash_offset, dashes, cap_style and join_style
These are straightforward and well documented.

A line is regarded as a long, thin filled rectangle. Line drawing is therefore affected by the filling, tiling and stippling components described below.

A line of line_width zero is special. X normally uses its own line drawing algorithm to determine which pixels are drawn for a line. This ensures that the behaviour is identical across different display hardware. If the line_width is zero, the X server will use the hardware's line drawing support to draw a 1 pixel wide line. This may not draw quite the same line as the X algorithm, but will generally be considerably faster.

16.4.5 Filling, tiling and stippling

fill_style, tile, stipple, ts_x_origin, ts_y_origin and background
The fill_style describes how a region is filled; it can be FillSolid, FillTiled, FillOpaqueStippled and FillStippled. The tile is a pixmap that must be the same depth as the window that is being drawn on and stipple is a bitmap (a one bit deep pixmap) that is used as a mask.

FillSolid is obvious; the foreground pixel (background for odd dashes of dashed lines) in the GC is used as the source pixel.

FillTiled simply tiles the area being drawn with the tile pixmap.

FillStippled works like a stencil; the foreground pixel (background for odd dashes of dashed lines) in the GC is used as the source pixel and is drawn in areas where the stipple has a one. Where the stipple has a zero the destination is unchanged. FillOpaqueStippled is similar except that where the stipple has a zero the background pixel from the GC is drawn. Use FillOpaqueStippled if you want to draw the same bitmap in different colours.

The origin components allow the application to adjust the origin of the tile or stipple so that it lines up with the area being drawn. The following example draws the same bitmap with three different colour pairs:

stipple

```
void create_gc (w)
    Widget w;
{
    ...
    white = alloc_colour (w, "white");
    grey50 = alloc_colour (w, "grey50");
    grey90 = alloc_colour (w, "grey90");
    black = alloc_colour (w, "black");

    if (XReadBitmapFile (display, XtWindow (w),
                    "/usr/include/X11/bitmaps/mensetmanus",
                    &width, &height, &bitmap,
                    &hot_x, &hot_y) == BitmapSuccess) {
/* Create GC for stippled drawing */
        values.stipple = bitmap;
        values.fill_style = FillOpaqueStippled;
        mask = GCStipple | GCFillStyle;
    }
    gc = XCreateGC (display, XtWindow (w), mask, &values);
}

void draw_bitmap (w, x, y, width, height, fg, bg)
    Widget  w;
    int     x, y, width, height;
    Pixel   fg, bg;
{
    XGCValues values;

    values.foreground = fg;
    values.background = bg;
    values.ts_x_origin = x;
    values.ts_y_origin = y;
```

```
/* Set GC foreground and background, then draw filled rectangle through the
stipple mask */
    XChangeGC (XtDisplay (w), gc, GCForeground | GCBackground |
                    GCTileStipXOrigin | GCTileStipYOrigin, values);
    XFillRectangle (XtDisplay (w), XtWindow (w), gc, x, y, width, height);
}

do_expose (w, client_data, call_data)
    Widget   w;
    XtPointer client_data;
    XtPointer call_data;
{
    create_gc (w);
    draw_bitmap (w, 0, 10, 161, 145, white, grey50);
    draw_bitmap (w, 161, 10, 161, 145, grey50, grey90);
    draw_bitmap (w, 322, 10, 161, 145, black, grey90);
}
```

The output is shown in Figure 16.6.

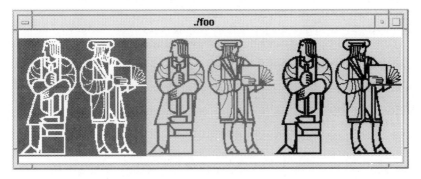

Figure 16.6 *Using FillOpaqueStippled to draw a bitmap in different colours*

A number of other GC components are relevant to fill drawing operations.

fill_rule

Specifies the algorithm used to determine whether a point is inside or outside the path in XFillPolygon(). This only makes a difference if the path intersects with itself. Experimentation will probably be required to achieve the desired effect.

arc_mode

Controls filling in XFillArcs(). The values ArcPieSlice and ArcChord accurately describe the effect.

16.4.6   Other GC components

subwindow_mode

This mode allows the application to specify whether drawing on a window will be clipped by child windows (ClipByChildren, the default), or whether the drawing will go over the children (IncludeInferiors). This latter mode is often useful when doing animated dragging, where the user wants to drag over another widget.

By drawing on the root window with IncludeInferiors, you can draw on any part of the display.

graphics_exposures

Setting this Boolean component determines whether the server will generate GraphicsExpose events when this GC is used in an XCopyArea() and similar requests. Section 7.4.3 describes the use of XCopyArea() and the handling of GraphicsExpose events in some detail.

clip_x_origin, clip_y_origin and clip_mask

The clip_mask is a one bit deep pixmap that is used to decide whether destination pixels will be drawn or not. They are only drawn where the mask has a bit set. This mask can be set by providing a bitmap, but is more usually set with XSetClipRectangles() or XSetRegion(). There is an example of this in Section 7.4.1.

To reset the clipping (i.e. allow all drawing through) use:

```
XSetClipMask (display, window, None).
```

16.5   Drawing text

font

The font component of the GC is used by text operations such as XDrawString().

Text drawing operations require both the text to be drawn and a font to draw it in. The font is normally taken from the GC provided. This is all somewhat complicated by the introduction of internationalised text and font sets in X11R5. Font sets are discussed in Chapters 15 and 20.

16.5.1   Fonts

Fonts can exist as both client and server side data structures. The server needs the font so that it can draw the characters onto the display. The client needs the font so that it can make calculations about how big a piece of text would be if it were displayed. Client applications frequently need to make this sort of calculation if they are displaying text that is to be aligned or centred, or if they want to draw other graphics in relation to the text (such as a surrounding box).

A font is loaded into the server, using XLoadFont(); it is then referenced by a font ID. This ID is stored in a GC before it is used to draw text.

A client can obtain information about a font by calling XQueryFont(). The information (which is painfully detailed) is stored in an XFontStruct.

16.5.2 Text drawing functions

The basic text manipulation functions are:

- XTextWidth() - Get width of text using a font structure.
- XTextExtents() - Get text extents using a font structure.
- XQueryTextExtents() - Get text extents using a font ID (which requires a round trip to the server).
- XDrawText() - Draw text items using specified font IDs, or the font from a GC.
- XDrawString() - Draw char* text using the font from a GC.
- XDrawImageString() - Draw char* text using the font from a GC, filling the background at the same time.

For each of these functions there are versions for 8 bit characters (as above), 16 bit (or 2 byte) characters (e.g. XDrawText16()), multi-byte strings (XmbDrawText()) and wide-character strings (XwcDrawText()). There are also functions for drawing Motif compound strings, described in Section 15.3.2.

16.5.3 Example of use

The following fragments of code can be used to perform word wrapping and line justification when drawing text.

First, a font is loaded with XLoadQueryFont(). This both loads the font on the server side and creates the XFontStruct client side data structure. A graphics context is created with the font component set to the font ID from the font structure:

textdraw

```
XFontStruct *font;
GC gc = 0;

void create_gc (w)
    Widget w;
{
    XGCValues values;

    if (gc != 0)
```

```
                    return;
            /* Load the font into the server, and query font info */
                font = XLoadQueryFont (XtDisplay (w),
                                "-*-lucidabright-medium-i-*-*-18-*-*-*-*-*-*-*");
                XtVaGetValues (w, XmNforeground, &values.foreground,
                                XmNbackground, &values.background, 0);
            /* Put font ID into GC */
                values.font = font->fid;
                gc = XCreateGC (XtDisplay (w), XtWindow (w),
                                GCForeground | GCBackground | GCFont, &values);
        }
```

The next function, build_items(), converts a char* string into an array of
XTextItem. An XTextItem contains a text string and some additional spacing (a
delta) to be allowed before the string is drawn:

```
        int build_items (text, text_items)
            char        *text;
            XTextItem   *text_items;
        {
            char  *chars = text;
            int    wp = 0;
            int    ch_count = 0;

            text_items[0].chars = chars;
            while (*chars) {
                if (*chars == ' ') {
                    /* Found beginning of next word */
                    text_items[wp++].nchars = ch_count;
                    ch_count = 0;
                    text_items[wp].chars = ++chars;
                } else {
                    ch_count++;
                    chars++;
                }
            }
            text_items[wp].nchars = ch_count;
            return wp;
        }
```

The function display_line() calculates the spacing and draws the text. The
function is passed the number of words, the width of the output area and the
combined width of the words. The spacing is calculated by dividing up the
difference between the output width and the text width. The delta component of the
XTextItem is set to the appropriate value, to specify an additional increment before

the item is drawn. The text is drawn using XDrawText(), which draws the supplied
XTextItems:

```
void display_line (w, gc, text_items, first_word, last_word, y, width, text_width)
    Widget        w;
    GC            gc;
    XTextItem     *text_items;
    int           first_word, last_word, y, text_width, width;
{
    int j;

    text_items[first_word].delta = 0;
    for (j = first_word + 1; j <= last_word; j++) {
        text_items[j].delta = (width - text_width) / (last_word - j + 1);
        text_width += (width - text_width) / (last_word - j + 1);
    }
    XDrawText (XtDisplay (w), XtWindow (w), gc, 10, y,
                    &text_items[first_word], last_word - first_word + 1);

}
```

The function display_text() calculates how many words will fit on a line. It
works its way through the array of XTextItems summing up the width of each
word. When the next word would cause the text width to be greater than the output
area width, display_line() is called to output the line.

Where the other functions have only used the font ID, here we need the
XFontStruct to calculate the width of each word:

```
void display_text (w, font, gc, text_items, w_count, width)
    Widget        w;
    XFontStruct   *font;
    GC            gc;
    XTextItem     *text_items;
    int           w_count, width;
{
    int    first_word = 0;
    int    text_width = 0;
    int    space_width = XTextWidth (font, " ", 1);
    int    y = font->ascent + 12;
    int    i, item_width;

    for (i = 0; i <= w_count; i++) {
        text_items[i].font = None; /* Use the font in the GC */
        item_width = XTextWidth (font, text_items[i].chars,
                        text_items[i].nchars);
        if (text_width + item_width + space_width * (i - first_word) <= width)
            text_width += item_width;
```

```
            else {
               if (i > first_word) {
                  display_line (w, gc, text_items, first_word, i - 1, y, width,
                        text_width);
                  text_width = item_width;
               } else {
                  display_line (w, text_items, first_word, i, y, width, text_width);
                  text_width = 0;
               }
               y = y + font->ascent + font->descent + 2;
               first_word = i;
            }
      }
      display_line (w, gc, text_items, first_word, w_count, y, width, text_width);
   }
```

These functions can then be put together with an expose callback, to produce the results shown in Figure 16.7.

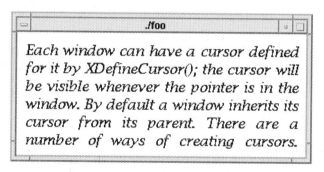

Figure 16.7 *Displaying text with variable spacing*

16.6 Cursors

Each window can have a cursor defined for it by XDefineCursor(); the cursor will be visible whenever the pointer is in the window. By default, a window inherits its cursor from its parent.

There are a number of ways of creating cursors; the easiest is XCreateFontCursor(), which creates any of the cursors defined in <X11/cursorfont.h>.

The following functions can be used to set the busy cursor on a shell widget and all its popup children. Passing an ApplicationShell to these routines will cause the cursor to be set for all the windows in an application.

busycursor

```
#include <X11/cursorfont.h>
#include <X11/IntrinsicP.h>

static Cursor wait_cursor = 0;

busy_cursor (widget)
    Widget widget;
{
    int       i;
    Display   *display = XtDisplay (widget);
    if (wait_cursor == 0)
        wait_cursor = XCreateFontCursor (display, XC_watch);
/* Set cursor on this widget's window and those of all popup children */
    XDefineCursor (display, XtWindow (widget), wait_cursor);
    for (i = 0; i < widget->core.num_popups; i++)
        if (XtIsRealized (widget->core.popup_list[i]))
            XDefineCursor (display, XtWindow (widget->core.popup_list[i]),
                          wait_cursor);
    XFlush (XtDisplay (widget));
}

unbusy_cursor (widget)
    Widget widget;
{
    int       i;
    Display   *display = XtDisplay (widget);
    XUndefineCursor (display, XtWindow (widget));
    for (i = 0; i < widget->core.num_popups; i++)
        if (XtIsRealized (widget->core.popup_list[i]))
            XUndefineCursor (display, XtWindow (widget->core.popup_list[i]));
}
```

⚠️ This code looks into the widget's internal data structures to find the popup children.

⚠️ It is important to flush the connection to the X server in busy_cursor(), otherwise the cursor may never appear. This does not have to be done in unbusy_cursor(), as (presumably) the application will return from there to the main loop, which flushes the server connection as a side-effect of polling for events.

CHAPTER 17

Grabs

A grab is a mechanism which changes the way in which events are reported. In one sense, it is a way of taking exclusive control of an input source - the mouse or the keyboard. It also allows applications to get around some of the problems caused by the asynchronous nature of the X protocol.

Grabs are used (sparingly, on the whole) by Xt and the Motif toolkit. Applications do not usually need to get involved with grabs explicitly, as the sort of grab that an application usually needs is provided by Xlib as a default (automatic grabs). However, they have their uses (such as keyboard accelerators on buttons) and, if an application does need to use grabs, it also needs to be aware of the way in which grabs are used by the toolkit and the way in which various levels of grab interact.

Normally, an event that occurs on a window is reported to the corresponding widget, or ignored. This is usually appropriate, but an application may sometimes want to change the way in which events are reported, either to have them reported to different widgets from the usual, or to ignore them altogether. This can often be done by modifying the behaviour of the event loop, but this is rather messy. Instead, you can use Xlib and Xt mechanisms called *grabs*.

The grabs provided by Xlib and those that Xt gives you are rather different in use and intent. Xlib grabs let an application or window take control of an input device (keyboard or mouse), so that application or window will receive all the device events, even if they happen on a window belonging to another application.

Xt grabs change the way event dispatching works within an application, but still allow other clients to receive input. Xlib grabs are useful if you need to get events that would normally be reported to some other window, or if you need to stop the server sending events for a brief period while you get ready to receive them. Xt grabs are used to restrict the windows within an application that can receive input events, so as to support modal popup menus and dialogs.

The Motif modal dialog behaviour (defined by the mwmInputMode resource of VendorShell) uses a combination of Xt grabs in the toolkit and Xlib grabs in mwm, and should be enough in itself to control modal dialogs. In any case, the way Motif uses Xt grabs makes it dangerous to use them in an application. However, an understanding of Xlib grabs can be useful, especially as they will happen without any explicit request from the application, so these are discussed in some detail.

Note that you can also grab the entire X server, stopping any event processing. This is impolite and so is not described here.

17.1 Xlib grabs

An Xlib grab causes device events to be diverted to a 'grab window', instead of being reported to the normal window. It may also freeze the server's device event processing temporarily. Xlib grabs come in three sorts: active, passive and automatic.

An active grab takes place immediately when an application requests it and stays in effect until explicitly released. An application will normally request an active grab in response to some device event, so there is a round-trip delay between the action on the server which generates the event and the time when the active grab request reaches the server and the grab comes into effect.

A passive grab avoids this round-trip delay, by allowing an application to specify in advance that a grab should take place immediately whenever a specified combination of mouse buttons and keys is pressed.

One use of grabs is to support a click-drag-release style of interface for moving objects. By grabbing the pointer, an application can ensure that the ButtonRelease event is reported to the same window as the ButtonPress, even if it actually happens outside the boundaries of the window. This is such a common requirement that, if no active or passive grab applies, the X server will put into effect an automatic grab whenever a mouse button is pressed. Automatic grabs only grab the mouse.

Xlib provides a set of functions to manipulate Xlib grabs, but these are paralleled by a set of Xt functions (XGrabPointer() and XtGrabPointer() and so on). An Xt application must use the Xt versions, otherwise it may lock the keyboard or the mouse.

17.1.1   Active grabs

Grabbing the pointer

An active pointer grab is initiated by a call to XtGrabPointer() (which calls XGrabPointer()). The Xt version of the function takes a widget rather than a display and window, but they otherwise have the same parameters and return values.

The grab widget must have a viewable window, so the widget must have been realised and its window mapped. In practice, most active grabs are in response to a device event on a widget's window, so the window is likely to be viewable:

```
int XtGrabPointer(grab_widget, owner_events, event_mask, pointer_mode,
               keyboard_mode, confine_to, cursor, time)
    Widget          grab_widget;
    Boolean         owner_events;
    unsigned int    event_mask;
    int             pointer_mode, keyboard_mode;
    Window          confine_to;
    Cursor          cursor;
    Time            time;
```

When the active pointer grab is in effect, mouse events (ButtonPress, ButtonRelease, EnterNotify, LeaveNotify, MotionNotify and KeymapNotify) are reported to the grab window - the window belonging to grab_widget - if and only if they are selected for by the event_mask. However, if owner_events is True and a mouse event would have been reported to some other window of the same application if the grab were not in effect, then it is reported to that window as normal. In other words, all mouse events that occur outside of any of the windows of the application (perhaps on the root window) are reported to the grab window, but you can choose whether or not this happens for mouse events within the application.

Mouse events are only reported if they are selected for by the grab event mask. In particular, further ButtonPress events and ButtonRelease events are not reported by default.

Events other than mouse events are reported as normal.

The event_mask is a bitwise OR of ButtonPressMask, ButtonReleaseMask, EnterWindowMask, LeaveWindowMask, PointerMotionMask, PointerMotion-HintMask, ButtonMotionMask, Button[1-5]MotionHintMask and KeymapState-Mask. These select for events as described in Table 12.2.

The pointer_mode and keyboard_mode flags are used to freeze event processing; this is described below.

While the grab is in effect, you can choose to confine the cursor to a particular window, specified by confine_to. Note that this is a window, not a widget and need not be the same as the grab window. The symbol None specifies that the cursor should not be confined.

The cursor can also be changed; specify None for the usual cursor.

Finally, the timestamp passed in time should normally be that of the event that caused the application to grab the pointer. Passing the symbol CurrentTime will also work.

 It is important to check the return status. See the Xlib documentation for details of the return values.

An active grab stays in effect until it is explicitly released by a call to XtUngrabPointer(). No other application will receive mouse events until the grab is released. The event mask and cursor of an active pointer grab can be changed using XChangeActivePointerGrab(). There is no XtChangeActivePointerGrab().

A typical active pointer grab might look something like this:

```
grab_pointer (grab_widget, confine_to_widget)
    Widget   grab_widget;
    Widget   confine_to_widget;

{
    Cursor cursor;
    cursor = XCreateFontCursor (XtDisplay (parent), XC_coffee_mug);
    XtGrabPointer (grab_widget, False,
                ButtonPressMask | ButtonReleaseMask,
                GrabModeAsync, GrabModeAsync,
                XtWindow (confine_to_widget), cursor, CurrentTime);

}
```

Grabbing the keyboard

An active grab on the keyboard is similar to an active pointer grab, but affects the processing of KeyPress and KeyRelease events, rather than mouse events. An active keyboard grab is initiated by a call to XtGrabKeyboard() (which calls XGrabKeyboard()):

```
int XtGrabKeyboard (grab_widget, owner_events, pointer_mode,
                keyboard_mode, time)
    Widget   grab_widget;
    Boolean  owner_events;
    int      pointer_mode, keyboard_mode;
    Time     time;
```

The parameters are essentially the same as for XtGrabPointer(). There is no event mask (KeyPress and KeyRelease events are always reported) and you cannot specify a cursor change or a window to confine the cursor.

While an active keyboard grab is in effect, all KeyPress and KeyRelease events are reported to the window of the grab_widget, except that those keyboard events that would normally have been reported to another window of the grabbing application will be reported as normal, if owner_events is True.

An active keyboard grab is released by a call to XtUngrabKeyboard(). No other application can receive keyboard events until it is released.

17.1.2   Passive grabs

An active grab takes effect as soon as it is requested, but subject to delays in propagating the request across the network. A passive grab is set up in advance and takes effect instantly when the server detects a given combination of mouse button and key states.

When the server detects a key or button press, it searches for a passive grab which has been set to trigger on that key or button. It starts the search at the root window and works down towards the window in which the event 'happened'. It stops searching at the first window which has a suitable passive grab and activates it. This changes the way in which events are reported and the change is applied to the event that triggered the grab, and subsequent events until the grab is released.

Because the search order is from the root window down, a passive grab set up on a widget at the root of a widget hierarchy can be triggered by events anywhere within the corresponding dialog. This can be used to implement reliable keyboard accelerators for XmPushButtons in dialogs (see Section 11.4.3).

Passive pointer grabs

A passive pointer grab is set up using XtGrabButton() (which calls XGrabButton()). The widget does not have to be realised at the time of the call; if it is not (and so has no window), Xt will delay the call to XGrabButton() until the widget is realised and the window created:

```
void XtGrabButton (grab_widget, button, modifiers, owner_events,
                   event_mask, pointer_mode, keyboard_mode,
                   confine_to, cursor)
        Widget          grab_widget;
        int             button;
        Modifiers       modifiers;
        Boolean         owner_events;
        unsigned int    event_mask;
        int             pointer_mode, keyboard_mode;
        Window          confine_to;
        Cursor          cursor;
```

For the most part, the parameters are the same as for an active grab. The button and modifiers parameters are used to specify the mouse/keyboard state that makes the grab go active; button may be Button[1-5] or AnyButton; modifiers is a mask - a bitwise OR of ShiftMask, LockMask, ControlMask and Mod[1-5]Mask or the symbol AnyModifier.

The grab becomes active just as if the pointer had been actively grabbed when the specified button is pressed and the specified modifiers are in effect. There must be no other mouse buttons down and no other modifiers in effect. If modifiers is AnyModifier, the grab will become active when the button is pressed with any combination of modifiers (including none) in effect.

The grab remains active until all the mouse buttons are released. Note that this means that the grab can remain active, even if the button that activated it is released. For instance, if a passive grab is set up to activate on Button1, the event sequence <Btn1Down>,<Btn2Down>,<Btn1Up> will leave it active. Not until Button2 is released will it revert to a passive state.

The function XUngrabButton() will remove a passive pointer grab. If the grab is active at the time, it remains active until all mouse buttons are released, then disappears altogether.

Passive keyboard grabs

Passive keyboard grabs are set up using XtGrabKey(). As with pointer grabs, the widget does not have to have a window at the time this is called:

```
void XtGrabKey(grab_widget, keycode, modifiers, owner_events,
                pointer_mode, keyboard_mode)
    Widget      grab_widget;
    KeyCode     keycode;
    Modifiers   modifiers;
    Boolean     owner_events;
    int         pointer_mode, keyboard_mode;
```

Again, the parameters are similar to the active grab, but a keycode and modifiers mask specify the circumstances under which the grab becomes active. The modifiers mask is as for a passive pointer grab. The keycode is a server-dependent value, usually derived from a keysym via XKeysymToKeycode():

```
XtGrabKey (widget, XKeysymToKeycode (XtDisplay (widget), XK_a),
            ControlMask, False, GrabModeAsync, GrabModeAsync);
```

A passive keyboard grab becomes active when the specified key is pressed and the specified modifiers (but no others) are in effect. It is released when the key is released.

17.1.3 Automatic grabs

An automatic grab is the server's last resort. If it sees a ButtonPress event and there is no relevant active or passive pointer grab, it will put a default active grab into effect. The grab window is the window the event is reported to, the event mask contains those pointer events selected for by the grabbing client on the event window and the owner_events flag is set if the client has selected events with OwnerGrabButtonMask on the event window. This will take care of the commonest click-drag-release processing, by ensuring that the button release is reported to the same window as the button press.

17.1.4   Event freezing

The Xlib grab examples above all used GrabModeAsync for the pointer mode and keyboard mode. This means that the server will continue processing mouse and keyboard input, although it may change the way in which it reports the resulting events. It is also possible to freeze the server's input processing by specifying GrabModeSync in an active or passive grab. Mouse and keyboard input can be frozen separately.

This is usually called 'event freezing'. However, it freezes more than just event reporting; it freezes event generation. While the freeze is in effect, the X server does not process device input to generate events. Rather, it (notionally) queues the input, then generates events from it when the freeze is released by a call to XAllowEvents(). In the intervening period, of course, the application which requested the freeze can change the arrangement of windows; the events generated when input processing is unfrozen will reflect the arrangement at that time, not the arrangement at the time when (say) the user pressed the keys or buttons. It is also possible to unfreeze events in such a way as to replay the event that activated a passive grab without activating the grab again.

Event freezing is a specialised technique and falls well outside the scope of this book. It is usually used to implement features like reliable popup menus and the Motif toolkit takes care of this for you. Typically, event freezing is needed if the application, when it receives a certain mouse or keyboard event, needs some time to prepare for further input. If you find yourself with this requirement, you should consult a number of the Xlib texts and preferably somebody who has experience of this technique.

17.2   Xt grabs

Xt grabs are similar to Xlib grabs in that they change the way events are reported, but they work entirely within the application - in XtDispatchEvent() - and so do not affect other applications using the same server.

Xt maintains a list of widgets called the grab list. If the grab list is non-empty, only the widgets on the list and their descendants receive input events; think of the grab list as a list of shells; only those dialogs whose shells are on the list receive input.

When a widget is added to the grab list, it can be added as exclusive or non-exclusive. The active set of the grab list is the part from the most recently added exclusive widget to the end and only widgets in the active set (and their descendants) will receive input events. In other words, adding a widget to the grab list exclusively keeps input away from all the widgets that are already on the list (and their descendants).

Xt grabs are usually used in conjunction with popup shells. For instance, if a shell is popped up with an exclusive grab, only that dialog can receive input; it is modal. This use is so common that the function used to pop up a shell - XtPopup() - takes a parameter for the kind of Xt grab to be used: XtGrabNone, XtGrab-Nonexclusive or XtGrabExclusive. It is also possible to add a widget other than a shell to the grab list by calling XtAddGrab().

A widget can be added to the grab list as exclusive or non-exclusive. It can also be added as spring-loaded or not. This should only be done via a call to XtPopupSpringLoaded(), not a direct call to XtAddGrab() and is provided for popup menus. The essential feature of a spring-loaded popup is that it receives a copy of every input event (provided the popup is in the active set of the grab list), both those that occur within the grab list widgets and those outside. In other words, if there is a spring-loaded popup in the active set of the grab list, input events occurring in the active set are reported twice: once where they occurred and once to the spring-loaded popup and input events occurring outside are reported to the spring-loaded popup, but not to the widget where they occur. In a popup menu, it gives the menu shell widget the opportunity to detect ButtonRelease events and pop itself down.

17.2.1   Xt and Xlib grabs

Both Xt grabs and Xlib grabs can affect the way in which events are reported. In particular, an event that triggers an Xlib passive grab may be discarded or remapped by an Xt grab and not delivered to the widget that owns the grab window. This is particularly unfortunate if the passive grab freezes input events, as it is usually the receipt of the triggering event that causes the application (eventually) to unfreeze events. If this does not happen, events will remain frozen indefinitely and the keyboard and/or mouse locks up.

To avoid this, Xt keeps a list of the passive grabs, maintained by XtGrabButton() and XtGrabKey(). If the event dispatcher sees an event which will have triggered a grab and does not deliver it normally because of an Xt grab, it calls XUngrabPointer() or XUngrabKeyboard() to release the Xlib grab. If the passive grab was set up with XGrabButton() or XGrabKey(), Xt has no record of the passive grab and cannot release it if it triggers inappropriately. Only a little ingenuity is then required to lock the input devices.

17.2.2 Xt grabs and Motif

As the previous section indicates, the Xlib grab model is not perfectly attuned to the requirements of Xt, and the latter has to do some layering to provide its own form of grab and to make sure that it does not interfere with the Xlib grabs. This would not be so tragic if the Xt model were well suited to Motif, but it is not and the Motif toolkit implementers have added yet another layer. This layer is, however, private and completely undocumented.

The most obvious difference between the Motif approach and that of Xt is that Xt treats the widgets on the grab list as a cascade; if a widget is removed from the list, so are all the widgets that were added after it; you can imagine that this is sensible for a set of cascading menus. Motif uses Xt grabs to implement modal dialogs; if there are two modal dialogs visible, popping down the older (which removes its Xt grab) should still leave the younger on the grab list. To achieve this, Motif maintains a parallel grab list; when it removes a widget from the Xt grab list, it puts back on all those widgets that were after it.

Clearly, if an application adds and removes Xt grabs using the Xt mechanisms, the Xt grab list and the Motif list will be out of step. While it is not certain that this will interfere with the toolkit, it seems likely. The advice has to be to avoid using Xt grabs in an application, except via the Motif modal dialog mechanisms.

CHAPTER 18

Selections

To write this book, we have made frequent use of cut and paste; in particular the ability to select some source code from an application being edited in an xterm window and paste it into the text being edited in our desktop publishing application. This works because both applications are prepared to cooperate in inter-client communications designed to transfer data. X calls these, coordinated data transfers selections.

For applications to have a chance of communicating, they need to be operating to the same conventions. As you will want your applications to cooperate with applications written by developers who do not know you, you will want to follow some external set of guidelines and must hope that they will do the same. These guidelines are set out in the Inter-Client Communication Conventions Manual, or ICCCM (Scheifler and Gettys, 1972 pp. 610-628). Fortunately you do not need to read this document; the various layers of toolkits give you some help with getting it right.

In this chapter we look at the mechanisms provided by Xt for generically handling selections and their development by Motif to support a persistent clipboard. We do not examine the underlying Xlib functions in any depth.

18.1 Selection mechanisms

The ICCCM describes the selection protocol and lays down guidelines to give applications some chance of achieving a meaningful conversation. A selection is:

- Global to the server.
- Named by an atom.
- Owned by a client.
- Attached to a window.

The ICCCM identifies three selections and suggests their general use.

PRIMARY

For the principal means of communication between clients.

SECONDARY

For communication where either the primary selection is not to be disturbed, or where both a primary and secondary are required (perhaps for a swap).

CLIPBOARD

As a repository for data that is being transferred. This is really only different from the other selections in that the ICCCM suggests that there might be a special clipboard client which immediately requests the selection value, whenever a client asserts that a selection is available for the CLIPBOARD. This special client can then maintain the selected data even when the original client has died. This is discussed further in Section 18.2.

18.1.1 An overview

The selection mechanisms work by defining a simple protocol which allows two clients to communicate and providing the communication channel through which the data is passed. The Xt toolkit encapsulates this into a simple widget-based interface (XtOwnSelection() and XtGetSelectionValue()). The actual implementation simply sends events around and stores data in a known property.

When an application wants to designate something as selected, it calls XtOwnSelection() to claim exclusive ownership of the specified selection and to specify the window to which it is to be attached. The application also specifies three functions which are to be called when:

- The data is requested (convert_proc).
- The selection is claimed for a different widget (lose_proc).
- The data transfer is complete (done_proc).

When an application wants to request the data from a selection, it calls XtGetSelectionValue(), which specifies which selection it wants to get the value of, the type of data that it is prepared to accept and a function which will handle the incoming data (request_callback).

If an application wants to drop its claim on the selection (for example, if the selected data is deleted), then it calls XtDisownSelection().

The actual data transfer is accomplished by Xt. On the requestor's side it sends a SelectionRequest event to the owner of the selection. On the owner's side it then stores the data, which it obtains using the convert_proc registered by XtOwnSelection(), in a property on the requestor's window and sends back a SelectionNotify event. When this event is received by the requestor, Xt extracts the data from the property and invokes the callback registered by XtGetSelectionValue().

Or, to look at it another way:

- User indicates he or she has made a selection - perhaps by clicking on an icon.
- Owner application calls
XtOwnSelection (convert_proc, lose_proc, done_proc).
- User indicates he or she wants to get a selection - perhaps by activating a paste menu item.
- Requestor application calls XtGetSelectionValue (request_callback).
- Xt for requestor sends SelectionRequest event.
- Xt for owner receives SelectionRequest and calls convert_proc.
- convert_proc gets the data and returns.
- Xt for owner sets property and sends SelectionNotify event.
- Xt for requestor receives Selection Notify event and extracts data from the property.
- Xt for requestor calls request_callback to use the data.
- Xt for owner calls done_proc if specified.

18.1.2 ICCCM compliance

For data to be satisfactorily exchanged between the two clients, they must agree on the form of the data. The ICCCM refers to targets; when the requestor calls XtGetSelectionValue(), it specifies a target which denotes the type of information that it is expecting from the selection. The selection owner's convert_proc is informed of the requested target. If it can satisfy that target, it returns True and sets the format_return parameter to describe the format of the actual data. The requestor's request_callback can then examine the format to decide how to decode the transferred value. The ICCCM suggests a list of possible target types that selections might be prepared to support.

A well-engineered application should make no assumptions about the applications with which it is communicating. If it claims the selection, it should be prepared to export it in a number of forms, in case it meets up with either a very simplistic or a sophisticated application. If it is importing a selection, it should be prepared to find out what targets the other application supports before calling XtGetSelectionValue() to actually transfer the selection.[1]

The ICCCM therefore requires that the owner should always respond to a target of TARGETS with a list of atoms representing the targets that it supports. The requestor can then make two calls to XtGetSelectionValue(); the first to get the list of available targets and the second, from inside the first's request_callback, to fetch the data for the target it prefers. Note that it is possible for the selection to change between the two calls (unless the server is grabbed).

The ICCCM also allows for the atomic transfer of data which is too large to be stored in a property. This is handled invisibly by the toolkit routines, using a MULTIPLE target.

So that your application correctly handles these special targets and therefore communicates effectively with other applications you should use the Xmu function XmuConvertStandardSelection() in your conversion procedures.

The example in Sections 18.1.3 and 18.1.4 illustrates these techniques.

18.1.3   Exporting a selection

This example simply extends an XmList widget so that the list selection is treated as the primary selection. The code is very simple, though somewhat lengthy.

First, a callback is added to the XmList widget which either claims or disowns the selection, depending on the number of items selected in the list:

```
void select_callback (w, client_data, cd)
    Widget      w;
    XtPointer   client_data;
    XtPointer   cd;
{
    XmListCallbackStruct *call_data = (XmListCallbackStruct *)cd;
    if (call_data->selected_item_count)
        XtOwnSelection (w, XA_PRIMARY, call_data->event->xbutton.time,
                        convert_proc, lose_proc, NULL);
    else
        XtDisownSelection (w, XA_PRIMARY,
                        call_data->event->xbutton.time);
}
```

export

---

1. Some targets represent the form of the data - COMPOUND_TEXT, BITMAP; others represent both form and content - HOST_NAME, USER. A third group have 'side-effects'; asking the selection owner to convert to the target DELETE is actually a request to delete the data.

```
        ...
        ac = 0;
        XtSetArg(al[ac], XmNselectionPolicy, XmMULTIPLE_SELECT); ac++;
        /* build list items etc. */
        list = XmCreateScrolledList (form, "list", al, ac);
        XtAddCallback (list, XmNmultipleSelectionCallback, select_callback,
                        NULL);
        ...
```

The conversion procedure convert_proc() has to convert the data into an appropriate type that can be transferred by the underlying mechanisms and be handled by the requesting application. To this end, it is passed in an atom which indicates the target that the requestor has specified. To illustrate the different methods of transferring data, we shall support XA_STRING and COMPOUND_TEXT targets.[1] As this is quite long, we will break it up into sections:

```
        Boolean convert_proc (w, selection, target, type_return, value, length, format)
            Widget          w;
            Atom            *selection, *target, *type_return;
            XtPointer       *value;
            unsigned long   *length;
            int             *format;
        {
            Atom COMPOUND_TEXT = XmInternAtom (XtDisplay (w),
                        "COMPOUND_TEXT", False);
            Atom TARGETS = XmInternAtom (XtDisplay (w), "TARGETS", False);
            XSelectionRequestEvent *request = XtGetSelectionRequest (w,
                        *selection, (XtRequestId) NULL);
```

XtGetSelectionRequest() returns the event that triggered the call to the conversion procedure. This is needed for XmuConvertStandardSelection(), but is not provided as a parameter to the conversion procedure, for historical reasons.

The conversion procedure has to return the type, value, length and format of the data corresponding to the selection. If the requested target is TARGETS, we have to return a list of the targets we are prepared to support as a list of atoms. The format is used for byte swapping between client and server (if required) and should be 32 for a list of atoms.

XmuConvertStandardSelection() will create the list for the targets it supports, so we only have to add the ones we handle:

---

1. Some atoms are predefined and we represent them by the symbol defined in <X11/Xatom.h>, such as XA_STRING. You will need to create other atoms from the corresponding strings by calling XmInternAtom(). These are given with no prefix: COMPOUND_TEXT. You should not assume that the useful atoms are predefined, nor that the predefined atoms are useful.

```
            if (*target == TARGETS) {
                Atom                *targets;
                Atom                *std_targets;
                unsigned long   std_length;
/* Get standard list of targets */
                XmuConvertStandardSelection(w, request->time, selection, target,
                            type_return, (caddr_t*)&std_targets, &std_length,
                            format);
/* Allocate extra storage for our extra targets and build a list. We return the
list via the value parameter */
                *length = std_length + 4;
                *value = (XtPointer)XtMalloc(sizeof(Atom)*(*length));
                targets = *(Atom**)value;
                *targets++ = TARGETS;
                *targets++ = XmInternAtom (XtDisplay (w), "MULTIPLE", False);
                *targets++ = XA_STRING;
                *targets++ = COMPOUND_TEXT;
/* Append standard list to ours, and free the standard one */
                bcopy((char*)std_targets, (char*)targets, sizeof(Atom)*std_length);
                XtFree((char*)std_targets);
                *type_return = XA_ATOM;
                *format = 32;
                return True;
            }
```

The XA_STRING target is commonly used to transfer text. Many simple applications, which do not bother to query the supported targets, just ask for this target. In this case, we extract the text of the selected items and build it into a list of char* strings. This is then converted to a text property which can then be transferred by the Intrinsics using XmbTextListToTextProperty():

```
            else if (*target == XA_STRING) {
                char                **tmp_value;
                XTextProperty   tmp_prop;
                int                 status = 0;
                XmString            *selected_items;
                int                 selected_count;
                int                 i;

                XtVaGetValues (w, XmNselectedItems, &selected_items,
                            XmNselectedItemCount, &selected_count, 0);
                if (selected_count == 0)
                    return False;
```

```
    tmp_value = (char **) XtMalloc (selected_count * sizeof (char *));
    for (i = 0; i < selected_count; i++)
       if (! XmStringGetLtoR (selected_items[i],
                XmFONTLIST_DEFAULT_TAG, &tmp_value[i]))
          tmp_value[i] = NULL;
    status = XmbTextListToTextProperty (XtDisplay (w), tmp_value,
                selected_count, (XICCEncodingStyle)XStringStyle,
                &tmp_prop);
    for (i = 0; i < selected_count; i++)
       XtFree (tmp_value[i]);
    XtFree (tmp_value);
    if (status == Success || status > 0) {
       *type_return = XA_STRING;
       *format = 8;
       *value = (XtPointer) XtMalloc ((unsigned)tmp_prop.nitems);
       memcpy ((void*)*value,
                (void*)tmp_prop.value,(unsigned)tmp_prop.nitems);
       XFree ((char*)tmp_prop.value);
       *length = tmp_prop.nitems;
       return True;
    }
}
```

The COMPOUND_TEXT target is another widely used text transfer target. It is capable of handling text with different font list tags. Although there is a public function XmCvtXmStringToCT(), we here use the unpublished _XmCvt-XmStringToCT(), as it also returns the length of the compound text:

```
else if (*target == COMPOUND_TEXT) {
    XmString    *selected_items, s1, s2, sep;
    int         selected_count;
    int         i;
    XrmValue    from_val, to_val;

    XtVaGetValues (w, XmNselectedItems, &selected_items,
                XmNselectedItemCount, &selected_count, 0);
    if (selected_count == 0)
       return False;

    s1 = XmStringCopy (selected_items[0]);
    sep = XmStringSeparatorCreate();
    for (i = 1; i < selected_count; i++) {
       s2 = XmStringConcat (s1, sep);
       XmStringFree (s1);
```

```
            s1 = XmStringConcat (s2, selected_items[i]);
            XmStringFree (s2);
        }
        from_val.addr = (char *) s1;
        if (_XmCvtXmStringToCT (&from_val, &to_val)) {
            *type_return = COMPOUND_TEXT;
            *format = 8;
            *value = to_val.addr;
            *length = to_val.size + 1;
            XmStringFree (s1);
            XmStringFree (sep);
            return True;
        }
        XmStringFree (s1);
        XmStringFree (sep);
    }
```

All that remains is to let XmuConvertStandardSelection() have a turn and failing that, return False to indicate that we do not support the requested target:

```
    else if (XmuConvertStandardSelection(w, request->time, selection, target,
                    type_return, (caddr_t*)value, length, format))
        return True;
    *value = NULL;
    *length = 0;
    return False;
}
```

The lose_proc() needs to deselect all the items in order to keep the correlation between the list's selection and the primary selection. This function will be called if another client of the server claims the primary selection (e.g. the user makes a selection in another application):

```
void lose_proc (w, selection)
    Widget      w;
    Atom        *selection;
{
    XmListDeselectAllItems (w);
}
```

With this implementation, the user can select items in the list and simply paste them into a Motif XmText widget or an xterm, by clicking Button2.

⚠   If the done_proc() is NULL, the Intrinsics will call XtFree() on the value returned from the convert_proc(), so it must have been allocated with XtMalloc(), XtRealloc() or XtCalloc().

⚠️ If the done_proc() is not NULL, the Intrinsics will not attempt to free the value returned and it should be deallocated in the done_proc().

18.1.4 Obtaining the selection

This example requests the selection when an XmPushButton is activated, converts the returned text (if any) into a compound string and sets the labelString of the XmPushButton. It does it in two phases, first requesting the supported targets of the selection owner, then requesting the data with a target of COMPOUND_-STRING if it is supported, or XA_STRING otherwise.

First, a callback is added to the XmPushButton which calls XtGetSelectionValue(), specifying a TARGETS atom as the required target. The event time is passed as client_data to the request callback, request_targets(), so that it can be used again in the subsequent call to XtGetSelectionValue():

import

```
void activate_callback (w, client_data, cd)
      Widget      w;
      XtPointer   client_data;
      XtPointer   cd;
{
      XmAnyCallbackStruct *call_data = (XmAnyCallbackStruct *)cd;
      Atom TARGETS = XmInternAtom (XtDisplay (w), "TARGETS", False);
      XtGetSelectionValue (w, XA_PRIMARY, TARGETS, request_targets,
                    (XtPointer)call_datRY, TARGETS, request_targets,
                    (XtPointer)call_data->event->xbutton.time,
                    call_data->event->xbutton.time);
}

button = XmCreatePushButton(form, "button", al, ac);
XtAddCallback (button, XmNactivateCallback, activate_callback, NULL);
...
```

The request_targets callback inspects the list of targets returned in value, decides which target to use and calls XtGetSelectionValue() again:

```
void request_targets (w, client_data, selection, type, value, length, format)
      Widget          w;
      XtPointer       client_data;
      Atom            *selection, *type;
      XtPointer       value;
      unsigned long   *length;
      int             *format;
{
```

```
            Time event_time = (Time) client_data;
            Atom COMPOUND_TEXT = XmInternAtom (XtDisplay (w),
                        "COMPOUND_TEXT", False);

        if (value) {
            int i;
            Atom *targets = (Atom *)value;

            for (i = 0; i < *length; i++)
                if (targets[i] == COMPOUND_TEXT) {
                    XtFree((char*)value);
                    XtGetSelectionValue (w, XA_PRIMARY, COMPOUND_TEXT,
                        request_callback, NULL, event_time);
                    return;
                }
        }
        XtFree((char*)value);
        /* Fallback position */
        XtGetSelectionValue (w, XA_PRIMARY, XA_STRING, request_callback,
                    NULL, event_time);
    }
```

The request callback request_callback() has to handle the incoming data in either XA_STRING or COMPOUND_TEXT format:

```
    void request_callback (w, client_data, selection, type, value, length, format)
        Widget          w;
        XtPointer       client_data;
        Atom            *selection, *type;
        XtPointer       value;
        unsigned long   *length;
        int             *format;
    {
        Atom COMPOUND_TEXT = XmInternAtom (XtDisplay (w),
                    "COMPOUND_TEXT", False);

        if (!value)
            return;

        if (*type == XA_STRING)
        {
            XTextProperty tmp_prop;
            char **tmp_value;
            int num_vals;
```

```
    int i, status;

    tmp_prop.value = (unsigned char *) value;
    tmp_prop.encoding = *type;
    tmp_prop.format = *format;
    tmp_prop.nitems = *length;
    num_vals = 0;
    status = XmbTextPropertyToTextList(XtDisplay(w), &tmp_prop,
                &tmp_value, &num_vals);
    if (num_vals && (status == Success || status > 0)) {
        XmString     s1, s2, s3;
        XmString     sep = XmStringSeparatorCreate ();

        s1 = NULL;
        for (i = 0; i < num_vals ; i++) {
            s2 = XmStringCreateLtoR (tmp_value[i],
                    XmFONTLIST_DEFAULT_TAG);
            if (s1) {
                s3 = XmStringConcat (s1, sep);
                XmStringFree (s1);
                s1 = XmStringConcat (s3, s2);
                XmStringFree (s3);
                XmStringFree (s2);
            } else
                s1 = s2;
        }
        XmStringFree (sep);
        XFreeStringList(tmp_value);
        XtVaSetValues (w, XmNlabelString, s1, 0);
        XmStringFree (s1);
    } else
        return;
}

if (*type == COMPOUND_TEXT) {
    XmString s = XmCvtCTToXmString ((char *) value);
    XtVaSetValues (w, XmNlabelString, s, 0);
    XmStringFree (s);
}

XtFree((char*)value);
}
```

Using this implementation, the XmPushButton widget will change its labelString whenever it is activated to the value of the current primary selection if one exists.

18.1.5 Choice of targets

It is obviously good practice to try to use the targets suggested by the ICCCM, so that other clients can use the data in the selection. However if you want to restrict the data so that it can only be imported by certain applications, then there are some simple techniques that can be applied.

If you choose your own target name, then only the applications which request that target - presumably those that you write - will be able to import the data. If you want to restrict the data so that it can only be imported into a different part of the same application, then manufacture a target name using the ApplicationShell window ID as part of the name. Note that this allows you to simply pass some kind of reference to the data, rather than the data itself; the application can then access the data from internal structures. This technique is probably more relevant to drag and drop, which is covered in Chapter 19.

18.2 The clipboard

There is nothing particularly special about the CLIPBOARD selection, except that the ICCCM suggests a method in which it can be used and the Motif toolkit provides some functions that support this method. The intention is that data which is in some way deleted or copied from an application is stored on the clipboard so that it is available to other applications. The ICCCM suggests the implementation of a clipboard client, which always owns the CLIPBOARD selection and which can maintain the data should the client which owns it die. The default MIT distribution of X11 provides a sample clipboard client.

The Motif toolkit, whilst not precluding this option, takes this slightly further by actually copying the data to the server and storing it in a property on the root window. Other Motif clients can therefore access this property to retrieve the information, even when the providing client has died, or if the CLIPBOARD selection is not owned.

The functions provided and the techniques for using them are well documented in the Motif documentation and in the other Motif books listed in the bibliography. The Motif clipboard does not appear to be widely used in applications. Most applications seem to allow transfer of data via the PRIMARY selection with an XA_STRING target, but implement cut and paste type operations themselves.

CHAPTER 19

Drag and drop

The drag and drop facilities provided in Motif are extensions of the generic selection mechanism described in Chapter 18.

The basic concept is that users are able to pick up an object with the pointer, move it to another location (possibly in another application) and drop it onto a valid drop site. What happens internally is that when the drag is started, the toolkit grabs the server and provides the animation and validation for the dragging. When the drop occurs, the data is transferred, using the Xt selection mechanism.

Although this sounds simple, the toolkit has included a great deal of flexibility which allows for some very sophisticated interaction between clients, but can make it a little daunting for the developer. This chapter first examines a simple example, which uses as much default behaviour as possible. Later sections then build on this example to illustrate the full potential of the mechanisms provided.

19.1 Simple drag and drop

Imagine an application which draws a few bitmaps on an XmDrawingArea and which has a Pixmap type XmPushButton (see Figure 19.1).

The application maintains internally a structure of bitmaps and bitmap file names.

Figure 19.1 *Example application for drag and drop*

```
typedef struct Bitmap_s {
    char     *name;       /* The file name */
    char     *data;       /* bitmap format data */
    int      width;       /* The width */
    int      height;      /* And height */
    Pixmap   bitmap;      /* The data as a bitmap */
    Pixmap   pixmap;      /* The data as a pixmap */
    Widget   state_icon;  /* Drag state icon */
}Bitmap_t, *Bitmap_p;
```

simple

The user is allowed to drag a bitmap and drop it onto the XmPushButton, at which point the XmPushButton should display the bitmap. We will look at the code required to implement this in the order that it would be executed.

19.1.1   Creating the drop site

The drop site is created by registering the XmPushButton widget as a drop site with XmDropSiteRegister():

```
XtSetArg(al[ac], XmNlabelType, XmPIXMAP); ac++;
button = XmCreatePushButton (form, "button", al, ac);
ac = 0;
import_targets[0] = XA_STRING;
XtSetArg(al[ac], XmNimportTargets, import_targets); ac++;
XtSetArg(al[ac], XmNnumImportTargets, 1); ac++;
XtSetArg(al[ac], XmNdropProc, import_bitmap); ac++;
XtSetArg(al[ac], XmNdropSiteOperations, XmDROP_COPY); ac++;
XmDropSiteRegister (button, al, ac);
```

XmDropSiteRegister() takes an argument list which contains settings for some of the resources of an XmDropSite object. An XmDropSite is not a widget or gadget, but it does have resources. The dropProc is a callback function that will be called to initiate the drop operation if the user attempts to drop on the drop site. The importTargets resource specifies the targets that this drop site might accept - in this case, only STRING (which we will use to pass the name of a bitmap). The dropSiteOperations resource specifies the operations that the drop site will implement.

19.1.2 Initiating the drag

Assume that the XmDrawingArea has an input callback which detects Button2 presses, determines which bitmap it is over and calls the function drag_bitmap():

```
void drag_bitmap (w, bitmap, event)
    Widget      w;
    Bitmap_p    bitmap;
    XEvent      *event;
{
    Widget   drag_context;
    Arg      al[10];
    int      ac = 0;
    Atom     export_targets[1];

    export_targets[0] = XA_STRING;

    XtSetArg (al[ac], XmNconvertProc, export_bitmap); ac++;
    XtSetArg (al[ac], XmNclientData, bitmap); ac++;
    XtSetArg (al[ac], XmNexportTargets, export_targets); ac++;
    XtSetArg (al[ac], XmNnumExportTargets, 1); ac++;
    XtSetArg (al[ac], XmNdragOperations, XmDROP_COPY); ac++;
    drag_context = XmDragStart (w, event, al, ac);
}
```

Here we are initiating the drag using XmDragStart(), which takes an argument list specifying values for the resources of an XmDragContext object. The convertProc resource specifies an Xt conversion procedure, exportTargets contains the list of targets that the conversion procedure is prepared to convert to, and the dragOperations resource specifies which operations the drag initiator is prepared to support.

Note that we store a pointer to the appropriate bitmap structure in the clientData resource of the drag context; we will need this in the conversion procedure.

In XmDragStart(), the toolkit calls XtOwnSelection() for the Motif drag selection. It also creates a drag icon on the screen representing the thing being dragged and arranges for it to follow the pointer. The toolkit will handle all the visuals, so that the user will get feedback when the pointer is over a drop site which indicates that it might be prepared to accept a drop.

19.1.3 Accepting the drop

When the user releases the mouse button over a drop site, the dropProc callback function import_bitmap() is called.

Note that it will be called, regardless of whether the targets or operations match. It is up to this function to decide how to handle the drop. It does this by setting up an argument list, then calling XmDropTransferStart(). This creates yet another non-widget object, an XmDropTransfer:

```
void import_bitmap (w, client_data, call_data)
    Widget      w;
    XtPointer    client_data, call_data;
{
    XmDropProcCallback        drop_data;
    XmDropTransferEntryRec    transfer_entries[1];
    Arg                       al[5];
    int                       ac;

    drop_data = (XmDropProcCallback) call_data;
    ac = 0;
    if (drop_data->dropAction != XmDROP || drop_data->operation !=
                XmDROP_COPY) {
        XtSetArg (al[ac], XmNtransferStatus, XmTRANSFER_FAILURE);
                ac++;
    } else {
        Atom     *export_list;
        int       export_count, i;
        Boolean  ok = False;
/* Check that there is a compatible target (we need STRING) */
        XtVaGetValues (drop_data->dragContext,
                    XmNexportTargets, &export_list,
                    XmNnumExportTargets, &export_count, 0);
        for (i = 0; i < export_count; i ++)
            if (export_list[i] == XA_STRING) {
                ok = True;
                break;
            }
        if (ok) {
```

```
      /* We want a single STRING transfer */
              transfer_entries[0].target = XA_STRING;
              transfer_entries[0].client_data = (XtPointer) w;
              XtSetArg (al[ac], XmNdropTransfers, transfer_entries); ac++;
              XtSetArg (al[ac], XmNnumDropTransfers, 1); ac++;
              XtSetArg (al[ac], XmNtransferProc, transfer_bitmap); ac++;
              drop_data->operation = XmDROP_COPY;
          } else {
              XtSetArg (al[ac], XmNtransferStatus, XmTRANSFER_FAILURE);
                      ac++;

          }
      }
      XmDropTransferStart (drop_data->dragContext, al, ac);
  }
```

This processing is similar to the processing for determining matching targets in normal selection processing. In this case, rather than doing a selection transfer, we find out the export targets from the dragContext entry in the drop_data. It is important to do this, so that if the targets do not match the transferStatus resource can be set to TRANSFER_FAILURE, which will cause the toolkit to supply the correct visuals to indicate that the drop has not occurred.

Calling XmDropTransferStart() (indirectly) causes the toolkit to call XtGetSelectionValue() for the Motif drag selection, the request_callback() being the function specified by transferProc. This will therefore in due course cause the convert_proc() for the selection to be called.

 The dropProc callback function must call XmDropTransferStart(), even if it does not want to transfer any data, as the drag initiator will be waiting for a reply.

19.1.4 Exporting the data

The conversion procedure export_bitmap() is called in response to the drop site initiating the drop. It is very similar to the conversion procedure illustrated in Section 18.1.3:

```
      Boolean export_bitmap (w, selection, target, type_return, value, length,
                      format, max_length, client_data, request_id)
          Widget        w;
          Atom          *selection, *target, *type_return;
          XtPointer      *value, client_data;
          unsigned long  *length, *max_length;
          int            *format;
      {
          Bitmap_p       bitmap;
```

```
XTextProperty  tmp_prop;
int                  status = 0;

if (*target != XA_STRING)
        return False;
/* Get bitmap name from clientData resource of the drag context and convert
to property */
XtVaGetValues (w, XmNclientData, &bitmap, 0);
status = XmbTextListToTextProperty (XtDisplay (w), &(bitmap->name), 1,
                    (XICCEncodingStyle)XStringStyle, &tmp_prop);
if (status == Success || status > 0) {
    *type_return = XA_STRING;
    *format = 8;
    *value = (XtPointer) XtMalloc ((unsigned)tmp_prop.nitems);
    memcpy ((void*)*value,
                    (void*)tmp_prop.value,(unsigned)tmp_prop.nitems);
    XFree ((char*)tmp_prop.value);
    *length = tmp_prop.nitems;
    return True;
}
return False;
}
```

The widget passed in here is the drag context widget returned by XmDragStart().
The client_data passed in is not the clientData of the drag context, but this can be
fetched as shown. The function should support the standard selection targets as
well, but these are omitted for brevity.

19.1.5   Importing the data

Once the drag initiator has converted the data, it is delivered by the selection
mechanisms and the requestor is notified by the request callback, in this case
transfer_bitmap(). Again, this is very similar to the request callback in
Section 18.1.4. The widget parameter here is the widget that received the drop:

```
void transfer_bitmap (w, closure, seltype, type, value, length, format)
        Widget            w;
        XtPointer         closure;
        Atom              *seltype;
        Atom              *type;
        XtPointer         value;
        unsigned long     *length;
        int               *format;
```

```
{
    Widget      widget = (Widget) closure;

    if (*type == XA_STRING) {
        XTextProperty  tmp_prop;
        char           **tmp_value;
        int            num_vals;
        int            status;
/* Extract bitmap name into tmp_value */
        tmp_prop.value = (unsigned char *) value;
        tmp_prop.encoding = *type;
        tmp_prop.format = *format;
        tmp_prop.nitems = *length;
        num_vals = 0;
        status = XmbTextPropertyToTextList(XtDisplay(widget), &tmp_prop,
                    &tmp_value, &num_vals);
        if (num_vals && (status == Success || status > 0)) {
            Pixel fg, bg;
/* Get pixmap and set labelPixmap resource */
            XtVaGetValues (widget, XmNforeground, &fg, XmNbackground,
                    &bg, 0);
            XtVaSetValues (widget, XmNlabelPixmap,
                    XmGetPixmap (XtScreen (widget), tmp_value[0], fg, bg),
                    0);
            XFreeStringList(tmp_value);
        }
    }
}
```

19.1.6   Interaction with default drag and drop sites

The implementation shown above will allow the user to drag a bitmap from the XmDrawingArea and drop it on the XmPushButton. If two copies of the application are running, the bitmap can be dragged from the XmDrawingArea in one to the XmPushButton in the other.

    Motif also provides some default drag initiators and drop sites. The XmLabel and XmPushButton widgets will initiate a drag if Button2 is pressed on them. They export the targets COMPOUND_TEXT and XA_PIXMAP. They do not, however, export the target XA_STRING, so our new XmPushButton drop site cannot accept a drop of the labelString resource.

    The XmText and XmTextField widgets both support dragging of the primary selection with an XA_STRING target, so the user could type the name of a bitmap file into an XmText widget, select it and drag it to our XmPushButton to see it displayed. Similarly, both the XmText and XmTextField widgets are drop sites which will accept XA_STRING targets. The user can therefore drag a bitmap from the XmDrawingArea and drop it in an XmText widget to find out its name.

19.2   Dropping non-text data

Although the example above allows the user to initiate a drag by selecting a bitmap and to set a XmPushButton's labelPixmap by dropping on it, this is achieved by transferring textual data. This can equally be achieved by transferring the Pixmap itself as the data. The only real difference is in the conversion procedure and request callback called to export and import the data.

The drop site is registered with an extra import target of XA_PIXMAP:

pixmaps

```
import_targets[0] = XA_STRING;
import_targets[1] = XA_PIXMAP;
XtSetArg(al[ac], XmNimportTargets, import_targets); ac++;
XtSetArg(al[ac], XmNnumImportTargets, 2); ac++;
XtSetArg(al[ac], XmNdropProc, import_bitmap); ac++;
XtSetArg(al[ac], XmNdropSiteOperations, XmDROP_COPY); ac++;
XmDropSiteRegister (button, al, ac);
```

The drag is started with an extra export target:

```
export_targets[0] = XA_STRING;
export_targets[1] = XA_PIXMAP;

XtSetArg (al[ac], XmNconvertProc, export_bitmap); ac++;
XtSetArg (al[ac], XmNclientData, bitmap); ac++;
XtSetArg (al[ac], XmNexportTargets, export_targets); ac++;
XtSetArg (al[ac], XmNnumExportTargets, 2); ac++;
XtSetArg (al[ac], XmNdragOperations, XmDROP_COPY); ac++;
drag_context = XmDragStart (w, event, al, ac);
```

When accepting the drop, the application has to decide which of the targets it wants to accept. In import_bitmap(), the PIXMAP target is preferable:

```
...
Atom       *export_list;
int        export_count, i;
Boolean    got_pixmap = False;
Boolean    got_string = False;

XtVaGetValues (drop_data->dragContext, XmNexportTargets,
```

```
                        &export_list, XmNnumExportTargets, &export_count,
                        0);
        for (i = 0; i < export_count; i ++)
            if (export_list[i] == XA_STRING)
                got_string = True;
            else if (export_list[i] == XA_PIXMAP)
                got_pixmap = True;
        if (got_pixmap || got_string) {
            if (got_pixmap)
                transfer_entries[0].target = XA_PIXMAP;
            else
                transfer_entries[0].target = XA_STRING;

        ...
```

The drag initiator's conversion procedure export_bitmap() has to export the pixmap. This is very simple, bearing in mind that a pixmap is a server resource, so only its ID need be transferred:

```
    if (*target == XA_PIXMAP) {
        Pixmap *pixmap = (Pixmap *) XtMalloc(sizeof(Pixmap));
        *pixmap = bitmap->pixmap;
        *value = (XtPointer) pixmap;
        *type_return = XA_DRAWABLE;
        *length = sizeof(Pixmap);
        *format = 32;
        return True;
    }
```

Finally the requester's request callback transfer_bitmap() has to handle the incoming data:

```
    if (*type == XA_DRAWABLE) {
        Pixmap pixmap = *(Pixmap *)value;
        if (pixmap == XmUNSPECIFIED_PIXMAP)
            XtVaSetValues (w, XmNtransferStatus, XmTRANSFER_FAILURE,
                        0);
        else {
            int          x, y, status;
            Window       root_win;
            unsigned int width, height, border, depth;
            Pixmap       new_pixmap;

            status = XGetGeometry (XtDisplay (widget), pixmap, &root_win, &x,
                        &y, &width, &height, &border, &depth);
```

```
                          new_pixmap = XCreatePixmap (XtDisplay (widget), XtWindow
                                  (widget), width, height, depth);
                          XCopyArea (XtDisplay (widget), pixmap, new_pixmap, gc, 0, 0,
                                  width, height, 0, 0);
                          XtVaSetValues (widget, XmNlabelPixmap, new_pixmap, 0);
                      }
                  }
```

   Note that a copy of the pixmap is made by the receiver. The pixmap is a server side data structure owned by the drag initiator. If we simply reference it, it will become invalid if the drag initiator subsequently dies or destroys the pixmap.

This assumes that the incoming pixmap and the destination widget are of the same depth. It would probably be safer if the code checked the depths and failed if they did not match, or possibly attempted a conversion.

Note that the code checks for UNSPECIFIED_PIXMAP and fails by setting the transferStatus resource in the drop transfer widget.

Using this code, the application could drag pixmaps from any XmLabel widget with labelType set to PIXMAP, as this is implemented by default and drop them onto the new drop site.

19.3   Drag and drop operations

The Motif drag and drop system introduces a concept which it calls an operation. An operation can have the following values:

- DROP_NOOP - No operation is valid.
- DROP_MOVE - The data is to be moved from the drag initiator to the drop receiver.
- DROP_COPY -A copy of the data in the drag initiator is to be made in the drop receiver.
- DROP_LINK -A link is to be established from the drop receiver to the data in the drag initiator.

These values are specified by the drag initiator and drop receiver to indicate which operations they are prepared to support. As the drag enters a drop site, the toolkit examines the operations supported by the drag context and the drop site and determines whether the drop site is valid. In addition, if the drag context or drop site supports more than one operation, the user can request a particular one using modifier keys: Shift for DROP_MOVE, Control for DROP_COPY and Shift Control for DROP_LINK. The user can (and probably will) change his or her mind about the operation during the course of the drag by pressing different modifiers. When the drop actually occurs, the toolkit notifies the receiving application of the required operation; the receiving application can ignore this and perform some other operation if appropriate.

Dragging an icon representing a file provides an easily understood illustration of the different operations available.

DROP_COPY

The example in Section 19.1 illustrates DROP_COPY, where a copy of the pixmap is made in the drop site.

Dragging a file icon suggests that a copy of the file is made at the destination. A print or compile service application normally works this way.

DROP_MOVE

This is very similar to DROP_COPY, except that the drag initiator should delete the data when the drop is complete. There are two ways this might be achieved. The drag initiator could specify a dropFinishCallback that examines the operation component of the call_data and deletes the appropriate data. Alternatively, the drop receiver could request a special target, which would cause the drag initiator to delete the drag data. The latter method is adopted by the Motif Text widgets. When they have successfully received a drop, they add a transfer entry to the drop transfer, requesting a DELETE target. Text widget drag initiators respond to this target by deleting the text currently selected. This is illustrated in Section 19.8.2.

Using the DROP_MOVE operation for a file would indicate that the file is to be deleted after the drop. Typically this would be used for a waste bin application.

DROP_LINK

The intention of the DROP_LINK operation is that the drag initiator retains the original data and the drop receiver creates a link to that data. In order for this to be viable, the data should be:

- Common to both applications (i.e. they are the same application).
- External to both applications (i.e. it is held in the operating system, perhaps as a file).
- Held by the X server (e.g. a window which can now be drawn on by both clients. The receiver can select for events to handle exposures, configuration and destruction).

Applications can ensure that a drag is limited to a drop only in the same application by constructing targets from strings containing a common window ID.

The use of DROP_LINK for a file icon might indicate that a file system link is to be created for a desktop application, but more typically it could be handled by simply passing the name of a file into another application which could then read it when appropriate.

19.4   Drag and drop visuals

The advantages of the drag and drop facilities over the conventional selection mechanism are in the visual feedback that can be provided. Motif provides two sets of visuals: those provided by the drag initiator (drag-over visuals) and those provided by the receiver (drag-under visuals).

19.4.1   Drag-over visuals

Whilst the drag is in progress, a drag icon is displayed. This icon is made up of three sections which are "blended" into a single icon. These sections are:

- The source icon - this is intended to give some indication about what is being dragged. For the example above, this might be set to the pixmap being dragged.
- The state icon - this should indicate the current state of a possible drop. Possible states are: VALID_DROP_SITE, the drag is over a drop site which would accept the drop; INVALID_DROP_SITE,[1] the drag is over a drop site which is not prepared to accept the drop (probably because the targets do not match); NO_DROP_SITE, the drag is not currently over a drop site.
- The operation icon - this shows what kind of operation would occur if the drop were started. The operation can be DROP_COPY, DROP_MOVE, DROP_LINK or DROP_NOOP.

The toolkit provides defaults for these icons using resources in the screen widget for the application. This allows the application to make the drag-over visuals consistent for the whole application, even if the drag initiators are those included as part of the toolkit by default.

See Section 19.6 for examples of drag-over visuals.

19.4.2   Drag-under visuals

The receiver drop site can change its visuals to indicate that it is prepared to accept a drop. A number of standard visuals (highlight, shadow-in, ...) are supported by the toolkit and will be displayed if the animationStyle resource is set on the XmDropSite (see Section 19.7). Non-standard visuals can be implemented in the drag-under procedure if the dynamic protocol is being used.

---

1. Had the choice been ours, we would have chosen a name that did not suggest a place where ambulances can make deliveries. Perhaps that is why the documentation inaccurately refers to XmDROP_SITE_INVALID.

19.5   Drag and drop protocols

As usual, there are two ways of handling the communication between the drag
initiator and the drop requester; the easy way and the hard way. The choice
determines the flexibility of visual feedback available. The actual protocol used
depends on resources in the XmDisplay widget for the initiator and receiver
applications and may therefore change during the drag as the user drags over
different applications. This is examined later.

The two protocols only affect the way the drag is handled. Once the drop
actually begins, it completes using the Xt selection mechanism, as we have already
seen.

19.5.1   The easy way - preregister drag protocol

In this mode, the toolkit handles all the drag-under visual processing using
resources supplied by the drag initiator and the drop site. The receiving application
is not involved in the process until the drop begins. The visuals for the receiver are
updated automatically, depending on the information supplied in the drop site and
drag context.

The advantages are that it is simple to implement, minimises network traffic and
large pixmaps can be used for the drag icons.

The disadvantages are that the server is grabbed, the drop site cannot
dynamically determine whether it is prepared to accept the drop until it actually
occurs and it can only use the standard drag-under visuals.

19.5.2   The hard way - dynamic drag protocol

In this mode, the initiator's toolkit communicates with the receiver whenever the
pointer enters a window which contains a drop site, allowing the receiver to
dynamically decide whether it is prepared to accept the drop and to update its
visuals accordingly.

The advantages are that the server is not grabbed and so can respond to other
event sources, the receiver can dynamically decide whether it is prepared to accept
the drop and can implement sophisticated visuals.

The disadvantages are that it requires more work on the part of the application,
there is additional network overhead as messages are passed to allow the receivers
dragProc to be called and the drag icons are restricted to cursors, which are likely
to be of limited size.

19.5.3   The choice of protocol

The protocol used for the drag is determined by examining the dragInitiatorProtocolStyle resource for the XmDisplay widget in the initiator's application and the
dragReceiverProtocolStyle in the receiver's XmDisplay widget whenever the
pointer moves into a window. These resources can be set in a resource file or can
be explicitly set by the application. They can take the following values:

- DRAG_NONE - Do not participate in drag and drop at all.
- DRAG_DROP_ONLY - Treat drag and drop just like the conventional
selection mechanism. The drag icon is displayed during the drag, but there are
no drag-over or drag-under visuals.
- DRAG_PREREGISTER - Use the preregister protocol.
- DRAG_PREFER_PREREGISTER - Use either protocol, but prefer
preregister. This is the default for dragReceiverProtocolStyle.
- DRAG_PREFER_RECEIVER - Use the protocol that the receiver specifies.
This is specified only by initiators and is the default for dragInitiatorProto-
colStyle.
- DRAG_PREFER_DYNAMIC - Use either protocol but prefer dynamic.
- DRAG_DYNAMIC - Use only the dynamic protocol.

If either the initiator or receiver has specified DRAG_NONE, then
DRAG_NONE will be used. If either have specified DRAG_DROP_ONLY, then
DRAG_DROP_ONLY will be used.

If the initiator specifies DRAG_PREFER_RECEIVER, obviously the
receiver's protocol is used.

If there is a direct conflict of DRAG_DYNAMIC for one side and
DRAG_PREREGISTER for the other, then DRAG_DROP_ONLY is used.

If there is a conflict of preferences (i.e. one side is DRAG_PREFER_PRE-
REGISTER and the other is DRAG_PREFER_DYNAMIC), then the initiator's
choice takes precedence.

If both sides specify the same value, then that protocol is used.

If one side specifies a firm choice and the other a preference (e.g.
DRAG_PREFER_PREREGISTER and DRAG_DYNAMIC), then the firm choice
is used.[1]

19.5.4   Drag and drop callbacks

A large number of callback functions can be called during a drag and drop
operation. Many of these are optional and exist largely to support sophisticated
visual effects. All of these functions are represented as resources of the three

1. This is neatly illustrated by a table in the Motif documentation.

objects involved in a drag and drop transaction: XmDropSite, XmDragContext and XmDropTransfer. XmDropSite is a persistent object in the receiving application. XmDragContext is a transient object in the initiating application, but a copy of it is made in the receiver; it lasts only as long as the drag is in progress. XmDrop-Transfer is a transient object in the receiver, created when the drop starts and persisting only until the drop is complete (see Table 19.1).

Table 19.1 *Drag and drop callbacks*

Callback	Object	Notes
dragProc	XmDropSite	Only with dynamic protocol - used for special drag-under visuals
dropProc	XmDropSite	Called (in receiver) when drop starts
transferProc	XmDropTransfer	This is the Xt selection callback procedure
convertProc	XmDragContext	This is the Xt selection incremental conversion procedure
dragDropFinishCallback	XmDragContext	Called when the entire transaction complete
dragMotionCallback	XmDragContext	Called when pointer moves
dropFinishCallback	XmDragContext	Called when drop completes
dropSiteEnterCallback dropSiteLeaveCallback	XmDragContext	Called when pointer enters/leaves a drop site
dropStartCallback	XmDragContext	Called (in initiator) when drop starts
operationChangedCallback	XmDragContext	Called when operation changes during a drag
topLevelEnterCallback topLevelLeaveCallback	XmDragContext	Called when pointer enters/leaves a top-level (shell's) window or changes root window

Figure 19.2 shows an annotated trace of the callbacks called in a simple drag and drop without moving outside the top level window. The XmDragContext callbacks (those invoked in the initiating application) are in the left-hand column; those on the right are receiver callbacks in the XmDropSite or XmDropTransfer.

19.6 Drag contexts

XmDragContext is a widget-based data structure used to hold information about the drag. It is created by the toolkit when the application calls XmDragStart() and is destroyed automatically. Although it is not a conventional widget, it does respond to the normal resource setting conventions from resource files, at create time, and by XtSetValues().

```
                          /* drag initiated by user */
        topLevelEnterCallback
        dragMotionCallback
        ...
        dragMotionCallback
                                     dragProc/* first is before drop site enter */
        dropSiteEnterCallback
                                     dragProc
        dragMotionCallback

                          /* drop initiated by user */
                                     dragProc
        dropSiteLeaveCallback
        topLevelLeaveCallback
                                     dropProc
        dropStartCallback
        convertProc
                                     transferProc
        dropFinishCallback
```

Figure 19.2 *Interaction of drag and drop callbacks*

The widget is created initially in the initiator's application. A shadow copy is created in the receiver's application for the dropProc and dragProc call_data.

19.6.1   Interesting resources

blendModel, sourceCursorIcon, sourcePixmapIcon, operationCursorIcon and stateCursorIcon

These resources are combined to create the drag icon that is visible whilst the drag is in progress. The blendModel resource indicates which Icon resources are used. The Icon resources are objects created by XmCreateDragIcon(), which is described in Section 19.9.

There are resources in the XmScreen widget for the state icon for the three different drag states (VALID_DROP_SITE, INVALID_DROP_SITE and NO_DROP_SITE). If the stateCursorIcon in the XmDragContext widget is set to NULL, the appropriate icon from the XmScreen widget is displayed in the drag icon as the drag progresses. It seems incongruous that there are no equivalent resources in the XmDragContext itself and to achieve a state-specific source icon requires the use of the dragMotionCallback. This is illustrated below.

Either the sourceCursorIcon (DYNAMIC) or the sourcePixmapIcon(PRE-REGISTER) is used as the basis for the drag cursor depending on the drag protocol in effect.

Setting any of the icons other than sourcePixmapIcon to an XmDragIcon which has a depth of more than one is silently ignored.

cursorForeground, cursorBackground, invalidCursorForeground, noneCursorForeground and validCursorForeground
Specify the pixel values used for the cursor foreground and background depending on the state of the drag. This can give a good indication to the user of what will happen if the drag is terminated.

clientData

   As we have already seen, this is very useful for passing round contextual data. The Motif documentation states that this is passed as the client_data to the convertProc, but this is only true if incremental is False. The data can easily be fetched from the widget in the convertProc anyway.

convertProc
The selection conversion procedure which will be called to export the data.

dragOperations
The operations that the drag initiator is prepared to support. These are used by the toolkit to match with the dropSiteOperations of the drop site when determining the drag state.

exportTargets and numExportTargets
The targets the drag initiator is prepared to export. These are used by the toolkit to match the importTargets of the drop site when determining the drag states.

dragDropFinishCallback, dragMotionCallback, dropFinishCallback, dropSiteEnterCallback, dropSiteLeaveCallback, dropStartCallback, operationChangedCallback, topLevelEnterCallback and topLevelLeaveCallback
These callbacks get called at various stages during the drag and drop process. They can be used to modify the visuals, decide whether a drop site is valid and clear up after the drag and drop has completed.

iccHandle
This is an undocumented resource. It is used to store the atom of the selection owned by the drag context. It is particularly useful if the receiving application wants to transfer some data to validate a potential drop site. This is illustrated in the example in Section 19.7.2.

19.6.2 Examples of use

We can modify our example application so that the drag icon displays the pixmap being dragged when the pointer is over a valid drop site. The drag_bitmap() function body becomes:

drag_icon

```
            ...
            export_targets[0] = XA_STRING;
            export_targets[1] = XA_PIXMAP;

            if (bitmap->state_icon == NULL)
            {
                XtSetArg (al[ac], XmNpixmap, bitmap->bitmap); ac++;
                XtSetArg (al[ac], XmNwidth, bitmap->width); ac++;
                XtSetArg (al[ac], XmNheight, bitmap->height); ac++;
                bitmap->state_icon = XmCreateDragIcon (w, "drag_icon", al, ac);
                ac = 0;
            }

            XtSetArg (al[ac], XmNconvertProc, export_bitmap); ac++;
            XtSetArg (al[ac], XmNclientData, bitmap); ac++;
            XtSetArg (al[ac], XmNexportTargets, export_targets); ac++;
            XtSetArg (al[ac], XmNnumExportTargets, 2); ac++;
            XtSetArg (al[ac], XmNdragOperations, XmDROP_COPY); ac++;
            drag_context = XmDragStart (w, event, al, ac);
    /* Register callbacks for entering and leaving drop sites */
            if (drag_context) {
                XtAddCallback (drag_context, XmNdropSiteEnterCallback,
                            drop_site_enter, (XtPointer) bitmap);
                XtAddCallback (drag_context, XmNdropSiteLeaveCallback,
                            drop_site_leave, NULL);

            ...
```

The drop_site_enter() callback examines the call_data to determine the state of
the drag and sets the stateCursorIcon accordingly; the drop_site_leave() callback
simply resets the icon:

```
        void drop_site_enter (w, client_data, call_data)
            Widget       w;
            XtPointer    client_data;
            XtPointer    call_data;
        {
            Bitmap_p bitmap = (Bitmap_p) client_data;

            if (((XmDropSiteEnterCallbackStruct *)call_data)->dropSiteStatus ==
                        XmVALID_DROP_SITE)
                XtVaSetValues (w, XmNsourceCursorIcon, bitmap->state_icon, 0);
        }
```

```
void drop_site_leave (w, client_data, call_data)
    Widget      w;
    XtPointer    client_data;
    XtPointer    call_data;
{
    XtVaSetValues (w, XmNsourceCursorIcon, NULL, 0);
}
```

Note that this example is contrary to the intended use of the drag icons. The source icon should probably always display the pixmap and the state icon should change, to indicate that the drop site was valid.

Further examples can be found in Section 19.9.2.

19.6.3 Watch out for

 The convertProc is always an XtSelectionIncrProc regardless of the setting of incremental.

 The call data passed to some of the XmDragContext callbacks includes a dropSiteStatus member. Setting this to INVALID_DROP_SITE in, say, the dropSiteEnterCallback, does not stop the drop from starting; it only affects the visuals.

19.7 Drop sites

XmDropSites are data structures created and destroyed automatically by the toolkit. They are created by calling XmDropSiteRegister(), which takes a widget argument and resource list. They are associated with the widget for which they were created and resources for them are set and fetched, using XmDropSiteUpdate() and XmDropSiteRetrieve(). The function XmDropSiteUnregister() can be used to remove a widget from the list of drop sites.

19.7.1 Interesting resources

animationStyle
Specifies the type of drag-under visuals used when a drag enters a valid drop site. The resource can be set to the following values:

* DRAG_UNDER_HIGHLIGHT - The highlight border is drawn around the drop site.
* DRAG_UNDER_SHADOW_OUT - The drop site is drawn with a raised shadow.

- DRAG_UNDER_SHADOW_IN - The drop site is drawn with a recessed shadow.
- DRAG_UNDER_PIXMAP - The pixmap specified in animationPixmap is drawn in the drop site.
- DRAG_UNDER_NONE - The toolkit is not to provide any drag-under visuals. If the drag is using a DYNAMIC protocol, the application may provide drag-under visuals in its dragProc.

animationMask, animationPixmap and animationPixmapDepth

These are used to specify the drag-under visual when the animationStyle is DRAG_UNDER_PIXMAP. The animationPixmapDepth will default to the depth of the animationPixmap and these should both match the depth of the drop site's window or be one.

dragProc

If the drag protocol is DYNAMIC, the dragProc callback function will be called when the drag enters or leaves the drop site and for motion events while the drag is over the drop site.

Section 19.7.2 illustrates the use of the dragProc to validate the data being dragged.

dropProc

This resource specifies a function that is called to initiate the drop. Note how it is used to validate the drag initiator's export targets in Section 19.1.

dropSiteType

Drop sites can be either DROP_SITE_SIMPLE (the default) or DROP_SITE_-COMPOSITE. A drop site should be set to DROP_SITE_COMPOSITE if the widget has descendants that are to be registered as drop sites. Descendant drop sites are used to clip their parents and each other where they overlap. XmDropSiteQueryStackingOrder() and XmDropSiteConfigureStackingOrder() can be used to examine and change the stacking order of drop sites.

dropRectangles and numDropRectangles

These resources can only be specified for drop sites which are not DROP_SITE_-COMPOSITE. By default the whole of the widget is used as the actual drop site. These resources can be used to specify a subregion.

dropSiteActivity

Specifies whether a drop site is active (DROP_SITE_ACTIVE) or inactive (DROP_SITE_INACTIVE). An inactive drop site is treated as if it and any child drop sites were not registered.

dropSiteOperations
Specifies the operations (DROP_MOVE, DROP_COPY, DROP_LINK or DROP_NOOP) that the drop site is prepared to accept. The resource is compared with the drag context's dragOperations when the toolkit determines the drop site status.

importTargets and numImportTargets
Specifies the list of target atoms that the drop site is prepared to accept. The toolkit compares this with the drag context's exportTargets when determining the drop site status.

19.7.2 Examples of use

We can extend our basic example a little further to illustrate a variety of the drop site features.

Creating the drop site
The code for creating the drop site is modified, so that only a small region of the widget is used. If a PREREGISTER protocol drag is used, this draws a raised shadow to indicate that the drop site is valid. A dragProc function is specified to handle DYNAMIC protocol drags:

dynamic_drag

```
XRectangle rect[1];

...

rect[0].x = 10;
rect[0].y = 10;
rect[0].width = 30;
rect[0].height = 30;
XtSetArg(al[ac], XmNdropRectangles, rect); ac++;
XtSetArg(al[ac], XmNnumDropRectangles, 1); ac++;
XtSetArg(al[ac], XmNdragProc, drag_proc); ac++;
XtSetArg(al[ac], XmNanimationStyle,
            XmDRAG_UNDER_SHADOW_OUT); ac++;
XmDropSiteRegister (button, al, ac);

...
```

Handling DYNAMIC protocol drags
The dragProc function drag_proc() is going to set the drop site status to INVALID_DROP_SITE if the drag is for a non-square Pixmap. If the drag is for a square pixmap, it is going to set the pixmap on the XmPushButton while the drop site is valid. Drags of XA_STRING will be handled using the toolkit visuals.

To do this, the drag receiver has to transfer the pixmap from the drag initiator using the Xt selection mechanism when the drop site is entered, so that it can validate that it is square. The selection atom is stored in the drag context by the toolkit and so it can be fetched from the shadow copy of the drag context provided in the dragProc's call_data. The original pixmap is restored when the drop site is left. The call_data is passed through to the transfer's request callback, drop_site_validate():

```
void drag_proc (w, client_data, cd)
    Widget      w;
    XtPointer   client_data;
    XtPointer   cd;
{
    XmDragProcCallbackStruct *call_data
                        = (XmDragProcCallbackStruct *)cd;
    static Pixmap enter_pixmap;

    if (call_data->reason == XmCR_DROP_SITE_ENTER_MESSAGE &&
                    call_data->dropSiteStatus == XmVALID_DROP_SITE)
    {
        Atom selection;

        XtVaGetValues (call_data->dragContext, XmNiccHandle, &selection,
                    0);
        XtVaGetValues (w, XmNlabelPixmap, &enter_pixmap, 0);
        XtGetSelectionValue (w, selection, XA_PIXMAP, drop_site_validate,
                    (XtPointer) call_data, call_data->timeStamp);
    }
    else if (call_data->reason == XmCR_DROP_SITE_LEAVE_MESSAGE)
        XtVaSetValues (w, XmNlabelPixmap, enter_pixmap, 0);
}
```

The request callback for the selection transfer (drop_site_validate()) simply checks the width and height of the pixmap and sets the labelPixmap of the drop site widget. Note that the pixmap is not copied, on the assumption that the original is going to survive for the duration of the drag:[1]

```
void drop_site_validate (w, closure, seltype, type, value, length, format)
    Widget          w;
    XtPointer       closure;
    Atom            *seltype;
    Atom            *type;
    XtPointer       value;
    unsigned long   *length;
```

---

1. This is not a particularly safe assumption and indeed this example is somewhat dubious in its assumption that the transfer will occur within the lifetime of the DragProcCallbackStruct. However, it does seem to work.

```
    int             *format;
{

    XmDragProcCallbackStruct *call_data = (XmDragProcCallbackStruct *)
                    closure;

    if (*type == XA_DRAWABLE) {
        Pixmap pixmap = *(Pixmap *)value;
        int x, y, status;
        Window root_win;
        unsigned int width, height, border, depth;

        status = XGetGeometry (XtDisplay (w), pixmap, &root_win, &x, &y,
                    &width, &height, &border, &depth);
        if (width != height)
            call_data->dropSiteStatus = XmINVALID_DROP_SITE;
        else
            XtVaSetValues (w, XmNlabelPixmap, pixmap, 0);
        call_data->animate = False;
    }
}
```

19.7.3   Handling help requests for drop site

The user can request help for the drop site while the drag is in process by pressing the osfHelp key. The application can respond to this by showing a help dialog which enables the user to proceed with or cancel the drop. The toolkit will display the drag icon over the drop site until the application calls XmDropTransferStart().

The dropProc callback import_bitmap() can check the dropAction field of the drop data to determine the action that the user is taking. An InformationDialog is displayed with appropriate callbacks to process the user's actions (proceed or cancel). The drop site widget and the drop data are saved in global variables, so that they can be used in the callback to simply call import_bitmap() with the dropAction suitably amended. This is an unsophisticated example, but it serves to illustrate the basic principle:

drag_help

```
void import_bitmap ();

static Widget help_dialog;
static Widget help_drop_site;
static XmDropProcCallbackStruct help_drop_data;

void drop_from_help (w, client_data, call_data)
```

```
        Widget      w;
        XtPointer    client_data;
        XtPointer    call_data;
{
/* Proceed with drop - modify client_data and pass to dropProc */
        XmDropProcCallback drop_data = (XmDropProcCallback) client_data;
        drop_data->dropAction = XmDROP;
        XtDestroyWidget (help_dialog);
        import_bitmap (help_drop_site, NULL, client_data);
}


void cancel_from_help (w, client_data, call_data)
        Widget      w;
        XtPointer    client_data;
        XtPointer    call_data;
{
/* Cancel drop - modify client_data and pass to dropProc */
        XmDropProcCallback drop_data = (XmDropProcCallback) client_data;
        drop_data->dropAction = XmDROP_CANCEL;
        XtDestroyWidget (help_dialog);
        import_bitmap (help_drop_site, NULL, client_data);
}


void import_bitmap (w, client_data, call_data)
        Widget              w;
        XtPointer            client_data, call_data;
{

    ...
    if (drop_data->dropAction == XmDROP_HELP)
    {
        XmString s = XmStringCreateLocalized ("Drop it here");
        XtSetArg (al[ac], XmNmessageString, s); ac++;
        help_dialog = XmCreateInformationDialog (appshell, "help_dialog", al,
                    ac);
        help_drop_site = w;
        ac = 0;
        memcpy (&help_drop_data, drop_data, sizeof
                    (XmDropProcCallbackStruct));
        XtAddCallback (help_dialog, XmNokCallback, drop_from_help,
                    (XtPointer) &help_drop_data);
        XtAddCallback (help_dialog, XmNcancelCallback, cancel_from_help,
                    (XtPointer) &help_drop_data);
        XtManageChild (help_dialog);
        return;
```

```
    }
    ...
```

19.7.4 Watch out for

 In Motif up to release 1.2.2 drop sites are still active, even when the widget to which they are attached is unmapped.

19.8 Drop transfers

XmDropTransfer is a widget-based data structure used to hold information about the drop currently in progress. It is created by the toolkit when the application calls XmDropTransferStart() and destroyed automatically. Although it is not a conventional widget, it does respond to the normal resource setting conventions from resource files, at create time and by XtSetValues(). The XmDropTransfer widget is used to track the progress of a drop.

XmDropTransferStart() should only be called from a dropProc of a drop site, as it requires an XmDragContext widget parameter.

19.8.1 Interesting resources

dropTransfers and numDropTransfers

The dropTransfers resource specifies an array of XmDropTransferEntryRec, which is used to request the transfer of a number of targets from the drag initiator.

The XmDropTransferEntryRec is a structure that contains a target atom and a client_data pointer. For each of the targets that should be transferred, create an entry in the array and set the target field to the appropriate atom. The client_data component is passed in as the closure parameter to the transferProc function.

Setting numDropTransfers to 0 at any time before or during the progress of the transfer indicates that it is complete. Once the transfer has begun, additional transfers can be included in the list by calling XmDropTransferAdd().

incremental

Set this resource to True if you want to use the incremental Xt selection mechanism.

transferProc

This resource specifies an XtSelectionCallbackProc function used to receive the selection values. This is the request callback used in XtGetSelectionValues().

transferStatus

Indicates the current state of the transfer. Setting this to False causes the correct visuals to be displayed if the receiver does not accept the drop, either before the transfer starts, or if the transfer data is rejected.

19.8.2   Examples of use

We can illustrate the use of the drop transfer widget by modifying the basic program to support the DROP_MOVE operation. The best way to let the drag initiator know that it is safe to delete the data is to use a selection transfer once the data has been successfully received by the drop receiver.

First, we must register the drop site for DROP_MOVE operations:

drag_move

```
    ...
    XtSetArg(al[ac], XmNdropSiteOperations,
                    XmDROP_COPY | XmDROP_MOVE); ac++;
    XmDropSiteRegister (button, al, ac);
```

The drag must also be initiated with DROP_MOVE:

```
    ...
    XtSetArg(al[ac], XmNdragOperations,
                    XmDROP_MOVE | XmDROP_COPY); ac++;
    drag_context = XmDragStart (w, event, al, ac);
```

When the drop begins, we want to allow the DROP_MOVE operation; once the main data transfer is complete, we want to add an additional transfer entry if the operation is DROP_MOVE. This complicates the code for import_bitmap() somewhat, as the transfer_bitmap() function does not know what the operation is and the closure parameter is already being used to store the destination widget. The only solution to this is to store the widget and the operation in a data structure and pass a pointer to this in the closure parameter. We then need to add a destroyCallback to the XmDropTransfer widget to deallocate the storage used for this structure:

```
    typedef struct Transfer_s {
        Widget          widget;
        unsigned char   operation;
    } Transfer_t, *Transfer_p;

    void transfer_bitmap (w, closure, seltype, type, value, length, format)
        ...
    {
```

```
     Transfer_p transfer = (Transfer_p) closure;

          ...

          if (transfer->operation == XmDROP_MOVE)
          {
/* We have successfully completed a move - tell the initiator to delete the
information transferred by requesting transfer of the target 'DELETE' */
          transfer_entries[0].target = XmInternAtom (
                    XtDisplay (transfer->widget), "DELETE", False);
          transfer_entries[0].client_data = (XtPointer) NULL;
          XmDropTransferAdd (w, transfer_entries, 1);
          }
}


void drop_transfer_destroy (w, client_data, call_data)
     Widget       w;
     XtPointer    client_data;
     XtPointer    call_data;
{
     if (client_data)
          XtFree ((char *) client_data);
}

void import_bitmap (w, client_data, call_data)
          ...
{
     Widget       drop_transfer;
     Transfer_p   transfer = NULL;

          ...
/* Support both move and copy */
     if (drop_data->dropAction != XmDROP
     || (drop_data->operation != XmDROP_MOVE
     && drop_data->operation != XmDROP_COPY)) {
          XtSetArg (al[ac], XmNtransferStatus, XmTRANSFER_FAILURE);
                    ac++;
          XtSetArg (al[ac], XmNnumDropTransfers, 0); ac++;
     } else {
          ...
          if (ok) {
/* Initially request single transfer of STRING target. The transferProc will
request transfer of DELETE target when it has got the STRING */
          transfer = (Transfer_p) XtMalloc (sizeof (Transfer_t));
          transfer->widget = w;
          transfer->operation = drop_data->operation;
          transfer_entries[0].target = XA_STRING;
```

```
                    transfer_entries[0].client_data = (XtPointer) transfer;
                    XtSetArg (al[ac], XmNdropTransfers, transfer_entries); ac++;
                    XtSetArg (al[ac], XmNnumDropTransfers, 1); ac++;
                    XtSetArg (al[ac], XmNtransferProc, transfer_bitmap); ac++;
                }
                ...
            }
            drop_transfer = XmDropTransferStart (drop_data->dragContext, al, ac);
            if (drop_transfer)
                XtAddCallback (drop_transfer, XmNdestroyCallback,
                            drop_transfer_destroy, transfer);
        }
```

Finally, the drag initiator needs to handle the DELETE target in export_bitmap(). It has to delete the bitmap (where 'delete' is interpreted in the context of the application and here means just making the bitmap non-draggable) and respond with a NULL value:

```
        Boolean export_bitmap (w, selection, target, type_return, value, length,
                            format, max_length, client_data, request_id)
            ...
        {
            Bitmap_p bitmap;
            ...
            if (*target == XmInternAtom (XtDisplay (w), "DELETE", False)) {
                XtVaGetValues (w, XmNclientData, &bitmap, 0);
                bitmap->draggable = False;
                *type_return = XmInternAtom (XtDisplay(w), "NULL", False);
                *value = NULL;
                *length = 0;
                *format = 8;
                return True;
            }
            return False;
        }
```

This method is compatible with the Motif Text widgets which will request a DELETE transfer when they receive a DROP_MOVE drop and will respond to a DELETE request by deleting the text currently selected.

19.8.3 Watch out for

⚠ XmDropTransfer is derived from Object and not Core. It is therefore not valid to pass it as a parameter to XtDisplay(), etc.

19.9   Drag icons

The XmDragIcon widget is specifically intended for use within XmDragContext widgets. It simply consists of resources used by the toolkit to build up a drag cursor. See Section 19.4.1 for discussion of how several XmDragIcons are put together to form a drag cursor.

19.9.1   Interesting resources

attachment, offsetX and offsetY
These resources specify how a stateCursorIcon or operationCursorIcon is attached to a source icon in an XmDragContext widget. Attachment can be ATTACH_HOT, ATTACH_CENTER or one of eight compass points. The offset resources specify the amount by which the origin of the cursor is to be offset.

depth, width, height, pixmap and mask
These resources specify the pixmap used to build the cursor.
   If the pixmap is specified, then the width and height must also be specified. If the specified pixmap has depth greater than one, then the depth resource should be appropriately specified.

hotX and hotY
Specify the cursor's hot spot. These are used for XmDragContext source and state icons.

19.9.2   Examples of use

The default drag cursor, supplied by the toolkit if no Icon resources are set when XmDragStart() is called, is shown in Figure 19.3.

Figure 19.3 *Default drag cursor, blendModel = BLEND_ALL*

The following code produces the drag cursor shown in Figure 19.4:

```
#include <X11/bitmaps/woman>


    ...
    Pixmap   bitmap;
    Widget   source_icon;
```

```
bitmap = XCreateBitmapFromData(XtDisplay(w), XtWindow(w),
                    sorceress_bits, sorceress_width, sorceress_height);
XtSetArg (al[ac], XmNpixmap, bitmap); ac++;
XtSetArg (al[ac], XmNwidth, sorceress_width); ac++;
XtSetArg (al[ac], XmNheight, sorceress_height); ac++;
source_icon = XmCreateDragIcon (w, "drag_icon", al, ac);
ac = 0;

XtSetArg (al[ac], XmNsourceCursorIcon, source_icon); ac++;
XtSetArg (al[ac], XmNblendModel, XmBLEND_STATE_SOURCE); ac++;
...
drag_context = (XmDragContext) XmDragStart (w, event, al, ac);
...
```

Figure 19.4 *Drag cursor, blendModel = BLEND_STATE_SOURCE*

The following code adds a custom state icon (perhaps in one of the drag callbacks) and produces the drag cursor shown in Figure 19.5:

```
#include <X11/bitmaps/Fold>

...
bitmap = XCreateBitmapFromData(XtDisplay(w), XtWindow(w),
                    Fold_bits, Fold_width, Fold_height);
XtSetArg (al[ac], XmNpixmap, bitmap); ac++;
XtSetArg (al[ac], XmNwidth, Fold_width); ac++;
XtSetArg (al[ac], XmNheight, Fold_height); ac++;
XtSetArg (al[ac], XmNoffsetY, -Fold_height/2); ac++;
XtSetArg (al[ac], XmNoffsetX, 5); ac++;
XtSetArg (al[ac], XmNattachment, XmATTACH_EAST); ac++;
state_icon = XmCreateDragIcon (w, "drag_icon", al, ac);
XtVaSetValues (drag_context, XmNstateCursorIcon, state_icon, 0);
...
```

Figure 19.5 *Drag cursor, blendModel = BLEND_STATE_SOURCE*

19.10   Display

The XmDisplay widget contains only three resources, of which two are relevant to drag and drop and recorded here.

There is a single XmDisplay widget for each display accessed by the application. The XmDisplay widget is created automatically the first time a shell is created for a display. An application can obtain the XmDisplay widget, using XmGetXmDisplay().

19.10.1   Interesting resources

The resources for an XmDisplay widget can only be specified in a resource file or set with XtSetValues(). There is no way of the application specifying them at create time.

defaultVirtualBindings
Although not relevant to drag and drop, this is where the toolkit stores the default virtual bindings (the definitions of the osf keysyms).
Note that there is no symbolic constant XmNdefaultVirtualBindings. If, for some reason, you need to set the resource, use "defaultVirtualBindings".

dragInitiatorProtocolStyle and dragReceiverProtocolStyle
The required drag and drop protocols for this application. See Section 19.5 for a description of how these resources are used to determine the drag protocol.

19.10.2   Examples of use

If an application provides sophisticated drag-under visuals (for example, those illustrated in Section 19.7.2), the following line might be included in the application resource file:

    XApplication*dragReceiverProtocolStyle: PREFER_PREREGISTER

⚠️   The protocol styles can also be set in code using XtSetValues() on the XmDisplay widget, although the documentation denies this.

19.11   Screen

The XmScreen widget contains a number of resources relevant to drag and drop, so they are recorded here.

There is a single XmScreen widget for each screen accessed by the application. The XmScreen widget is created automatically the first time a shell is created for a screen. An application can obtain the XmScreen widget, using XmGet-XmScreen().

19.11.1   Drag- and drop- related resources

The resources for a screen widget can only be specified in a resource file or set with XtSetValues(). There is no way of the application specifying them at create time.

defaultCopyCursorIcon, defaultMoveCursorIcon and defaultLinkCursorIcon
The XmDragIcons used to indicate the current operation in an XmDragContext if operationCursorIcon is NULL.

defaultInvalidCursorIcon, defaultNoneCursorIcon and defaultValidCursorIcon
The XmDragIcons used to indicate the current state of an XmDragContext if stateCursorIcon is NULL.

defaultSourceCursorIcon
The XmDragIcon used to indicate the drag source of an XmDragContext if source-CursorIcon is NULL or unusable.

CHAPTER 20

Internationalisation

Many applications these days are used in different parts of the world in different languages. Ideally, they are written so that this can be done without change to the application itself. X provides some support which (although it stops short of natural language translation) makes this a feasible proposition.

The Motif and X toolkits neatly encapsulate these mechanisms, so that you need do little short of following a few basic guidelines to make your application adaptable for different international requirements. This chapter gives you those basic guidelines. It does not discuss the philosophy and practice of internationalisation, nor the intricacies of X support.

One feature of the X internationalisation support is that an extra process - an input method - may be used to process keyboard input. This chapter uses the xwnmo input method for illustrations. It is supplied with the X11R5 contributed sources, along with other example input methods.

20.1 Locales and localisation

A locale is an ANSI concept. It identifies a set of information that characterises a particular international location. For example, the locale might be set to be "En_UK" to denote that the locale is UK English, "En_US" for US English or "ja_JP.ujis" for a version of Japanese. The setting of a locale makes certain C library functions operate in different ways, defining the collation order, number format and so on (a locale has pieces known as categories - LC_COLLATE, LC_NUMERIC, ...). It is also used to define the encoding, which is the mapping between characters in a text string and their index in a font. This latter function is of primary interest when writing internationalised X programs.

Although locale support should be provided by your operating system, some systems only support the C locale (in which functions behave as C programmers expect them to). Xlib conveniently provides a set of locale support functions that can be used as an alternative and which support a number of other useful locales.[1]

It is important to distinguish between internationalisation and localisation. Internationalisation is what you, the application developer, have to do to make sure that your application can be successfully adapted for different locales without code changes. The localisation may be done by you (if you are also a linguist) or it may be done by a distributor or end-user. The major part of localisation is the actual translation of labels and messages into the native language. Internationalisation is the inclusion of mechanisms so that the same application can be localised to a variety of locations and the exclusion of mechanisms that would prevent this.

20.1.1   Application internationalisation

Internationalising an application requires little effort. It is mostly a matter of ensuring that language-specific and culture-specific resource values are not hard-coded. An application also has to establish the locale, so that the locale support functions (for date support and so on) can do their job.

Establishing the locale

An application has to call setlocale() to establish the locale to be used. The X toolkit provides good support for an application to do this and allow the user to specify the locale, using a resource or an environment variable. By default, no locale is specified and the application will run using the C locale. If the application wishes to enable the internationalisation facilities it should call:

XtSetLanguageProc (NULL, (XtLanguageProc)NULL, NULL)

before opening the display. This installs the default Xt language procedure. XtOpenDisplay() determines the required locale, by searching (in a locale independent way) for the xnlLanguage resource in the command line arguments (set using -xnllanguage) or in the RESOURCE_MANAGER property on the root window of the default screen and calls the installed language procedure passing this locale as a parameter.

The language procedure is responsible for setting the locale and returning the locale name that is set. The default Xt language procedure calls setlocale() to set

---

1. If you have X11R5 sources, compile with -DX_LOCALE and -DX_WCHAR. See the X release notes.

the locale in all categories to that determined by XtOpenDisplay() and falls back on the C locale if the chosen locale is not supported. You can supply your own language procedure if you wish to provide additional methods of setting the locale, or only provide support for certain locales, but in most cases the default language procedure should be sufficient.

If the locale is not set by resource, the empty string will be passed through to setlocale(), which will indicate to the system that it should determine the locale from an environment variable (commonly LANG).

Strings and fonts

Clearly, the application should not hard-code any strings. These should be specified in a resource file so that they can be localised. Fonts should also be specified in a resource file, as the fonts used limit the characters that can be displayed.

Icons, bitmaps and pixmaps

It is tempting to assume that pictures constitute a universal language, but the reality is rather different. Any icons used in your application may have to be localised and so should be represented in external bitmap or pixmap files.

The Motif pixmap routines, XmGetPixmap*(), use a file search path which depends on the locale, so an application that uses only this can easily be localised. The Xlib pixmap routines and the XPM pixmap library do not. If you use these, you can layer a search path on top using XtResolvePathname() or simply distribute different sets of icon files to be installed according to the locale of the user.

Layout

Translating the strings used in an application will usually change the size of those widgets that display static text. Changing the font will change text input widgets as well. If you use a fixed layout, you should ensure that the positions are given in a resource file. If you use a layout determined by XmForm attachments, it will generally work without alteration if the component widgets change size, but particularly gross changes can render anything invalid. Again, you should define as much as possible of the layout in the resource file. Motif provides a string-to-widget type converter, so you can specify resources like leftWidget in a resource file.

20.1.2 Application localisation

Given a properly internationalised application, localisation is fairly straight-forward.

Resource files

Resource files are the obvious place to localise much of the application. The user has full control over the text displayed if it is specified in a resource file. The application-specific class resource file (application defaults file) is located by the intrinsics toolkit, using the algorithm detailed in Section 10.4. In theory you should provide an application defaults file for each of the locales that you support.

Font sets

A locale will often require more than one font encoding to display all the required characters. For example, the Japanese locale ja_JP.jis7 requires three different encodings:

- iso8859-1 - for Latin characters.
- jisx0208.1983 - for Kanji ideographic characters.
- jisx0201.1976 for Kana phonetic characters.

To create a font set use one of the techniques described in Section 15.2.1. The important thing is that the font set contains elements to cover all the encodings required by the locale. The simplest way to do this is to specify it as a resource with * in most of the font segments.

20.2   Internationalised text output

Xlib provides functions which can display text using a font set, choosing the appropriate font, using encoding information buried in the text string. These are automatically used by the compound string functions when a font list element containing a font set is used to output a string. The Motif widgets which display compound strings (XmLabel derivatives) therefore automatically support internationalised text output as long as they have a fontList which has a font set complete and valid for the current locale.

A font list entry that is tagged with the current locale will match compound string segments tagged with the default tag. This is not particularly useful, as fonts will generally be specified in a resource file; the resource file for each locale can simply contain a font set appropriate to that locale with the default tag.

20.3   Internationalised text input

X11R5 provides additional mechanisms to support internationalised text input. An application can connect to another client process - an input method - dedicated to handling input. Input methods are supported by the Motif Text widgets.

20.3.1   Input methods

Input methods provide the solution to the problem of input for languages (such as Japanese) where the number of ideographic characters available make the conventional one character to a key paradigm unworkable. Instead characters are composed by several keystrokes and may require user interaction to select from a number of possible options. One common method is to base the required keystrokes on the phonetics of the language. These phonetic characters are then converted to the required ideographic character on request from the user. If there are several possible ideographs, the input method presents a list to the user and the user selects the appropriate one.

Obviously the application toolkit writers do not want to get involved in this, so it is carried out in a separate client, which intercepts keyboard input and returns composed characters in a buffer. The process of composing characters from multiple keystrokes and user interaction is called pre-editing.

The example input method used in this section is xwnmo.

Input method components

The input method attaches itself to the shell that contains the widget which requires the text input (see Figure 20.1).

Conventional XmText widget

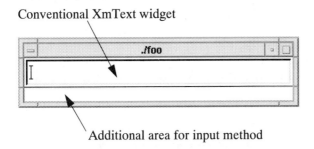

Additional area for input method

Figure 20.1 *Internationalised text input*

Input methods typically use two areas: the pre-edit area and the status area. Once the Text widget gets the keyboard focus, the input method comes to life and displays the current status. In Figure 20.2, the status area shows that the input method is in 'Romaji Hiragana' input mode. The pre-edit area contains some partially composed text and the Text widget contains a completed character.

In Figure 20.2, the pre-edit area is superimposed on the Text widget for which it is accepting input. This input style is called OverTheSpot. The xwnmo input method also supports an OffTheSpot input style. Here the pre-editing is done in the input method window at the bottom of the shell (see Figure 20.3).

Conversion conflicts

The input method can resolve conflicts in the conversion of Hiragana to Kanji, by allowing the user to select the appropriate ideograph from a popup menu (see Figure 20.4).

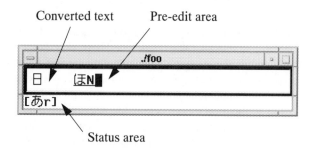

Converted text   Pre-edit area

Status area

Figure 20.2 *Input method areas*

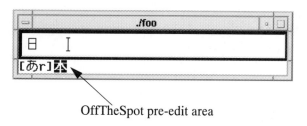

OffTheSpot pre-edit area

Figure 20.3 *Input method with OffTheSpot pre-edit style*

Figure 20.4 *Selecting from optional translations*

20.3.2   Examples of use

A Motif Text widget will attempt to connect to an input method if its fontList resource contains a font set. This is fortunate, as it means that you do not need to do very much work; as long as you use Motif Text widgets for text input and allow their fonts to be specified in a resource file, your application is internationalised.

Here is the simplest internationalised text input program:

textinput

```
#include <X11/Xatom.h>
#include <X11/Intrinsic.h>
```

```
#include <X11/Shell.h>
#include <Xm/Xm.h>
#include <Xm/DialogS.h>
#include <Xm/Text.h>

int main (argc,argv)
    int     argc;
    char  **argv;
{
    Arg             al[5];
    register int    ac = 0;
    XrmValue        from_value, to_value;
    XtAppContext    app_context;
    Display         *display;
    Widget          shell = (Widget) NULL;
    Widget          text = (Widget) NULL;
/* Use default language procedure to set locale */
    XtSetLanguageProc ((XtAppContext) NULL, (XtLanguageProc) NULL,
                    (XtPointer) NULL);
    XtToolkitInitialize ();
    app_context = XtCreateApplicationContext ();
    display = XtOpenDisplay (app_context, NULL, argv[0], "XApplication",
                    NULL, 0, &argc, argv);
    if (!display) {
        printf("%s: can't open display, exiting...\n", argv[0]);
        exit (-1);
    }
    XtSetArg (al[ac], XmNallowShellResize, True); ac++;
    XtSetArg (al[ac], XmNargc, argc); ac++;
    XtSetArg (al[ac], XmNargv, argv); ac++;
/* Set inputMethod to use xwnmo */
    XtSetArg (al[ac], XmNinputMethod, "_XWNMO"); ac++;
    shell = XtAppCreateShell (argv[0], "XApplication",
                    applicationShellWidgetClass, display, al, ac);
/* Let Xlib find a font set appropriate to the locale */
    ac = 0;
    from_value.addr = "-*-*-*-*-*-16-*-*-*-*-*-*;;:";
    from_value.size = strlen(from_value.addr)+1;
    to_value.addr = NULL;
    XtConvertAndStore(shell, XmRString, &from_value,
                    XmRFontList, &to_value);
    XtSetArg(al[ac], XmNfontList, *(XmFontList*)to_value.addr); ac++;
    text = XmCreateText (shell, "text", al, ac);
    XtManageChild (text);
```

```
        XtRealizeWidget (shell);
        XtAppMainLoop (app_context);
    }
```

Running this program with the locale set to ja_JP.jis7 displays the window shown in Figure 20.2.

The progress of the display for a typical user input sequence is shown in Figure 20.5.

20.3.3   Interesting resources

There are resources in both the Motif VendorShell widget and the Text widgets used in conjunction with input methods.

xnlLanguage

A per display resource used to identify the required locale. This can be set from the command line. The example program in Figure 20.2 was run using -xnllanguage ja_JP.jis7. The locale can also be set by the LANG environment variable.

inputMethod

A Motif VendorShell resource which indicates which input method the application is to connect to. In the example program in Section 20.3.2, the inputMethod resource is set to "_XWNMO" to indicate that the xwnmo input method should be used. This can also be achieved by the user setting the XMODIFIERS environment variable. In this case, it would be set to "@im=_XWNMO". It is unlikely that this resource should ever be hard-coded as in the example, as this then denies users the opportunity to use the input method of their choice.

preeditType

This Motif VendorShell resource is used to configure the input method. There are three basic pre-edit types:

- Over the spot - The pre-edit area is overlaid on the Text widget, as illustrated in Figure 20.2.
- Off the spot - The pre-edit area is in the application window, but not over the Text widget, as illustrated in Figure 20.3.
- Root window - The pre-edit area is in a separate application window, controlled by the input method.

The preeditType resource takes a comma-separated list of preferred pre-edit types (the default is OverTheSpot,OffTheSpot,Root). This is matched against the input styles supported by the input method and the best match is used.

The user types h

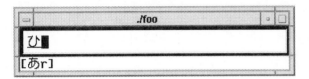

The user types i, the Hiragana for "hi" is displayed

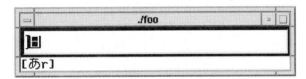

The user types the "Kanji" key to convert the symbol to Kanji

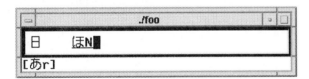

The user types hon for the next symbol

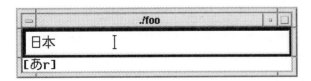

The user types the "Kanji" and "execute" keys and the input is complete

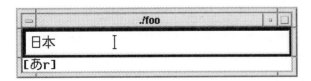

Figure 20.5 *The progression of input using an OverTheSpot input method*

fontList

The presence of a font set in a Text widget's fontList resource causes the toolkit to attempt to connect to an input method.

Bibliography

This short bibliography includes some books that all X and Motif programmers should have, and a sampling of other useful books. Many other sources are available.

Reference manuals

Open Software Foundation, **OSF/Motif** (5 vols). Prentice Hall, 1990, 1991, 1992.
OSF/Motif Style Guide
OSF/Motif Programmer's Guide
OSF/Motif Programmer's Reference
OSF/Motif User's Guide
OSF/Motif Application Environment/Specification (AES) User Environment, Revision 3

These books are the definitive reference guides on Motif. Note that the **Programmer's Guide** contains a section on UIL.

O'Reilly and Associates, **The X Window System Series** (7 vols).
O'Reilly and Associates, Inc., 1988, 1989, 1990, 1991, 1992.
Volumes 0, 2, 3 and 5 are lightly edited versions of the MIT manuals. Volume 1 discusses Xlib. Volume 4 on the X Toolkit has a Motif edition, but the Motif-specific material is very basic. Volume 6 is devoted entirely to Motif.

The newest versions of these books cover both X11 Release 4 and Release 5 and Motif Version 1.2. As of this writing, volumes 3 and 6 are not available for these new releases.

Other books

Asente, Paul J. and Swick, Ralph R., **X Window System Toolkit.**
　Digital Press, 1990.
The definitive guide to the X toolkit. It contains an excellent and comprehensive tutorial on using and writing widgets, as well as a complete specification to the toolkit.

Scheifler, R.W. and Gettys, J., **X Window System, third edition.**
　Digital Press, 1992.
The definitive reference to Xlib, X Protocol, ICCCM and XLFD, from the originators of the X Window System.

Young, Douglas A., **X Window System: Programming and Applications with Xt, OSF/Motif Edition.**
　Prentice Hall, 1990.
A good tutorial on writing programs using the X toolkit and Motif.

Young, Douglas A., **Object-Oriented Programming with C++ and OSF/Motif.**
　Prentice Hall, 1992.
This book provides helpful solutions to the problems of building C++ programs which use the Motif toolkit.

Index